D1268810

THE MASK OF MERLIN

Topix Picture Service

Lloyd George in Bardic robes, when, with his family, he acted as Castellan at St. Donat's Castle, Glamorgan, to entertain the Gorsedd of Welsh Eisteddfod Bards at a banquet served with medieval splendour.

THE MASK OF MERLIN

A Critical Biography of David Lloyd George

BY DONALD McCORMICK

HOLT, RINEHART AND WINSTON

NEW YORK CHICAGO SAN FRANCISCO

First Published in the United States
August 1964.

Library of Congress Catalog Card Number: 64-20102

First Edition

85551-0114
Printed in the United States of America

ACKNOWLEDGMENTS

It is impossible to thank adequately all the many people whose knowledge of and interest in David Lloyd George helped me to write this book.

Various private collections of papers, pamphlets, diaries and letters have been perused, in addition to which I have had the inestimable value of the services of the staffs of the Reading Room, Manuscripts Room and Newspaper Library of the British Museum, and the Public Records Office, for which I am deeply grateful.

I wish to thank the executors of Mr. Vivian Phillipps, the former Liberal Party Chief Whip, for allowing access to Mr. Phillipps' papers and contemporary memoranda and for permission to quote from the same: Mrs. E. A. Morgan for permission to reproduce extracts from letters and diaries of the late Mr. Moses Roberts; Mrs. E. Lycett Green for reminiscences of North Wales of the Lloyd Georgian era; Mr. B. Schofield, Keeper of the Department of Manuscripts of the British Museum.

In addition there have been many people who have known Lloyd George personally, or worked for him, who have provided help and advice anonymously. I should like to emphasise that I have consulted many who, though they strongly opposed some of my own interpretations of events and personalities, nevertheless co-operated willingly. In this connection I should like to thank Mr. Reginald Orlando Bridgeman, who had an intimate knowledge of British foreign policy in the years immediately before and after the Russian Revolution. Though our respective outlooks on the Lloyd George policy towards Russia were sometimes diametrically opposed, he provided a salutary counterblast to my own contentions and did much to induce me to re-write a whole chapter on this subject.

Similarly I must warmly acknowledge the valuable criticism and constructive suggestions of Mr. Malcolm Elwin and Sqn.-Ldr. Ronald Ladbrook, Senior History Master at Stanbridge Earls School. In fairness to each I must admit that, while I gladly accepted some of their suggestions, in other instances, rightly or wrongly, I begged to differ.

Much assistance has been given to me from other countries. In particular I wish to acknowledge my thanks to Professor Frank Freidel, the biographer of President Roosevelt; Mr. Adolf A. Berle, Jr.; the late Mr. Wythe Williams, of New York; Dr. L. de Jong, of Amsterdam;

Herr H. Hausofer, of Hartschimmel; Dr. Weis, Director of the W.K.B. at Stuttgart; various friends in the Quai d'Orsay in Paris.

I gratefully acknowledge permission for the use of copyright material from:

Earl Haig and Mr. Robert Blake, who are trustees of the Haig Papers;

Mr. Robert Blake and Eyre & Spottiswoode Ltd., for extracts from *The Private Papers of Douglas Haig*, *The Unknown Prime Minister* and *The Baldwin Age*;

Sir Harold Nicolson and Constable & Co. Ltd., for material from *King George V, His Life and Times*;

Cassell & Co. Ltd., for extracts from *A King's Story* by H.R.H. the Duke of Windsor;

Lord Beaverbrook and Hutchinson & Co. Ltd., for extracts from *Men and Power: 1917–18* and from a broadcast review of *The History of The Times*;

Sir Winston S. Churchill and Odhams Press, Ltd., as publishers and proprietors of the copyright, for extracts from *Great Contemporaries* and *The World Crisis*;

The Editor of *The Observer* for extracts from Kenneth Harris's interview with Sir Harold Nicolson;

Mr. F. M. Maurice for extracts from the papers and correspondence of General Sir Frederick Maurice;

The Times Publishing Co. Ltd., for extracts from *The History of The Times*;

Professor H. R. Trevor-Roper and Weidenfeld & Nicolson Ltd., for extracts from *Hitler's Table Talk*;

Mr. Malcolm Thomson and Hutchinson & Co. Ltd., for extracts from *David Lloyd George*;

Mr. Kingsley Martin and the *New Statesman & Nation*, for extracts from that journal;

Mr. J. P. W. Mallalieu, M.P., and the Editor of the *Evening Standard* for extracts from an interview with General Gough;

George Allen & Unwin Ltd., for extracts from *Dame Margaret* by Earl Lloyd-George;

Mrs. Eirene White, M.P., for extracts from Dr. Thomas Jones' *Lloyd George* (Oxford University Press);

J. M. Dent & Sons, Ltd., for an extract from Dylan Thomas's poem, "O Make Me a Mask" from *Collected Poems: 1934–52*.

More than 130 books have been consulted (though not necessarily all used as sources) as well as vast quantities of press cuttings and documents and, though a bibliographical list is included, it is far from being a complete bibliography of Lloyd George, as new material on the man is still being either published or unearthed. Nevertheless, the list given should enable readers who wish to delve further into this subject to obtain an objective and well-documented picture of the Lloyd Georgian era. Students wishing to check on other sources will find them given in chronological order in the bibliography under chapter headings.

I should, however, acknowledge my special indebtedness to Dr. Thomas Jones' *Lloyd George*, a short but extremely workmanlike biography which can usefully be regarded as a text-book on the subject; to Sir Winston Churchill's *The World Crisis*; to Mr. Frank Owen's *Tempestuous Journey*; to Sir Harold Nicolson for the time he kindly spared to discuss with me the subject of Lloyd George; to Lord Beaverbrook's various illuminating and well-documented books on the period, for no student of Ll. G. can fail to benefit from his revelations; and *The Life of Lord Oxford and Asquith* by H. A. Spender and Cyril Asquith.

CONTENTS

ILLUSTRATIONS

The illustrations of Dame Margaret Lloyd George and Michael Collins are from the Radio Times Hulton Picture Library, and that of F.M. Earl Haig from Bassano Ltd.

I

THE RIDDLE OF THE WIZARD

"A fiery soul, which working out its way,
Fretted the pygmy body to decay."
John Dryden

Llanystumdwy is still an unspoilt village with nothing particularly remarkable about it until one comes to the ancient three-span bridge under which flows the River Dwyfor. Here is the kind of Tennysonian stream which onomatopoeically "bubbles into eddying bays and babbles on the pebbles". A tumultuous, gay little river, meandering and cantering like a Celtic goblin, a stream which has never quite grown up.

This is the river so beloved by David Lloyd George that, when he received an earldom, he chose Dwyfor as part of his title. To see the river is to appreciate the bond between the two; each share the same characteristics—waywardness, directness when the path ahead is clear, deviousness when there are obstacles to be circumnavigated, gaiety in the sunlight and a reflective note of warning when the clouds gather.

Not to know Llanystumdwy is not to know Lloyd George. Here he was reared and here he returned to die. Here also he has left behind a clue to his elusive character and to the legend of the Cambrian Wizard who, for the best part of a century, cast a sparkling pattern of magic, of rhetoric and of a brittle, fragile charm over the valleys of North Wales. Once that magic left the valleys and ventured into more sophisticated regions it became tainted and sullied. It was as though Ariel had given place to Puck, and Puck, in turn, had changed into a scheming, tortuous faun.

Llanystumdwy. The name has a pleasant, sleepy softness about it, much more eloquent than its rather clumsy English translation—"the church at the bend of the Dwyfor River". Across the bridge from the Pwllheli road is the Lloyd George Museum, where are to be found the caskets and rolls of the many cities of which Lloyd George was made a Freeman and the policeman's helmet which he wore when escaping from an angry mob at Birmingham Town Hall during the Boer War. Further on along the Criccieth road is the tiny, ivy-covered cottage where he spent his boyhood days. On the Criccieth side of the river is Lloyd George's grave in the exact site he chose for himself, among the trees on a bank of the rushing Dwyfor. A small garden of memory in the form of an enclosed shrine has been designed by Clough Williams Ellis, the Welsh architect.

The Welsh love their rivers with a passionate fervour and imbibe from them a deep spiritual comfort. The theme of the "little stream, meandering down the mountain-side" on its way to the sea, is a constantly recurring *motif* in the lyrical and dramatic *hwl*, that torrential peroration with its sing-song delivery which marks the end of a Welsh preacher's sermon.

Symbolically, and not merely sentimentally, the Dwyfor seems to provide the one permanent background to Lloyd George's life. All else was a frenzied scene-changing in a feverish revue. The Lloyd Georgian era was one of quicksands and follies. The constant threat of war from the continent of Europe, the pitfalls of a foreign policy built on expediency and not on principles, the passage from Victorian sobriety and solidity through Edwardian frivolity to the butterfly way of life of the nineteen-twenties, all these things were merely an echo of earlier history. For the Coalition Government of Lloyd George read the crooked counsels of the Cabal. In Dryden's bitter satire on Lord Shaftesbury there is an echo of that other False Achitophel from Llanystumdwy. . . .

"A fiery soul, which working out its way,
Fretted the pygmy body to decay."

In an historical context it is impossible in any attempt to assess Lloyd George to avoid posing the question: Could a man who was hailed as the saviour of civilization, the master-mind behind the Allied victory over the Central Powers in 1918, the architect of social security, be an evil genius rather than a benevolent wizard?

At Llanystumdwy it is least easy to answer this question. The old magic comes back to one and, with it, a question mark. Is it dust thrown in the eyes by unseen Celtic goblins? Or is the phrase "Welsh wizard" just a happy piece of alliteration thought up by a propagandist? Neither is quite true. There is an ancient tradition of wizardry in Wales that brings the word naturally to the lips of any Welshman who wishes to describe genius. Another Welsh-born Prime Minister, Billy Hughes of Australia, was the first politician to liken Lloyd George to the Arthurian wizard when he referred to his statecraft as "the magic of Merlin".

The most difficult task of any biographer of Lloyd George is to explain and interpret the magic without being mesmerised by its spell. One must avoid, for example, so surprisingly sweeping an assertion as that of Mr. A. J. P. Taylor who writes: "Lloyd George was the man who won the war and, as the years recede, he stands out as the greatest political genius that the twentieth century produced in this country."

Stanley Baldwin was, perhaps, wiser when he said: "It will take ten men to write his life." More than twice this number have individually attempted the task, yet a clear picture has not yet emerged.

The modern tendency in biography is to sublimate any inspired sense of history to a desire to be dispassionate at all costs. The result is a series of books which pretend that nothing is either black or white, but an all-embracing greyness. It is history as Whistler might have painted it on a misty November morning looking out on the Thames from Chelsea Embankment.

Yet his contemporaries never saw Lloyd George in other than black or white, either hating him or idolising him. An impassioned local orator, carried away by his own eloquence at Rhyl in 1919, introduced Lloyd George to his audience as "the greatest man since Christ".

It would be utterly untruthful to assert that this is a dispassionate biography. Indeed, it is not intended to be a biography in the conventional sense, but rather a critical interpretation of one of the most baffling political figures of our time. Beyond this basic aim there is a broader purpose to be developed, and if the book has a theme other than its main subject it is to show how power corrupts. For Lloyd George undoubtedly undermined the moral structure of British public life and began the moral degeneration which is the greatest political problem of the present day.

It has been necessary to examine the legend of Lloyd George and to check the facts with that legend, to separate the wheat of truth from the chaff of idolatry. More especially has it been important to fill in the gaps in the Lloyd George story left by other biographers.

The legend of Lloyd George has come down to a generation to whom he is a complete stranger. All this generation knows, or is told about him, is that he was the man who won World War I, or, as Sir Winston Churchill has put it: "He was the greatest Welshman which that unconquerable race has produced since the time of the Tudors." There have been greater occupants of No. 10 Downing Street in the past century, but Lloyd George was easily the most fascinating premier since the days of Disraeli and possibly the most remarkable human enigma ever to have resided there. During his lifetime, well fed by a skilled propaganda machine, aided and abetted by a national Press that saw in him a heaven-sent boon to cartoonists, the legend blossomed into extravagant imagery. In his last days it had become somewhat shabby and tawdry, but in the years since his death various biographers have resurrected the fading picture and restored the halo.

The biographical pictures so far drawn of Lloyd George have been largely uncritical and incomplete. "Although I have it on good authority that the Lloyd George bibliography is probably the most extensive of that of any man living" (his father was still alive when this was written), writes his son, Earl Lloyd-George, "I have yet to read one biography that does David Lloyd George justice. Certainly all of them that have come under my eye are either full of inaccuracies or sadly lacking in important facts—or both."

Even allowing for the books published since this date, a modern student of the Lloyd George bibliography, having no other facts to go on, might decide that the edifice which was the great Welshman had very few cracks. The evidence which builds up this picture is formidable. In its obituary of Lloyd George *The Times* stated: "His countrymen will remember that he wrought greatly and daringly for them in dark times, in peace and in war, and will admit without distinction of class or party that a great man has passed away." And again, Sir Winston Churchill has commented: "As a man of action, resource and creative energy he stood, when at his zenith, without a rival. Much of his work abides, some of it will grow greatly in the future, and those who come after us will find the pillars of his life's toil upstanding, massive and indestructible." Field-Marshal Jan Smuts declared that Lloyd George was the "supreme architect of victory in the First World War". Dr. Thomas Jones, who as a senior civil servant was very close to Lloyd George, does, it is true, admit his master had faults, but somewhat extravagantly claims that he "took hold of flabbiness and muddle" at a great crisis in history, and "by his own energy turned flabbiness into resolution, muddle into system and purpose".

But when one examines the base of this edifice it is found to be far from durable. There are yawning chasms of omission in the narratives, many controversies are glossed over. Even Dr. Thomas Jones honestly confesses that "I have tried to rid myself of prejudice and partiality, but I am not so foolish as to think I have succeeded. For the fact must be faced that he was not universally trusted".

The hesitations of his biographers have been echoed by various critics. "People will go on writing books about him and remain not quite sure what to say," was the summing-up of Mr. Kingsley Martin in *The New Statesman and Nation*, reviewing Frank Owen's book, *Tempestuous Journey*. "So the mystery of Lloyd George remains . . . what was his secret?" was the cryptic question put in an unsigned review in *The Economist*. The *Daily Worker*, on the left, headed its review of the same book, "If Only the People Had Known"—a dark hint and nothing more—while the *Evening Standard*, on the right, asked, "Was he a failure after all?"

Possibly his fellow-countryman, Aneurin Bevan, came nearest to finding a clue to the truth about Lloyd George when he wrote in the *News Chronicle:* ". . . The explanation is that we are looking in the wrong place. The secret of the career of Lloyd George is to be sought in the character of British political institutions and in the conduct of the people influenced by them. We are much more the creatures of social institutions than we care to admit."

Lloyd George's collected papers, including official documents, private correspondence, Press-cuttings and other records (an immense accumulation of material, weighing several tons) have been carefully preserved. Yet it requires only a little preliminary research to prove that there is too much "evidence" and that what exists tends to obscure vital facts.

How, for example, can one find in dusty documents the answer to this poser by Mr. Robert Blake, who, in his introduction to his collection of the late Earl Haig's diaries, mentions that "there was something in Lloyd George, a love of intrigue, a lack of fixed principle, a curious inconsistency, which at once puzzled Haig and aroused his suspicion. What lay behind the charm, the wit, the swift ripostes, the romantic oratory? Lloyd George's closest friends could not always tell. Was he a man of principle pursuing by devious means a consistent end, or was he an opportunist who relied upon his intuition to gratify at every turn his love of power and office? To this day it is not an easy question to answer. Lloyd George remains—and perhaps will long remain—an enigma to the historian."

It is strange that not even his Welsh biographers have attempted to convey the real background and atmosphere of Lloyd George's early life in any detail. Not one of them has captured the sultry, smouldering evangelism of the Welsh valleys, with its undertones of sexual obsession, in the sixties and seventies of the last century. Yet the Wales of his boyhood is a subject which is inextricably linked with the man's character and outlook. Clues to the riddle of the Wizard may be found in many unusual places, and more in his associations with men who worked behind the scenes than in his relations with the greatest statesmen of his age. Mr. Dingle Foot suggests that Lloyd George's reputation can only suffer at the hands of Lilliputians, but Lilliputians can get around in places where larger men would not deign to go. They can ferret out facts close to the ground, while the Brobdignagian biographers stand, arms akimbo, surveying the landscape from too great a height. The latter see the main highways of Lloyd George's political career, but ignore the narrow, hidden footpaths through the corn.

For much of Lloyd George's political planning was done stealthily, working in the shadows with trusted accomplices who shared his love of intrigue and secrecy. In his hey-day these puppets, unknown to the general public, exercised more real power and influence than any of his Cabinet colleagues.

* * * * *

The charm of Lloyd George is, perhaps, the most difficult thing of all to capture. I was eight years old when I first heard him speak and that is still an unforgettable experience. He pleaded, he cajoled, he amused, he dramatised. He was the subtlest wooer of a crowd since Mark Antony made his funeral oration over the body of Julius Caesar, and it is strange that he should have taken the pseudonym of Brutus when first he wrote for the Press.

No other British orator of this century could compare with Lloyd George in his capacity for thrilling and enthralling an audience. He could, said Dr. Thomas Jones, "charm a bird off a tree". The day I first heard him speak he gave a two minutes' peroration in Welsh at the end of his main speech. Those brief moments were the high-light of the meeting. If he was eloquent in English, he was positively mesmeric in Welsh.

Years later, as a young reporter, I had to interview him. I recall most of all his large, shiny head and the flowing mane of white hair that glistened in the early morning sunlight. There was about him a fresh, polished look as though he had just emerged from a bath and a session with the hairdresser. It was mostly his sunshine mood that morning, talking about his "New Deal". Yet, curiously enough, in conversation on political subjects he was far less impressive than on the platform. One felt that his gestures and histrionics were false, that he was often groping for his own meaning. He seemed to lack erudition, to chase ideas like a cat playing with a mouse. When talking of trivialities he could be charming and witty, but in expounding his new political philosophy he mumbled a lot of platitudes. Throughout the interview he grasped every opportunity to steer the talk away from too close questioning on his economic plans and I suspect he never really mastered the ideas of Maynard Keynes. But apart from this he contributed to the conversation much that was memorable and illuminating.

He decried the fact that modern politicians were by and large poor speakers. "Even the aristocrats have lost their touch," he commented. "They miaow and puke out the words from their mouths as though the very syllables are too much for them. Perhaps it's the B.B.C. that has emasculated the English language, but there's no bite in it any more. Churchill is the last of the great Parliamentary orators and he's just an odd man out anyhow."

"Is it true," I asked, "that you never know exactly how your speech is going to work out when you get up to make it?"

"That is what they say. But don't you believe that, or take it too literally. In most cases I stick to my brief. Only in crises, or when the meeting I address contains a challenge, do I improvize. Then I feel my way along. I——"

He dropped the apple he was munching and clutched the air as though to draw a word from the heavens. "I pause. I reach out my hand to the people and draw them to me. Like children they seem then. Like little children."

There was nothing of the ham actor about this dissertation, nothing insincere. I swear that he really believed what he said and that in fact he could become intoxicated by the presence of a crowd. But there was something in the tone in which he said it that was more than a little Merlinesque. As Dryden put it:

> "Great wits are sure to madness near alli'd,
> And thin partitions do their bounds divide."

Here, one felt, was that hint of megalomania which often infected Lloyd George, though he kept it under control through his sense of humour and native subtlety. In a flash Lloyd George had suddenly ceased to be himself: he was Danny, the conceited young Welsh servant in Emlyn Williams's play *Night Must Fall.*

He went on: "It is emotion which counts most at these times. If a meeting seems flat, I throw out a challenge on the spur of the moment —perhaps a little story that will bring a throb to their hearts. Or, if the meeting is hostile, I try to get an opponent to toss me a lifebelt."

"You mean?"

He threw back his head and chuckled. "Well, there was an occasion when I was speaking to some Welsh farmers. Tory farmers, of course. I was talking about Home Rule. When I talked about it, I tried to make people feel it was not just an ideal for Ireland, but for England, Scotland and Wales, too. 'We want Home Rule not only for Ireland, but for Wales as well,' I told them. 'Aye, and for hell, man, I suppose?' shouted some drunken lout. 'Yes,' I said, 'I like to hear a man stand up for his own country.' That changed the mood of the meeting.

"Then there was another meeting in the East End of London when a boozy-faced old harridan called out: 'Is it true that most of the Cabinet have illegitimate children?' I was at a loss to reply for a moment. Then, in a flash, the words came: 'It's a wise old mare who knows the best stallions,' I parried. Laughter and applause. But it isn't always so easy."

It is difficult to evoke from mere shorthand notes the spirit of a raconteur such as Lloyd George. He was completely unsophisticated and yet still a man of the world. There were no epigrams, but his wit sparkled and bubbled. His voice would drop almost to a whisper, then rise in a sudden burst of glee. He was as irrepressible as a schoolboy. Yet, when talking of some politicians of the day, his eyes would glower and his whole countenance take on a ferocious expression. The very mention of Neville Chamberlain was enough to transform him into a Biblical prophet denouncing the evils of the world. Few who witnessed it will ever forget his scathing denunciation of Sir John Simon when the latter crossed the floor of the House to vote with the Tories. With his finger twisting a tortuous trail in the air, he scornfully referred to the "right honourable gentleman who crossed the floor, leaving a trail of slime behind him".

A few other things he said during our interview shed light on his affinity with the River Dwyfor and the mountains of North Wales. "When I seek for strength and courage I always say 'go to the mountains and the little streams for these qualities'. That is where the greatest preachers of Wales have found their inspiration. You cannot beat it. 'The Banner of the Dawn', 'The mists of the mountains, which as they begin to rise give promise of a brighter day.' There you have it all. I often feel that perhaps the speech of mine which gave me the most pleasure was at the Cardiff City Hall on the occasion of the unveiling of the statues to the 'Great Men of Wales', presented by Lord Rhondda. I relied on the mountains for that speech. This is what I said:

"'The great men of any nation are like mountains. They attract and assemble the vitalising elements under the heavens and distribute and direct them into the valleys and plains to irrigate the land.

"'Without great men a nation would be a desert or a morass, a fen of stagnant waters. Wales without its great men would be a wretched swamp.'"

* * * * *

Lloyd George was not by nature introspective; he drew his inspiration from external sources rather than from communion with himself. Sometimes he steeped himself in gloom as foreboding as one of the cloudy days in his native valleys and his gaiety would easily evaporate. But he was remarkably resilient and it was one of the quirks of his character that optimism in others depressed him, yet when confronted by prophets of doom he was provoked into a quixotic and taunting optimism himself. Away from him, having escaped his magic, men found it easy to be angry with him and to criticise. But in his presence the anger even of his enemies usually melted away. Had he lacked the charm, he might have been routed by his enemies on many occasions. Even so outspoken a critic as Lord Croft was once so overcome by Lord George's personal magnetism that he seized him by the hand and said, "Sir, you would have made the greatest Conservative Prime Minister of all time, if you had only joined our Party in 1919."

Mr. J. S. Barnes, an observant critic from inside the Foreign Office, wrote that Arthur Balfour "allowed himself to be hypnotised by personalities. He watched Lloyd George, fascinated like one entranced by the beauty of a firefly". Indeed, this can be the only explanation of how A.J.B. allowed one of his most formidable political enemies to lure him into a Government about which he must have had the mo profound misgivings.

Asquith, to his cost, mistook emotional appeals by his adversary fc sincerity. Even so discerning a judge of character as King George V, who never really liked or trusted Lloyd George, once so far forgot himself as to say: "He is a very great man. I am sorry he is leaving Downing Street, but he will come back again."

The real genius of Lloyd George was a subtle combination of personal magnetism and an innate Machiavellianism. The two traits worked together in his heart and mind. They proved an intoxicating mixture, for he lacked the devotion to an ultimate aim which Machiavelli had in great measure, while too often relying on charm to obscure lack of principles. At times one felt that Lloyd George believed the means justified the end, for he was proud rather than ashamed of his chicaneries. This, more than anything else, was his undoing and made him a master of self-deception, a factor which developed the most dangerous characteristics he possessed—a fatal facility for making a complete *volte-face*, of seeing black as white. The man who could fight for the rights of little nations with the fire of a Garibaldi could also laud the advent of Hitlerism. The statesman who professed liberalism as a creed could behave as Prime Minister like a dictator and tyrant.

Mr. A. J. Sylvester, who was for many years his right-hand man, has written of him: "A great pacifist . . . a believer in humanity . . . a democrat . . . such was the character he always presented as his. But those of us in daily contact with him recognised he had few of these qualities in his heart. Lloyd George was a pacifist just as long as pacifism didn't involve humiliation, or interfere with his plans. In his personal affairs he was the most autocratic of men. He would never admit he was in the wrong. He suffered from an inferiority complex which explains his jealousies and suspicions."

Was Lloyd George a great man, or was greatness merely thrust upon him? Was he a Liberal Democrat or a dictator? A zealous social reformer or a demagogic charlatan? A statesman or a mountebank? A patriot of the highest order, or a self-seeker who would stoop to treachery and treason?

These questions pose extreme viewpoints. In some cases the facts will show the answers come down positively one way or the other. Sometimes the answers lie between two extremes. But whatever picture must finally emerge from the reader's point of view the fascination of the personality of Lloyd George is undeniable and will remain so throughout the ages.

2

BIBLE AND BUNDLING

"I often think we can trace almost all the disasters of English history to the influence of Wales. Think of Edward of Carnarvon, the first Prince of Wales, then the Tudors and the dissolution of the Church, then Lloyd George, the temperance movement, Nonconformity and lust stalking hand in hand throughout the country, wasting and ravaging."

Dr. Fagan in Evelyn Waugh's
Decline and Fall

It was a world of optimism into which David Lloyd George was born on January 17, 1863. The tide of liberalism was flowing fast, engulfing the New World and the Old. On New Year's Day slavery was abolished by proclamation of President Lincoln. Gladstone had not yet reached his hey-day, but the forces of democracy throughout Europe were on the march.

Young Lloyd George's father belonged to an ancient Pembrokeshire family. At the end of the eighteenth century the Georges lived in a farm at Tresinwen near Stumble Head. In 1797 a French expedition landed on the coast only a short distance from the Georges' farm. Among the farmers' and fishermen's wives who donned red cloaks and massed on the cliff-tops to trick the French into believing that a formidable detachment of redcoats was awaiting them was Mrs. Timothy George, Lloyd George's great-grandmother.

During the First World War, when "gallant, little Belgium" was the hero among nations, Lloyd George allowed it to be given out at a Welsh reunion in London that, although Welsh by birth, he was Flemish by origin. The Brussels newspaper *Soir* on July 29, 1920, stated that "from private information in our possession it appears that Lloyd George is descended from a family which emigrated to Pembrokeshire from Menin, Comines or Warneton".

William George left the family farm to become a teacher. He seems to have had the same kind of restless urge as his son, for he taught in London, Liverpool, Haverfordwest, Pwllheli and Newchurch before finally settling in his last post at Manchester. While at Pwllheli he met Elizabeth Lloyd of Llanystumdwy. They married and in 1862 went to Manchester where, in a two-storied house, No. 5 New York Place, his son David was born.

The climate of this city did not suit William George and his health suffered in consequence. Eventually he returned to Pembrokeshire, gave up teaching and rented a small farm. The year after David's birth he caught pneumonia and died.

His widow went to live with her shoemaker brother, Richard Lloyd, in Llanystumdwy in her native Caernarvonshire. It has often been suggested that Lloyd George was a fatherless waif, a story to which Ll. G. himself subscribed on occasions, especially when speaking in a constituency where poverty was widespread. In some of his speeches he declared that he was "reared in poverty", that his sole luxury was "half an egg on Sundays". Such statements were misleading and a travesty of the truth. It is true that his father had little money to leave, that his mother was expecting a third child when her husband died, but he had as stable a family background in his infancy and youth as any average boy of his time. A Mr. Evan Thomas, of East Orange, New Jersey, who knew the family in Lloyd George's childhood, wrote to the *New York Times* on January 20, 1945, criticising these reports which were repeated in the paper's account of his elevation to the peerage. "He was always well fed and the George boys were among the best dressed at the local school," wrote Mr. Thomas. "Lloyd George should be regarded as a child of good fortune." Yet Ll. G. said of his early days: "We scarcely ever ate fresh meat."

His uncle was no ordinary shoemaker, but a remarkable man of great strength of character who amply filled the place of a father who died before he could have made any impression on his son. Richard Lloyd has been described as "an uncanonised Welsh saint", which may be Celtic exaggeration, but is a testimony which is corroborated by many who knew him. The present Earl Lloyd-George has recorded how in those days schooling in North Wales did not exist for children beyond their twelfth year. "But Richard Lloyd," he said, "did not hold with this custom. I have never heard of anything finer than what my great-uncle did. With heroic pertinacity, and at the end of a hard day's work at his cobbler's bench, he took on the task of himself learning Latin and Greek and French. . . . In addition he acquired textbooks on English Common Law and laboriously mastered their contents. Thus he equipped himself with at least sufficient knowledge to further the schooling of his children."[1]

To understand fully the influences which moulded Lloyd George's character one must also appreciate not only the religious revolution of the period, but the influences of Wales dating back to the twilight world of Celtic folk-lore. The Welsh nation has its roots deep in pre-Christian Celtic legend. Even its Christianity is peculiarly conditioned

[1] *Dame Margaret* by Earl Lloyd-George.

by paganism, possibly because neither Roman culture nor the Norman conquest made the same impression here as in England.

The Welsh mountains formed the one bulwark which shielded Welsh nationality when the invader threatened; they were father and mother to the Welsh people, guardian and inspiration. This explains the passion for mountain names in Welsh nonconformity—Mount Sion, Mount Horeb and Mount Ararat, as so many of the chapels are named. From the earliest days the mountains were the source and subject of songs and from these songs came the national love of music.

Giraldus Cambrensis (1146–1223) has said of the Welshman's love of music: "In their musical concerts they do not sing in unison like the inhabitants of other countries, but in many different parts. They have the gift of making the human voice a musical instrument."

This gift Lloyd George had in great measure. Allied to it was the influence of the mountains which was never so marked as in an early World War I peroration of his:

"I knew a valley in the north of Wales between the mountains and the sea—a beautiful valley, snug, comfortable, sheltered from all the bitter blasts. It was very enervating and I remember how all the boys were in the habit of climbing the hill above the village to have a glimpse of the great mountains in the distance and to be stimulated and freshened by the breezes which come from the hill-tops. We have been living in a sheltered valley for generations. We have been too comfortable, too indulgent, many, perhaps, too selfish, and the stern hand of fate has scourged us to an elevation where we can see the great everlasting things that matter for a nation—the peaks of honour we had forgotten—duty, patriotism, and, clad in glittering white, the pinnacle of sacrifice, pointing like a rugged finger to heaven."

This is the heady wine of speech which dulls the head and warms the heart. Analysed, it amounts to little more than tub-thumping. No one in these years of disillusionment since the First World War would risk such a blatant appeal to the emotions. Nevertheless it has the quality of a "musical instrument", to which Giraldus referred, and it illustrates perfectly the influence of those native mountains.

* * * * *

At the beginning of this chapter there is a quotation from one of Mr. Evelyn Waugh's most brilliant social satires. "The Welsh," said Dr. Fagan in *Decline and Fall*, "are the only nation in the world that has produced no graphic or plastic art, no architecture, no drama. They just sing and blow down wind instruments of plated silver. They are deceitful because they cannot discern truth from falsehood, depraved because they cannot discern the consequences of their indulgence." This is exaggeration in a Shavian sense of magnifying facts to reveal a truth, but it is unjust for the English to wax indignantly about Welsh faults when one recalls that subjection by the English created a social degeneration in Wales and brought such despair to the hearts of the bards that the court poet of Llewellyn cried: "Woe is me for my Lord. Do ye not see that the world is done? A sigh to thee, O God, that the sea might come overwhelming the land. Why are we left to wait?"

The publication of the Welsh New Testament and Prayer Book by William Salesbury brought about the revival of the Welsh language and lit the torch of Welsh patriotism after centuries of despair under English subjection. Towards the end of the seventeenth century Stephen Hughes founded the Welsh Trust to fight the notorious ignorance and lack of religion in the country. Then a new evangelical movement began within the Established Church with Howell Harris as its spearhead. He toured Wales, preaching indoors and out, suffering persecution at the hands of mobs who often assaulted him. "We must agitate the very soul to its foundations," he thundered, and when he died in 1773 some 20,000 souls from all parts of Wales were sufficiently "agitated" to attend his funeral and moan as well as mourn his passing.

Howell Harris was the first of a long line of evangelist preachers who ranted, raved and whipped themselves into a frenzy. Jeering mobs brought a sense of persecution and persecution begot masochism. In their twin tides sex and religion merged into an emotional whirlpool. Howell Harris seems to have realised this danger of playing on the emotions: "It provokes strange manifestations of religious hysteria," he said. But evangelism spread throughout the country. It reached villages in remote country districts where religion had been unknown for years, perhaps centuries. Preaching became a national occupation. Anyone who felt like it packed his bags and sauntered out into the byways, Bible in hand. Even Anglican curates were enthused to such an extent that one of them, Daniel Rowland, once preached for six hours without pause or, more remarkably still, interruption.

The Methodist Revival gave the movement further impetus, and soon the Calvinistic Methodist Church became in effect a Welsh National Church. It was essentially a Church for the common man, as democratic in its administration as the Presbyterian Kirk in Scotland. The democracy of the Church revealed itself in the insistence on plain, simple grey stone chapels. Religious revivalism touched off a demand for education. "On Sunday the whole nation was turned into a school," declared O. M. Edwards. "They not only read the Bible in the fields, but debated its meaning, and the geography of Palestine became more familiar than that of Wales itself." It may be that Lloyd George's passion for Biblical place-names and his pre-occupation with the Middle East in 1919–23 was a relic of those days.

Bibles were regarded as the most precious of possessions, but it was mainly preaching which revived the Welsh language and brought about the renaissance of Welsh verse. Goronwy Owen, son of a drunken tinker, became Wales's greatest poet. Until the early nineteenth century the Welsh Revival was almost entirely religious, but the industrial revolution reshaped revivalism, directing it into political channels. The unrest and agitation which developed from the revolution soon spread to Wales. Low wages, long hours, child and female labour and bad housing caused protests against the fixed payments for tithes and toll-gates when the Highway Act of 1855 was passed. And Chartism produced an unusual and typically Welsh by-product, Rebeccaism. Rents had been inflated during the Napoleonic Wars and there was little capital to enable smallholders to carry out improvements to property. The main source of vexation was the toll charged on lime, but Rebeccaism developed as an organised attack on all the toll-gates of the various Turnpike Trusts. Church rates, tithes, high rents and the new Poor Law were all attacked in turn.

The leader of the Rebeccaite movement was a mysterious, anonymous figure. An old print shows "Rebecca" as a woman armed with a stock leading an attack on a toll-gate. But while some claim "Rebecca" was a woman, others are equally emphatic that *he* was a farmer who signed his manifestoes "Rebecca" and that, as a disguise, he ordered his lieutenants to dress themselves in women's gowns and bonnets and called them "Daughters of Rebecca". After the demolition of each toll-house the "Daughters" rode away and presumably returned their bonnets and gowns to their wives. "Rebecca" was also a Nationalist, writing in one manifesto that "it is a shameful thing for the sons of Hengist to have domination over us Welshmen".

This may seem a far cry from Lloyd George, but, according to the late Thomas Charles Williams, a celebrated preacher from Menai Bridge, Ll. G. at one time toyed with the idea of reviving the tactics of Rebeccaism in the ranks of the Welsh Nationalists with the object of organised attacks on the Established Church and the squirearchy.

Feeling in Wales in the middle of the nineteenth century became steadily more antagonistic to England. Already, through the industrial revolution, the miseries of Victorian capitalism had been inflicted on Wales by English employers. And when the British Government decided to send a Commission of Enquiry to Wales in 1846 they added insult to injury. The Commission was comprised of Englishmen, mostly lawyers, who made no attempt to conceal their prejudices against Wales. Much of what they discovered as a result of extensive tours of the country was appalling indeed. They found that almost every man who lost his job could get a post as a teacher regardless of his ability. "Teaching is one of those vocations which serve as the sink of all others," stated the Commission's report. "The Welsh language is a vast drawback to Wales and a manifold barrier to the moral progress and commercial prosperity of the people. . . . The Evil of the Welsh language is fearfully great . . . it distorts the truth, favours fraud and abets perjury. . . . There are few countries where the standard of minor morals is lower. Of these immoralities the worst and most common is sexual incontinence, the peculiar vice of the Principality." Mr. Waugh's Dr. Fagan might well have written this report!

The Commission's unanimous conclusion was that Wales must get rid of its language. Understandably, the report created a furore throughout Wales and, far from killing the Welsh language, it stung the Welsh Nationalists to campaign for even more extensive use of their native tongue. Some immediate results of this campaign were the founding of *Baner Cymru* by Thomas Gee and the publication of a Welsh encyclopaedia in 1854. Through the columns of the former Gee did much to influence Welsh political thought and *Yr Amserau*, with which *Baner Cymru* was amalgamated in 1859, and the encyclopaedia were vital sources of young Lloyd George's education.

Yet even as late as 1866 *The Times* was arguing that the "Welsh language is the curse of Wales". Instruction in the schools was given in English and children were punished for speaking in Welsh. In many schools a blackboard bearing the legend "Welsh Stick" was hung in the class-room. If any pupil was caught speaking Welsh, this blackboard would be hung round his neck for a whole week, at the end of which a severe flogging was inflicted on him. At the school in Lloyd George's own village a girl pupil was made to walk to and from school wearing a dunce's cap bearing the words, "Welsh Fool".

If violence was not shown towards "the enemy from across the border" it was due very largely to the pacifist teaching of the religious revival. The first Welsh M.P. to make something of an international reputation for himself was a pacifist, Henry Richard, who was secretary of the Peace Society and who, from 1845 to 1884, expounded the need for disarmament both in and out of Parliament and as far afield as Brussels, Frankfurt and Paris. Henry Richard was the inspiration for Lloyd George's bitter opposition to the Boer War.

All these events helped to mould the opinions and stimulate the ideas of the youthful Lloyd George. He grew up against a background of revolt against the social order of the day, the domination of the English and widespread poverty. The Wales of his boyhood was marked by radicalism and militant Nonconformity arising after a long period of indifference to religion. Religious fervour stirred the valleys from apathy; the desire was to revolt, but the emphasis was on intellectual action rather than the use of brute force. Religion coloured and formed the political outlook. The bitter passions which might so easily have resulted in riots were put through the sieve of pulpit exhortation, thus making religion the natural outlet for the emotions of a passionate race.

But, in staving off the dangers of violent nationalism, this religious emotionalism frequently turned in on itself. The Nonconformist section of the nation, now by far the largest section of the population, leavened its Calvinistic pre-occupation with sin with an obsession with sex. Exultation of the spirit, far from mortifying the flesh, inflamed it, and in the period from 1850 to 1906 the picture drawn by Dr. Fagan of "Nonconformity and lust stalking hand in hand" is certainly not overdrawn. Calvinism and paganism united to make sex and religion a patch-work quilt of idealism, exhibitionism and sexual indulgence.

Nowhere was the pagan tradition stronger than in North Wales, and here the religious revival achieved its emotional zenith and produced the most marked excesses. Revivalist preachers were adored and doted on with as much extravagant enthusiasm and frustrated passion as is now bestowed on pop singers. After family prayers and Bible reading bundling followed as a matter of course in the most strictly religious of North Wales households.

Llanystumdwy was no exception to the general rule. There were two Nonconformist chapels in the village besides the parish church, but Richard Lloyd and his family worshipped at the Church of the Disciples of Christ at Penymaes, a small chapel two miles away. The Disciples were a sect which had broken away from the Baptist denomination because of an insistence on following more closely the precepts of the New Testament. Preaching festivals were held at regular intervals and the emphasis in religion was always on the preacher. There could hardly have been a better training ground for a future public speaker than this part of Caernarvonshire, for the ablest preachers in Wales and the most outstanding orators of the era all came here in turn. In his later years Lloyd George always acknowledged this, saying: "I owe nothing to the university. I owe nothing to secondary schools. Whatever I owe is to the little *bethel*.'[1] He learned the arts and technique of public speaking by listening to the great preachers and the effect of the *hwl* in their sermons conditioned the purple parts of his own oratory.

It was an intoxicating brew of oratory which these preachers served up. Of one of them, Hugh Price Hughes, Ll. G. said: "The greatest personal force my race has turned out for a generation. That was the atmosphere Hugh Price Hughes brought in my youth. We had then preachers who believed passionately in heaven and hell, God and Satan, damnation, salvation and redemption."

Lloyd George was baptised by immersion at the age of twelve. "Washing for Jesus" was how the irreverent non-Baptists regarded this ritual: they were strangely intolerant of each other's sects. The Calvinistic Methodist preacher would declaim from his pulpit against the practices of Baptists, while a little crowd of unruly village toughs

[1] Church.

would gather around the immersion pool, lewdly jeering behind cupped hands at the parson immersing men, women and children in loose-fitting night-shirts. In Welsh the Baptists would intone:

> "In the water
> He will wash us,
> He will wash us,
> He will wash us."

Devout Baptists such as Richard Lloyd may have been unaffected by such manifestations of mocking irreverence around them, but many testified to the soul-warping nature of such ceremonies under the public gaze.

* * * * *

In researches around Llanystumdwy the author was given extracts from letters written by a friend of Lloyd George's youth, a man named Moses Roberts, who hailed from Caernarvon and later emigrated to Patagonia. These letters shed fascinating light on the period in which Lloyd George grew up and on the man from Llanystumdwy himself.

"I shall always remember the day young Ll. G. and I went to a convention at Blaenau Festiniog. There were about thirty churches and chapels in Blaenau at the time and the place was full of tuberculosis. I remember Ll. G.—he was about fifteen then, a clever boy and full of big ideas about the future—saying that T.B. was due to English Church and that it was a regular scandal. What he meant was the custom of English Church of passing the same cup round at Communion, and all those coughing and spitting people passing the germs on to one another this way. Of course he was quite right, but I had never thought of this before. Shows how his brain worked even at that age.

"At Blaenau we attended two convention meetings in the morning and the big meeting at night. They had been quiet meetings with not much interest until the big show at night.

"I shall never forget it was a lovely balmy summer evening and the young people of the district had gathered in groups outside the *capel*, wondering whether to go in or just to walk the streets. Then one young girl came in, knelt down in front of everyone and confessed that she had sinned greatly, but was now willing to testify to the Great Lord Jesus.

"Young Lloyd George was deeply moved. He kept crying 'Amen' and then the other young people, probably curious to know what the girl had said, flocked into the *capel* and everyone singing and praying all at once. The preacher's full name I cannot recall, but his Christian name was Evan. We all knew that Evan was a secret drinker and that was why he had never made the great name for himself that as a preacher he deserved.

"'I am a sinner,' cried Evan. 'We are all sinners here. But don't do as I do, do as I tell you. The glory of the Lord lies in overcoming our sins and being sorry for them. If we have no sin, we have nothing to be sorry about.'

"At the end of his sermon he closed the meeting with a prayer, shouting out in a paroxysm of ecstasy: 'O Lord, let us make our sins glorify Thy Name. That is not the cry of blasphemy, but of true repentance. Oh, Lord, bend us!'

"There was a great commotion in the congregation as men and women tumbled on their knees, some whimpering and crying softly, others shouting 'Alleluia!' Then I opened my own eyes as I heard someone fall down beside me. It was young Lloyd George. He was prostrate on the floor, with the sweat pouring off his brow. And young women gathered around him, wiping away the sweat and whispering to him. When he came to he told me: 'From this day I am ready to go out and preach to the world like that man. I know exactly what my message is.'"

Anyone in Nonconformist circles in North Wales who wished to preach could do so: he did not have to be ordained or to receive any formal blessing. Youths started to preach spontaneously and on the inspiration of a single experience at a convention. The sinners were even more prone to preach than those who had lived virtuous lives. Personal experience of sin became a cult. Nor was this revivalism a short spasm in the life of Wales. It sparked, flared, ebbed and burst forth again into great flames of emotionalism throughout the first forty years of Lloyd George's lifetime. The last great Revival in Wales was that inspired by Evan Roberts, a man with a handsome, almost semitic countenance. From 1904 his oratory and influence spread from Loughor to Angelsey, from Newcastle Emlyn to Ammanford. Whereas the Methodist Revival was educational in substance, that of Lloyd George's childhood was theological, but the final Revival of 1904 was unadulterated emotionalism. Indeed, it is probable that in 1904 Revivalism reached its zenith and gradually burnt itself out.

Aneirin Talfan Davies, the B.B.C.'s West Wales representative, has given an account of one of Evan Roberts's meetings: "On the Sunday evening . . . Evan Roberts asked those who had given themselves of the Lord to remain in the chapel. The doors were locked. Evan Roberts then gave them a simple prayer, 'Send the Holy Spirit now, for Jesus Christ's sake.' Each member of the congregation was to repeat it in turn, but before they were half way through the number present something happened and there was an outburst of pentecostal fervour. . . . People came groaning under the burden of sin; others, confessing, and others shouting: 'Hold Thy Hand, O Jesus, I can't stand any more.'"

In the neighbourhood of Llanystumdwy and especially at Caernarvon there were many Irish and Spanish labourers, mostly working in the slate quarries. Many of these infused something of their own native emotionalism into the Pentecostan dances which so often followed the Revivalist meetings. Terpsichorean abandon was the handmaiden of religious mania so that its participants danced wildly around while proclaiming the glories of the Lord in a fashion which would have done more credit to West African fetishists than to sober Nonconformists. They invariably ended up in sexual orgies.

Moses Roberts of Caernarvon seems to have been a close crony of Lloyd George in his early teens. He tells us that together they "Took part in the Pentecostan dances and afterwards were sorely tempted by two Irish girls. I do not dare to imagine what Richard Lloyd would have said! He did not hold with anything that deviated from the strict tenets of the Disciples. Ll. G. and I were in fine fettle that night, a little merry maybe, but just stimulated by the preaching and we did nothing wrong, only taking the girls to their lodgings for *caru gwely*.'

Caru gwely means literally courting in bed, or, more accurately, bundling. It is an ancient custom in Wales, dating back several centuries, and in the last century was the general form of courting, even though frowned upon by some deacons of the chapels. *Caru gwely* was practised in various forms and the liberties which courting couples could enjoy were carefully regulated according to the district in which they lived. There were strict rules and they had to be kept, or social ostracism would follow. Sometimes the parents or guardians of the girl would put the couple to bed, tuck them in and place a pillow or plank between them. On occasions the girl would be sewn up in a sack to make complete seduction almost impossible. But when the boy and girl were both faithful members of a chapel such restrictions were regarded as an insult to their religious senses, so they were put on their honour not to exceed the bounds of decency. As to the conception of "decency" considerable latitude was allowed. In theory this may suggest that all reasonable precautions for controlling bundling were taken, but in practice, as Evan Price Davies once denounced *caru gwely* in an anti-bundling sermon:

> "Deep down in hell let them there dwell
> And bundle on that bed,
> Then turn and roll without control
> Till all their lusts are fed."

The Anglican Church in Wales frowned on bundling. The Rev. William Jones, Vicar of Nevin, had this to say on the custom in North Wales: "In England farmers' daughters are respectable. In Wales they are in the constant habit of being courted in bed. In the case of domestic servants the vice is universal. I have had the greatest difficulty in keeping my own servants from practising it. It became necessary to secure their chamber windows with bars to prevent them from admitting men. Of course, they are Nonconformists and heretics, so what can you expect. I am told by my parishioners that unless I allow the practice, I shall very soon have no servants at all."

So if Lloyd George went bundling in his youth he must be judged by the custom of his fellow countrymen. A chaplain to the Bishop of Bangor, the Rev. J. W. Trevor, declared that "fornication was not regarded as a vice, scarcely as a frailty, by the common people of Wales. It is considered as a matter of course and laughed at without shame or scruple by both sexes alike. In Anglesey and Caernarvonshire householders absolutely encourage the practice."

It is important to realise the effects of such practices as *caru gwely*, the unhealthy religious emotionalism and the local attitude to sex relations in assessing the peccadilloes of Lloyd George's later life. Though the full details of his amorous life may never be told, it is possible now to show how Lloyd George's character and career were injured by this weakness. Not since the days of Palmerston had a British Prime Minister shown so few inhibitions in his private life as Ll. G. Certainly none has been so careless of his reputation in private life, or risked so much to satisfy the smallest whim. How he escaped unscathed in a country so prone to outbursts of moral indignation is one of the social miracles of our time. During his lifetime he saw Dilke and Parnell crucified on the altar of British hypocrisy, yet he never heeded the warnings. Luck was always with him in his private, if not his public life.

Many a Sunday night sermon acted as an unconscious spur to bundling, or to provoking sexual thoughts. In one such sermon preached in near-by Nevin during Lloyd George's youth the congregation were told in the middle of a *hwl* peroration: "Our native mountains raise themselves like paps to show to God their affinity with humanity. These mountains are God's monuments to the glory of Woman, and when the sun sets on them and lights them up in an aura of pink, one can look upon them as those roseate buds of a woman's breasts which offer us life and hope."

Doubtless that preacher had the same ideas as Somerset Maugham's missionary in *Rain* when he was disturbed in his dreams by the likeness of the mountains of Nevada to the breasts of the prostitute he was trying to reform.

Mountains and breasts, running streams and the surging, babbling source of love and religious fervour, God and Satan, Mary and the Whore of Babylon, harp-playing angels and hell-fire. This was the black-and-white, all things clear-cut forthrightness of the Wales of the era. It was a heady brew for the simple-minded; for a young man of intelligence and avid curiosity, of passion and enthusiasm, it must have stimulated to an incalculable extent.

3

"THE BLACKEST TORY PARISH IN THE LAND"

"Llanystumdwy, the place from where I came, was the blackest Tory parish in the land."

David Lloyd George

The Bethel and the Bible, politics and bundling: these were the diverse ingredients of Lloyd George's youth. In the background, like an Avenging Angel, reminiscent of an Old Testament prophet, was the stern figure of Uncle Richard. There was little time for idling. Even bundling was something to be snatched furtively "in between a Band of Hope meeting and a walk home."[1] Work all the week and lessons late at night from Richard Lloyd; the journey on foot three times each way on Sunday to the chapel at Penymaes; Band of Hope meetings at Moriah and singing classes in Llanystumdwy; Sunday School and occasional visits to the conventions as far afield as Caernarvon and Bala; a walk into Pwllheli once a week to borrow the London papers: it was a full life and certainly not a dull one, far fuller and more exciting than civilised suburban life in Victorian England.

Village schooling may have been defective in many ways, but it was thorough in the emphasis it placed on speaking clearly and correctly, the trained Welsh ear being unable to tolerate any spoken word that was unmusical. Lloyd George commented: "I learned to speak clearly and correctly so that all could hear me when I was four years of age. We had singing lessons in the village from a farmer's son who was a fine interpreter of tonic sol-fa. He taught us to strike the right tones truly, to enunciate clearly and to use our voices correctly. He would force us to sing again and again until every word was intelligible."

The chief battle which waged in the hearts of the people of North Wales in the sixties and seventies of the last century was that against the power and domination of the Established Church. Llanystumdwy was no exception to the general rule. There was a bitter hatred in this village of the tyranny of a Church which, through Squire and Rector, tried to stamp out the Welsh tongue, persecuted schoolchildren and even forced them to repeat the Catechism by threatening the direst penalties against their parents if they disobeyed. The Church of

[1] Moses Roberts.

England clergymen of the area were feeble characters, the lackeys and lickspittles of the Squire, far more intent on doing his bidding than preaching the philosophy of Christ.

Richard Lloyd, who was morally and intellectually head and shoulders above his fellow-villagers, was one of the stoutest opponents of the Established Church, not on bigoted grounds—he was friendly enough with the Rector to borrow his papers—but because he saw it as an instrument to bolster up a class system.

"The English Church," said Richard Lloyd, "is but a milk-and-water copy of Papism, with all its follies and frills." He impressed on his nephew the need for resisting the attempts of the local schoolmaster to wean his pupils towards the Established Church.

This war between the branches of the Church of Christ must have made its mark on Ll. G. early in life. The knowledge that there could be open war between practising Christians would induce cynicism in so intelligent a boy. Doubtless this inter-denominational strife and bickering between Churches created in his mind the doubts he always held privately about organised religion and the increasing unorthodoxy of his theological views in later life.

From 1715 to 1870 there was not a single Bishop in Wales who could speak Welsh. This deepened the class conflict and fanned the spirit of nationalism. The extension of the franchise in 1867 made a difference: for the first time the ascendancy of the Church of England and the Tory landlords was challenged. It was, however, odd, yet at the same time significant of the resilience of the English Church, that a devout member of that Church, perhaps the greatest lay member it has ever had, should become the rallying figure for the aspirations of the Welsh Nonconformists. William Ewart Gladstone gradually cast his spell across the sombre valleys of Wales until in many a humble cottage a picture of the familiar and formidable visage of that statesman held a place of honour beside the coloured prints of Old Testament patriarchs.

From 1870 onwards there was open war between the forces of Liberalism and Nonconformity on the one hand and those of Toryism and the Established Church on the other. The landlords, especially those of North Wales, were among the worst in Britain. In rapaciousness and lack of charity they can only be compared to the early nineteenth century English landlords in Ireland. When the Liberals won the elections of 1868, the landlords were sufficiently aroused to realise that this was a threat to their authority and they used their powers to crush this dangerous new doctrine, which, as they saw it, was filling the people's minds with ideas above their divinely allotted station in life. The election ballots were not secret in those days and many tenants who had not voted for Tory candidates were evicted from their land and cottages. This happened at Llanystumdwy, and Lloyd George's earliest memories must have been of neighbours—often mothers in the last stages of childbirth—thrown out into the street with their few belongings and driven to the fields to find what shelter they could in some distant hayrick. Even then they might be charged as vagrants and hounded out of the district.

Other landlords were more subtle. They merely raised the rents of those who had voted Liberal and reduced those of the faithful Tories. Liberals who owned shops were boycotted; their children were brought before the courts on some trumped-up charges of poaching. Is it to be wondered that this tyranny produced a reaction towards Socialism and even Communism in the next fifty years?

But in 1872 the Ballot Act checked these unscrupulous tactics and tenants were enabled to vote without being intimidated and the forces of Liberalism grew to combat the solid bloc of Tory landlords.

Young Lloyd George's schoolmaster wanted him to take up teaching. But to become a teacher in the parish school he would have had to join the Church of England and this, of course, was unthinkable. It was David's mother who suggested her son might become a solicitor and, with his uncle's assistance, he passed the preliminary examination of the Law Society in December, 1877, and in due course was articled to the office of Breese, Jones and Casson, of Portmadoc. By a happy coincidence Mr. Breese was not only Clerk of the Peace, but Liberal agent as well.

Sir Herbert Lewis recorded that in 1904, when Lloyd George was already established politically, the latter regretted he had not become a preacher. But, Sir Herbert added: 'Of one thing I am sure. If Ll. G. had gone into the pulpit he would have started a new sect."

Lloyd George's earliest attempts at public speaking and preaching were at local Temperance Society meetings. Coming from a teetotal household, he was made secretary of the local branch of the United Kingdom Alliance. Occasionally he read the lesson at the chapel at Penymaes, but his original ideas on preaching made him chary of conforming to the strict tenets of the Disciples. His first preaching engagement was at the age of eighteen in a Baptist chapel at Penmachno in Denbighshire.

About this time Richard Lloyd closed down his cobbler's business and moved with his family to Criccieth. This town must have been a constant reminder to Lloyd George of the traditions of Welsh nationalism. For the castle which towered above his new home was once held by Edward I. It was captured and destroyed in 1404 by Owain Glyndwr. Outside the Memorial Hall in the little town lay the ancient stone called *Carreg Orchest*, which means "Try your strength". "Whenever I passed that stone," Ll. G. used to say, "it always seemed to be addressing itself to me alone. It was that stone which prompted me to enter politics seriously."

Yet, despite the call of politics, he found time to join the Volunteers and even attend their camp at Conway. Little is known for certain about this brief and untypical episode in his life. Here he was preaching pacifism and attacking the British occupation of Egypt in the local Press, and at the same time a Volunteer. It has been suggested that he was asked to leave the Volunteers after he told a Liberal meeting at Caernarvon:

"I come from the blackest and wickedest Tory parish in the land. It is a parish in which the Squire turned the fathers of young children out of their homes because they dared to vote Liberal. But the political power of the landlords in Wales will be broken as effectively as the power of the Druids. The great rugged nationalist sentiments of Wales will rise against the English Ogre, this fiendish she-wolf whose lair is in Westminster. I shall not sleep in my grave until someone knocks and tells me '*Mae hi wedi mynd*' (She has gone)."

The Llanfrothen Burial Case, one of Lloyd George's first and greatest legal triumphs, has been described in great detail by many people, and if a brief summary of it is included in this chapter, the purpose is solely to throw light on that fiery outburst at Caernarvon and to show how even at the age of twenty-four Lloyd George was possessed of a fanatical, single-minded political opportunism.

Llanfrothen Churchyard had been enlarged by the gift of a piece of land which had been used for burials even though it was unconsecrated. In 1880 the Burials Act was passed, authorising the burials of Dissenters in Church of England graveyards with specific permission for services other than those of the Established Church. The Rector, who disliked the Act, persuaded one of the donors of the land to sign a deed insisting that burials must be conducted with Church of England rites.

Lloyd George followed this move on the part of the Rector with interest. With how great an interest his biographers do not tell us. But he evidently anticipated that one day the Act of 1880 would be tested, for he took counsel's opinion in London on such a hypothetical case. When he had received this opinion, he told his political mentor, Michael D. Jones, Principal of the Independent Theological College at Bala: "I see in Llanfrothen the chance of striking a mortal blow against the Church of England. We can make the plight of the downtrodden Welsh Nonconformists a political issue, not only in Wales, but far beyond its borders."

Michael Jones and Lloyd George had struck up a close friendship, and the latter's land reform policy was borrowed in almost every detail from the former. Together the two discussed a plan of action in the event of a Dissenter dying and desiring to be buried in Llanfrothen Churchyard. Michael Jones was somewhat shocked when the young solicitor insisted that the only way to defy the Rector was to "break down the gate if necessary and force through the burial".

According to Michael Jones, Lloyd George actually made a tour of the parish of Llanfrothen, inquiring of Nonconformists who had expressed a wish to be buried in the little churchyard. Then he was told of an ailing quarry worker named Robert Roberts, a Calvinistic Methodist, already destined for an early grave, whose daughter was buried in the annexe to the churchyard. Ll. G. visited the dying man, talked with his relatives and persuaded them to insist on his being buried beside his daughter. There is something rather ghoulish about these deathbed imbroglios, with Ll. G. whispering advice on how the poor man should be buried, but it is certain that the family of the quarry man would never have dared to challenge the might of the Established Church without the backing and encouragement of the solicitor from Criccieth.

When Roberts died the relatives informed the Rector that they wished his burial to take place in the churchyard according to Calvinist rites. The Rector refused, locked the churchyard gate and declined to hand over the key. The funeral procession was barred.

Lloyd George, who had foreseen that the relatives might capitulate, was near at hand. He told them that the Rector had said: "The man Roberts can be buried in the corner reserved for suicides and unbelievers." In fairness to the cantankerous old Rector it is only right to point out that there is no evidence he said any such thing. By misrepresenting the Rector Lloyd George may have stiffened the morale of the relatives, but he certainly caused them grievous pain. When the pain turned to anger, they accepted Lloyd George's advice to "break down the gate and bury him beside his daughter, using whatever service you desire".

This was done. The Rector sued the relatives of Roberts in the Portmadoc County Court and Lloyd George, now sure of gaining political kudos out of the incident, defended the case. The jury found in favour of the defendants, but the Judge not only made an inaccurate note of their findings, but gave a verdict for the Rector. When the appeal went to the High Court of Justice, the Judge's findings were reversed.

That case did more harm to the Established Church in Wales than any other single incident. It had wide publicity throughout Britain and was, perhaps, the final nail in the coffin of the un-Christian edifice of the Church of England as it functioned in Wales. For Lloyd George it did all he expected, enhancing his reputation and paving the way for a political career.

* * * * *

There is no positive proof of how and when Lloyd George first met Maggie Owen, the farmer's comely daughter. His notebook stated that on November 28, 1885, "after an election meeting" he "took

M.O. and her cousin home". Later entries seem to confirm that this was Maggie Owen, daughter of Richard Owen, a yeoman farmer of Mynydd Ednyfed, near Criccieth. "How and where they first met I never knew," wrote the present Earl Lloyd-George. "I do know it was not a case of love at first sight as far as my mother was concerned."

J. Hugh Edwards, however, recalled asking Mrs. Lloyd George whether she could remember the occasion on which she first saw her future husband. She replied that she "had a distinct recollection". It appears that, when they were small children, they used to pass each other in the main street as they accompanied their elders to their respective chapels. One Sunday morning the little boy who was Lloyd George arrived in his knickerbocker suit, displaying a pair of scarlet woollen stockings, which attracted her attention, with the result that, immediately after they had passed each other, she turned round to have another look "at so attractive a pair of stockings". As she did so, the boy turned round also and they smiled at each other.

There was immediate and vehement opposition to the match both from Lloyd George's family and that of Maggie Owen. Was not Ll. G. a fatherless waif, argued the Owens, and his uncle only a poor cobbler? They really knew very little about the relative well-being of Richard Lloyd and his brood. What dismayed them was that Ll. G. was a Baptist and a peculiar sort of Baptist at that. Besides he was a Radical Liberal, whereas the Owens were Calvinistic Methodists and lukewarm Liberals as well.

Richard Lloyd was so perturbed at the idea of a match with a Calvinistic Methodist that he set out to lure his nephew away from his heart's desire by inviting all the eligible daughters of Baptists to tea at his home, rather clumsily encouraging David to take them out. Moses Roberts, his friend from Caernarvon, seems to have been a close conspirator of Lloyd George at this time. Working on the principle that two's company, three's not, Lloyd George would persuade Moses to join him in these evenings and so thwart his uncle's purpose.

"You take her home, Moses, and mind you don't leave me alone with her, man," admonished young Ll. G. "I don't want Maggie Owen to hear I'm out and about chasing other girls. Already some people have given her that idea."

"And what do I do about all this? What do I get out of it, Dai *bach*?"

"Oh, you have the honour of taking her home. You can bundle with her if she'll let you. But I doubt your chances, knowing she's been chosen by the *Esgob* to keep company with me."

The *Esgob* (Bishop) was Ll. G.'s own nickname for Uncle Richard.

So Moses, as he used to relate in later years, was the chosen instrument to thwart the wishes of Uncle Richard. "Ll. G. used to tell his uncle that I was the fast one, that I knew more about courting them than he did. He always was one for telling a tall story. I don't think Uncle Richard ever forgave me for this. He forbade David to see me, saying I was a thriftless good-for-nothing."

Meanwhile Lloyd George had made up his mind that he was going to marry Maggie Owen as firmly as he had fixed his heart on entering politics. In love, as in politics, be showed immense cunning. When Maggie told him she had been forbidden to see him any more, he solemnly replied: "Don't you worry, *cariad* (sweetheart). Love will find a way without cheating. You have been told not to see me and I understand that. But we can write to one another."

"But you mustn't post the letters to my home, and if I write to you your Uncle Richard will know all about it. Then there'll be trouble."

"No need to use the post office for love messages," said Ll. G. soothingly. "I know a far, far better and much more romantic way to do these things."

And he pointed to a small crevice in a wall surrounding one of the Owen's fields. "This will be our post-box. I'll put my letters in here and you can come and collect them when no one is looking. And mind you put your answers in the same place."

So the hole in the wall was the sole method of communication for many weeks, if not months. Meanwhile David had found an unexpected ally in his campaign to win the hand of Maggie. She was Maggie's aunt who, differing from the rest of the Owen family, advised her niece: "Don't give him up. He has a great future."

Young Lloyd George paid frequent visits to this aunt, cajoling her into championing his cause more actively. But he did not trust to this method alone; he sought to ingratiate himself with Margiad, a faithful servant of the Owens, who was devoted to Maggie. With all the charm and persuasion at his command, he proceeded to impress his personality on Margiad just as he had on the aunt. But Margiad was not such an easy ally in the early stages. She knew that Lloyd George was not favoured by her employers and she was too fond of Maggie to want to risk ruining her happiness.

Moses Roberts wrote: "Ll. G. met his match in Margiad. She would have nothing to do with him at first. 'We don't want no Baptists round our farm,' she told him scornfully. 'You go back to the girls of Llanystumdwy.'

"But Ll. G. refused to be daunted. He tried all methods to win Margiad over. He was solemn and dignified, and when that failed he was gay and even flirtatious. He bought her little presents, most of which she gave back to him with a piece of her mind.

"'Well, Margiad, if this state of affairs goes on much longer, I shall have to propose to you instead. For if you don't want Maggie to be happy and marry me, why, then, you must want to marry me yourself! Is that it, my girl? Fie on you, you Jezebel! No, no, I don't really think that myself, so don't look so shocked and pained. But other people might think so and what would Maggie say then, eh? Come now, be a good girl, and take a message to your beloved mistress. We both love her, don't we, so we both want the same thing.'

"Margiad began to acquiesce in the persistence of this ardent suitor. He would put his arm round her shoulder and cuddle her and she would push him away. 'Don't you go touching me, Mr. George,' she would say. 'I'm not one of your Baptist girls.' 'Well, I can't cuddle Maggie, she's not here, so why not cuddle her best friend? Now, be sensible, Margiad, just do me the favour of telling Maggie Owen that I can kiss better than those Calvin louts. Tell her you know because I've tried it out on you. But you wouldn't dare to admit kissing a Baptist, would you now?'

"Ll. G. was a man who would never take no for an answer where girls were concerned."

Eventually it became apparent to Richard Lloyd that his nephew was not going to be palmed off with any Baptist maidens, and the Owens, partly persuaded by the aunt, but much more impressed by the young solicitor's growing prestige, agreed to a marriage. It took place on January 24, 1888, a few days after Lloyd George's twenty-fifth birthday, in the Presbyterian Chapel of Pen-cae-newydd. Significantly the wedding was solemnised in neither the bride's nor the groom's village; it was a very quiet affair and the choice of chapel was obviously a compromise to reconcile religious differences. There was still reluctance on both sides to a match that was now regarded as inevitable rather than desirable by the respective families. After a brief honeymoon in London the Lloyd Georges settled down for a while at Maggie's home near Criccieth.

Village legal triumphs did much to turn Lloyd George from the idol of the poachers and working men whom he defended into the rising hope of the Liberal Party in the district. On all sides it was agreed that he had all the attributes of a first-class public speaker. He had thrown his weight into the fight for Disestablishment of the Church in Wales and allied himself to the left-wing and nationalist fringe of the Welsh Liberals. At this time Gladstone was actively wooing the Welsh Liberals, and the G.O.M. in a speech at Swansea in 1887 had more or less invited the formation of a Welsh Parliamentary Party.

Lloyd George decided to follow up this lead from the mightiest political figure in Britain. His one idea at the time was to be leader of a Welsh Nationalist Party, a radical, reforming Party which would break away from the "she-wolf at Westminster".

Yet already he was displaying that ingratitude in political life which was such an unpleasant feature of his later life. When Gladstone spoke at Swansea in favour of the "just claims of Wales", Lloyd George lauded him as "this grand fighter for the liberties and rights of little nations". But the following year in a speech to the North Wales Liberal Federation he was supporting a resolution condemning Gladstone for his absence from a recent debate on Welsh Disestablishment and threatening him with the withdrawal of Welsh Liberal support if he did not mend his ways.

From four nominees the young solicitor was selected as prospective Parliamentary candidate for Caernarvon Boroughs. Some of the older men in the Party shook their heads at the choice. "Young George is too wild," they said. "He will lose us votes. He is too ambitious and will over-reach himself." But his popularity with the rank-and-file ensured his selection. Had he been turned down there would have been a revolt among the younger Liberals of the constituency. Young Lloyd George was a handsome, dominating figure, with his large head and commanding presence. It was audacity which was the quality which most of all in his younger days won him admiration, for audacity is rare in a politician.

His chance came unexpectedly. Just as he was setting off for a holiday with his wife news came that Edward Swetenham, Q.C., member for the division, had died suddenly. The by-election he had to fight early in 1890 was, appropriately enough, against his old enemy and tormentor, Squire Ellis Nanney. It was a piquant situation in which Lloyd George impishly delighted.

His programme was good, heady radical stuff—Home Rule for Wales as well as Ireland, Disestablishment and Land Reform, the abolition of plural voting and the removal of restrictions on fisheries, the last-named being a sure-fire vote-catcher in this constituency. He set about his election campaign with verve and zest, travelling round the scattered villages on foot as no candidate had ever done before; he knocked at cottage doors where a Parliamentary candidate had never previously been seen.

Lloyd George was declared the victor by 1,963 votes to 1,945—a narrow margin, but sufficient to cause great jubilation in the Liberal camp. Liberalism in Caernarvon had come into its own, and when he returned to Criccieth he was greeted by the glow of a score of bonfires on the surrounding hills.

4

YOUNG MAN IN A HURRY

"There is a path which no fowl
knoweth and which the
vulture's eye hath not seen."
Job, XXVIII, v.7

Above his bed in Downing Street in the days when he was Premier this text served as a reminder to Lloyd George both of the extremes of adversity and questing hope. He told Lionel Curtis that "more than once I have preached on this text, but it was not until the Boer War that I realised its full meaning. Then indeed I felt that I was on a path which no fowl knew and the eye of the vulture had not seen—a perilous mountain path that soared high into the mists."

But the text is typical of the young man in a hurry, eager to seek out paths that disappeared in the mists. From the moment he took his seat in the House of Commons on April 17, 1890, Lloyd George gave the impression of an impatient young man who had much to do and little time in which to do it. He made his maiden speech on the day Goschen introduced his Budget. "I was horribly nervous. I felt like a young student who had not even been to Bala to preach a sermon before John Elias."

Lloyd George missed the invigorating atmosphere of the cheering meetings of his own countrymen, felt the chilly hostility of the aristocrats who looked upon him as a Radical interloper. *Cassell's Popular Educator* was a poor substitute for Oxford. This sense of loneliness made him more of a rebel; for a time he turned his eyes back towards Wales and yearned for a Welsh Party that could employ the obstructive tactics of the Irish and dominate the scene at Westminster. Parnell became his hero for a while and Mabon was another strong influence. This rugged and impassioned Welsh miners' leader was a remarkable orator who made his mark with one of the most memorable rebuffs the House of Commons has ever witnessed.

Welsh Disestablishment was being discussed and Mabon was emphasising the grave handicap to the spiritual life of Wales which arose from the fact that so many of the clergy in the Church could not speak Welsh. Suddenly, and without warning, Mabon switched from English into a torrent of Welsh. The Tories hooted with laughter.

Mabon paused. He looked across the floor of the House and asked quietly: "Do you know what you were laughing at? That was the Lord's Prayer."

The effect of that remark was instantaneous. His critics were shamed and silent.

Outside Westminster Lloyd George pursued his role as crusader of the Nationalists. He always seemed to be one step ahead of Tom Ellis, son of a peasant farmer from Merionethshire, who was the acknowledged leader of the little band of Welsh Liberal M.P.s. In speeches at Cardiff and Merthyr Tydfil he demanded, "As complete a measure of Home Rule for Wales as for Ireland."

Then Tom Ellis was made Liberal Whip, and from that day Welsh Nationalism sadly lacked his selfless leadership. For Ellis was a loyal Party man, where Ll. G. was an opportunist. As Chief Whip Ellis put the Liberal Party's interests first and those of Welsh Nationalism second. "I was elected as a Liberal and to that creed I am pledged. Its interests come before anything else," he told fellow Welshmen. His attitude caused Ll. G. to sneer that, "Tom Ellis is a renegade and mere office-seeker." It was an unworthy remark.

After Ellis became Chief Whip, Lloyd George assumed the mantle of unofficial leader of the Welsh Nationalists, who were surprised and delighted when they found they had a more aggressive and colourful speaker than Ellis. "Welsh Nationalism," he told one meeting, "is not anti-Liberal. It is Liberal enthusiasm worked up to a glowing red by the blasts of patriotism."

Lloyd George was never a convinced "Home Ruler" on the subject of Ireland. While insisting on the need for Home Rule for Wales, he made it clear that he was not altogether happy about granting the same rights to Ireland. "Every argument in favour of Home Rule in Ireland would be equally if not more appropriate for Wales. There is the fear that Irish Home Rule would re-establish Roman Catholicism as the national religion of Ireland—not a step we Nonconformists would regard as necessarily progressive. This risk would be entirely absent in the case of Wales. And Wales has no Ulster."

His new plan for the nationalists was to rally the forces of Irish, Scottish and Welsh nationalism into a united front to press for a policy of "quadrilateral Home Rule". It was not a new idea, for the Scottish Nationalists had spent five years insisting that whatever was done for Ireland should be done for Scotland. Now Lloyd George, with the support of his friend, Sir Herbert Lewis, M.P. for Flintshire, argued for Scottish and Welsh Home Rule. A motion in favour of this was carried by 180 votes to 170. In 1895 a resolution expanded this to cover Home Rule all round and was seconded by Ll. G. This time the motion was defeated by 128 to 102.

By now the "young man in a hurry" was sizing up his colleagues in the House. For Gladstone he always had deep veneration mingled with impatience and sometimes outspoken criticism. He detested Lord Rosebery whom he regarded as a "Tory aristocrat masquerading under Liberal colours". Rosebery, for all his brilliance, shone with the tinsel glamour of a dilettante in the political field and was a constant and understandable thorn in the side of the radicals. But the original reason for Lloyd George's unconcealed dislike of Rosebery was the latter's reference to the Welsh as "natives of the Principality". "He talks about us as though we were some African tribe," grumbled Ll. G. "Stanley cheated the African tribes with empty jam-pots. That is the policy of the Liberal Government, giving us jam-pots from which others have had the jam."

But if the House of Commons had its Roseberys and other Liberals who still lived in the past, it also had on the Liberal benches a far stronger streak of genuine radicalism than it has ever seen since. One of these, Labouchere, was a man after Lloyd George's heart—"a gay spark who coruscates when he likes and doesn't give a damn for anyone", was the Welshman's summing-up of him. It was the irrepressible "Labby", last of the Liberal rakes, who, as the member for Northampton, supported the right of Nonconformists to be buried in Anglican churchyards. "I am in favour of religious equality not only above, but below the sod," said "Labby", employing a quip which might almost have come from the lips of the member for Caernarvon Boroughs. The man who, before entering politics, had gambled his way across Mexico, appeared in a circus in pink tights, billed as the "Bounding Buck of Babylon", taken part in a Californian gold rush in 1853 and fought a duel with an Austrian *chargé d'affaires*, was an exhilarating companion for the young Welshman whom he introduced to some of the less reputable of London night resorts. Both men had that touch of audacity without which radicalism can become arid and unexciting.

* * * * *

Whenever rumours about Lloyd George's private life developed to the extent of a court case—as they did on a number of occasions—the impression he managed to convey to the outside world was of an innocent man cruelly and wickedly victimised by malicious slander. This is a picture which has been iterated by many writers, but a re-examination of some of these charges will show that the portrait of injured innocence is somewhat overdrawn.

There was the divorce action of Edwards versus Edwards and Wilson, in July, 1897. The petitioner, Dr. David Edwards, a close friend of Lloyd George, of Cemmaes, Montgomeryshire, asked for leave to proceed without making a certain man, unnamed but referred to as "A.B.", the co-respondent. It was alleged that Mrs. Catherine

Edwards, his wife, had on August 19, 1896, given birth to a child of which the petitioner was not the father. Nine days before the birth of this child Mrs. Edwards had made a written confession to her husband mentioning the name of a man and alleging him to be the father of the child. The petitioner had been unable to obtain evidence which would corroborate this and meanwhile he had charged his wife with adultery with one, Edward Wilson.

The President of the Court stressed that a section of the Divorce Act was to ensure "that no man shall be convicted of adultery without the opportunity of clearing himself". He suggested that the unnamed man might put in a statement with reference to the course he intended to adopt.

Mrs. Edwards claimed her husband had forced her to make and sign the confession. Dr. Edwards had produced letters from "A.B." denying adultery with his wife in emphatic terms. The President of the Court then agreed that the petition should be allowed to proceed without making "A.B." a co-respondent. By this time it was common gossip in various parts of Wales that "A.B." was Lloyd George, but it was not until the case was heard again in the following November that suspicions became confirmed. Then Catherine Edwards's confession was produced. It stated that: "I, Catherine Edwards, do solemnly confess that I have on 4 February, 1896, committed adultery with Lloyd George, M.P., and that the said Lloyd George is the father of the child, and that I have on a previous occasion committed adultery with the above Lloyd George."

Counsel on both sides said they were "satisfied that the imputation against Lloyd George was without foundation". The respondent's confession was "an invention to protect a guilty man by naming an innocent one".

The co-respondent, who was stationmaster at Cemmaes Road railway station, said he was prepared to fight the case. Mrs. Edwards denied the charges of adultery made against herself and Wilson. The President then said the right course had been adopted in not pressing the case against Wilson, when once the petitioner had established his case against the "unknown adulterer", and Wilson was entitled to the benefit of his denial. Mrs. Edwards's adultery with a person unknown was clearly proved and there must be a decree nisi.

It was an unsatisfactory ending to a case which seems to have been deliberately confused on both sides. The allegation against Lloyd George was that on February 4, 1896, Dr. Edwards invited him to stay at his home. During the night Dr. Edwards had been called away professionally and did not return until the following morning. Did Lloyd George fool counsel on both sides and the President of the Court into the bargain? The reports of the case make no reference to statements which Lloyd George himself must have made to counsel.

In Mr. Frank Owen's book, *Tempestuous Journey*, we learn: "When the case came up for hearing Lloyd George produced to counsel records of the Parliamentary Division lists to show that on 4 February he had been until early morning voting in the House of Commons."

But on February 4, 1896, *Parliament was not sitting.*

The second session of the fourteenth Parliament of Queen Victoria was not opened until February 11 of that year. How then could Lloyd George clear himself on the grounds indicated by Mr. Owen?

Immediately the result of the case had been declared Lloyd George posed successfully as the injured martyr and was cordially congratulated by the Caernarvon Liberal Association on the "complete vindication of his character". Ll. G. wrote to the secretary of that association a long letter in which he said: "Our slander law is still uncivilised. Here was one of the greatest imputations on a man's honour that could ever be invented . . . and yet I was helpless in the matter. My accuser I could not bring to justice, as she had not 'published' the charge within the legal meaning of that term; a communication made by a wife to her husband does not constitute 'publication'. The horrible anguish of mind, the impairment to health, the possible loss of reputation counted for nothing in the eyes of our slander law. . . . Surely the law should be placed on a more humane footing?"

This scandal was indirectly the cause of a final split on the Welsh Home Rule issue between Lloyd George and D. A. Thomas (later Lord Rhondda). Originally Lloyd George's own scheme for the nationalists was to organise a highly disciplined Welsh Party which could link up with the Irish Party in challenging the House and forcing the Liberals to a more forthright Home Rule policy. Lord Oxford's biographers have spoken of the "studied want of consideration" with which Parnell, the Irish leader, treated his supporters and sympathisers. Lloyd George was reluctantly forced to draw the same conclusion. According to John Morley, Lloyd George actually made overtures to Parnell through Kitty O'Shea, the Irishman's mistress. But he received no encouragement from the chilly Parnell and when D. A. Thomas heard of his overtures he deprecated them strongly. There was no enthusiasm for Parnell among the Nonconformist Welsh M.P.s, who knew all about the liaison between Parnell and Kitty O'Shea. When Ll. G. put to a small group of them his plan for a Welsh Party on the Irish model he met with hostility. At this time Lloyd George was already involved in the scandal which eventually ended in the Divorce Courts, and D. A. Thomas heatedly asked him: "Do you want to repeat Parnell's blunders by ruining everything for Wales's future? You seem to think the Irish have everything to teach us. It would be better to learn from the lesson of where Mrs. O'Shea will lead Parnell—to Home Rule or the Divorce Court!"

This was a rebuke which Lloyd George never forgot and never completely forgave. Thomas, an extremely able man, who had been University light-weight boxing champion at Oxford, in the nineties, "counted for more in South Wales, which contained three-fourths of the people in the Principality, than the future Prime Minister," declared Llewellyn Williams, Q.C. This made Lloyd George extremely jealous of him, inclining him to the view that there was no room for two "kings" in Wales.

Consequently, wrote Lady Rhondda, Lloyd George "took the necessary precautions to ensure that there should not be. My father made one attempt to work with him in 1894, but he soon gave it up".

Lloyd George strove hard to bring the whole of the Welsh Nationalist movement into line with Cymru Fydd, the most fanatical of the Home Rule organisations. But his strength in North Wales was counteracted by his lack of influence in the south. D. A. Thomas supported Disestablishment, but he did not want Home Rule for Wales, and he disliked the idea of the South Wales Liberal Association, of which he was president, being merged into a wider organisation of which, without doubt, Lloyd George aimed to be the head. There was a split between south and north, and this finally proved fatal not only to Ll. G.'s plan for a militant Nationalist Party on the Irish model, but to the cause of nationalism generally.

In the House of Commons, Lloyd George deliberately set out to be the *enfant terrible* of Parliament. He was at his best in opposition and seemed happier when the Tories were back in power. *L'audace, l'audace, toujours l'audace:* Danton's policy became his guiding principle: to shock and to keep on shocking until the enemy was speechless in the face of his furious onslaughts. In June, 1899, in a debate on the Tithes Rent Charge Bill he flabbergasted the House with a scathing attack on the Church of England, making the more pious Tories gaze upwards as though they expected a thunderbolt from heaven to strike him down. "The Squire and the Parson," he decried, "have broken into the poor box and divided its contents between them. The Tammany ring of landlords and parsons are dividing the last remnants of the money between them."

But soon Tithes disputes, Welsh Nationalism and Disestablishment were forgotten in the sudden emergence of a far bigger issue—the South African War. With this even the "young man in a hurry" came into his own as a national figure, reviled and despised by a large section of the public, but by sheer force of personality compelling the people to listen to a series of unforgettable speeches condemning that war and all it stood for. In retrospect this period was Lloyd George's finest hour, morally a far greater achievement than his World War I premiership, even though the latter may have had more widespread results. Any student of the history and biographies of this era will recognise that it required supreme moral courage, allied to a defiant *panache*, to defy the overwhelming popular prejudice in favour of the war. One can best underline this statement by stressing how even the few other pro-Boer Liberals, such as Morley and Campbell-Bannerman, never effectively risked opprobrium by condemning the war in such vehement language as Ll. G. As to whether Lloyd George's uncompromising attitude and vehement hostility to the war were justified in the light of history is still a debatable point, but he succeeded in clearing the air of cant, humbug and nonsensical jingoism. The issue of the Boer War was never a clear-cut one of black and white, of right or wrong, as Ll. G. suggested. If there were unscrupulous capitalist adventurers on the British side, there were also on the Boer side men who permitted unspeakable indignities to be perpetrated on the African people. Probably the best summing-up of the war was that of Sir Edward Grey when he declared: "It has no right to be a popular war."

Lloyd George, the Nonconformist, developed a sectarian sympathy for the Boers. He mistook their Calvinist leaders for angels of light, whereas today their descendants seem more like princes of darkness bent on a fatal path of repression and segregation.

But, whatever their shortcomings, these Boers were excellent colonisers with a moral code that was far better than that of the money-grabbing, gold-seeking imperialist filibusters who were the friends of Cecil Rhodes. The virtue of Lloyd George at this period was that he showed immense moral courage, that he acted as a highly necessary antidote to the unthinking jingoism of a majority of the British people and that, for the first time since John Bright, he forced them to think about war and not just to accept it blindly as a national necessity.

In the nation-wide campaign from Bangor to Bristol, from London to Liskeard and from Caernarvon to Birmingham on which he embarked as a one-man crusade during the Boer War, his oratory was forceful and sincere, yet factual and well argued. Not only does it still read well, which cannot be said for many of his later speeches, but it is vital documentary material for any historian of that period.

The war hardened the hearts of the Afrikaners not only against the British but against human nature. It built up such a barrier of mistrust of Britain that not even the generous settlement made later by a Liberal Government could repair the damage done. It is not surprising that if Cromwell is still an issue in Eire and George III a hated figure in the American school, the crimes of Joseph Chamberlain are still realities in the minds of Afrikaners.

In many ways Chamberlain was an English version of Lloyd George—a demagogue and anti-royalist when it suited him, a reactionary imperialist and contemptuous of the rights of small peoples on other occasions. Fickle, disloyal, erratic, vain and deceitful, often stooping to the most outrageous intrigues, Chamberlain came as near to ruining the Tory Party as Lloyd George did to obliterating Liberalism.

Thwarted from power in the Liberal Party by a Grand Old Man who hung on to the leadership until he was almost blind, Chamberlain changed his Party allegiance without a pang. Seeing Home Rule for Ireland as a goal about to be achieved, he pressed Captain O'Shea to cite Parnell as a co-respondent to bring about his downfall and so divide the nation on the Irish question. When Chamberlain met Baron Sonnino, the Italian Foreign Secretary, a Jew, he made the appalling ill-mannered declaration at a dinner table: "Yes, sir, I have been called the apostle of the Anglo-Saxon race, and I am proud of that title. I think the Anglo-Saxon race is as fine as any race on earth. Not that I despise other races. There is only one race I despise—the Jews, sir. They are physical cowards."

This pathological outburst to Baron Sonnino sums up the mentality of the man who, despite all attempts to prove otherwise, encouraged the Jameson Raid which caused the South African War and made an injured martyr out of a barely disguised saboteur of the peace in the person of Cecil Rhodes. Though the inquiry into the Jameson Raid of 1895, when five hundred troopers of the Chartered Company invaded the Transvaal, revealed that Rhodes was culpable, Chamberlain, as Colonial Secretary, went out of his way to present Rhodes with an unblemished character. Such condonation of a man who had treated Chamberlain badly is quite inexplicable unless Rhodes or somebody else was in a position to hold a threat over the Colonial Secretary. In Gardiner's *Life of Harcourt* the assumption is made that "a member of the Rhodes group had come to the House with copies of missing telegrams and prepared to read them, if Chamberlain's attitude had not proved satisfactory".

The Committee of Inquiry were extremely reticent on Chamberlain's complicity in what was a flagrant piece of aggression in the name of the British flag. Lloyd George fastened on to the far more sinister aspect of Chamberlain's vested interests in imperialist adventures in South Africa—the big profits reaped by the Colonial Secretary's relatives from arms supplied for the conduct of the Boer War while Chamberlain was a minister.

If there was any doubt as to Chamberlain's culpability for the war, the views of Sir William Butler, High Commissioner and Acting Governor of South Africa, should suffice. Chamberlain ordered Butler to move troops to the Transvaal frontier; Butler refused, expressing the opinion that such a provocative gesture would inevitably cause war. If Chamberlain had genuinely desired to keep the peace, he could have accepted the advice of the man on the spot. Instead he insisted on the recall of Butler, with the result that troops were sent to the frontier and the Boer President, Kruger, sent an ultimatum to the British Government, demanding their withdrawal. The ultimatum, which was regarded as a bluff, was ignored and so the war began.

The views of the "Liberal Imperialists" who supported the war reluctantly once it had started—Rosebery, Grey, Asquith and Haldane —were summed up by Lord Haldane in his autobiography: "If a war is clearly wrong, then it cannot be right to support it even if one's own country is involved. But if a new situation has developed itself, one in which the nation is no longer fighting for what is wrong; if in the course of time issues are raised on which one's own country is in the right, and which have to be fought out by our own people for the sake of dear life, then those involved in the struggle ought to be supported with the full strength of the nation."

Haldane took his stand on the Kruger ultimatum and the invasion of Natal. But both these situations could have been avoided by tactful diplomacy by Chamberlain. The only new situation which developed was that Britain, in embarking on this war, found the Boers a much tougher proposition than had hitherto been imagined. In short, Britain's prestige was at stake and every nation in Europe was cock-a-hoop at the prospect of a severe twist for the tail of a blustering lion.

The Boers quickly proved themselves adept at concentrating secretly in unexpected places, such as farm-houses in the veldt. The British answer to this was to burn and destroy all farm-houses whether they were fortified or not, and to drive the inhabitants into concentration camps where they were barbarously treated and died of starvation and disease. Lloyd George challenged the morality of the war when the mood of the British people was one of frenzied and thoughtless jingoism. It was not only in the public houses and the streets that the Boer War fever raged, but in the salons of Mayfair and among the somewhat mediocre poets of the day. Lord Salisbury, with a cynical gesture, had made Alfred Austin, a hack propaganda writer for the Tory Party, the Poet Laureate. Austin offered his propaganda to the Muse in these words:

"Wrong! Is it wrong? Well, maybe:
But I'm going, boys, all the same.
Do they think me a Burgher's baby,
To be scared by a scolding name?
They may argue and prate and order;
Go, tell them to save their breath:
Then, over the Transvaal border,
And gallop for life or death!"

The date of this Tory hand-out in verse was January 8, 1896, and its title *Jameson's Ride*.

For Lloyd George the years of the war were fraught with fears of what the future might hold: financial disaster, political ruin, the path of an outcast. His attitude on the Boer War meant his taking a line against his own Party leaders, only Campbell-Bannerman and Morley being critical of the war and neither man showed the same spirit of opposition as the member for Caernarvon Boroughs.

Gone was the old-time pacifism of the Welsh; instead Lloyd George met with cold hostility, ostracism, even threats to his legal practice. In Llanystumdwy he was cold-shouldered. In Bangor he was greeted by howling mobs who stoned him, shouting "Pro-Boer" and "Traitor". That he stuck to his convictions was due partly to a feeling that there could be no turning back, but even more to the high moral courage of his wife. The rôle Margaret Lloyd George played in those dark days was invaluable to her husband in sustaining him in a diversity. For him there was always the escape which flights of oratory provided, the courage which he could pluck from the air by the knowledge of his own mastery of words. For her there were financial embarrassment, the torment from neighbours who had been friendly but now turned their backs on her, and, even worse, the news in letters that her own children were bullied and victimised at school because their father was hated.

Those who knew both Ll. G. and his wife in this period doubt whether he could have withstood the strain without the loyal support of Mrs. Lloyd George. Mr. Arthur Porritt, former editor of the *Christian World*, wrote: "Mrs. Lloyd George said in the Boer War that she would rather take in washing than sacrifice principles." Hugh Edwards related that at one stage, when several clients had left him, Ll. G. suggested that his wife had better stay in North Wales and that he would find a room in an attic for a few shillings a week. Without one moment's hesitation the brave little woman replied: "The children can go to Criccieth, but I will come and share the attic with you."

In his early speeches against the war he showed a sense of foreboding of what it would ultimately bring about. "The Transvaal Boers are a nation of farmers, one hundred thousand of them, against whom we are massing the might of forty millions. I want Wales to be free of this business. I have a deep-felt belief that this horror and injustice can do us no good. Its misery may turn back upon us and we shall see in this fair land of Cambria poverty and unemployment because war has eaten up the means for providing pensions for the needy and jobs for the able."

Chamberlain was the chief target for Lloyd George's attacks. Not an easy target, but he made gaffes of which Ll. G. took instant advantage with his quick, darting mind and ready retort. "The Transvaal, the country we created," said Chamberlain with characteristic arrogance: "The Birmingham version of the Scriptures," sneered Lloyd George. "In the beginning Joseph Chamberlain created heaven and earth—including the Transvaal. And he divided the earth, too. Yea, he quoth, there shall be those who shall have the fruits of the earth and those who shall not."

The "Khaki Election" in October, 1900, gave the Tories just the chance they wanted. "Every vote for a Liberal is a vote for the Boers" was the cry, and Liberals, whether Imperialists supporting the war, or radicals against it, were tarred with the same brush. As the election drew near many of Lloyd George's supporters in his constituency left him. There was even a move to dissuade him from standing.

"But Ll. G.'s ear was close to the ground," wrote Moses Roberts. "He paid no attention to his agent who whispered that he was almost certain to lose. His trusted unofficial agent was a Calvin and he went out for the Calvin vote. He made great play with the fact that the Boers were Calvins, 'sober, God-fearing Nonconformists like ourselves.' In my opinion these tactics won him the day."

Perhaps, too, the singular incompetence of the pedestrian politician who was opposing him in the Conservative interest, the mild and ineffectual Colonel Platt, gave him quite a few additional votes. On October 6 he was re-elected member for Caernarvon Boroughs by his biggest majority yet—296 votes.

In the new House of Commons there were 402 Tories against 186 Liberals and Lloyd George was now the main target for Tory attacks. In his diary he wrote: "Was warned that the Tory rioters threatened to kill me." Certainly he was assaulted on a number of occasions and once his wife was nearly seriously injured by rioters. The story of his escape from Birmingham Town Hall in a policeman's uniform has been told with a wealth of detail by many writers. What has not before been revealed is the extent of Joseph Chamberlain's responsibility for the riot and the reason for it. In 1884, when he was still a radical, Chamberlain had been implicated in a riot at Aston, in which Lord Randolph Churchill was only just saved from assault. Lord Randolph blamed Chamberlain and declared: "A contest in Birmingham is not a contest such as is carried on in other constituencies in England between Party and Party. It is a contest between popular self-government and corrupt oligarchy."

Before Lloyd George's visit it was noticeable that the Liberal-Unionist Press (Chamberlain's own political interest) was far more vituperative towards the visit of the member for Caernarvon than were the Tory papers. The former opened their correspondence columns to the most abusive, provocative and threatening letters, many of them anonymous. One writer, "Pax", wrote: "A riot is inevitable."

Lloyd George had aroused local hatred because he had attacked the Birmingham firm of Kynochs as suppliers of arms for the Boer War and complained of the Chamberlain family interest in the firm. He himself was hesitant about going to Birmingham, and through the intercession of Labouchere asked Chamberlain whether he was prepared to make an appeal for a fair hearing for him in Chamberlain's home city. Chamberlain's reply was: "If Ll. G. wants his life, he had better keep away from Birmingham. That is the only advice I am prepared to give him. If he doesn't go, I will see that it is known he is afraid. If he does go, he will deserve all he gets."

This uncompromising reply incensed Lloyd George, and even his wife, who fully realised the risks of physical violence, insisted that it was his duty to go to Birmingham.

Chamberlain had reason to be frightened about the visit to Birmingham. For Lloyd George, intent on mischief, had threatened Chamberlain—again through Labouchere—to reveal in Birmingham how a cheque for £10,000 was paid by Cecil Rhodes into the Irish Home Rule funds to secure the sympathies of the Nationalist Party and Charles Parnell without leading a Tory Government to suspect the character of Rhodes's "patriotism". This was a reference to the events leading up to the formation of the Chartered Company to exploit Rhodesia. In addition Lloyd George and Labouchere had obtained proof of how, as a direct result of the Jameson Raid, Rhodes had netted a profit of more than half a million pounds within a few years.

Tickets for the Birmingham meeting were forged by the Liberal-Unionists with the object of smuggling rioters into the Town Hall. Lloyd George's picture was printed on large pamphlets and given to hooligans so that they could identify him. In a large space normally reserved for commercial advertising, the time at which Ll. G. was due to arrive at New Street station was published, an obvious incitement to attack. But Lloyd George came by an earlier train and missed the first wave of rioters, or he might have been lynched before the meeting began.

Nobody could have heard more than a few sentences of Ll. G.'s speech that night. But he found time for one characteristic comment before the mob rushed the platform. "The Union Jack," he said, "is the pride and property of our common country and no man who really loves it could do anything but dissent from its being converted into Mr. Chamberlain's pocket handkerchief."

Chamberlain was in Birmingham that night. He asked to be informed of what happened at the meeting at regular intervals. A telegram was sent to him by his hooligan agents saying "Lloyd George the traitor was not allowed to say a word. Two hundred citizens passed a resolution of confidence in the Government and admiration for your unique and fearless efforts for King and Country."

Some doubt was cast on the story of Lloyd George's escape from Birmingham Town Hall, disguised as a policeman, by a cryptic remark by the present Earl Lloyd-George that all the versions of this incident he had read were inaccurate. In his biography of his mother Earl

Lloyd-George declined to disclose the "real story" of what happened that night.

The most indisputable evidence of what transpired seems to be that of Police-Constable James Stonier, of Olton, Birmingham:

"The Chief Constable of Birmingham was convinced that the mob would kill Lloyd George if they got him. So his chief concern was how to smuggle him out of the Town Hall. Then he remembered that a few months previously the American police had saved President McKinley's assassin from being lynched by disguising him in police uniform.

"At first Lloyd George wouldn't hear of this plan. He thought it would make him look ridiculous. However, he finally agreed and I was chosen to exchange clothes with him.

"I can well remember that night, but I have no souvenir of it. The uniform, the helmet and the telegram I found in Lloyd George's coat pocket are all museum pieces in glass cases.

"I was a bigger man than Lloyd George so you can imagine I had a struggle to get his clothes on. The uniform was never worn again, for the day afterwards I became a plain-clothes man in the C.I.D. I had to get the uniform back so that I could hand it back to the store.

"I had been out since 5 a.m., and it was just twenty-four hours later that I reached home, complete with uniform and having smoked a cigar I found in Lloyd George's pocket."

Mr. Stonier died in 1954. It is a little ironic that the man whose life he saved became Prime Minister while he himself remained a police-constable until he retired.

5

VERMIN AMONG THE ERMINE

"I have a deep and ineradicable hatred in my heart for the Tories. As far as I am concerned, they are lower than vermin."

Aneurin Bevan in a speech at Manchester in 1950

Aneurin Bevan's speech at Manchester in 1950, when he delivered a violent and, as it proved, vote-losing speech attacking the Conservative Party, was received with gasps of astonishment from a new generation which had become accustomed to mild-mannered and even mealy-mouthed Tories.

But Bevan's speech was an echo of the past, a summing-up of Toryism in the first forty years of this century. He was echoing what Dickens said, in describing an election at Ipswich in 1835: "Never have I set eyes on such a ruthless set of bloody-minded villains as the Tories. Would you believe that a large body of horsemen, mounted and armed, who galloped on a defenceless crowd yesterday, striking about them in all directions, and protecting a man who cocked a loaded pistol, were *led* by clergymen and magistrates?"

If this were true in Dickens's day, it was to a large extent applicable from 1900 to 1914. It was to be seen not only in the hooliganism of Chamberlain-controlled Birmingham, but in the combination of Tories and clergymen supporting the Education Bill directed against the Nonconformists, in the policy in South Africa and the jingoism it encouraged at home, in the "Khaki Election" of 1900. But political "verminism" reached its zenith after the Tories' shattering defeat in the 1906 elections. So overwhelming a defeat not only frightened the Tories, it enraged them. They stooped to tactics which showed a complete disregard for the traditions of Westminster and, coming from the supposedly "respectable" party, were as monstrous as the obstructionism of the Irish M.P.s in the eighties. The attire and accents of these Conservative M.P.s were impeccable, but their antics were those of the Bowery.

When the Balfour Government resigned in November, 1905, Lloyd George was recuperating from tonsilitis at Rapallo. He hurried back to London to find that Campbell-Bannerman had nominated him for the Presidency of the Board of Trade. Balfour had resigned rather than dissolve Parliament because he thought the deep schisms within the Liberal Party would make it impossible for Campbell-Bannerman to form a Cabinet. But he underestimated C-B. The quiet, pawky Scottish Liberal, not without difficulty, managed to produce a Cabinet that reunited all wings of the Party and was by general consent exceptionally talented. It was not surprising that when the General Election followed in the New Year, the Liberals acquired a record majority. The Tories, discredited by the feeble leadership of Balfour and his metaphysical evasions, and disrupted by the quarrelling between aristocratic Free Traders and middle-class Protectionists, were in full retreat, as Lloyd George put it: "The retreat of saboteurs and anarchists bent on pulling everyone else down with them."

During the election Lloyd George himself descended to tactics that were quite as bad as anything the Tories employed. He raised the cry of "Chinese slave labour in the South African mines", and told the electors in his constituency that the Tories who supported this might easily approve of slavery in the Welsh quarries. There was a come-back to this speech when F. E. Smith made his debut in the House of Commons. Quoting from Lloyd George's speech—"Slavery on the hills of Wales! Heaven forgive me for the suggestion"—the debonair Tory recruit sarcastically remarked: "I have no means of judging how Heaven will deal with persons who think it decent to make such suggestions."

The new Liberal Government was individually an able, even a brilliant administration. But it was a little top-heavy. Some of its leaders were spiritually of the Victorian age, men who had lived under the banners of John Stuart Mill and Richard Cobden, but who had little in common with the feeling of the masses that so great and prosperous an empire ought to provide some kind of social umbrella for its peoples. To the relief, tinged with sadness, of most Liberals, Lord Rosebery had discarded himself by petulant fits of temperament. But if Rosebery had gone, the people in whose "tabernacle" he would not serve included such faded relics of Gladstonian Liberalism as John Morley and Lords Ripon and Elgin.

Grey, at the Foreign Office, had the right instincts and a stern sense of patriotism allied with an equally uncompromising ethical approach to politics, but he was a Whig rather than a Liberal. The Foreign Office welcomed Grey's appointment for they knew that he would approach the tasks of diplomacy with orthodoxy. This, in Ll. G.'s opinion, was a fatal weakness: Lloyd George had little time for experts, diplomatic or otherwise, and was irked by an orthodox approach to problems.

The dominant figure in the Government was Herbert Henry Asquith, who towered above his colleagues with his massive intellect, absorbing problems and turning out the answers with the unerring accuracy of a precision machine. Asquith never needed to thrust for power, as did Lloyd George. The traditional "effortless superiority" of the Balliol man of the Jowett era automatically marked him out as the next Prime Minister.

Otherwise it was the tail that wagged this Government, the vigorous tail of Lloyd George at the Board of Trade, Haldane at the War Office, the brilliant young C. F. G. Masterman and that ex-Tory recruit to the Liberal ranks, the young and ebullient Winston Churchill. Already Churchill and Lloyd George, both with a keen nose for, and almost aesthetic delight in, political mischief, had struck up a warm friendship, each regarding the other with admiring envy as a buccaneer. Soon Churchill was speaking on the same platform as Lloyd George at Caernarvon, telling the people that "the fact remains clear and undeniable that Mr. Lloyd George is the best fighting general in the Liberal Army".

Meanwhile Lloyd George brought to the Board of Trade a mind that was fresh and untrammelled. It was a mind from which he deliberately purged his demagogic urges and set in their place the lawyer's skill at negotiation and an empirical approach. "What can I do for commerce?" was his first question at the Board of Trade, and big business was duly impressed.

This period at the Board of Trade saw the emergence of a new Lloyd George, a man immersed in every facet of his job, with a zest for finding out for himself technicalities that ministers were normally expected to leave to their subordinates. Big business was not slow in telling him how he could help, and the shipowners quickly informed him that a new Merchant Shipping Bill was long overdue. They had long been incensed against the Plimsoll Line, claiming that, while thousands of lives had been saved by this measure which was designed to fix a safe and satisfactory load line for ships, tens of thousands of pounds had been lost to shipowners because of the smaller loads carried. Their case was that, while overloading had been checked in British ships, foreign vessels did not have to observe this regulation and therefore gained an advantage.

When the Conservatives had been in office a committee comprised entirely of Board of Trade officials, with no representatives of ships' masters or seamen, had recognised this problem and recommended the raising of the load line. The shipowners immediately pressed Lloyd George to implement this proposal. They found him, writes Mr. Malcolm Thomson, "to their surprised delight, not only very well-informed about their affairs, but remarkably understanding and conciliatory". Well they might have done, for Lloyd George proceeded to do exactly what they wanted and more. In his Merchant Shipping Bill he raised the Plimsoll Line to permit ships to carry heavier cargoes, and also made it obligatory on foreign ships entering British ports.

This at once raised criticism from the out-and-out Free Traders in the Liberal Party, who insisted that this was a barely disguised form of Protectionism for British shipping. Had the object of the Bill been to improve the lot of merchant seamen, as was claimed, the cry of "disguised Protectionism" might well have been a tedious academic quibble. Mr. A. G. Gardiner records that Lloyd George incorporated in the Bill "valuable provisions for improving the life of the seamen". When Ll. G. worked out the details of this Bill, added Gardiner, he took a voyage to Spain and learned about ships. The visit to Spain was, in fact, made at the request of the shipowners to see how foreign competition under inferior conditions of service was injuring them.

There were some sops for the seamen included in the Bill; part of Lloyd George's bargain with the shipowners was that, if they wished to raise the load line against the wishes of the merchant seamen, they must agree to mollifying them in some way. So the Shipping Bill laid down improved standards of food and accommodation and ensured medical attention for the seamen. The main object of the Bill was, however, that the Plimsoll Line should only be raised in ships of new construction, specially designed to carry heavier cargoes. After pressure from the shipowners, ships of the oldest pattern were also allowed to raise the line. Lloyd George was promptly charged with allowing officials at the Board of Trade to obtain dispensing power to permit some provisions of the Act to be disregarded: it was a charge which could hardly be disputed as the President of the Board of Trade had deliberately inserted Clause 78 to provide for this dispensing power.

The Bill might well have been a Tory measure. Ships were deliberately overloaded with the object of bringing bigger profits to the owners; in some cases the risk of losing a ship as a result of this was considered fully justified because the loss could be made good through insurance claims. Very soon the losses of both ships and men steadily increased.

In the House of Commons Lloyd George declared that the raising of the load line had reduced the number of ships foundering by twenty per cent. A letter dictated by him in 1912, but signed "H. P. Hamilton" on his behalf, stated that for the six years prior to June 30, 1906, the total number of vessels registered in the United Kingdom which foundered was 307; for the six years since that date the figure was 240, so beneficial had been the raising of the load line.

This juggling with figures was a typical example of Lloyd Georgian dishonesty, which was a technique frequently repeated throughout his political career. Included in the returns for the six years prior to the passing of the Bill were vessels of two, four, five and seven tons, where the question of the load line did not arise.

An example of how old ships were allowed to raise the load line is provided by the ship, *North Briton*. Before 1906 the freeboard of this ship was one foot four and a half inches. The Board of Trade allowed it to be reduced to a mere ten inches. In the first six months of 1912, when Lloyd George was no longer at the Board of Trade to face the mounting criticism, twenty-two British vessels were reported missing and forty-two had foundered (in thirty of the latter the load line had been altered). In this same year Sydney Buxton had to admit that more than 3,000 British seamen had lost their lives in a single year, "this being equal to a rate of one in seventy-six compared to one in 112 previously". The situation was by this time getting much worse because the vessels were older and more freights were being lost. Nevertheless, the much-boosted Shipping Act saved the owners an estimated £8 millions in building new ships which, by the original intention of the Bill, they should have provided.

The anger of the seamen's leaders at this state of affairs may be judged from the fact that on April 14, 1913, a meeting was called by the British Socialist Party at the Memorial Hall, Farringdon Street, London, for an address by Mr. H. M. Hyndman on the subject of "The Official Murdering of British Seamen by Mr. Lloyd George and the Board of Trade". Mr. Hyndman was no ignorant, feckless, cloth-capped tub-thumper, but the top-hatted, frock-coated Old Etonian who was founder of the Social Democratic Federation.

At this meeting Mr. Hyndman, referring to the "arch-humbug George", said that the "raising of the load line is one of the most shameful things done to the working-class of this country. I say that Lloyd George has been officially murdering the seamen of British vessels in the interests of the ship-owning class. This man George is an unscrupulous and murdering rascal. I challenge him to bring an action for criminal libel against me. I tell you he won't dare to do so."

"Mr. Lloyd George is poor in honesty and statesmanship and rich in humbug," was the comment at the same meeting by Robert Williams of the Transport Workers' Federation.

Both in his Shipping Bill and in the Patents and Designs (Amendments) Bill, Ll. G. showed that the moral principles of Free Trade meant very little to him. In the latter Bill he laid down that a British patent could only be retained to protect a manufacture carried on in Britain, a principle which would have horrified the Victorian Liberals by its narrow nationalism.

Perhaps the clearest proof that at the Board of Trade Lloyd George so frequently appeared as the ally of big business was the statement made in the House by Bonar Law: "During the time the Right Hon. gentleman was at the Board of Trade the Opposition on almost every occasion supported and agreed to his proposals. That I attribute entirely to the fact that in his administration of the Board of Trade he treated every question on its merits."

Nevertheless Lloyd George made a great reputation for himself in this office and he undertook and initiated far more legislation than had his predecessors. To his credit he set out to study foreign trade and transport installations. When he turned his attention to the docks, he travelled abroad to investigate port facilities at Hamburg, Antwerp and elsewhere. His great merit was his passion for finding out for himself, an asset which was shared by only a few of his colleagues in the Government. The Port of London, he rightly decided, was hopelessly antiquated and in need of a drastic overhaul. Competition between the various companies in the port, which at first brought rapid expansion, had ended by crippling each other and harming trade. Even the provision of such necessities as deeper dredging to take larger ships had been neglected through lack of money. A deadlock occurred when the conservators saw no reason for dredging a channel for ships of deeper draught before the dock owners lowered the cills of their docks. The owners on their part refused to spend the money on reconstruction until the channel had been dredged.

Most of Lloyd George's biographers give Ll. G. the full credit for bringing the Port of London under a single authority. But it was Asquith who took the initiative in this matter, according to Sir Joseph Broodbank, author of the *History of the Port of London*. "Mr. Asquith had some acquaintance with port questions, as he was briefed as counsel in some dock cases, invariably, I think, against the dock companies. But as an Elder Brother of the Trinity House he took a very keen interest in port management and outlined the proposals which led to the ultimate solution."

Sir Joseph sums up the part played by Lloyd George in establishing the Port of London Authority as follows: "He had sounded the dock companies as to purchase, and had come to terms with the leading company. He had disarmed City opposition by proposing that the new authority which was to control the docks and the river channel should be without state or municipal guarantee. He had given an additional safeguard to the private wharfingers by allowing them to have representation in the management of the new body.

"Giving the impression to everyone who went to him with their tale of hardship that he was desirous of acting equitably to all and even to be tender to vested interests, Mr. Lloyd George eventually had the satisfaction of seeing his measure placed upon the Statute Book."

That the creation of the P.L.A. was his greatest achievement at the Board of Trade must be conceded, but his methods of achieving his object were so circuitous that the machinery of the new organisation was in many ways cumbersome. By assuring the dock owners that the P.L.A. would be without state or municipal guarantee he prevented the rapid improvement of the port so urgently needed. The P.L.A. took over an imperfect system of docks and the £11,500,000 which was spent by the authority from 1910 to 1926 was not disbursed in the best possible manner to secure the highest financial return, with the result that the Port of London continued to lose in prestige. The policy of the authority was to spend the greater part of its money on works on unsuitable sites in the lower reaches of the Thames, while the south side, which possessed deep-water facilities at low tide, was for years utterly neglected.

To sum up, Lloyd George's achievement in this direction was an adroit effort at negotiation, but not a measure of far-sighted, radical reconstruction.

His talent for skilful negotiation was the real secret of his success at the Board of Trade, and the reason for the speed and smoothness with which he accomplished what he set out to do. He dealt successfully with trade disputes in the cotton, engineering and shipbuilding industries and managed to prevent a strike by the railwaymen which caused Campbell-Bannerman to write to King Edward VII and say: "The country was largely indebted for so blessed a conclusion to the knowledge, skill, astuteness and tact of the President of the Board of Trade."

* * * * *

Sonia Keppel, Somerset Maugham and other nostalgically minded authors have painted a picture of Edwardian days as an England bathed in the gold and silver of a Lehar waltz, with God in his Heaven and all right with the world. It is true that the landed aristocracy, in spite of Harcourt's death duties, had not yet begun to feel financial pressures upon them and that a mass of cheap domestic labour enabled a clerk's wife to employ a teenage girl full-time for not more than £12 a year, sometimes less. But the real value of money was already slowly melting away and a closer investigation of the Edwardian scene shows growing discontent in the working classes and increasing threats of violence and use of violence every year. It is perhaps not generally realised that between 1900 and 1914 there were far more unofficial strikes than occur today and that more working days were lost by strike action than at any time in our history.

A Liberal Government had arrived far too late in the day to be fully effective, despite its remarkable record of social legislation. "Verminism" existed not only in the political ranks, but among employers who, far from wishing to come to terms with organised labour, frequently sought to crush it. A typical example of the indifference and callous attitude of employers was the sequel to the Senghenydd Mine disaster, costing 439 lives. Proved gross negligence and disregard of safety regulations by the colliery manager resulted in a fine of £22: to assess the value of miners' lives at a shilling a man was scarcely a slogan to encourage the unity of classes.

That Lloyd George was conscious of these things there is no doubt. Such scars and blemishes on the good name of the nation moved him deeply. But it was anger more than compassion that he felt, hence he frequently wasted his invective in Party polemics rather than in focusing it on the need for a higher all-round standard of living. His experience at the Board of Trade had whetted his appetite for a bigger job and he began to throw himself wholeheartedly into the attack on the obstructive tactics of the House of Lords. In language that was often intemperate he proceeded to inform the nation of the menace of "the men in ermine". It was language which shocked the more orthodox Liberals as well as angering the Tories, but it cannot be denied that it was provoked by the irresponsible conduct of the peers who tried to thwart the will of the electorate. "The House of Lords is petrified Toryism and has lost its use," he declared, and promptly scorned the peers' claim to be the watchdog of the nation. "A mastiff?" he asked. "No. It is the right honourable gentleman's (Balfour's) poodle. It fetches and carries for him. It bites anybody that he sets it on to."

Welsh Nationalism, as far as Ll. G. was concerned, was almost a thing of the past. So much so that on January 17, 1907, at a meeting at Caernarvon, Lloyd George said: "I will say this to my fellow-countrymen. If they find the Government manœuvring its artillery into position for making an attack on the Lords, Welshmen who worry the Government into attending to anything else until the citadel has been stormed ought to be pushed into the guardroom."

This speech caused a furore in the Nationalist ranks. It was immediately interpreted as an indication that the Government had given up the policy of Disestablishment. In fact it was directed against D. A. Thomas, who lost no time in counter-attacking. From Robertson Nicoll, editor of the *British Weekly*, came stern criticism of the President of the Board of Trade: "Mr. Lloyd George is detained by mysterious providence these days from appearing at Nonconformist gatherings, but he will have to explain himself to the nation that has trusted him."

The quietus to the critics was given in sobbing rhetoric at a convention of the Nonconformist League at Cardiff. "Am I going to sell the land I love?" asked Ll. G., with a histrionic catch in his voice. "God knows how dear to me is my Wales." If the Deity understood, Welsh Nonconformists could hardly doubt the heavenly judgment.

Lloyd George has so frequently been hailed as the architect of social security in Britain that this claim needs to be analysed. It would be a mistake to detract from his genuine achievements towards this end, achievements without which he could never have risen to his subsequent supremacy. He was the spearhead, the propagandist and the executioner of the revolutionary measures of social security introduced by the Liberal Government. But no one man and certainly no single Party can honestly pretend to be the architect of Britain's social revolution of the past sixty years. If the Tories of the Edwardian era were more anti-social than at any time since the Reform Bill, it must be admitted that Disraeli, Lord John Manners, Lord Shaftesbury and Lord Randolph Churchill had all tried to breathe some moral purpose into the domestic policy of the Conservatives at a time when Gladstonian Liberalism was far too pre-occupied with Ireland. The real drive towards the awakening of the social conscience to the need for fairer shares and greater security came primarily not from the Socialist politicians, but from the artists and writers and philanthropists of an earlier period, from Coleridge, Byron, Godwin, Hazlitt, Wilberforce, Clarkson and the Wedgwoods. This was long before Cobbett and Robert Owen paved the way for Ruskin's generation and the dilettante Socialists such as William Morris, and Oscar Wilde's brief flirtation with social security in that often forgotten, but still most thought-provoking essay in the English language, *The Soul of Man under Socialism.* Later Shaw and the Fabians converted romantic appreciation of an ideal into more practical pamphleteering.

Asquith, A. D. D. Acland, Sydney Buxton and Haldane co-operated with Sydney Webb, Bernard Shaw and other members of the Fabian Society. It is interesting to note Mrs. Sydney Webb's view of Asquith. "Asquith," she said, "supplies all the ideas. He is the best of the lot and the greatest radical of them all."

This sidelight on Asquith has never been given, even by his own biographers, the prominence that it deserves. Modest, content to let others take the credit, indifferent to what other people thought of him, ready with advice, yet never one to flaunt it, the part he played in paving the way towards "the greatest happiness for the greatest number" has been under-estimated. Lloyd George was given and readily took the credit for the Old Age Pensions measure which the Liberal Government introduced. But the initial work, the long-term planning and the honour belong in no small measure to Asquith. While at the Exchequer he planned the whole scheme of Old Age Pensions, and by wise and prudent financial management saved the cash to pay for them. A. G. Gardiner wrote of him: "No great cause will ever owe anything to him in its inception, but when he is convinced of its justice and practicability, he will take it up with a quiet, undemonstrative firmness that means success. It was so in the case of Old Age Pensions. He made no electoral capital out of them, seemed indeed to be unsympathetic." This is a misleading picture. Asquith, according to Mrs. Sydney Webb, planned the details of Old Age Pensions fifteen years before they were introduced.

How Asquith handled his Budget to achieve this is still a classical model of financial resourcefulness. Not only did he provide the cash for pensions, but he reduced the sugar tax by more than a half and reduced the National Debt by £47 millions. No one remembered this lesson when Hugh Dalton with "a song in my heart" helped to lay another stone in the still unsecure foundation of the Welfare State of today. Yet in the official biography of Lloyd George we are told: "No doubt Asquith deserved a large measure of the credit. . . . But popular instinct has been right in this matter. It recognised in Lloyd George the man who chiefly inspired and fought for the complex of progressive and ameliorative social legislation carried out by the Liberal Government between 1906 and 1914, of which the Old Age Pensions was one of the biggest items."

The importance of Lloyd George's rôle in introducing social security was his genius for simplifying the issues, for turning arid and complicated financial details into a neat phrase that humanised his proposals. No other man in the Cabinet, not even John Burns, could have achieved this, and the achievement is greater when one realises how neither the "haves" nor the "have-nots" had been politically educated to appreciate the benefits of these measures. This is admirably illustrated by a recollection by his son, Lord Tenby, in a tribute he made to the Ministry of Pensions on the fiftieth anniversary of national insurance in Britain.

"He (Ll. G.) was very glad to have been able to do something for the old people, but he said, 'I am much more worried about the young. The man with a small family, unemployed through no fault of his own because his work may be seasonal, the mother who has just borne a child, or the family with sickness in the house without means to meet the medical expenses.'

"There is much I could say about the hostility with which his proposals were received in many quarters—our family doctor argued at great length that the Bill would ruin him. I well remember my father's reply, 'How many families do you attend here knowing full well you will never be paid? I will mention one to you now,' and he gave the name. Then said my father, 'Do you ever refuse to go?' The doctor said, 'Of course not.'

"My father told him that he would in future be paid; but the doctor insisted that the Bill would ruin him. The argument appeared unending and it was finally closed by my father saying, 'Look, if you are not getting paid for those cases you attend without payment now, I'll be glad to give you a turkey next Christmas.' Our doctor never claimed the turkey!"

When Campbell-Bannerman resigned and Asquith became Premier, Lloyd George was appointed Chancellor of the Exchequer. Thus it was that he introduced the pensions scheme which Asquith had initiated and so unobtrusively worked for. But the medical insurance scheme owed an immeasurable debt to his first-hand knowledge of how the poor lived, how the doctors in areas of unemployment functioned, and even more to his vision and vigorous determination to ram home self-evident points to people obstinately declining to admit their truth. The hypocrisy of the Tories on these subjects was typical of their

The house at 5 New York Place, Chorlton-On-Medlock, Manchester, where Lloyd George was born.

Topix Picture Service

His home in Llanystumdwy.

Topix Picture Service

The young Lloyd George.

irresponsible attitude to all social reforms in this period. On the one hand they pretended the country could not afford the measures, on the other they claimed they were not enough. Even so responsible and usually statesmanlike a Tory as Lord Lansdowne made the astonishing remark that "expenditure on the South African War had been a better investment than Old Age Pensions. This Bill," he argued, "will cost the nation as much as a great war. There will be this difference —that you may pay your war debt by making sacrifices in order to do it. A war, terrible as are its consequences, has at any rate the effect of raising the moral fibre of the country, whereas this measure I am very much afraid is one that will weaken the moral fibre of the nation."

The nation not only could afford the pensions scheme, but the fall in the real standard of living demanded it. Between 1898 and 1910, in spite of the growth of population, the consumption in Britain of wheat, sugar and meat actually declined, as did the sales of beer and spirits, yet the gross assessments on Schedule D of Income Tax were fifty-five per cent up and between 1905 and 1914 an extra £2,000 millions was invested abroad. The Liberal welfare legislation of this period, including the 1909 Budget and the 1911 Insurance Acts, was in fact only redistributing one per cent of the national income.

The Licensing Bill provided ample evidence that the brewers were the masters of the Tories' soul. What happened in recent years in France, when their most outstanding prime minister for twenty years was thrown out of office by the "liquor lobby" because he tried to stamp out the evils of widespread alcoholism, was preceded in Edwardian Britain by the unedifying spectacle of a Tory Party financed and dominated by the brewers. "An un-Christian measure" was the most blatantly impudent description which the Tories gave to the Licensing Bill. Though some bishops supported the Liberal Government in its efforts to stamp out drunkenness and control the liquor trade, many of the clergy backed the brewers even from the pulpit. One clergyman even held a service of protest on behalf of the brewers, but perhaps the depths of political "verminism" were reached in the Peckham by-election, which was hailed as a victory for the liquor trade. Casks of free beer were doled out to lubricate the consciences of the semi-literate. While placards in Peckham screamed "Thou shalt not steal" —an oblique and obscure reference to the Government's licensing project—hundreds of pounds were spent by brewers in backing the Tory candidates.

While attacking the Lords for their sabotage of social measures, Lloyd George threw himself enthusiastically into the quest for bringing new means of security to the British people. He liked to give the impression that his projects were thwarted at every stage by members of the Cabinet. "You are concerned with your friends, the dukes," he told Lord Loreburn, according to Sir Herbert Lewis.

It is hard to believe he could have had any just cause to make such an offensive remark to a Lord Chancellor who was a radical above all else, but it is part of the Lloyd Georgian myth that he brought social security to Britain in the face of a partially hostile Cabinet. What he did achieve was mastery of his subject so that in Cabinet discussions he could argue from first-hand experience of social legislation in other countries, resulting from his visits to Austria, Germany and Belgium. He learned much from studying on the spot Belgium's "Ghent System" of insurance against unemployment, and he was deeply impressed by the higher standard of health achieved in Germany through her national insurance scheme against ill-health. He borrowed some ideas from all these various schemes and worked out his compulsory and contributory health insurance plan on a simple, if sketchy outline which was handed over to C. F. G. Masterman to thrash out. Oddly enough, the one man in the Cabinet who was most critical of all this was the Socialist John Burns. Burns regarded the projects as "mainly propaganda for Lloyd George. In many ways," he added, "this insurance scheme does not go far enough and the proposals for raising the money are fundamentally unsound."

When he introduced the "People's Budget" in the House in 1909, Lloyd George paid tribute to the social legislation of the countries he had visited. He referred to Bismarck's "superb scheme" of insurance for workmen and their families and he commented: "I hope our competition with Germany will not be in armaments alone . . . to put ourselves on a level with Germany is to make some further provision for the sick, for the invalided, for widows and orphans."

His actual Budget speech was often diffuse and lacking in lucidity, suggesting he had no real grasp of the complicated details of his newly created fields of revenue. "The performance," recorded Dr. Thomas Jones, "was a parliamentary failure."

A sum of approximately £16 millions had to be raised in additional revenue. Lloyd George was careful to point out that the building of eight "Dreadnoughts" under the naval programme would add nearly 4*d.* on to income tax, but the crux of his Budget was that £8 millions had to be raised to preserve nearly 700,000 old people from the "horror of the workhouse". "The workhouse," declared Ll. G., "may be better than hunger, but it is a humiliating end for men whose honest toil won for them through life at least freedom, if not plenty. It (the Budget) provides another million or two for the emancipation of the pauper who is still in the grip of the Poor Law. There are at least 200,000 of these aged toilers who stand at the gates wistfully awaiting the turn of the key with nothing between them now and their redemption but the greed of the Lords."

The extra money required to finance his proposals Lloyd George planned to raise as follows:

Income Tax	£3,500,000
Estate duties	2,850,000
Liquor duties	2,600,000
Tobacco duties	1,900,000
Spirits duties	1,600,000
Stamp duties	650,000
Tax on motors & petrol	600,000
New land taxes	500,000

The increases in direct taxation, though they raised a howl from the Tories, were moderate enough. The idea of an autonomous fund from motorists to pay for new roads and their upkeep has long since proved to be a mirage. The weakest link in the financial provisions was the land duties. Bearing in mind that Lloyd George had to carry not only the Commons, but the Lords, too, in accepting his highly necessary, but nevertheless revolutionary proposals, the land duties were a foolish and unnecessarily provocative measure. It was almost entirely due to the land taxes that the Budget increases were not accepted by the Opposition. Lloyd George was warned that any move to bring in a comprehensive system of land taxes on unearned increment of land values and on undeveloped land would be rejected by the Lords. So it was, by 350 votes to 75.

Lloyd George's idea of "minus site value" was declared by the Scottish courts to be nonsensical. The land taxes produced very little revenue and were soon abandoned. One of their worst features was that they caused a decline in house-building which had serious and lasting effects.

The "People's Budget" and the much publicised Limehouse speech in which Ll. G. lashed out at the landowners produced an instantaneous reaction by the Tories who set up anti-Budget Leagues all over the country. The Duke of Beaufort told his tenants: "I would like to see Churchill and Lloyd George in the middle of twenty couple of doghounds."

Equally extravagant and inflammatory speeches were made by Ll. G. A particularly ill-timed jest on the singularly inappropriate occasion of the presentation of his portrait to the Law Society was his boast: "I have no nest-eggs. I am looking for someone's hen-roost to rob next year."

This irresponsible remark from the Chancellor of the Exchequer cost the Liberals many votes. In worst taste was his flamboyant challenge: "Who is going to rule the country? The King and the Peers? Or the King and the People?"

The rejection of the Budget by the Lords led to the constitutional crisis between the House of Lords and the Liberal Government. After a General Election, in which the Liberals were returned with a reduced majority, the Budget of the previous April was eventually passed by the Lords on April 28, 1910, without a division. But by now the Liberals knew that no major measure of reform could be passed as long as the Lords held the power of the veto. So the Parliament Bill was introduced by the Prime Minister, providing that any Bill which had been passed three times by the Commons must be accepted by the Lords.

Meanwhile, despite the constant shadow of obstruction by the House of Lords, the Liberal Governments of the period from 1906 onwards had given the country many measures of lasting value. Old Age Pensions, the Labour Exchange Act, the Medical Inspection of Schoolchildren, the Education (Provisions of Meals) Act, all paved the way towards a form of Welfare State. If they were modest measures compared with what has been achieved since, it must be remembered that the task of a Liberal Government, even with a large majority, was always hampered by the disgraceful manner in which the Tories invoked the Lords' power against the will of the people.

One final comment might usefully be made to illustrate the muddled and antediluvian thinking of the Tories of Edwardian days. It was provided by the gambling spendthrift, Mr. Henry Chaplin, when speaking in the House of Commons on the Old Age Pensions Bill: "It had ever been the purpose of my life to do nothing that would sap the foundations of thrift among the poor."

Sir Harold Nicolson, a most moderate, detached and keenly intellectual observer of the political scene, recently told Kenneth Harris[1] that he joined the Labour Party because "I've always hated the Tories". This statement more clearly perhaps than any other explains how the behaviour of the Tories in the days before 1914 aroused hatred in the breasts of those of their own class who tried to think honestly and preserve a social conscience. Asked how he first became aware of "hating" them, he replied: "When I was ten. It seemed to me that a certain number of people who used to come to my father's house—as a diplomatist he entertained all parties, of course—believed above all in pomp and grandeur. It was an indefinite idea, but the feeling I had about them was positive. The idea became definite when I was between seventeen and eighteen. My father was then Ambassador to Russia and I went out to spend a vacation with him at St. Petersburg. I saw the behaviour of the Russian Court. I thought it was horrible. I transferred my hatred of their cruelty, indifference and selfishness to their opposite numbers at home—the Tories."

If the effect of the Tories on Nicolson, a patrician, was such, then political "verminism", coupled by the abysmal ignorance in the Tory

[1] *Observer*, 1961.

ranks, easily explains, though it does not excuse, the adoption of Tory tactics in his speeches by Lloyd George. Indeed, in the light of his own softness towards vested interests when at the Board of Trade, it makes these tactics appear strangely insincere. By employing them he began to destroy the confidence of the floating voter in Liberalism. Admittedly the electorate needed an infusion of forthright and dynamic oratory which would in simple terms and by brilliant similes show them what the Tories really stood for. This Lloyd George gave the people, but in the long run it was the Labour Party that benefited from it. Ll. G. did the spade work for the Labour Party in those days; it was a more effective spade than that wielded by the mystical and fastidious Mr. Ramsay MacDonald.

Fortunately the political bitterness of those days is something which has never been witnessed in Britain since. But in 1910 the words "Traitor!" "Swine!" and "Liberal Scum!" were frequently heard in the House of Commons, and even the Prime Minister was prevented from speaking by the prolonged and organised uproar by the Opposition. "For God's sake defend him from the cats and the cads," was the plea of the Prime Minister's wife in a hastily scribbled note sent from the gallery to Sir Edward Grey.

6

THE BID FOR POWER

"Of these the false Achitophel was first,
A name to all succeeding ages curst.
For close designs and crooked counsels fit,
Sagacious, bold and turbulent of wit. . . ."

John Dryden

For the constitutional battle that raged around the subject of the veto by the Lords A. J. Balfour must take considerable responsibility. As far back as the General Election of 1906 he had laid down the principle that the Conservative Party "whether in power or whether in opposition should still control the destinies of the country".

In spite of the threat to create sufficient new peers favourable to the Liberal Government to secure the passage of the Parliament Bill, the Lords held out. Towards the end of King Edward's reign the loyalty of the peers to the Crown was a little strained. King Edward, though always a strict constitutionalist, was suspected by some of being more favourably disposed to the Liberals than the Tories. This was not an accurate diagnosis of the King's attitude. The fact was that, in contrast to his mother, who had never disguised her pro-Tory sentiments, King Edward, by his strictly neutral approach, appeared to be sympathetic to the Liberal Government in its acute dilemma over the Lords controversy. The King had surprised his critics when he came to the throne by displaying a serious-mindedness which had never been apparent in the play-boy Prince. His common sense and gift of humour had also enabled him to be popular with all classes and he had a flair for understanding the European scene a great deal better than some statesmen. He had no illusions that, if the monarchy was to survive, it must appear to be far more constitutional than had been the case in the Victorian age. He made close friends with one or two members of the Liberal Cabinet, of whom Haldane was perhaps the favourite. With the Liberal War Minister he travelled incognito in Germany and Austria, drinking coffee at roadside cafés and having tea with the monks at Teppel.

Yet the controversy over the House of Lords clouded the last years of his life. He heard the whispers of some Tory peers that he was secretly encouraging the Liberals and that he had "betrayed his class" and "sold the Lords for the messpot of the Cassels"—a disgraceful and utterly untrue reference to his friendship with Sir Ernest Cassel—"the King's dam' banker and moneylender" as some Tories called him. Such scurrilous gossip hurt the King deeply.

Lloyd George's views on the King varied with to his moods. According to his brother, Mr. William George, in one diary entry after he had settled a railway strike, Ll. G. wrote: "The King was against the working-man in the matter of the strike. . . . He is a Tory at heart and I came away hating all kings." Yet on another occasion he described King Edward as "a shrewd and sensible old boy and our first real constitutional monarch".

When the King died a truce was called in the constitutional crisis. The Tories, some of whom had been openly gleeful at the old King's passing, believed that King George V, who was more conservative by nature than his father, would side with them and resist the plan to create additional peers to give the Liberals a majority in the Lords. It was a foolish illusion.

Nevertheless the new King sought to take advantage of the Party truce by proposing a conference on the constitutional question. On the Liberal side the Prime Minister, Lloyd George, Augustine Birrell and Lord Crewe were joined at the conference table by Balfour, Austen Chamberlain, Lord Lansdowne and Lord Cawdor for the Tories. It was this abortive conference which marked Lloyd George's first open bid for power.

The questions to which the conference was supposed to limit itself were, first, the relation of the two Houses regarding the passing of financial measures; second, provision of some machinery to deal with the persistent disagreement between the Houses; and, third, the possibility of coming to some agreement as to change in the composition and numbers of the House of Lords to ensure that it would act fairly between the two major parties in the state.

The idea of resuming the political controversy immediately the new King came to the throne was repugnant to Asquith, and doubtless he felt there were moral advantages for the Liberal Party in offering to explore the possibilities of a compromise. That the Tories were suspicious of Liberal motives can be judged from Lord Lansdowne's comment on a suggestion that the conference should meet during the summer at Lord Crewe's country house: "Will not criticism at the hands of our friends be much more severe, if it can be said that we had been 'softened' by the excellence of Crewe's champagne and the other attractions of a hospitable and luxurious country house?"

But if there was any "softening" with champagne or any other luxurious attractions, it would seem that the Chancellor of the Exchequer rather than the Tories was the victim. Did Lloyd George mellow under the influence of closer and more informal contact with the Tory leaders, or did he see this conference as a means to paving the way to a Coalition Government in which he would eventually hold the reins of power? However strange it may seem in the light of his earlier speeches, the most virulent critic of the Lords in public speedily became the chief exponent of compromise in private. In honeyed whispers he was heard at the dinner tables of Mayfair to give the words "Coalition Government" a melodious and seductive air. Though the conference was strictly confidential, leakages occurred and it is significant that they nearly all came from Lloyd George.

It was the Liberal Chancellor who, regardless of the fact that it meant a betrayal of the wishes of a majority of the British people and the end of any further ambitious social legislation, suggested privately to Balfour that there should be a "National Government". His plan was to concede to the Tories a stronger Navy, which they had been wanting and he had been condemning, to have compulsory military service (which the Tories on their own would have never dared to suggest), a compromise on Home Rule for Ireland, for Asquith to remain Prime Minister temporarily, but to go to the House of Lords. There was no mention of Disestablishment of the Church in Wales, to which Lloyd George was now committed absolutely.

Arthur Balfour, as nimble as a monkey in his political acrobatics, cynically encouraged the idea, while hypocritically commenting (as Mr. Roy Jenkins tells in *Mr. Balfour's Poodle*): "Now, isn't that like Lloyd George. Principles mean nothing to him—never have. His mind doesn't work that way. It is both his strength and weakness."

When *The Times* recorded the death of Lord Balfour in 1930, in referring to these events it stated that "a common programme of a Ministry was laid down, Mr. Asquith being excluded. Balfour, however, declined to take part in this intrigue." Why, if Balfour had originally encouraged the idea, did he now turn it down? One must deduce that he saw this as a subtle move by Lloyd George to oust Asquith. Obviously, with a Liberal majority in the country, Lloyd George could have demanded the Premiership in any National Government.

Asquith's biographers took the view that Asquith was "certainly aware that Mr. Lloyd George was conferring with Mr. Balfour". How much Asquith knew of the intrigue they do not say, but it is almost equally certain that he viewed the whole affair with tolerant amusement, knowing full well that nothing was likely to come of it.

Winston Churchill was undoubtedly involved in the National Government proposal at an early stage. Mr. Malcolm Thomson tells us that Churchill "as Ll. G.'s intimate friend was aware of the discussions", and that he wrote to Ll. G. saying, "Let us dine on Tuesday and talk to Grey about it all." "This," adds Mr. Thomson, "underlines the fact that up to this point most of the Cabinet were in complete ignorance of Lloyd George's secret negotiations with Balfour."

After twenty-one meetings the conference broke down owing to the rigidity of the Tory Diehards. But it showed that Lloyd George could switch from violently partisan campaigning one day to plotting with the Opposition the next, without a care about the betrayal of political principles any such surrender would involve. For the truth is that a "National Government" in 1910 or 1911 would have been more of a mockery than either the Lloyd George-controlled Coalition of 1916–23 or the Tory-manipulated National Governments of 1931–40.

In the end Asquith obtained from the King a pledge to create 250 new Peers in the event of the Lords again throwing out the Parliament Bill, and this pledge proved decisive. Lord Simon described the final scene in this prolonged melodrama as a "climax not to be forgotten". Margot Asquith, in more vivid vein, told how "there were Diehards and other Peers who were fighting each other; friend attacked friend and the issue remained uncertain until the last moment . . . the Archbishop of Canterbury was cursed and blessed as he moved from group to group, persuading and pleading with each to abstain".

In the end the Parliament Bill was passed by the narrow margin of seventeen votes, most peers abstaining from voting. Thus the House of Lords had its weapon of the veto rendered harmless and democracy prevailed. From across the German Ocean the Prussian war lords hailed this "storm in a teapot"—the Kaiser's own description—as a sign of the frivolity and decadence of the British nation.

* * * * *

The years between 1908 and the outbreak of war in 1914 witnessed a slow but significant metamorphosis in Lloyd George's political outlook. Though he took pains to hide the fact in public, he became much less of a Party man. His friendship with Churchill had brought him into contact with the younger Tories, and in F. E. Smith he found a companion who was witty, amusing and preferable to some of the staider Liberals.

Lloyd George's visits abroad became more frequent and these encouraged him to develop ideas of his own on foreign policy. In 1908 he went to Germany, met the Vice-Chancellor of the German Empire and expressed his enthusiasm for the "German way of doing things", allowing himself to be freely quoted by a reporter of *Neue Freie Presse* of Vienna, warmly advocating an Anglo-German understanding. Back at home he was criticised for his intrusion into foreign policy. Later, after a visit to Stuttgart, the *Daily News* declared that Lloyd George would resign from office if more than four new capital ships were laid down.

The least doctrinaire of men, impatient of tradition and theory,

Lloyd George's mind was unburdened by what Hazlitt called the "regular gradations of a classical education". To many this would have been a disadvantage; to Lloyd George it was an asset. Because he was free from the inhibitions of learning, his mind ranged far and wide, picking up and storing away information which many politicians would have disregarded. Whatever he lacked in education and administrative training was compensated for by his insatiable curiosity and constant questioning of people. He picked other people's brains, but, unerringly, he knew what to reject and what to accept. His "private intelligence service" was talked about as a joke in the smoking room of the House of Commons some years before the war, but it was much more comprehensive and better organised than was generally realised at that date. From the time he was at the Board of Trade, Ll. G. had built up in haphazard, but certainly not ineffective, fashion a system of contacts in all continents, providing him with a wealth of industrial, naval, military and political intelligence. Between 1908 and 1923 he was one of the best-informed men in Europe, and in Cabinet discussions he was frequently better briefed than departmental ministers on subjects within their own province.

One of the principal links in his private intelligence chain was a fellow-countryman named Isaac Roberts, a relative of his youthful friend from Caernarvon who had emigrated to Patagonia. It was Isaac Roberts who aroused Ll. G.'s interest in the Welsh settlement in Patagonia and in trade with Argentina, an interest which was later developed by his close association with Viscount St. Davids. Roberts, who had contacts in many countries, urged Lloyd George to concentrate on finding out how Britain's control and influence over all areas where oil was to be found could be extended. It was this preoccupation with the subject of oil that led Ll. G. to form an acquaintanceship with one of the strangest characters ever to have sat in the House of Commons—Ignaz Trebitsch, otherwise known as Ignatius Timothy Trebitsch Lincoln, the Hungarian Jew who became an English clergyman, a member of Parliament, a spy against Britain and, finally, a Buddhist monk.

As a young man Trebitsch had met Isaac Roberts in South America where he had acted for him as an adviser on oil prospects in the Americas. When, having been ordained a deacon of the Church of England by the Archbishop of Montreal, Trebitsch came to Britain in 1903 he was appointed curate at Appledore in Kent. Later, armed with a letter of introduction from Isaac Roberts, he made the acquaintance of Ll. G. One of Trebitsch's churchwardens at Appledore has told how Lloyd George came more than once to listen to the curate preach: "One day he told me he was going to London to see Lloyd George. If the interview was satisfactory, Trebitsch said, he would leave the Church."

Presumably the interview was satisfactory, for Trebitsch gave up his curacy, went to live in Hampton and changed his name to Timothy Lincoln. Lloyd George welcomed the new recruit to the Liberal fold and promised to sponsor him. Then Mr. Seebohm Rowntree, the cocoa manufacturer and a philanthropist of the Society of Friends, engaged Lincoln as a research specialist, sending him all over the continent to investigate the conditions of the labouring classes. Years afterwards Rowntree explained: "For three and a half years Lincoln was my head investigator in Belgium, France, Germany, Hungary and Switzerland. I chose him because he was an accomplished linguist, being able to speak ten languages, and also because of a personal recommendation from Mr. Lloyd George."

It is not without some significance that the man whom Mr. Rowntree selected upon Lloyd George's recommendation was engaged on the very type of research which Ll. G. himself most urgently required in connection with his schemes for national insurance.

Nothing could have suited Lincoln's purpose better than these trips round the continent with all expenses paid by Rowntree. Under the guise of a student of the lot of the working classes he was able to collect all sorts of information useful to him, not only to further his ambitions for a political career, but to establish business contacts and, ultimately, for espionage.

When his naturalisation papers were granted he was adopted as Liberal candidate for Darlington in April, 1909. Two facts about this nomination are of interest: the meeting at which he was adopted was private and, though Darlington was a Quaker stronghold, Lincoln did not owe his candidature to his employer. Seebohm Rowntree later repudiated that he had sponsored Lincoln's political career in any way, though he admitted that some of the money he advanced to him may have been used for election expenses.

Whoever foisted Lincoln on to the Liberals of Darlington remains somewhat of a mystery, but it is possible that Lloyd George played a part in it. Certainly Lincoln received on the eve of poll the following letter from Ll. G.: "You have my heartiest good wishes in your contest at Darlington. A win at Darlington would be a great victory for Free Trade and Liberalism, and I am fully confident that the vigour with which you have conducted your campaign and the excellence of our case will combine to defeat the forces of reaction and Protectionism."

Liberals looked askance at this black-bearded eccentric, but Lincoln attracted to his side the more advanced radicals as he expounded a fiery, left-wing brand of Liberalism. Despite his broken English, his oratory made a considerable impression on audiences, and his election programme in January, 1910, was notable for a remarkable address to constituents which was headed: "This is the last will and testament of we, the people of Great Britain and Ireland, defenders of our faith in the country we call our own, in which we have been graciously permitted by the Lords to exist."

This was the bitterly fought Commons versus Lords election, and Lincoln made a devastating attack upon the upper House with the slogan: "That which God hath given let not the Lords take away."

Whether the electorate was apathetic, amused by this phenomenon in their midst, or bemused by his mixture of patriotic and religious fervour, one cannot tell, but he was elected by a majority of twenty-nine votes and soon important Liberals, business men, stockbrokers and company promoters were flocking to the London home of the new M.P.

Lloyd George was at this time closely interested in the Galician oil-fields and Lincoln was his chief informant on the subject. Lincoln, however, lost so much in speculations in this part of the world—undoubtedly it was not his own money—that he was unable to raise the funds to stand for Parliament at the next election. When his creditors were called together early in 1911 he had gross liabilities of £17,118, due, he claimed, to the investment of some £20,000 in the proposed amalgamation of certain pipe-lines and oilfields in Galicia.

According to Moses Roberts, Lloyd George "Used Trebitsch Lincoln as an adviser on the oil market. This arrangement dated back many years and I believe Ll. G. actually met Lincoln through Isaac Roberts in the Argentine in 1896."

This association may amount to little more than a minor political diversion in Lloyd George's career, but it indicates how the Welshman cultivated the strangest and most diverse personalities when he felt they could be of use to him.

* * * * *

Lloyd George's usually ebullient spirits were at their lowest ebb in the months which preceded the first shot in World War I. The Liberal Government was wilting under the blows of the Ulster rebels who were openly threatening civil war in Ireland, and Ll. G. was profoundly pessimistic about the future. In this he showed a great deal more imagination than some of his colleagues, though his deductions were somewhat wide of the mark. He feared there would be war, yet sought excuses for avoiding rather than averting the calamity. His moods took on a dangerously escapist form and he retreated more often to Caernarvonshire, there to consort with some of his former pacifist cronies and talk of quitting politics altogether.

Lloyd George wanted to know the strength of pacifist feeling in the country and whether he could waft himself to power as its sole articulate interpreter in the Government. "Intimate peace-loving friends in Wales," wrote Dr. Thomas Jones, "had been urging Lloyd George to stand for isolation and keep the country free from foreign entanglements, and he was aware that his own strong distaste for armaments was shared by many Liberals."

Early in January, 1914, he gave to the *Daily Chronicle* what Asquith called "a heedless interview", calling for economy in the naval estimates and arguing that there was an improvement in Anglo-German relations. F. E. Smith attacked these views as being those of a "clumsy amateur whose hands are already too full and who has never lost an occasion in compromising and injuring this country in attempts to advertise himself".

It is notable that, though Lloyd George did not take kindly to any criticism, he never seemed to mind the sharpest barbs from F. E. Smith's tongue. Their personal friendship remained unimpaired.

Immediately after giving his *Daily Chronicle* interview Lloyd George went to Algeria for a holiday. This was an admirable time and place for an exodus from Britain's winter gloom, but relaxation was not what he had in mind. He chose Algeria because he had been tipped off by Trebitsch Lincoln that oil had been tapped in this annexe of Metropolitan France and that there was an excellent chance for Britain to obtain concessions.

Proof of this was supplied by a former official of the *Société d'Etude et Recherche du Pétrole*, who was asked to make a report of Ll. G.'s Algerian visit for French oil interests. "We knew all about Trebitsch Lincoln," he said, "and both the Deuxième Bureau and private oil interests were watching his activities for we suspected he was a double agent for Britain and Germany.

"That was what alarmed us, for we feared that Lincoln, with his known friendship for Lloyd George, was planning to divide up North African oil areas by working out concessions for Britain and Germany.

"Lloyd George was very astute. He asked several questions about the extent of our prospecting, how much capital we needed. He even forecast that the oil area in Algeria would prove to extend into Tunisia from Cap Bon across the Kairouan pocket to Sfax, Gafsa and the Isle of Djerba. It wasn't until after World War II that this forecast was actually confirmed."

The Chancellor of the Exchequer must have acted promptly in advising that Britain should invest in Algerian oil, for, in 1915, one of his oldest associates in the Liberal Party, the Master of Elibank, went out there on behalf of the oil company of S. Pearson and Company and tried to get concessions. By then the French Government suspected that this was part of a deeply laid British Government plot and they flatly refused to co-operate. Yet in 1919 Lloyd George tried again, this time through the medium of Sir Basil Zaharoff, who secured concessions to the extent of one-third for the British and two-thirds for the French.

In the next few months of 1914 Lloyd George began a campaign to organise a movement towards pacifism in the radical Press. He argued that "if we went on spending and swelling the Navy's strength, we should wantonly provoke other nations".

His campaign brought him into opposition to Admiral Jellicoe, a vendetta he pursued vindictively for some years.

But the Tories, while noisily demanding more warships, were behaving as though the only menace on the horizon was not Germany, but the Irish Nationalists. D. W. Brogan traces this "unprecedented collapse of the political sense of the English governing class" in the years before the war to humiliations inflicted by the Boers being destructive to imperial self-esteem. But the truth was that since the passing of the Marquis of Salisbury there had been no stern hand to keep in check the delinquent aristocrats and irresponsible filibusters who formed the hard core of Toryism.

So the Curragh episode, one of the most deplorable in modern history, became a mutiny simply because there was, as A. P. Ryan has summed up, "A classic confusion of orders." Thus it was that a group of Army officers, urged on by the Tories, encouraged in a disgraceful manner by Sir Henry Wilson (who deserved to be dismissed from the Service), made it known that they were not prepared to carry out their duties to the Crown by putting down any attempt at armed insurrection by Ulstermen against Home Rule. The political temperature in Britain in these months can only be compared to that of France when the *Croix de Feu* was rampant, or Spain shortly before the Civil War.

* * * * *

Politically, Trebitsch Lincoln had during his brief Parliamentary career followed a policy which was very similar to Lloyd George's. Some of his speeches, indeed, might almost have contained phrases written by Ll. G. In one such speech at Darlington, Lincoln told his constituents: "It is no use, it is worse than useless, to cry out against the building of big ships while we employ methods of diplomacy and carry on a foreign policy which gave birth to dreadnoughts. People say we must have a strong Navy and I say, too, we must have a strong Navy, but let us change our foreign policy and then other nations will follow.

"Let us encourage a policy of peace and then we shall be able to diminish our armaments. Our relations with Germany are much better than they were a few years ago. They could be better still with a different approach. We should regard each other not as rival nations, but as two great Empires."

In July, 1914, little more than a week after the assassination of Franz Ferdinand at Serajevo, Lloyd George told a group of bankers at the London Guildhall: "In the matter of external affairs the sky was never more perfectly blue." No one so shrewd and well informed as the Chancellor of the Exchequer could possibly have believed that this was other than a travesty of the facts. Not even the bland assurance of Sir Samuel Hoare early in 1939 that "a golden age of prosperity" was "just around the corner" can compare with this tergiversation. Lloyd George went on to say: "Take a neighbour of ours." This was a reference to Germany. "*Our relations are very much better than they were a few years ago.* There is none of that snarling which we used to see, more especially in the Press of these *two great, I will not say rival nations, but two great Empires.*"

The italics emphasise those parts of Lloyd George's speech which were practically identical with what Lincoln had said a year or two earlier. Was it just a coincidence that the Hungarian Jew and the Welshman thought on the same lines and that they used the same phrases? Or could it be that Lloyd George had employed Lincoln as a sounding board for his own opinions and had, in fact, supplied him with material for some at least of his speeches?

As Chancellor of the Exchequer Lloyd George skilfully set out to mobilise financial and City opinion against participation in the war by Britain. Long dealings with the City had convinced him that businessmen generally were always against war unless they could get something out of it. Thus he sought in the City right-wing allies who would make uncomfortable but seducible bedfellows for the left-wing pacifists.

One finds ample evidence of the way his mind was working by his statement in *Pearson's Magazine* in March, 1915, that "a poll of the electors of Great Britain would have shown ninety-five per cent against embroiling this country in hostilities. Powerful City financiers, whom it was my duty to interview this Saturday (August, 1914) on the financial situation, ended the conference with an earnest hope that Britain would keep out of it."

Lloyd George's Guildhall speech must have been just what the Prussian Junkers wanted to hear. If anything were needed to encourage the belief that Britain would remain neutral, that was it. Ll. G. was, in effect, the appeaser-in-chief of Germany.

Just as Montagu Norman, Lord Stamp and other bankers were pro-German during 1934–39 so in 1914 was there a partiality towards Germany and a peace movement in the City of London. Business and banking interests in London were closely linked with their counterparts in Berlin and Vienna. So it was comparatively easy for Ll. G. to find allies in financial circles.

Sir Walter Cunliffe, Governor of the Bank of England, an upright but ineffectual man, was told by the Chancellor that "this war storm will produce a financial crisis of the first magnitude". Furthermore, said Ll. G., he had evidence from an unimpeachable source on the continent that international financiers in Paris and elsewhere were deliberately fomenting war to stir up a crisis. "This war talk is all a ramp by cosmopolitan bankers. If we stand firm and aloof from what is going on in Central Europe, everything will settle down normally."

What was the unimpeachable source on the continent? French intelligence reports of the period insisted that Trebitsch Lincoln was "feeding anti-French stories of speculation on the Paris Bourse to the English Chancellor".[1] After March, 1914, there is no evidence that Lloyd George and Lincoln maintained any direct contacts. If they did, it must have been a carefully guarded secret. But equally is there no evidence that Lloyd George repudiated Lincoln who, when war came, was still a member of the National Liberal Club and for several weeks after the outbreak of war worked as a censor of Hungarian and Rumanian correspondence at the War Office and Post Office.

Sir Walter Cunliffe consulted colleagues in the banking world. In a state of panic, after they had heard the Chancellor's warnings, they asked Cunliffe to go back and urge on Lloyd George that they were totally against Britain being drawn into war. Once again the capitalist forces were on the side of the big battalions.

On the very day, July 23, that Austria was handing an ultimatum to Belgrade, the Chancellor announced in the House of Commons that "next year there will be a substantial economy without interfering in the slightest degree with the efficiency of the Navy". Eight days later he assured the Cabinet that Britain could not afford a war, which would mean "immediate bankruptcy for her".

The panic in the City of London at the end of July, 1914, was something unprecedented. The utter chaos in the financial structure should have provided ample justification for nationalising the Bank of England immediately. The merchant bankers had absolutely no knowledge of modern economic theory at this time. Indeed none of them knew exactly what foreign balances the nation held. How could they? There was no means of knowing; even the Treasury was completely in the dark.

Lord Morley in his *Memorandum on Resignation* cast some light on these intrigues between Lloyd George and the City when he referred to "a very remarkable piece of intelligence communicated to the Cabinet" by the Chancellor of the Exchequer. According to Morley, Ll. G. told the Cabinet:

"He had been consulting the Governor and Deputy Governor of the Bank of England, other men of light and leading in the City, also cotton men and steel and coal men in the north of England, in Glasgow, etc., and they were all aghast at the bare idea of plunging into a European conflict; how it would break down the whole system of credit with London at its centre, how it would cut up commerce and manufacture

[1] *Documents politiques de la guerre.*

Topix Picture Service

A portrait in his early days as M.P.

Radio Times Hulton Picture Library

Dame Margaret Lloyd George.

—they told him—how it would hit labour and wages and prices and, when winter came, would inevitably produce violence and tumult."

Asquith was caustic about the panic in the City. "They are," he said, "the greatest ninnies I ever had to tackle. I found them all in a state of funk like old women chattering over their teacups in a cathedral town." It was an apt commentary. No one could either believe or understand what was happening in financial circles. Confidence had disappeared overnight; everyone was screaming to sell and stock-brokers were rushing around stampeding the market; withdrawals from the banks assumed abnormal proportions. London, the financial centre of the world, was revealed in those days as the House of Usher of banking circles. Within a few days its legend of stability and omniscience was destroyed for all time. Up went Bank Rate to ten per cent. There was a clamour for gold such as Midas could never have imagined. But if the City panicked, Lloyd George had certainly done everything to stimulate the stampede and by word of mouth and lack of action to publicise stories of a financial crisis.

Later poor Cunliffe, who considered he had been disgracefully misled by the Chancellor, said: "Mr. Lloyd George was indeed lucky that Bank Holiday fell on August 3 and so allowed a day's grace for measures to be taken to avoid a serious crisis. If it hadn't been a Bank Holiday, the whole finance of the nation would have collapsed in ruins."

In the event the holiday for the banks was extended a further three days to enable safety measures to be taken. These could and should have been carried out earlier.

Yet it was unlike Lloyd George to neglect to take action swiftly when a crisis developed: this failure to do so may perhaps be explained by his increasing doubts about how the threat of war should be met. Three years previously, despite his occasional pacifist speeches already mentioned, he had shown his concern about the international situation by writing this letter to Winston Churchill:

"I have been reading the Foreign Office letters. They are full of menace. . . . I am not at all satisfied that we are prepared, or that we are preparing. Weeks ago when I thought war a possibility I urged upon Grey the importance of Russia as a factor. I wanted him to ascertain definitely what Russia would do, and could do, in the event of war. . . . We ought to know what R. is capable of before we trust the fortunes of Europe to the hazard. We are even now almost at the point whence we can't recede."

In another letter to Churchill he showed even greater foresight, urging that "150,000 British troops supporting the Belgian Army on the German flank would be a much more formidable proposition than the same number of troops extending the French line. It would force the Germans to detach at least 500,000 men to protect their lines of communication".

But the mood of 1911 had been replaced by pessimism in the summer of 1914. Lloyd George as Chancellor stressed again and again that in his opinion war would mean financial ruin. Did he deliberately delay taking the requisite financial measures because he hoped that by doing so he would confront the Cabinet with a picture of economic chaos if Britain entered the war? No one, least of all his colleagues, could quite say what was going on in his mind. His activities do not seem to have been confined to financial and economic matters in those last desperate days of July. Long afterwards Count Mensdorff, Austrian Ambassador in London in 1914, stated that at the end of July he received "assurances from a very prominent British politician" that Britain would in "no case intervene if war broke out". This politician was certainly not Sir Edward Grey, the Foreign Secretary, who had conversations with the Ambassador on July 28 and left him in no doubt that Britain could not stand on one side. The archives of the Austrian Foreign Office show that Count Mensdorff, "Had constant access to Lloyd George who was consistently in favour of a peace policy at this time and regarded Austria's case as a strong one and Servia's as unsatisfactory. He saw no reason to support Servia in any circumstances."

In case this seems to savour of propaganda on the part of Austrian archivists who might be searching for excuses after the event, it is interesting to note that Asquith himself in his contemporary notes shared this viewpoint to some extent. He wrote on July 26: "The curious thing is that on many, if not most, of the points, Austria has a good and Servia a very bad case." But he obviously differed from Lloyd George in his interpretation of the situation, for he added: "But the Austrians are quite the stupidest people in Europe. There is a brutality about their mode of procedure which will make most people think that this is a case of a Big Power wantonly bullying a little one."

Meanwhile the battle in the Cabinet went on: at what point was the honour and word of Britain committed to standing behind France, Belgium and Russia in their hour of peril? That was the vital question on which no one but a conscientious pacifist had any moral right to dissent. Asquith, Churchill, Grey and Haldane had no doubts whatever. Any infringement of the neutrality of Belgium meant that Britain must enter the war, or her word in future would be worthless and suspect.

Lloyd George, Lord Beauchamp and John Simon were the waverers, ever seeking excuses for inaction; Morley and Burns, taking at least an honest pacifist view, were adamant against war at any cost. Asquith's diary comment on his Cabinet at the time was: "Winston, who has a pictorial mind, brimming with ideas, is in tearing spirits at the prospect of war, which to me shows a lack of imagination; Crewe is wise and keeps an even keel; no one can force Grey's hand; Ll. G. is nervous; Haldane, Samuel and McKenna very sensible and loyal."

It was touch and go at this time as to who would break up the Cabinet first—Churchill, straining at the leash to mobilise the Fleet, or Lloyd George, painting a picture of financial doom and chaos. Between Churchill and Lloyd George passed a barrage of staccato messages trying to establish a bridge between their opposing points of view. On August 1, Churchill wrote to the Chancellor: "I am most profoundly anxious that our long co-operation may not be severed. I implore you to come and bring your mighty aid to the discharge of our duty."

The turning point for Lloyd George came when he acquiesced in the decision to send an ultimatum to Germany. Only Burns and Morley resigned from the Cabinet. What may have caused this change of mind was an intimation that, if he persisted in opposing intervention, the Tories would be prepared to join in a Coalition Government from which he would be excluded.

There is, however, a more illuminating clue to his sudden switch from being the exponent of pacifism to that of the driving force in the conduct of the war in Walter Runciman's description of his state of mind in *Master and Brother*, by A. C. Murray:

"When the crisis came it found Lloyd George vacillating. Right up to tea-time on Sunday, August 2, he was doubtful of the action he would take. He told us that he would not oppose the war, but he would take no part in it, and would retire for the time being to Criccieth. He would not repeat his experience of 1899–1902. I remember him saying that he had had enough of 'standing out against a war-inflamed populace'. Right up to the moment we received news that the Germans had crossed the Belgian frontier, he left us in doubt as to what was his view and what action he would take."

Moral obligations, the honouring of pledges and treaties had no place then in his mental acrobatism. In the Cabinet he argued that if Germany did no more than trespass on a small corner of Belgium, "it might be overlooked". At the back of his mind was a firm determination never again to be on the losing side, never again to face the mass disapproval of his pro-Boer days. Had that experience cut deeper into his soul than he himself thought possible at the time? This tendency to "overlook" marked a further stage in the disintegration of his character.

If he had doubts as to what his countrymen thought, they must have been quickly dispelled at midnight on August 4, when, with the tolling of Big Ben, the tocsin of patriotism sounded in the hearts of the crowds who gathered outside Buckingham Palace and sang "God Save the King". For a brief hour Britain was in mafficking mood again and short shrift was given to pacifists and doubters. Later that mood was to be mellowed by the noble fatalism of Rupert Brooke, but it was also to allow itself to be transmogrified into hysterical flag-wagging, the distribution of white feathers by foolish spinsters of uncertain age and a Germanophobia which was more intent on destroying so stalwart a patriot as Haldane than on concentrating on overcoming the supreme symbol of the Junkers, the wretched, envious German Emperor who telegraphed to his wife:

"Pleased to be able to tell you that by the Grace of God the battles of Cambrai, St. Quentin and La Fère have been won. The Lord has gloriously aided. May He further help."

7

THE LIE THAT SINKETH

"'Tis not the lie that passeth through the mind, but the lie that sinketh which doth the harm."

Francis Bacon

When Asquith was quizzed in the House of Commons in 1910 on his plan of action if the Lords continued to thwart the will of the Commons, he made four answers which were later to be twisted into one of the worst examples of distortion ever employed in the history of British newspapers.

These answers were:

"We had better wait and see."

"I am afraid that we must wait and see."

"The hon. member had better wait and see."

"The noble lord must wait and see."

The request to "wait and see" was remembered by Lloyd George. Before the war had long been in progress he was cajoling Lord Northcliffe to use it out of its context as a useful quotation for misrepresenting the Prime Minister as one who believed in "waiting and seeing" as a policy for waging war. By that time only students of Hansard could remember on which occasion the phrase was first used.

This was but one typical example of the technique of the "lie that sinketh" by which various politicians of the period sought to wage war for their own personal aggrandisement. It was a heedless phrase that dogged Asquith for the rest of his political life so that "wait and see" was the image by which he came to be wrongly recognised by a new generation. Thus it was in World War I that politicians, newspaper magnates and mere wishful thinkers welcomed lies that helped to make their wishes become realities; they combined to use the misfortunes of war for besmirching their enemies and scrambling over their shoulders to arrive in comparative comfort at "the pinnacle of sacrifice pointing like a rugged finger to heaven".

On the morning of August 5 the Chancellor went back to the Treasury to wrestle with financial problems. Possibly the chaos which faced him took his mind away from the war. He was no economist, nor had he a flair for abstruse monetary posers, but he was exhilarated by the discovery that the experts at the Treasury were often completely baffled by the conundrums which war posed and that almost as often their assessments of a situation were glaringly inaccurate. The truth is that Treasury experts and the cosseted, donnish economists had lived too long in the cloistered calm of middle-class Edwardian stability, smug and safe in the knowledge that the pound sterling was the world's safest currency and that God was, in His heaven, looking down benignly on the paladins of monetary witchcraft. From Cunliffe to John Maynard Keynes—the latter was predicting "financial ruin" if specie payments were suspended—they were all wrong at some time or other.

When the experts were proved wrong, Lloyd George took puckish pleasure in their discomfiture. He seemed to draw strength from the errors of others. Their confusion gave him a chance to jump ahead of them and he would cover up his own ignorance of the intricacies of high finance by alternately bullying and coaxing officials. At the Treasury he showed boldness, power of decision and imagination, but he rarely stopped to look beyond an immediate problem. He was the architect of creeping inflation. Money was wanted at once. All right, take it and spend it. It could always be borrowed. Never mind the cost, or future inconvenience. Forget the National Debt. There were always sinking funds which could be diverted.

"At the Exchequer, Mr. Lloyd George's work was not as successful as at the Board of Trade," wrote Charles Mallet. "The truth is he did not always master very thoroughly the financial problems with which he had to deal. There are stories, well authenticated, of Treasury officials who saw with dismay important papers tossed aside, while the Minister invited them to talk to him instead."

Lloyd George never let the prospect of inflation worry him and he was guilty of encouraging it by failing to increase taxation until after people had liberally and ostentatiously adapted themselves to rising incomes.

From the New World the financial tactics of the Chancellor and his haphazard, makeshift plans for buying goods from U.S.A. were noted with alarm by shrewder experts. Mr. H. P. Davison, a leading partner in the House of Morgan and wholeheartedly behind the Allied cause, was distressed to observe "the helter-skelter and at times almost frantic" fashion in which different Allied purchasing agencies were bidding against each other in the American markets. The recklessness with which the British agencies in particular forced up prices and wasted their money offended him, according to his partner and biographer, Thomas Lamont.

But for Lloyd George it was now war at all costs. By September 19, 1914, he had so far forgotten his suggestion that a minor trespass on Belgian territory might be overlooked that he could tell a gathering at the Queen's Hall with all the fervour at his command:

"I am fully alive to the fact that whenever a nation is engaged in war she has always invoked the sacred name of honour. Many a crime has been committed in its name; there are some being committed now.

"But all the same, national honour is a reality and any nation that disregards it is doomed. Why is our honour as a country involved in this war? Because we are bound by an honourable obligation to defend the independence, the liberty and the integrity of a small neighbour that has lived peaceably, but she could not have compelled us because she was weak.

"The man who declines to discharge his debt because his creditor is too poor to enforce it is a blackguard."

To some of his Cabinet colleagues this last sentence must have appeared as the very quintessence of hypocrisy when they recalled his obstructiveness only a few weeks previously. But, oblivious of the irony of his political metamorphosis, the Chancellor proceeded to fascinate the nation with a series of passionately patriotic speeches, shot now with silky cadences, then with forceful condemnation. His energy was indisputable. He worked long hours at the Treasury, while finding time to make speeches outside Parliament, and gradually began to take the keenest interest in military operations. John Buchan wrote: "Of all the civilians I have known, Lloyd George seems to have possessed in the highest degree the capacity for becoming a great soldier. But he might have lost several armies while he was learning his trade."

Most of the Cabinet were disposed to leave purely military problems to the experts. Only Churchill and Lloyd George set themselves up as exponents of strategy, and the latter rapidly developed a contempt for several of his colleagues whom he rated as incompetent when it came to the arts of waging war. Within a few months of war starting, Lloyd George had come to dislike Field-Marshal Lord Kitchener and both inside and outside the Cabinet it often appeared that he deliberately tried to antagonise the War Minister.

In choosing Kitchener as an adversary, Lloyd George fastened upon the one man in the Government who, at the beginning of the war, was a national hero and enjoyed the confidence of the greatest number of people. On August 3, 1914, Kitchener was on his way back to Egypt as H.M. Consul-General, but he had hardly boarded the channel boat at Dover than he was ordered back to London by Asquith. Without any preamble the Prime Minister told him he was to be Secretary of State for War. This was a popular move in that it took the direction of the military right out of the sphere of party politics, a highly desirable change in view of the Curragh rebellion and the open hostility of some of the Ulster-born generals for the Liberal leaders. "The Constable of Britain," as Churchill called Kitchener, was at this time the most powerful man in the country; he had his defects; he was shy, saturnine and secretive and had been too long away from Britain to be acclimatised to its political processes. His mistrust of politicians was well known; Asquith was one of the few in whom he had complete trust.

True, he neglected to take full advantage of the Territorial Army created by Lord Haldane, but he raised in fourteen months, without either compulsion or a national system of registration, an army of 2,257,521 men in the United Kingdom alone. He forecast that it would be a long war and overruled those—Lloyd George was among them—who said it would be finished in nine months. "The Chancellor of the Exchequer will find war is not a matter of simple gestation," he told the Cabinet. "It will last for three to four years."

Nor was he a man who would rely solely on expert advice. When his civil servants at the War Office insisted that no modern war could possibly last a year and that 50,000 soldiers would be enough for a volunteer army, he gave them a scathing look, said nothing, but added a nought on their draft for a recruiting appeal.

Without question the war thrust a great strain on the looseness of Cabinet procedure which, though workable in peacetime, lacked the cohesion and impetus to swift action so vital in fighting for survival: as Sir Edward Spears said, "The old coat of democracy, never intended for wear at Armageddon, was showing white at the seams."

That was an understatement; the seams had already burst and an unwieldy Cabinet could not satisfactorily cope with the day-to-day problems of war. John Terraine wrote that "Cabinet meetings were not minuted; there was no 'follow-through' of any Cabinet decision, beyond the sense of responsibility of individual Ministers; there was not even a precise 'official' definition of the decisions arrived at. The fact that this system ever worked at all is a remarkable tribute to the innate orderliness of the British character".

It was really a tribute to the type of minister which Asquith most liked to have around him: men like Grey, Haldane, Crewe and Samuel. Such men could make even so obviously outdated a system work, but to Lloyd George and Churchill, both essentially impatient men, it was anathema.

At the end of November, 1914, the opposing sides had dug themselves into positions which, except for minor changes, they were to occupy for the rest of the war. Stalemate had been reached. It was then that the feud between the "Easterners" and the "Westerners" on the conduct of the war developed. Grey, as Foreign Secretary, was a redoubtable "Westerner", like Asquith; that is to say, he believed the war must be won in the west and that diversions in the east, however much they held the attractions of a "short cut to victory", tended to weaken the effort in the west. Grey had an unerring judgment for what was practicable. Thus he never did anything to upset relations with the United States at a time when American commerce with the

Central Powers had almost ceased, with disastrous results for the U.S. economy. "With a skill and foresight which one can only admire, the British Foreign Office now advanced over the thin ice presented by this delicate problem," wrote the American Walter Millis in *Road to War*.

Lloyd George's mind was like a flight of swallows questing restlessly for the dawn of spring that would break the monotony of winter deadlock on the Western front. With Churchill he was the chief protagonist of the strategy of the "Easterners", who took the view that imaginative surprise thrusts could shorten the war by making a quick drive for victory in the east at far less cost of life than the toll taken by the bloody struggle in the mud of Flanders.

Churchill and Lloyd George both pressed this viewpoint on Asquith and the Prime Minister agreed to set up a committee of the Cabinet, in effect a War Council, to consider "all purposes connected with the higher direction of the war". This was an improvement on the slow and cumbersome machinery of the Cabinet for examining new strategic proposals.

The ill-fated Dardanelles expedition was its unfortunate first progeny.

* * * * *

Two vital factors in modern history have been largely ignored by those who have dealt with the events of the first two years of World War I. First was the reckless and improvident custodianship of the Treasury by Lloyd George, a heritage which has never since been eradicated and which has made creeping inflation through increased Government spending an insidious and persisting malaise in the British economy. Second, and the sole reason that the deadliest effects of Lloyd George's financial policy were never fully felt for some years, was American aid to Britain.

When Roosevelt announced "Lease-Lend" and when General Marshall launched his brave European Recovery Programme, each was following a tradition established in World War I not by an American Government, but by private bankers. In the first instance the loans by these bankers were dictated by a natural desire to recover from the depression of the autumn of 1914 and to pave the way to the business revival in U.S.A. in 1915 by enabling the Allies to purchase munitions in America.

In the United States isolationists took a less realistic view. *La Follette's Magazine* castigated the bankers and arms merchants with the rhetorical query: "What do Morgan and Schwab care for world peace when there are big profits in world war? We are underwriting the success of the cause of the Allies. We have ceased to be neutral in fact as well as in name."

But this was a narrow and unfair view. Neither Britain, nor the other Allies, could buy the sinews of war without dollar credits, a difficulty foreseen by American bankers long before it was appreciated in London or Paris. J. P. Morgan and Company were alarmed by the recklessness of Lloyd George: "He has no thought for the final bill," declared Morgan. They were sufficiently alarmed to take the initiative in finding an answer to it. That answer was the flotation of a war loan whereby the American people could continue to supply the Allies by providing them with the money to pay for the supplies.

Lloyd George at first declared himself "uninterested" in this plan, but when the crisis became acute and Britain faced bankruptcy, an Anglo-French Joint High Commission, headed by Lord Reading, went to New York for the purpose of selling to the Americans the first big Allied war loan.

Except for the generous and bold initiative of J. P. Morgan and Company and the financial backing which they gave in 1915, Britain must have suffered the biggest financial crash in her history. From that day onwards sterling lost its dominance in world finance and Britain became irrevocably entangled in a state of indebtedness to the United States. But, looking at the situation from a broader viewpoint, it now meant that the economies of the Old World and the New were so closely linked that each was concerned in the fate of the other. It would be churlish not to pay tribute to the fact that J. P. Morgan and Company took incredible risks in the early days solely because their sympathies were wholeheartedly with the Allies. The policy of this banking house was bold, imaginative and enlightened; it sign-posted the routes which governments have followed.

Lloyd George's increasing interest in strategic matters was one reason why he failed to come to grips with the problems besetting the Treasury. The whispering campaign against Kitchener grew; it was the same reckless technique of half-lies which had led to the downfall of Haldane. Half-lies soon grew into the "lie that sinketh", so that in his autobiography Haldane told how "my motives and the nature of my efforts when I went to Berlin in 1912 were grossly misrepresented by some newspapers. Every kind of ridiculous legend about me was circulated. I had a German wife; I was the illegitimate brother of the Kaiser; I had been in secret correspondence with the German Government . . . on one day, in response to an appeal in the *Daily Express*, there arrived in the House of Lords no less than 2,000 letters of protest against my supposed disloyalty to the interests of the nation . . . I had gone to Germany too often and had read her literature too much, not to give ground to narrow-minded people to say that Germany was my 'spiritual home'".

The whispering campaign against Kitchener took a more insidious form. No newspaper dared at this stage to criticise openly the man who was a national hero, but in the lobbies of the House of Commons malicious gossip was bandied around. Kitchener, said the gossips, was effeminate, his handwriting was like a woman's; he had a passion for collecting wild flowers; it was even asserted as proof of his "madness" that, as a young subaltern in Cyprus, he had kept a bear as a pet. In fact the bear was the pet of a Cyprus police officer, Lord John Kennedy, with whom Kitchener had shared a house.

The image grew of Kitchener as an obstinate, antediluvian character who had rigid views and too orthodox a training for modern war. Yet his military career had not been purely conventional, and he was balloonist and intelligence officer with the French in the Franco-Prussian war, he had made a survey of Palestine and even spent one of his periods of leave roaming around Egypt, disguised as a Levantine, collecting information about Arabi Pasha's revolt, and he was sufficiently interested in the broader aspects of life to make a study of Ottoman law and to work out a scheme for rescuing the Egyptian fellahin from moneylenders. But at the War Office, with intrigue, malicious gossip and wicked slander emanating from back-biting politicians, he was unhappy and ill at ease. The more he was attacked in Cabinet the more silent he became. Yet Asquith found him "most pleasant to work with".

He detested the popular Press and not without reason. The ridiculous optimism of some of these papers angered him with their stories of "Belgian victories" and Germans starving and committing suicide, when in fact the Allies were being steadily forced further back into France.

The Lloyd Georgian opinion of Kitchener can be judged from his remarks to Max Aitken (later Lord Beaverbrook): "Kitchener talked absolute twaddle, Max. No, that's not quite right. Let me put it this way: he has a mind like a revolving lighthouse. Sometimes the beam lights up all Europe and the opposing armies in vast and illimitable perspective. Then the shutter comes round and for several weeks you get blank darkness."

As the war progressed Lloyd George courted the Press increasingly. Not content with having the ear of the radical papers, he sought the friendship of the right-wing newspaper proprietors, Beaverbrook, Northcliffe and Riddell. Of these men Max Aitken, as he then was, was easily his shrewdest friend and critic, and the relationship between them survived for a lifetime, despite all their many differences on policy. On the other hand, Lloyd George's friendship with Northcliffe was a stormy, brief-lived affair which eventually proved an embarrassment to the politician.

Leakages of Cabinet business—mainly in the Northcliffe Press—were continually occurring. Mrs. Asquith noted in her diary: "When I point out with indignation that someone in the Cabinet is betraying secrets, I am counselled to keep calm. Henry is as indifferent to the

Press as St. Paul's Cathedral is to midges, but I confess that I am not and I can only hope that the man responsible for giving information to Lord N—— will be heavily punished. God may forgive him: I never can."

It was unfortunate that Henry Asquith did not listen to his wife's warnings. He, with Grey, Haldane and Kitchener, were the chief victims of a smear campaign that not only criticised their rôles in the war, but went so far as to suggest that Asquith's own family were pro-German. Margot Asquith was at length driven to bring a libel action in the Law Courts against the *Globe* and was awarded £1,000 damages. But still the lies were published. It was her husband's gravest error that he did not seek a show-down with Lloyd George early in the war and dismiss him from the Cabinet for revealing state secrets. The Prime Minister abhorred suspicion and intrigue and would have shrunk from taking such drastic action against an old colleague. He maintained that the essential task for a Prime Minister was not to waste time on what he wrongly regarded as futile matters, but to wage war; not to break up a Cabinet, but to settle differences of opinion and achieve unity of purpose. With Lloyd George in a Cabinet that was an almost impossible task. By this time lust for power had become a drug to Ll. G. He wanted new fields to conquer, finance bored him. There was no glamour in juggling with figures; the glamour lay in juggling with vast armies on the chessboard of the battlefields which he had previously despised.

The year 1915 saw a series of events which gradually worked in Lloyd George's favour. He himself had gloomily heralded the New Year with a letter to the Prime Minister complaining that "I can see no signs anywhere that our military leaders and guides are considering any plans for extricating us from our present unsatisfactory position".

Then came the calamity of the Dardanelles, an amphibious enterprise which, by the magnitude of its failure, was to prove a valuable lesson in how not to wage war during 1939–45.

The Dardanelles operation was, perhaps, the sole chance the Allies had of successfully breaking into enemy territory in the east. This was the one occasion on which Asquith concurred in the strategy of the "Easterners". But this brilliantly conceived Churchillian adventure was unhappily doomed from the start by its author. Churchill's weakness had been to put a sentimental regard for a colleague before a realistic appreciation of his demerits. The error which led to his downfall in World War I was his recall of "Jacky" Fisher to the Admiralty. Both before and during the Dardanelles expedition and the Gallipoli campaign the quixotic behaviour and disgraceful display of tantrums by Lord Fisher ruined all hope of success. Fisher not only hated the conception of the Dardanelles operation, he obstructed its execution when it was being carried out.

Mr. Alan Moorehead in an admirable narrative of the Gallipoli campaign has shown that the naval attack, if pressed, would have succeeded, and he vindicates Churchill from the charge that he wantonly threw away lives in an operation doomed to failure. But, more important, he showed what the hastily drawn conclusions of the Dardanelles Commission failed to explain—that Turkey might have been kept out of the war quite easily. This Mr. Moorehead was able to do because he had studied Turkish sources of information not hitherto available. Yet, in being an out-and-out enthusiast for the Gallipoli campaign, Mr. Moorehead neglected to examine the obvious alternative to that campaign which his research should have pointed out to him. That alternative was not Salonika, but by diplomatic and Secret Service channels to detach Turkey from the Central Powers.

If Fisher was the stumbling block to effective naval-military co-operation in the campaign, certainly failure to take full advantage of the weaknesses in the Turkish political situation was an equally decisive factor. Diplomacy in this area was timorous, though the obvious answer to this criticism must be that put forward by Grey to the Dardanelles Commission—that "diplomacy was perfectly useless without military success" to back it up.

Lloyd George's part in the Gallipoli story was negligible, but this was another occasion on which he blundered into the diplomatic field and nearly upset the plans not only of Grey but of the Naval Intelligence Department of the Admiralty. According to Admiral Sir Guy Gaunt, Ll. G. was convinced against all available evidence that a gift of a million pounds to Enver Pasha would change the policy of Turkey and even bring that nation over to the Allied side. The idea behind this suggestion was sound: it would have been wiser to have tried to detach Turkey from Germany before launching a full-scale operation. But the method proposed was little short of madness; there was never the slightest evidence from intelligence sources that it had any chance of succeeding.

Yet, so convinced was Lloyd George, that he wanted to send a note through an intermediary, saying: "I authorise you to make such arrangements on my behalf as you may deem desirable to guarantee British financial assistance under these conditions." Grey was furious and absolutely forbade the note to be used.[1]

A much sounder scheme was that evolved by the N.I.D., under Admiral Hall. Hall had always been interested in the Balkans and his N.I.D., which did as much towards winning the war as any single intelligence agency, knew a great deal about Turko-German relations. Hall's aim was to try through his agents to persuade Turkey to break with Germany and to promote revolution against Enver Pasha and

[1]*Documents politiques de la guerre*

the "Young Turk" Party then in power, or to encourage the more reasonable members of the Party to make peace with Britain.

A message came through to the famous Room 40 in Naval Intelligence H.Q. that prayers were being offered up in a mosque for the arrival of the British. Acting on his own initiative and without telling the Cabinet, Hall sent negotiators a letter guaranteeing £3 million for the success of a reconciliation with Britain plan. Further, Hall was prepared to pay £500,000 for the complete surrender of the Dardanelles and the removal of all mines.

For a few weeks it seemed as though, unknown to the Cabinet, Hall would bring off the biggest coup of the war. The Turks were short of ammunition; Turko-German relations were at their worst and the chances of success were promising. Hall, from the intelligence reports before him, knew that the forcing of the narrows would be a hazardous task for the Royal Navy and that disaster might confront the Fleet if all precautions were not taken. But he appreciated the importance of a political coup in this theatre of war. The First Sea Lord, Fisher, however, always either hostile or lukewarm about the Dardanelles Plan, ruined all chance of success by putting an end to negotiations.

Thus was a great opportunity lost and when Lord Fisher, in his own words, "pulled down the blinds" and walked out on his job, that was the beginning of the end of the Liberal Government. The bombardment of the Dardanelles had failed, a military and naval disaster followed. Churchill was blamed for Fisher's criminal neglect and lack of resolution and a Coalition Government was formed with Asquith at its head and with Bonar Law bringing in the Tories.

Mr. Malcolm Thomson has written that "Bonar Law, Balfour and Carson consulted with Ll. G." before the new Government was formed and that "Bonar Law offered Ll. G. the Prime Ministership—an indication as to how far the Tories had moved from their hatred of him—but Ll. G. refused to supplant his chief". Instead, we are told, Lloyd George went to see Asquith, told him about the Tory approaches and found the Prime Minister very willing to agree to a Coalition. This story is, however, not sufficiently corroborated from other sources for one to accept it at face value. It sounds very like an alibi for Lloyd George, and there is no evidence that at this stage any Tory would have been prepared to serve under Ll. G.

During the Gallipoli campaign there was further indication of how Lloyd George used his private intelligence service to obtain information from the battle-fronts. Some of this information came to him direct from war correspondents, sometimes confidential dispatches from the latter were passed on to him by Northcliffe and others. On October 4, 1915, Kitchener had sent a private cable to General Sir Ian Hamilton warning him about a "flow of unofficial reports from Gallipoli" criticising G.H.Q. Later Kitchener became convinced that other confidential reports intended for him alone, and which he had assumed to be safe in the War Office files, had been disclosed to Lloyd George. Sir Basil Thomson, head of the Special Branch at Scotland Yard, was called in to investigate the leakage. Within a few days he discovered that a clerk in the War Office had passed on copies of certain papers to the Ministry of Munitions to which Lloyd George had been transferred from the Exchequer. Later Kitchener told Sir George Arthur: "The man ought to have been summarily dealt with. All I am informed is that it was 'all a mistake' and that the man will be sent to another Ministry. You can be sure he will find a billet with Lloyd George."

One of the principal mischief-makers during the Gallipoli campaign was an impressionable, erratic and easily influenced war correspondent from Australia named Keith (afterwards Sir Keith) Murdoch. In a lengthy document, painting a picture of conditions approaching mutiny, Murdoch told a grim tale about Gallipoli. It was a document which should have been treated with the greatest mistrust and checked with other sources.

"Sedition," wrote Murdoch, "is talked around every tin of bully beef on the Peninsula." A copy of this letter came into Lloyd George's hands. In Mr. Moorehead's book *Gallipoli* it is stated: "It is only fair to assume that Lloyd George was sincerely moved by its terms, but he was also an opponent of Lord Kitchener. . . . He urged Murdoch to send a copy to Mr. Asquith."

8

MANPOWER OR GUN-POWER?

"All that is moulded of iron
Has lent to destruction and blood."
Herbert Edward Palmer

During the latter period of the Liberal Government, Lloyd George had been the leading figure in a Cabinet Munitions Committee set up to co-operate with Lord Kitchener at the War Office. Its activities had been marked by increasing friction due to Lloyd George's self-appointed rôle of defender of the private arms manufacturers against the War Office, a novel task for one who had lambasted the munitions makers during the Boer War.

Then Asquith put Lloyd George in charge of munitions in a newly-created department. There was a suggestion at the time that Ll. G. should either be Joint-Secretary of State for War with Kitchener, sending the latter out to the Western Front as Commander-in-Chief, or that he should completely supersede Kitchener. It was a typical feeler, put out by the new Minister of Munitions and cautiously ventilated in the Press, as to how far he could extend his powers, but, not unexpectedly, Kitchener refused to consider any such arrangement.

Much has been written about the shell shortage of 1915, a great deal of it arrant nonsense that suggests it was solely a British defect. Sensational journalism has been blithely accepted as fact by far too many historians of this war. The whole question of the shell shortage needs to be studied against the background of a war which had developed on a scale which neither belligerent had believed possible.

Practically every expert on both sides had been proved wrong not only in confident assertions that the war could not last a year, but in equally emphatic forecasts about the amount of ammunition required. The Germans expected a *blitzkrieg* in 1914 as much as they did in 1939; the truth was that both belligerents had a shell shortage. The gigantic consumption of munitions in this most wasteful and futile of all wars had far exceeded the expectations of the commanders in the field.

Naturally, the Germans, who had been preparing for war for years, had an initial advantage over the British in this respect, but by the end of 1916 they were themselves in a grave position owing to shortage of munitions. The German General Staff had believed the war could be finished and won in one short, sharp battle. The French General Staff had anticipated a war of only a few months' duration and, while they had provided for repairing guns, had made no provision for replacing them.

Until the Battle of the Marne neither of the two adversaries had seriously thought about the problem of supplies, if the war lasted beyond two years. When the shell shortage occurred it really amounted to two irreconcilable problems—manpower and gun-power—and the poser for the politicians was which should receive priority.

In his *War Memoirs* Lloyd George summed up thus: "The War Office was hampered by a traditional reactionism. Its policy seemed ever to be that of preparing, not for the next war, but for the last one or the last but one. . . . The whole business (i.e. *supplies of munitions*) was at the outset jealously retained by the War Office in its own hands. The result was shortage, delays, misfits and muddles."

It was Lloyd George's case that Kitchener was personally responsible for the shell shortage and that the War Minister hampered the activities of the Ministry of Munitions. Statistics show that in the first fourteen months of the war Kitchener expanded the production of shells twenty-seven-fold, the production of trench mortars by fifty-five-fold and that of hand-grenades by 6,000-fold. Admittedly this still was insufficient for the type of war that was being waged, but the achievement was unparalleled in history and no similar ratio of increased production was realised at any other period of the war.

From a study of the records of the German General Staff it is apparent that there was a shell shortage in Germany *before the end of 1914*. In 1915 General Sixt von Arnim referred to the "overwhelming British artillery" and "a shortage in our reserve supplies of munitions".

Kitchener had from the beginning taken the view that shell consumption was going to be vastly in excess of what the experts claimed. Indeed, Kitchener was almost the only military man in Britain who accepted the conception of long-drawn-out trench warfare as expounded by M. Emil Bloch of France, who had also been a prophet without honour in his own country. Field-Marshal Lord Roberts, a brave soldier but an unimaginative general, had contemptuously dismissed Bloch's views on ammunition consumption in a major war as "Bloch's tosh".

Shell production in December, 1914, was 871,700; by the same month in 1915 it had increased to 23,663,186; at the end of 1916 it had risen to 128,460,113. These are impressive figures, but, while Lloyd George can claim to have improved the output after he became Minister of Munitions, the two sets of ratios cannot properly be compared. In fact, Lloyd George benefited from the impetus originally provided by Kitchener and he also had a free hand and the full backing of the Prime Minister in a new department specially designed to cope with the problem. Similarly with small arms: production had been stepped up ten-fold by Kitchener, but only two-fold by Lloyd George. Apart from this there is the indisputable fact that the Battle of the Somme was fought entirely on ammunition supplied by the War Office alone. These supplies may not have been enough, but they are eloquent testimony to what Kitchener achieved. Indeed in April, 1915, when he was made Minister of Munitions, Ll. G. told the House of Commons that the output of munitions had been increased nineteen-fold under the Kitchener administration.

These figures and criticisms are not meant to belittle Lloyd George's substantial achievements at the Ministry of Munitions, but to reply to his unfair criticisms of Kitchener and even more to those of Ll. G.'s two-faced ally among the generals, the erratic and unreliable Sir John French, who raised the question of the shell shortage as an excuse for his own failures. French, who indulged in political intrigue of a type which should have called for disciplinary action, had never forgiven the War Minister for a personal intervention against him in France in 1914. Lloyd George now saw in him a welcome ally with whom to hammer both Kitchener and the War Office.

While French was writing letters to Asquith in fulsome terms, he was also sending secret messages to Ll. G. complaining about the lack of shells and seeking to undermine the Government in general and Kitchener in particular. The War Minister summed up the situation in a note which he circulated, claiming that, against his own judgment, he had "yielded to the pressing importunities of Sir John French and consented to send out infantry before the supply of artillery ammunition had reached the proper scale. If the Government have made a mistake, it has been, in Lord Kitchener's opinion, due not so much to their failure to produce ammunition in greater quantities, as giving in to persuasions to send out more troops. Lord Kitchener feels that it would be a grave mistake for the Government to repeat this and does not wish to send out reinforcements until the supply of artillery ammunition has reached the standard of seventeen rounds per day for the existing Force and has expanded sufficiently to enable the same proportion of ammunition to be supplied to the new troops as they go out."

The British front, alleged Lloyd George, was being starved of supplies. Yet he himself at the same time was illogically arguing that the way out of stalemate on that same front was to double its length. This, it was pointed out, could only aggravate the munitions shortage. He, the amateur strategist, wanted to mobilise the engineering firms which were outside the armaments industry, but the War Office insisted that, if this were done, it would not mean more munitions, but a vast quantity of faulty munitions. Lloyd George replied that almost anything would be an improvement on the Ordnance Department of the War Office which, he said, was "a failure in the past, chaos in the present and hopelessness in the future".

There is no doubt that the Ordnance Department needed a thorough reorganisation and that Ll. G. had pinpointed serious faults in it. But it was a defect of the Minister of Munitions that he would drag personalities into his criticisms, that he would seek to destroy and replace rather than to adapt and improve. Certainly he showed great foresight in appreciating that a huge arsenal of munitions was the nation's most urgent requirement. As Minister of Munitions he showed more flair than at the Exchequer; his dynamism, his zest for finding out for himself and his restless mind caused a great influx of ideas where they had been sadly lacking. He had found at Woolwich Arsenal "stacks of empty shells which were being slowly and tediously filled, one at a time, with ladles by hand from cauldrons of seething fluid. The production of the fuses for detonating the shells was governed by the same lack of imagination and consequently there was a similar deficiency in output."

But it was easier to propound the urgent need for changes in methods of production, but less easy to carry them out swiftly and effectively through private firms. In the first place the Army was fast absorbing the skilled labour which could make munitions. Lloyd George, who had established unofficial contacts with private manufacturers and industrialists who were anxious to make money while war lasted, insisted that these firms could produce munitions in greater quantities than the Ordnance Department. Kitchener had little faith in the promises of these industrialists that they could achieve this, and in the first year of the war he was largely right. Many of these firms were incompetent and eager only to win contracts. They not only failed to deliver the goods on scheduled dates, but often produced faulty work.[1]

Nor had the private manufacturers, in the early stages at least, the technical expertise or the skilled labour to do a proper job. Von Donop, of the Ordnance Department, stressed that there must be no risk in arms manufacture of the use of materials "too far below the accepted standards". Kitchener expressed his view that both he and the Prime Minister would have been "hanged on the gallows of public opinion if any such catastrophe had happened to the British as befell the French, who lost 800 guns and many lives and suffered a serious set-back in their plans through the use of defective shells".

This was the crux of the problem: how most effectively to step up shell production. To stress it is not to denigrate Lloyd George's efforts, or his remarkable drive at the ministry, but the appearance of getting

[1] By May, 1915, the Army should have had from private contractors 481,000 H.E. 18-pounder shells: only 52,000 were then delivered.

on with the job had to be weighed against the risks of too sudden changes. Thus it was that those who considered these risks often appeared to be hampering the war effort, and Lloyd George through Northcliffe saw that they were so presented to the public.

The root of the shell problem was that, with the best will in the world, it was no use trying to catch up on the Germans' lead in munitions supplies by turning out increased shells of the same type with which the war was started. Kitchener insisted that he must first find out exactly what type of shell was most needed and then concentrate on its production. When Lloyd George was glibly talking about shells in 1915 as though they were all alike, no one knew with any marked degree of certainty whether it was shrapnel or high explosive that was needed at the front. It took some months to convince the experts that high explosive was the answer for field artillery.

This was the background to the arguments that ranged from across the Cabinet table to the dinner tables in Mayfair, from golf course chats at Walton Heath to newspaper offices in Fleet Street. But if the shell shortage was the excuse, there was little doubt that Asquith was the main target. "Ll. G. and Co. are out to smash the Prime Minister, but Grey and I intend to stand on each side of him to protect him from such baseness," Haldane wrote to Mrs. Asquith.

Kitchener's comment to Asquith, when asked why he was so secretive and had not told the Cabinet something which he had only mentioned casually to the Prime Minister, was: "You I can trust, but all these damned politicians talk to their wives, except for Ll. G., who talks to other people's wives."

Once after a munitions row with Ll. G., Kitchener tried to resign in the middle of a Cabinet meeting and was only stopped by the Postmaster-General, who backed to the door of the Cabinet Room and so cut off the War Minister's line of retreat.

An obvious solution to the munitions problem might well have been state control over all manufacturers and industries concerned with arms production. It would have been the only way for more shells to have been produced safely, speedily and adequately. But in 1915–16 Lloyd George did not suggest such a measure. The one-time pacifist was almost indecently eager to give the arms manufacturers the chance to make huge profits, providing they gave him the shells. Had he produced a radical plan to control arms production and curb profits, he might have avoided the labour troubles with which the country was confronted in the last years of the war. It might be argued that any such plan would have been exceedingly difficult to realise because neither the Tories nor business men would have submitted to controls, and the Labour leaders would not have agreed to conscription of labour. But Lloyd George made no move in this direction, not even an attempt to get business men and Labour leaders round a conference table to reach some compromise. The only thing he seemed anxious to control was the liquor trade. Asquith wrote: "This volatile personage goes off at a tangent on the question of drink. His mind apparently oscillates from hour to hour between the two poles of absurdity, cutting off all drink from the working man—which would lead to something like a universal strike—or buying out the whole liquor trade of the country and replacing it by a huge state monopoly."

Yet, when Lloyd George gave evidence before the Royal Commission on the Private Manufacture of and Trading in Arms in 1936, he took a very different line. Then he argued in favour of a state monopoly for arms manufacture and completely contradicted the attitude he had adopted in 1914–16. "When in 1914 it came to the need for increasing our supply of munitions on an enormous scale, private arms firms broke down completely. Private manufacture broke completely down in the war. Orders were given and accepted, but not fulfilled. It is a lamentable story of failure."

These were the very arguments which both Kitchener and von Donop used; the only difference was that they did not carry them to the logical conclusion of seeking fuller control over the manufacturers. In World War I there was an unanswerable case for state control of the armaments industry from every point of view, from the test of efficiency, safety and speed of production, and certainly on the grounds of expenditure and on ethical considerations. The appalling loss of life of which Ll. G. so frequently complained, the failure to supply the Russians with arms in adequate quantities, the profiteering and racketeering of the industrialists at home, all these things could have been avoided or mitigated if Lloyd George had urged in these years what he so vigorously proclaimed in 1936.

Not unexpectedly the Lloyd Georgian view was opposed at the Royal Commission's sitting by those directly interested in arms manufacture, men like Sir Charles Craven and General Sir Herbert Lawrence, while Colonel Sir Maurice Hankey (now Lord Hankey), as Secretary to the Cabinet and Committee of Imperial Defence, said that "the prohibition of private trading in arms would be disastrous to Imperial defence".

At a time when a major switch-over from the production of shrapnel to high explosive shells would have meant a disastrous delay of ten weeks, Lloyd George was writing to the Prime Minister: "Private firms cannot turn out shrapnel because of the complicated character of the shell, but the testimony is unanimous that the high explosive is a simple shell and that any engineering concern could easily produce it."

This was again contradicted by Ll. G. in his diatribe against the private arms firms before the Royal Commission. Yet in 1915 he added in his note to Asquith: "This has been the experience of France."

This claim was not substantiated by facts which ought to have been in his possession as Minister of Munitions. Previously Ll. G. had urged that shrapnel could and should be manufactured by private firms. Far from preventing what Ll. G. called "the horrible loss of life", any big switch-over to high explosives would "not have produced," stated Kitchener, "any high explosive shell for ten weeks or more, and during this period the provision of the absolutely necessary amount of ammunition for the field-guns would have been seriously imperilled just when Sir John French was pressing for every round."

This was a typical example of Lloyd George "playing politics" with shell production, swearing that black was white in order to gain some political kudos. As far as the argument that "the high explosive is a simple shell that any engineering concern could easily produce it", this was a deliberate attempt by Lloyd George to mislead his own Prime Minister. The whole question of the right design for this type of shell was still a matter of research and experiment not only in Britain but in France. According to the French War Office their leading ordnance specialist at that time was "still not finally satisfied as to the right pattern of the high explosive shell, the best fuse to be employed for it and the nature of its filling".

So much for the claim that "this has been the experience of France"!

* * * * *

While at the Ministry of Munitions, Lloyd George was once again the friend of big business and the industrial-financial oligarchies with whom he curried favour when at the Board of Trade. He was caught up too deeply in the mesh of international armaments intrigues to be a free agent. For the man to whom he turned for help and advice was Sir Basil Zaharoff, chief agent of the Vickers Company, with a roving commission to go where he liked and sell arms to whomever he could at a commission. When war came in 1914 Zaharoff was at the zenith of his power and, with the aid of Lloyd George, soon filled the rôle of unofficial chief inter-Allied munitions agent.

With Zaharoff, Lloyd George made an ingenious bargain that enabled the Welshman to show how he was obtaining more shells at lower cost. An essential part of this bargain was that Zaharoff should co-operate in reducing costs on the understanding that he was personally allowed to make larger profits by selling more shells and guns. Thus as Minister of Munitions Lloyd George was able to claim that he had reduced the cost of eighteen-pounder shells from 22*s*. 6*d*. each to 12*s*. and of Lewis guns from £165 to £35 each. It was, of course, a considerable achievement.

True, the profits of the British armament industry were limited by law during the war; it was not permitted for them to exceed by more than 20 per cent the average net profit of the last two business years before the war. Any excess had to go to the Treasury. But the orders were so vast that profits still remained high and Vickers increased its capital during World War I from £10 million to £13,500,000, an increase which by no means indicated the extent of its profits.

In January, 1916, Lloyd George was once again making a dangerous personal and unauthorised incursion into the realms of foreign policy. On January 14 he dined with Colonel House, the roving Ambassador of President Wilson. Ll. G. was in expansive mood and he told House that the war could only be ended by the *neutral* intervention of President Wilson.

"This should come about," he said, "round about September next, when the slaughter that is now being planned rebounds on the heads of the planners and proves once again to be utterly ineffective. Terms should then be dictated by the President, terms which the belligerents would never agree upon if left to themselves."

A complex statement, but it left Colonel House in little doubt as to its implications. Fortunately, before he got in touch with Washington, House repeated what Ll. G. had told him to Grey and Balfour. The latter, aghast at what had been suggested, hastened to explain that this was simply Lloyd George's idea and that he had never mentioned a word of that kind to the Cabinet. They left House in no doubt that it was contrary to British policy.

Meanwhile the so-called "Shell Scandal" and the growing demand for conscription within the Cabinet were all used as excuses for attempting to clip Kitchener's powers. First it was Lloyd George alone who forced the issue; then, as events seemed to move against the War Minister, Carson and Bonar Law began to murmur against his authority.

The vital issue was conscription. Again it was Lloyd George, the former pacifist, who was the most vigorous exponent of the necessity for conscription. With Churchill and Carson, Ll. G. would have supported compulsory military service much earlier in the war. Indeed, as far back as the Constitutional Conference of 1910, as has already been mentioned, in a secret memorandum proposing a Party truce, Ll. G. had asked that the question of compulsory military service should not be shirked. Kitchener was against conscription. When a memorial service to mark the anniversary of the war's outbreak was proposed for St. Paul's Cathedral, Kitchener commented: "I want this service to be a great recruiting occasion. The Archbishop could, in a short sermon, stir up the whole congregation, which would be a far better way of doing things than all this intrigue about conscription."[1]

Certainly there was no clear-cut desire among the population for conscription sooner than 1916. Even then the measure had to be steered skilfully through a House of Commons which contained a Liberal majority to whom compulsory military service was anathema.

[1] *Autobiography* by Margot Asquith

It is still debatable whether conscription improved the military situation, though it removed the causes of much bitterness and controversy because at least each citizen was now treated alike. Auckland Geddes, who was Minister of National Service in the later years of the war, expressed the view afterwards that "with, perhaps, more knowledge than most of the working of conscription in this country, I hold the fully matured opinion that, on balance, the imposition of military conscription added little if anything to the effective sum of our total war effort".

* * * * *

Kitchener, worn out with the strain and responsibilities of office and the growing intrigues against him, was ageing visibly. As War Minister he had worked longer hours than most of his colleagues and, never a gregarious man, he tended to avoid social life increasingly and in consequence to rely more on his own judgment and less on that of his subordinates. Without doubt the nagging feeling that he had enemies in the Cabinet and in the newspaper world preyed heavily on a mind that was far more sensitive than was generally realised and this seriously affected his judgment and sapped his energies.

The War Minister's attention was in the early months of 1916 preoccupied with the problems of Russia. Whatever his shortcomings in other directions he had great foresight on this subject. He was convinced that the fate of Russia was of paramount importance to the Allies, and he frequently foretold of an attempt by underground forces in Russia to compel the Russian Government to make a deal with Germany and contract out of the war.

Kitchener stressed the need for giving Russia greater military support and supplies. He sneered at the "Easterners" for being blind to what constituted the Allies' most vital line in the east—the Russian front. It was, he argued, much more vital than any "Balkan diversions". Here again he clashed with Ll. G., bitterly reproaching the Minister of Munitions for failing to keep his promise to Russia regarding supplies of munitions. Lloyd George insisted that munitions poured into Russia in excess of what Britain could legitimately spare might result in these arms being used against us on some future occasion. But, speaking before the Royal Commission on the private manufacture of armaments in 1936, he again told a very different story:

"Undertakings were given by our armament firms to the Russians with even worse results," he then said. "Not even any appreciable percentage of the obligations undertaken was ever discharged. The Russians depended upon them and found themselves with no means of defending their lives against the German attack. The feeling against the British firms, as I know, was exceedingly bitter in the Russian Army. The failure was attributed to breach of faith and, there is no doubt, partly contributed to the Russian collapse and the Russian disgruntlement with the Allies."

In making this statement in 1936, Lloyd George, without directly saying so, was admitting his own culpability in 1916. For the responsibility for supplying the Russians with arms was then clearly his.

Kitchener's reputation in military circles in Russia was great, and his influence and opinions carried great weight with the Czar. Through diplomatic channels the Czar indicated that he would welcome a visit from Kitchener. Early in May a secret invitation was sent to the War Minister from the Czar, quite apart from the confidential approach made to the British Government. It is also certain that Kitchener had been making overtures or writing letters himself either to the Czar or to someone else close to that monarch, for the Russian Ambassador in Holland told the British Ambassador in the Dutch capital: "Lord Kitchener's urgent representations and inspiriting messages have induced the Czar to consider the whole matter of *munitions supply* from a new angle. The Czar now believes that a visit from Lord Kitchener can boost morale in Russia among the fainthearts at the Court. The Czar wants advice and he thinks it might help if the control of *certain things, possibly supplies*, were taken into British hands."

The italics are the author's: it is important to note the emphasis on munitions and supplies generally. This would normally be a matter for the Minister of Munitions, but Lloyd George, no friend of the Czar and a great critic of the Russian Government, did not see eye to eye with Kitchener on this subject.

There are various and contradictory versions of this proposal to send a mission to Moscow. The Prime Minister, mindful of Kitchener's personal influence with the Czar and his high standing with Russian generals, strongly urged acceptance of the Russian invitation by the War Minister, but there is no evidence that he asked Lloyd George to accompany him.

On the other hand, Dr. Thomas Jones stated in his book, *Lloyd George*, that in April, 1916, "Asquith thought Lloyd George should go to Russia. For some days the composition of the mission was in doubt, until Asquith decided the matter by announcing in the House of Commons on May 25 that the Minister of Munitions had agreed to devote his energies to the promotion of an Irish settlement, which had been newly bedevilled by the Easter Rebellion."

This can hardly be correct, as in April the question of a visit to Russia had not yet been raised.

Mr. Malcolm Thomson's version is that "Lloyd George was planning to visit Russia with Kitchener. The Easter Rebellion upset this plan and Kitchener had to go alone at the last moment." Mr. W. F. Burbidge in *Wizard of Wales* stated: "Lloyd George was invited to accompany the mission (*to Russia*), but because of his interest in the problems of the Irish question he declined."

Ll. G.'s own version in his *War Memoirs* was that he had decided to go with Kitchener when he received a letter from the Prime Minister, asking him "to take up Ireland, at any rate for a short time. That letter saved my life. Much against my own inclination, I decided I could not refuse Mr. Asquith's request, so I had to tell Lord Kitchener I could not accompany him on his voyage."

In Asquith's papers there is no reference to Ll. G. having been invited to go to Russia either with or without Kitchener. It is certain that Grey would have opposed the idea of Ll. G. making the trip; the prospects of the mischief-making Munitions Minister, with his penchant for interfering in foreign policy, visiting the Court of the Czar are unlikely to have commended themselves either to Asquith or Grey.

Lloyd George's visit to Ireland had ended and he was back in London before Kitchener set off for Russia, so the excuse that it was the Irish Mission which caused the Russian visit to be cancelled does not hold. All the evidence seems to suggest that at one time Ll. G. would have liked to go to Russia alone and that, for some reason or another, he gave the impression to his staff at the Ministry of Munitions right up to the last moment that he expected to go with Kitchener. At a few hours' notice he sent for Mr. Leslie Robertson, of the Ministry, and deputed him to "take my place. I find I cannot go myself". Yet, according to his own statement in the *War Memoirs*, he had known he would not be going at least two weeks before this.

But equally all the evidence points to the fact that the Prime Minister did not intend, nor did he ask, Ll. G. to make the trip. Asquith's own private secretary at the time, the late Sir Maurice Bonham-Carter, had no knowledge of any such proposal and completely discounted it. Sir George Arthur, Kitchener's right-hand man, knew nothing of the matter and considered it "highly unlikely".

On June 5, Kitchener and the other members of the mission sailed in the cruiser *Hampshire* from Scapa Flow, destined for Archangel. When only a mile and a half from the shore between the Brough of Birsay and Markwick Head the ship hit a mine and sank within fifteen minutes. Kitchener went down with her.

9

THE AMATEUR STRATEGIST

"Pleas'd with the danger, when the waves went high
He sought the storms; but for a calm unfit,
Would steer too nigh the sands to boast his wit."

John Dryden

Kitchener's death profoundly affected the morale of millions of his countrymen in that midsummer of 1916. His prestige in the country, despite the whispering campaign against him, was as high as it had ever been.

For Lloyd George the way to the premiership was through the War Office and, with Kitchener out of the way, he was a natural candidate for the post. As soon as the news of Kitchener's death was received, he was plotting to succeed him. An inspired paragraph in *The Times* of June 12 stated that the new War Minister would "Almost certainly be Mr. Lloyd George. We learn that Bonar Law called on Asquith to press Lloyd George's claims".

Many ridiculous rumours circulated at this time, attributing Kitchener's death to a plot engineered by his enemies, both Lloyd George and Lord Northcliffe being mentioned as originators of the plot. There is, of course, no doubt that the *Hampshire* was sunk by a German mine and one can dismiss any such fantastic allegations without question. Nevertheless, Lloyd George's behaviour in the days immediately preceding Kitchener's departure is difficult to explain. There is the indisputable fact that Ll. G. himself gave the impression that he was going to Russia although he had never been asked to go. There is also abundant evidence that details of Kitchener's mission to Russia had been leaked to the Press and, though nothing was printed, news of the mission was known in Fleet Street eight days before the *Hampshire* sailed. Lord Riddell declared: "Lloyd George had a presentiment about the *Hampshire*. About a week before she sailed he told me that Kitchener was going in this ship and that he was glad he wasn't sailing in such an old tub." Probably Lloyd George's motives in the political activities which preceded the mission to Russia will for ever remain an enigma. All that seems certain is that he did divulge the information to certain people.

Within a few months of Kitchener's death Lloyd George was angling for support from Bonar Law in a scheme which, say the biographers of Asquith, "Ll. G. was hatching for a War Council with himself at the head of it, and to consider his plan for getting rid of Sir William Robertson, Chief of the Imperial General Staff, whom he considered to be a great obstacle to his schemes, by sending him on a mission to St. Petersburg."

Bonar Law, whose inability to make up his mind was at times a serious handicap, must have scented an unsavoury plot, for, according to Lord Beaverbrook, he then took the view that "in matters of office and power Lloyd George was a self-seeker and a man who considered no interests but his own".

Robertson, advised by some of Ll. G.'s enemies among the pro-Asquithians in the Cabinet that it was a scheme to get him away from the War Office, refused to go.

* * * * *

When Lloyd George succeeded Lord Kitchener at the War Office, Mrs. Asquith, with feminine intuition, wrote in her diary: "We are out; it can only be a question of time now when we shall have to leave Downing Street."

Few shared her misgivings; many reproached her for even thinking that Lloyd George might be disloyal to his chief. Even Asquith himself showed no signs of doubting the War Minister. Why should he when only the previous year he had recorded in his own diary: "Ll. G. declared that he owed everything to me, that I had stuck to him and protected him and defended him when every man's hand was against him and that he would (1) rather break stones, (2) dig potatoes, (3) be hung, drawn and quartered than to do an act or say a word or harbour a thought that was disloyal to me. . . . His eyes were wet with tears."

Yet, from the moment he went to the War Office, Lloyd George never ceased to intrigue for the premiership, sometimes in the guise of patriotic critic of the Cabinet of which he was a member, more often through his close relations with the Press lords, all of whom were eager for varying reasons to oust Asquith.

It has been suggested that Lloyd George was estranged from Asquith by some of his colleagues in the Cabinet. There is very little evidence that this was the case; indeed, if these so-called enemies of Lloyd George had vigorously opposed his appointment to the War Office, Ll. G. would never have acquired the influence he eventually wielded. Asquith's error was not that he allowed himself to be estranged from his War Minister, but that he disregarded the existence of intrigues and refused to enter into arguments with his critics. The Prime Minister's case went by default. Mr. J. A. Spender wrote: "I myself went to him several times and begged him to be on his guard. I tried to put it to him that this time he was faced with something more than the ordinary Press attacks which he had grown to despise, that there was in fact a concerted movement with important backing within his own Government to displace him. He said he was sick of all this gossiping and whispering and determined to take no notice of it."

Lloyd George stopped at nothing to denigrate the man who "protected him and defended him when every man's hand was against him". Thus was the legend preserved that in 1916 Asquith was flabby, lacking in drive and losing his grip, while Lloyd George was the selfless patriot trying to bring order out of chaos.

The events which led up to the resignation of Asquith have been described at great length by various authorities. But it is not true that "at a crisis of history Lloyd George turned muddle into system and purpose". John Terraine writes: "By the end of 1916, when Mr. Lloyd George became Premier, the outlook from his point of view—and he was the leader of those statesmen and some few soldiers who felt particularly depressed by the course the war had taken—seemed thoroughly black. After France's heavy losses in 1915 and the terrible strain that the Germans had inflicted upon her at Verdun at the beginning of the new year, the British Army had been forced, before it was really ready, to assume the main rôle in the West. The result had been the Battle of the Somme, with its 415,000 British casualties and the virtual destruction of Kitchener's volunteer armies, for the gain of a very narrow strip indeed of muddy ground in Picardy. The battle, with all its terrifying consumption of human life . . . had not prevented the Germans from detaching sufficient strength to crush Rumania almost as soon as she had thrown in her lot with the Allies."

That was one side of the picture. The truth is that there was no crisis in 1916 when Lloyd George made his bid for power. In November, 1916, Sir William Robertson, then Chief of the General Staff, attended an Allied conference at Chantilly. Of that conference he later wrote: "The exhausted condition of the German armies was not then as well known to us as it has since become, but we knew sufficient about it to realise the wisdom of taking full advantage of the successes gained in the Verdun and Somme campaigns, first by continuing to exert pressure on the Somme front as far as the winter season would permit, and secondly by preparing to attack the enemy early in 1917 with all the resources that could be made available before he had time to recover from his difficulties. The conference decided on a plan of this nature, but it was not carried out."

The man who failed to carry it out was the man who became Prime Minister a month later—Lloyd George.

In an apologia made in a speech to the Manchester Reform Club on December 6, 1919, Lloyd George alleged that "in December, 1916, Russia had practically collapsed". Yet this statement is completely contradicted by what he said on December 20, 1917: "... That in December, 1916, the Russian Army was better equipped with guns and ammunition than it had ever been during the whole period of the war."

Certainly the Russians had been weakened, but they had still managed to launch a brilliant offensive under General Brusiloff.

Lloyd George also claimed that at the end of 1916 the cause of the Allies was in peril and "would be doomed unless new energy could be imported into the struggle." Yet M. Hanotaux, who was French Foreign Minister, said that from November, 1916, he was convinced that victory had been assured, while Ludendorff, the most objective of the German generals, took the view that at the end of 1916 "the Germans were completely exhausted on the Western front".

Asquith's verdict on Ll. G.'s Manchester apologia was: "I am sorry to have to say it, but I say it with the utmost deliberation and emphasis, that a more slovenly travesty of quite recent history has never been presented by a responsible statesman."

In 1916 Britain fought the Battle of Jutland, which, however disappointing its immediate results may have been, sealed up the German High Seas Fleet and its ports from which it never again emerged. If victory were not actually within sight, it was at least "the beginning of the end".

It might be thought that in December, 1916, a man with drive anxious to turn what Dr. Thomas Jones called "flabbiness into resolution", would have urged on the Cabinet the need for hitting the Germans really hard with an immediate onslaught on the Somme front. That would have made sense in the light of the Chantilly discussions. But it was not what Lloyd George urged. Instead he was conspiring with the Press lords to paint a picture of his own "dark estimate and forecast of the situation". He was openly advertising his aversion to any big push on the Western front by complaining of the "bloody assaults on the Somme". Yet the series of operations on the Somme had in fact saved Verdun. Lloyd George knew that British public opinion had been shocked by the decimations of the Somme, but instead of succouring the downhearted and stressing the need for that "knock-out blow" of which he had talked so glibly not long before, he sought to capitalise the public's anguish in his favour and against Asquith.

On December 5, 1916, when the greatest need was for Cabinet unity to support to the fullest extent the military experts' plea for a new drive against the enemy, Lloyd George was harping back on the Rumanian debâcle in a letter to Asquith: "There has been delay, hesitation, lack of foresight and vision. The latest illustration is of our lamentable failure to give timely support to Rumania." Yet it was Lloyd George himself, as War Minister, who had the fullest responsibility for the arrangements for bringing in Rumania. On the Prime Minister's instructions he had gone to Paris the previous August to negotiate with M. Briand and General Joffre on this very question. Britain was then preoccupied with the battle of the Somme and there were no guns or ammunition to spare. All this had been explained to the Rumanians who had been warned that the only direct aid for them could come from the Russians. It had been made fully clear to the Rumanians that if they failed to get help from the Russians, they could expect no immediate aid from Britain.

This intelligence had been faithfully conveyed to the Rumanians by Lloyd George; he was fully appraised of the risks of the situation. To try to exploit the Rumanian debâcle as he did to Asquith was to deny his own responsibility in the matter.

Just how defeatist Lloyd George was during this period and how unfitted to win the confidence of the generals is shown in a quotation from Lord Hankey's book, *The Supreme Command 1914-18*. "We are going to lose the war," said Lloyd George to Hankey on November 9, 1916. It was his rejoinder to an illuminating remark of Hankey's: "I told him that personally I had never the smallest illusions about crushing Germany. The best I had ever hoped for at any time was a draw in our favour and a favourable peace extorted by economic pressure."

Here then is the clue to the malaise of panic, depression and intrigue which spread in the highest political circles at the end of 1916. For long the suggestion was that it was merely a desire to have a more vigorous conduct of the war which actuated the anti-Asquith politicians, but these varying comments of Lloyd George and Hankey, the two men in the land who knew most about the day-to-day developments of the war, reveal that it was an innate pessimism which was the real cause of the trouble.

The final break with Asquith came over Lloyd George's demand for a small War Committee being set up to run the day-to-day conduct of the war, thus removing it from what Mr. Malcolm Thomson in his book *David Lloyd George* surprisingly calls "the futile discussions of the Cabinet". In other words, Lloyd George would preside over a committee which settled war policy while his own Prime Minister became a mere rubber stamp for his decisions. Mr. Thomson adds: "It is also very clear that Lloyd George had no desire to displace Asquith. He did not covet the Premiership."

It is odd that Mr. Thomson should so boldly make this assertion when the root difficulty (according to Lord Beaverbrook) "was that Bonar Law had formed the opinion that in matters of office Lloyd George was a self-seeker and a man who considered no interests but his own." By now even so long-suffering and uncomplaining a man as Asquith had seen the dangers ahead sufficiently clearly to write to Bonar Law: "There is one construction, and one only, that could be put on the new arrangement—that it had been engineered by him (Ll. G.) with the purpose, not perhaps at the moment, but as soon as a fitting pretext could be found, of his displacing me."

Nevertheless Asquith did not entirely turn down the Lloyd George plan, and some accommodation could have been obtained if Lloyd George had wished. Instead there appeared in *Reynolds News* an article which, said Lord Beaverbrook, "Was like an interview with Lloyd George written in the third person." The gist of that article was that Ll. G. was prepared to resign if his terms were not granted. But any possibility of a compromise between Asquith and Lloyd George was ruined when on the following day it was obvious that the most confidential matters discussed between the two men on the previous evening had been disclosed to *The Times* to form the basis of a leading article.

Both the *Reynolds* and *Times* articles angered leading Tories as much as the Liberals, and at this stage it looked as though they would turn against Lloyd George and insist that he should submit to the Prime Minister's demand to be chairman of the War Committee. Had Asquith continued to insist on this point and had he called a secret session of the House of Commons, explained the situation and asked for a vote of confidence, there is little doubt that he would have won the day. Probably his trump card would have been the need for continuity of government at a time when the Chantilly conference decisions for a new drive on the Western front needed to be implemented. By forcing the fall of the Asquith Government, Lloyd George prevented a new assault from being put into action, thus not only prolonging the war an extra year, but causing tens of thousands of casualties which need not have occurred.

Bonar Law was in a dilemma. He had tried in his pawky, pathetic manner to keep friends on both sides. In doing so he had revealed his own colourlessness and lack of ideas, confused his Party and left himself temporarily isolated. Lloyd George, sensing this, urged that, if Asquith resigned, Bonar Law should be considered as his natural successor, always providing that Asquith would serve under him. But, if Asquith declined to serve under anyone, then he, Lloyd George, should be the choice. Bonar Law fell into a subtle trap. By accepting any such understanding, he threw away any chance he had for the premiership. This was fortunate for the country, for Bonar Law had neither the ability, the drive nor the temperament to be a successful War Premier. His innate pessimism would have brought about his own downfall.

Asquith was completely misled on all sides. He was misled in the first place into thinking that an accommodation could be made with Lloyd George, though he was under no illusion that it would be the last accommodation he could make without losing all his prestige. He was misled by those of his Liberal colleagues such as Edwin Montagu, who failed to warn him of Ll. G.'s plots because they desired to keep both men in the same team. He was deliberately deceived by Bonar Law who failed to inform him of the vital resolution which had been passed at a Conservative Party meeting. This resolution stated that:

"We share the view expressed to the Prime Minister some time ago that the Government cannot go on as it is. It is evident that a change must be made and in our opinion the publicity given to the intentions of Mr. Lloyd George makes reconstruction from within no longer possible. We therefore urge the Prime Minister to tender the resignation of the Government. If he feels unable to take that step, we authorise Mr. Bonar Law to tender our resignation."

This was indeed an incoherent and complex resolution which needs clarifying. It surely was essential that the Prime Minister should have seen the exact phrasing. Asquith made it clear in his book, *Memories and Reflections*, that he was never shown the document. Mr. Robert Blake, in his biography of Bonar Law, confirms this: "Bonar Law had the resolution in his pocket, but he never showed it to Asquith."

Bonar Law was not of the same view as the majority of his Conservative colleagues. They were angry with Lloyd George and wanted the resolution to make that clear. This the resolution obliquely implied, but certainly not strongly enough. By this time Bonar Law wanted Asquith to go, whereas most of the Conservatives merely wanted Lloyd George brought under control even if breaking up the Government was the only way of doing it.

At a meeting of Liberal Cabinet Ministers (Lloyd George was not present) full support for Asquith was pledged, and they undertook not to serve in any Government under Lloyd George or Bonar Law. But two factors undermined Asquith's position; first, the death blow dealt by Arthur Henderson, who declared that Labour would join a Lloyd George Government; secondly, the uneasiness felt by many Tories that a reconstructed Asquith Government, without Lloyd George, might mean an alliance between Asquith and Lansdowne with a bid for a negotiated peace. In this second factor existed an astonishing paradox. Lloyd George, the man who had told Hankey that "we are going to lose", was reluctantly but admiringly regarded by some of the Tory rank and file as the apostle of the "drive for victory"; Asquith, who unostentatiously believed the military position favoured the Allies, was suspected of being a secret ally of Lansdowne. Such uneasiness was utterly unjustified as Asquith, though respecting Lord Lansdowne, had not supported this Conservative's well-intended "Peace" memorandum which he thought was badly timed.[1] The Prime Minister did

[1] On November 13, 1916, Lord Lansdowne presented a memorandum to the Cabinet setting out his personal views on the case for a negotiated peace. Asquith was regarded with unjust suspicion because he had not joined in the reproaches levelled at Lansdowne.

not think the Allies could possibly get reasonable terms for peace at this stage of the war.

It is still hard to understand why Asquith did not seek to explain his viewpoint on the situation to a secret session of the House. Perhaps the liberalism of his temperament made him too proud to take this advantage; more probably he was weary of the internecine warfare within the Cabinet and reluctantly came to the conclusion that resignation was the only step he could take compatible with patriotism and dignity. He resigned and Bonar Law went to see the King. Charged with the task of forming a government, he went to see Asquith and invited him to serve in it. Asquith, as Lloyd George had anticipated, refused to serve. This was not so much due to stubbornness as the fact that Asquith never had a high regard for Bonar Law as a statesman. In his refusal he was fully supported by his other Liberal colleagues in the Cabinet. So Bonar Law returned to the Palace and recommended the King to send for Lloyd George.

Thus, on December 6, 1916, Lloyd George was requested by the King to form a government. At the age of fifty-three he became Prime Minister. As Churchill put it, he "Seized the main power of the state and the leadership of the Government. I think it was Carlyle who said of Oliver Cromwell: 'He coveted the place; perhaps the place was his.'"

Few will deny that "seized" was an apt word, but the reasons for the seizing of power could not be attributed to selfless patriotism. The war situation when Asquith resigned was better than it had ever been and far better than it was a year later. Indeed, Asquith may well have taken the view that if there was to be a change of government this was the most propitious moment for it, though this was a view certainly not shared by most military experts, especially as the combination of Asquith and Robertson had been working so well.

True, there was a weariness among the people, an acute desire for something dramatic to resolve the deadlock on the Western front, but in two years the Asquith administrations had made steady strides towards a victory which Kitchener had declared would only be achieved after three years. Military conscription had been steered successfully through Parliament at the right psychological moment. Hindenburg summed up the view of the German generals at the time when he said of the position at the end of 1916: "There was no doubt that the relative strength of our own and of the enemies' forces had changed still more to our disadvantage at the end of 1916 than had been the case at the beginning of the year."

Tirpitz was even more illuminating. He "seriously doubted whether we could hold out for another year". Field-Marshal Haig was able to tell French newspapermen at the beginning of 1917 that the prospects of victory "this year are rosy".

This, then, was the considered military opinion of both sides as to the true position when Lloyd George became Premier. Where is the justification for his "dark estimate and forecast"? More important, where was the drive to achieve some dramatic coup to end the deadlock. Nowhere is there any record that Lloyd George had any positive plan for ramming home the Allies' undoubted advantage at this time. Major-General Sir Frederick Maurice told us that "Ll. G. lacked the Duke of Wellington's 'one o'clock in the morning' courage"—the courage which in the midst of troubles and difficulties sees also the enemy's troubles and difficulties. "Unrivalled in a sudden crisis, he had not the temperament to endure a long-drawn-out battle and to give at its end that extra push which means victory."

Lloyd George was from the beginning of his Premiership impeded by his own pathological aversion to seeking a decision on the Western front. He had a fatal flaw as a war-time Prime Minister: he was incapable of trusting his own military leaders. He hated Sir William Robertson, the Chief of the Imperial General Staff, and would have liked to curtail the powers conferred on him by Asquith. His pet aversion, however, was Haig. He would have dismissed both men had he felt strong enough to withstand the storm of criticism such an act would arouse. But, failing to win any support for such a move at home, he sought to intrigue with the French to get rid of them. It would be unfair to deny that he was genuinely appalled by the loss of life with so little result to date on the Western front; the 415,000 British casualties on the Somme had deeply angered him. He was also intensely bitter at what seemed to him to be the unthinking prodigality of the generals in proposing to hammer away again on the same front. Notwithstanding all this, he had nothing very practical to offer in place of this war of attrition.

There is evidence that Lloyd George had been in touch with politicians and generals in France to bring about Haig's downfall long before he had been Premier. Marshal Lyautey, at one time French War Minister, testified that Ll. G., when in France, was continually denigrating Haig. He told Lyautey that Haig lived in "such blatant luxury that he never had any conception of what the fighting men had to put up with". An even more disagreeable trait was his attempt to play up to the Anglophobe French generals by stressing his Welsh ancestry. "You and I understand each other better than these English. My country and yours are culturally closer together. The English lack our fire and imagination. Why, the close resemblance of the French and Welsh words for 'church' prove our affinity," he told Colonel D'Alençon, General Nivelle's staff officer, who was an inveterate Anglophobe.

Within two days of becoming Prime Minister, Lloyd George, in league with M. Painlevé, the French Premier, was planning to send two British divisions to Salonika, thus disregarding the need for an immediate push on the Somme. Sir William Robertson sent a secret telegram to Haig, saying that this proposal was "most unsound. No military reasons can be produced to justify such a procedure".

Lloyd George's utter failure to carry a majority of the Liberals with him against Asquith was demonstrated by the complexion of the new Government. It contained seven Liberals, fourteen Conservatives and one Labour member, compared to the previous administration of fourteen Liberals, ten Conservatives and one Labour. By far the most important change which Ll. G. introduced and perhaps the most valuable contribution he made to governmental administration was the creation of a small War Cabinet of six members which met daily. He also initiated a Cabinet Secretariat and an Imperial War Cabinet which brought the Dominions more fully into sharing responsibility for the conduct of the war. These innovations definitely strengthened not only the constitutional machinery, but the bonds of Commonwealth, and from the long-term view of history they may go down as one of Lloyd George's most sagacious acts.

Until he came to power there had been no record kept of Cabinet discussions or decisions, largely due to the tradition of secrecy in the conduct of Cabinet business. Indeed, secrecy had been carried so far that in Victorian days black blotting paper was used in the Cabinet Room to prevent any tell-tale scribblings being revealed in the waste-paper baskets. But, since Lloyd George himself had shown such a cynical disregard for this tradition of secrecy, he had no hesitation in arranging that all business must in future be recorded and minutes of all conclusions reached in the Cabinet circulated to the ministers concerned. Lord Simon, who for part of his life was a political adversary of Lloyd George, stated in his book, *Retrospect*, that, "I am one of the few ex-Cabinet Ministers now living who has had actual experience at first-hand of both systems and there is not the slightest doubt that, when the comparison is made, the one which now prevails (i.e., that introduced by Ll. G.) is not only to be preferred, but is absolutely essential."

Though Lloyd George took the credit for the change, the idea originated with Sir Maurice Hankey. In the official biography of Lloyd George it is stated that Hankey talked with Ll. G. and "urged him to insist on a small War Cabinet being set up to run the day-to-day conduct of the war". Between Hankey, the soldier-civil servant, and Lloyd George there had developed a remarkable affinity for so incongruous a pair. How close and remarkable this association was may be judged by the manner in which each aired his pessimistic views on the other and how, two days after Ll. G. became Premier, he called Hankey to the War Office to condole with him as "the most miserable man on earth".

But while a small War Cabinet can be, as was proved in World War II, of the utmost value, it can also deteriorate into a thinly veiled form of dictatorship, which was exactly what happened under Lloyd George, often with disastrous consequences. It could never be said of Lloyd George's wartime government, as he himself said of the Asquithian Cabinets, that Parliament was the only thing it was afraid of. The larger Cabinet and the slower Asquithian method might have been laborious and seemingly less effective, but they were the essence of democracy and provided time for careful deliberation before decisions were reached. Slow as the old system might be in time of war, it could have prevented some of the blunders of 1917–18.

In the early months of 1917 Lloyd George wasted much time in exploring new schemes for switching the military initiative from the west to the east. At a conference of the Allies at Rome in January he produced a plan for transferring several divisions from France to the Italian front with the object of dealing a blow at Austria. This was kept secret until the last moment as Ll. G. feared opposition from his own military advisers, but hoped to forestall this by winning Italian support. But if he thought to find allies among the Italians in this matter, he was wrong: the Rome conference merely referred his plan to the generals.

When he returned to Paris, Lloyd George was informed by the French that General Nivelle had a scheme for breaking through the German lines on the Western front and achieving a speedy victory—possibly "in forty-eight hours". A month earlier Ll. G. would have decried the idea as half-baked and nonsensical and the antithesis of his own views on strategy. Now he made another right-about-turn, which showed how easily he could be swayed from one plan to another. Nivelle was invited to London for discussions, and when the Italians eventually reported favourably for action on their front, they found Ll. G. had changed his mind.

Thus within two months of his coming to power Lloyd George had squandered all hope of an early victory. He had refused to implement the Chantilly plan for a new drive on the Somme, he had advocated action on the Italian front and then repudiated his own project, and finally agreed to the hastily conceived and foolishly optimistic Nivelle plan at a time when the Chantilly decisions should have been translated into action. The extraordinary feature of this muddled, patchwork military planning by an amateur strategist, heedless of his advisers, was that for one brief period Lloyd George became a "Westerner" in strategy.

What had happened to bring about this change? The blindness and obtuseness of Lloyd George to the chances of victory through a major assault in the west at this period are most clearly illustrated in Haig's diary. The latter recorded: "I asked Mr. Lloyd George to look at the

Western front as a whole. He stated that, although he recognised the west as the principal theatre, he 'could not believe that it was possible to beat the German armies there—at any rate, not next year'." This was on December 15, 1916.

Yet if any proof were wanted that Germany was in a desperate situation and anxious to play for time it was surely contained in the "peace note" issued by the German Chancellor on December 12. The Chancellor suggested negotiations but gave no hint as to conditions. True, the note was arrogantly worded, but the intention was clear—to alienate the neutrals from the Allies, if the latter bluntly rejected the suggestions, and to play for time while the German armies were regrouped.

The reason for Lloyd George's policy switch was that Nivelle's plan gave him a chance to ignore the plans of Robertson and Haig, and by working with the French to diminish the authority of the British generals and relegate them to positions of less importance. It was a gamble, but, if it succeeded, Ll. G. would enhance his prestige at home and in Paris. Nivelle not only believed he had a formula for breaking through the German lines, but insisted that, if he failed, he would be able to break off the battle within forty-eight hours without great loss of life. Nivelle may not have been a great general, but he possessed the very qualities which Robertson and Haig lacked and which Lloyd George most admired—an imaginative approach to strategical problems and an easy and lucid exposition of his arguments. Even more important, he spoke fluent English and was able completely to win over Lloyd George by his insistence that his plan would mean "no more Sommes, but just one short, sharp battle".

One of the Prime Minister's quirks was a belief in phrenology. Throughout his life he asserted that the shape of a man's head was a sure sign of the extent of his abilities. Mr. Malcolm Thomson has told us that in 1884 Ll. G. went up to London and visited a phrenologist at Ludgate Circus, who "amazed him by the accuracy of his character delineation, but went far to ruin the impression by his diagnosis that Lloyd George would one day be Prime Minister". When he met Nivelle, Ll. G. was greatly impressed by the bumps on the French general's head and deemed them to be "deserving of every confidence and reminiscent of Napoleon."[1]

From Ll. G.'s point of view, it must be admitted that, superficially,

[1] How keenly Ll. G. was interested in this subject was revealed by Professor Millott Severn, a phrenologist who examined some 250,000 skulls in his lifetime. Professor Severn recalled Ll. G. coming to see him as Chancellor of the Exchequer: "Mr. Lloyd George has a wonderful amount of length of head, as well as base, which gives him physical stamina and sustaining power. It is my firm opinion that our present Prime Minister owes his success very largely to his knowledge of phrenology, not only insofar as his personal advancement is concerned, but also as to his ability to judge the mental calibre of his colleagues." This may or may not be, but it is on record that Lloyd George claimed that Neville Chamberlain's head was "enough to disqualify him from high office".

the Nivelle plan had many attractions. The Prime Minister was sufficient of a realist to know that he was mistrusted in certain high circles in London and that he needed a quick and devastating coup to overcome this antagonism to him. No one had a deeper personal distrust of the Welshman than King George V, though the Sovereign tried hard to conceal this and to get along with him. The King was seriously perturbed at Lloyd George's accession to the Premiership and feared an attempt by the Prime Minister to sack Haig. He was also afraid that the new Premier would mishandle the neutrals and especially U.S.A. Privately the King told Haig that he had written to Lloyd George advising him "to use the greatest caution in what he says in the House of Commons", referring to the German Chancellor's suggestions, taking the view that the enemy's peace proposals should not be rejected before the conditions were known so as not to antagonise the neutrals.

The King had been increasingly aware of Lloyd George's dislike of Haig, and been determined to protect him, for on December 28, Haig received by King's Messenger "a charming letter from the King in which he says, 'I have decided to appoint you a Field-Marshal in my Army. I hope you will look upon it as a New Year's gift from myself and the country.'" Promotion of Haig was certainly a blow at Lloyd George's scheming.

The comments of the military on Ll. G. during these days are particularly significant. General Maurice told Haig: "Lloyd George is so sketchy and goes into nothing thoroughly. He only pressed forward measures which he thinks will meet with popular favour." Even more damning, Maurice expressed the view that he did not think Ll. G. "really cares for the country, or is patriotic. It is, indeed, a calamity for the country to have such a man at the head of affairs."

When the Prime Minister sprung his project for putting the British Army under the French Commander-in-Chief's orders in February, 1917, Hankey told Haig and Robertson that "Ll. G. had not received full authority from the War Cabinet for acting as he was doing".

The Prime Minister had attempted to undermine Haig's authority by conducting secret negotiations with Major Bertier de Sauvigny, a French liaison officer attached to the British War Office. When the conference at Calais, at which the Premier's plan was to be put forward as a *fait accompli*, was arranged, no hint was given as to the main subject under discussion. It was stated that the purpose of the conference was to discuss transport difficulties on the French railways and, to lend credence to this idea, Sir Eric Geddes, who was in charge of railway transport at the War Office, was detailed to attend. Neither Haig nor Robertson had then been told about the proposal to put the British Army under Nivelle.

To put the British Commander-in-Chief, who was fully occupied on his own important front, under the control of the Commander-in-Chief of another army in the middle of an important phase of the war was militarily unsound whichever way one looks at it. The placing of British troops under an American general in World War II cannot be regarded as a parallel, for in this instance the plan was made before the campaign was launched. Similarly there is no comparison between the appointment of Nivelle in 1917 and that of Foch as supremo in 1918. But it was even more senseless when one considers that Nivelle was a new and inexperienced Commander-in-Chief and that the French Army was at this time showing unmistakable signs of mutiny. Haig, whose rôle was reduced by this move to little more than that of an Adjutant-General, privately told Robertson that he did not believe British troops in these circumstances would fight willingly or effectively under French leadership. General Micheler, of the French Army, stated that "It does not matter what the politicians may decide, the French soldier is not going to fight after the autumn."

That this was a most inauspicious moment for putting British troops under French leadership was confirmed by Briand, then French Premier, who was horrified at the idea of Lloyd George contemplating such a change in opposition to his two leading soldiers.

Nivelle seems to have been as much under Lloyd George's spell as the latter was under his. Doubtless the intrigues with Colonel D'Alençon had borne fruit. Ll. G. had already intimated to D'Alençon his desire that Sir Henry Wilson should be made head of the British Mission at Beauvais as soon as he returned from Russia. D'Alençon presumably must have passed this information on to Nivelle, for on February 28, the French general was writing peremptorily to Haig, more or less ordering that Wilson should be drafted to this post.

Haig's correspondence with the King on this subject may have been undesirable from a strictly constitutional viewpoint in these modern times: it is easy to see how secret communications between a general and his Sovereign behind the back of the Government could lead to a thoroughly dangerous situation besides being undemocratic. Yet it should be realised that the constitutional relationship between monarch, government and the Armed Forces has always been elastic, thus allowing scope for the intervention by the monarch in unforeseen circumstances, and also that in 1917 the evolution of this relationship from Queen Victoria's occasional outbursts of authoritarianism towards an absolutely neutral form of sovereignty had not been completed. If the King interfered in these matters, he could also claim that Lloyd George had undemocratically deceived his own Cabinet and was using his powers dictatorially and therefore unconstitutionally. The King was, in the last resort, the only man to whom Haig could legitimately appeal and, in the circumstances, there was some justification for this correspondence, especially as Lloyd George had not secured the full authority of the War Cabinet for what he was trying to do, and, what was even worse, had delayed for four days communicating to the King his decision to put Haig under Nivelle's command.

Lord Stamfordham, acknowledging Haig's letter to the King, wrote: "You can well understand it was anything but agreeable reading to His Majesty. The King was unaware either that the question of the Command on the Western front had been discussed at the War Cabinet, or that it was to be the principal matter for consideration at the Calais conference."

So Lloyd George had been guilty of withholding vital information from his Sovereign—information on a matter which concerned the safety and survival of the King's people. The King was now convinced that the Prime Minister was hoping to force Haig to resign: it was probably this knowledge which caused him to beg Haig to dismiss from his mind "any idea of resignation". It is hard to accept the view that this mild intervention was unconstitutional.

Nevertheless, as these intrigues on all sides (the King's, Haig's, Lloyd George's and all others) went perilously near to undermining constitutional government and military discipline, it is essential to examine differing viewpoints. Lord Beaverbrook, in a biting summing-up of Haig in *Men and Power*, commented: "With the publication of his Private Papers in 1952, he [Haig] committed suicide twenty-five years after his death." The brilliance of the epitaph obscures the real merits of Haig. In his diaries he made no effort to disguise his prejudices, his somewhat pathetic attempts to "get along" with Lloyd George, nor did he cover up his own intrigues. It must be conceded that Haig himself was not free of intrigue; he had, under great provocation, intrigued against French and to this extent was a disloyal subordinate, though as French was himself a prince of intriguers he made it extremely difficult for any subordinate to trust him. Equally there can be no question that Haig did not hesitate to trade on his friendship with the King and without doubt this was the one factor which prevented Lloyd George from sacking him. The most damning indictment one can make against Haig was that he countenanced wholesale slaughter of his troops on the Western front, but then so did many other commanders in the field and, though such slaughter never produced worth-while immediate results, it cannot be said that, if the war was to be won, it was unnecessary. Haig's critics have tried to have it both ways, pointing to his incoherence at the conference table, yet failing to admit his lucidity and ability on paper; damning him as an administrator and yet attributing his doggedness and lack of imagination in the field to stubbornness and vanity. Haldane, who worked closely with Haig when he was at the War Office, referring to the creation of the Imperial General Staff, said, "Haig had a first-rate General Staff mind . . . he grasped the situation completely and gave invaluable guidance in the fashioning of both the Regular first line and the Territorial second line."

Once the head of government starts to intrigue behind the back of his own Cabinet and his Sovereign, a chain reaction of counter-plots is almost inevitable. Ll. G. had infected his colleagues with his own deceits, and soon members of the Cabinet were writing behind his back to the generals and the latter in their turn were intriguing with Cabinet Ministers. The allegedly more united Cabinet was actually a hive of imbroglios, with Curzon and Derby writing to Haig without the knowledge of Lloyd George.

While these discussions were going on the Germans were escaping from the difficult position in which they had been placed on the Somme battlefield. The essence of the Chantilly plan for a new offensive on the Somme was that the French army, weakened by heavy losses, would have to play a secondary rôle to the British. Therefore, if the Chantilly plan had been carried through, there was more reason for giving complete command to a British than a French C.-in-C. But some French generals so hated the idea of playing a secondary rôle to Britain that they had campaigned for the replacement of Joffre by Nivelle with the result that French military policy was reversed against the wishes of most French politicians.

Nivelle's idea was that the French army should have a greater share in any new drive and the British army less. Lloyd George, ever with an eye to winning favour with the British public, approved the idea, believing that it would enhance his popularity by saving the British from further heavy losses and that, if all went wrong, the French could be blamed. He had always been cynical in his attitude to the French, whom he never really liked and against whom he had frequently intrigued. At the same time he was quite prepared to advertise to them his Welsh descent and to stress that they and he together were more than a match for the "unimaginative English".

Yet the British army early in 1917 was in a far better position to make a new drive against the Germans than were the French, and the new plan meant the British taking over a longer front—something Ll. G. had hitherto strongly deprecated—and thus being unable to maintain pressure on the Somme. This was more than the Germans had dared hope for. They immediately began their retreat to the Hindenburg Line.

This withdrawal by the Germans was interpreted by the British General Staff as a vindication of the British actions on the Somme, since it obviously implied a refusal by the enemy to fight the British on that ground. News of the retreat was reported to General Gough, but no action to follow through was taken by either the British or the French. In retrospect this dilly-dally policy by the Allies was the biggest blunder of the war. It prevented a possible victory for the Allies before the end of 1917 and hastened the collapse of the Russian armies. It was a prime cause of mutiny in the French army and, but for America's entry into the war, might have undone all progress towards victory and even resulted in the defeat of the Allies.

Under these conditions Nivelle's alternative offensive was launched. In the light of suggestions that the changes in political and military leadership in Britain and France resulted in a speeding-up of the war effort it is worth recording that the Nivelle plan, though originally timed for mid-February, *was three times delayed and was not put into action until two months later, by which time the Germans had learned all about it and had ample reserves to meet the push.* Within two days of the launching of the French offensive on the Aisne on April 16, it was clear that disaster lay ahead.

To make matters worse, there was a French political crisis at the time. Lyautey resigned after being shouted down in the Chamber of Deputies, and this speedily brought about the fall of M. Briand's government. The latter was succeeded by M. Ribot, but with the main power held by M. Painlevé, the new Minister of War, French morale was at a very low ebb.

Nivelle lost the support of his senior commanders, Micheler and Pétain, and finally of his Government. So the situation arose of a British army being under the command of a French general whom his own government did not trust. His offensive, it is true, was not as expensive in manpower losses as many contemporary actions, but it failed to achieve its object, revealed serious organisational defects and brought about Nivelle's immediate disgrace and widespread mutinies in the French Army.

Such was the state of affairs in the late spring of 1917. Ll. G.'s first attempt to overrule his military advisers was doomed to failure and, ironically, the one successful feature of the whole affair was the capture by Haig's army of the Vimy Ridge.

In November, 1916, the Chief of the General Staff had asked for an extension of the age of military service, knowing that there would almost certainly be a steady reduction in Britain's fighting strength if this were not done. Indeed this, perhaps more than anything else, was the crucial issue when the Asquith Government was being undermined in December, 1916. It was the most powerful argument why political differences should be shelved and prompt action taken. But the Government fell and the measures taken by Lloyd George were paltry and insufficient. Not until January, 1918, were some minor amendments to the Military Service Act of 1916 made, and these merely provided for an extra 100,000 men, far less than had been requested by the Army Council. Yet the British fighting strength was fast declining by midsummer, 1917. The result of this dilatory action by the Lloyd George Government was that not a single man of the additional 100,000 was trained to meet the German attack of March, 1918. The Prime Minister, so freely vaunted as the war-winner and statesman of resolution and speedy action, was in fact always too late, too slow and too obstinate to take expert advice.

This is what came about from having a dictatorial Premier determined to run a war in his own makeshift, amateur fashion. It nearly cost the Allies the loss of the war: in terms of human life it cost tens of thousands.

10

A CONSPIRACY OF SILENCE

"If you can keep your head when all about you
Are losing theirs and blaming it on you;
If you can trust yourself when all men doubt you,
But make allowance for their doubting, too;
If you can wait and not be tired by waiting,
Or being lied about, don't deal in lies,
Or being hated, don't give way to hating,
And yet don't look too good, nor talk too wise . . ."

Rudyard Kipling

To a generation which has committed *If* to the category of homespun texts framed on a cottage wall, or bracketed it alongside the works of Ella Wheeler Wilcox, these lines may have little meaning. But in World War I they were the soundest advice that could have been offered to British commanders in the field.

"Donkeys leading lions" is how one modern historian has described these commanders. Maybe the lions appreciated the stolid, if negative, qualities of the donkeys better than that historian. At least these lions did not mutiny against their commanders.

In the last two years of this appalling war the British people lived in a fog of bewilderment, an incoherent state of mind that fluctuated between the extremes of optimism and pessimism, between the flamboyant, bogus patriotism of the music-hall songs and the knowledge that out in Flanders the opposing armies were locked in a hopeless stranglehold in a sea of mud, winning a few yards this way or that at a cost of thousands of lives.

The Lloyd George Government preferred the fog to enlightening the people. That was why, though on the surface morale was higher in Britain in World War I than in World War II, the foundations of that morale were far less sure, much more easily eroded. The people in 1940, wrote Sir Harold Nicolson, "are disheartened by the fact that they do not know what they are fighting for." It is true that only after Churchill came to power in 1940 did the people become really war-minded and realised they were fighting for survival. In World War I the people were fed on imperialist illusions. The man-in-the-street never was in any doubt that Britain, the mistress of the seas, must win in the long run; he was confident of Britain's superiority and efficiency to a much greater extent than was the Prime Minister. That was the reason why Lloyd George never had to issue edicts against "alarm and despondency" as did Churchill in a later war. On this evidence it might perhaps be argued that a nation so fed on illusions of national superiority and the belief that "one Briton was the equal of three Germans" could not be told the truth. But to withhold the truth from the people in wartime is always a dangerous policy and, at its best, a risky expedient. With the advent of Lloyd George to the Premiership the subtle technique of the small "lie that sinketh" had given way to that of the "big lie", a method which Dr. Goebbels copied a generation later. There was no frank talking to the British people from their wartime leader, none of that confidential, fearless fireside homily which Sir Winston Churchill used in a later war. The music-hall soubrette and Horatio Bottomley were the recruiting sergeants and if a military disaster occurred the generals were always the culprits.

Many of the Liberals forming the Opposition had held positions in the previous Government and were therefore keenly aware of the need for not embarrassing the new régime in a critical stage of the war. Neither Asquith, nor his chief colleagues, attempted to make political capital out of their opposition to the Government. Though in private Asquith never minced matters in giving his opinions on the conduct of the war, his biographers have revealed that he deliberately refrained from making an "effective" speech because it might have been a "grave disservice to the Allied cause".

The Government itself was, perhaps, the strangest combination of politicians ever to have installed itself at Westminster. Most of the Tory ministers who had been eager to push Ll. G. out of the Asquith Government showed astonishing alacrity in jumping on to the Welshman's Coalition coach. Arthur Balfour, whom Ll. G. had tried to elbow out of the Admiralty, and whom Asquith had stoutly defended, "passed from one Cabinet to the other," said Winston Churchill, "like a powerful, graceful cat walking delicately and unsoiled across a rather muddy street." Indeed, so anxious were the Tories to scramble to power that they made it comparatively easy for the Premier to fill the places left by the pro-Asquithian members of the last Cabinet.

Lloyd George's astutest catch was Dr. Christopher Addison, who had been his Parliamentary Secretary at the Ministry of Munitions, and who was now given charge of this Ministry. It was Addison, an intriguer in the lobbies, who whipped up 126 Liberal M.P.s to pledge their support of the new Government.

The Labour supporters of the new Government Lloyd George was able to cudgel and charm into submission in turn: they were singularly inept and uncritical. The Prime Minister's ploy was to play off one

Tory minister against another; to smirk and joke about Curzon's pomposity to Bonar Law and Carson, to flatter Curzon to his face and to dazzle and bewilder Arthur Balfour with his buoyant and gay approach to day-to-day problems. To such a misanthropic cynic as Balfour such lighthearted resilience appeared like the alchemy of the human soul.

By this time Lloyd George had patched up his quarrel with D. A. Thomas (Lord Rhondda) and made him President of the Local Government Board. Not that Ll. G. had forgotten his marked dislike for Rhondda, but he felt it wiser to have an enemy in his camp than out of it. Rhondda was especially interested in infant mortality and he urged the creation of a Ministry of Health. The attitude of the Prime Minister to so progressive and sensible a proposal can be summed up by his indifferent comment: "Rhondda contracted quite a passion for the health of babies . . . however, the call of duty was powerful enough to interrupt that passion."

The "call of duty" was the summoning of Rhondda to tackle the Ministry of Food. Rhondda agreed to accept this onerous and unpopular office in return for a promise that a Ministry of Health would be established within five months. That promise was not kept. It is noteworthy that, despite pressure on the Cabinet, Rhondda was unable to get his food rationing plan put into force until February 25, 1918. Yet each week for months there had been as many as a million people standing in queues in the London area alone, many of them patiently waiting for the food which often enough was all gone by the time their turn came.

* * * * *

For a short time after the failure of Nivelle's attack, Lloyd George found himself in agreement with the British generals. Both Haig and Robertson made it abundantly clear that if the Germans were given any respite they would be free to crush the Russian armies which Kerensky was desperately trying to rally.

Meanwhile the Germans had intensified their submarine offensive. It has frequently been argued that Lloyd George had to force the convoy system on an unwilling Admiralty, and to some extent this is true. Admiral Jellicoe was unco-operative on the question of extending the convoy system and, indeed, in many ways he showed a deplorable lack of imagination for a Service chief. The Admiralty's timidity on the subject of convoys was also echoed by the Foreign Office who had what they considered "legitimate doubts" about extending the system too soon. The joint arguments of the Admiralty and the Foreign Office were that they were not antagonistic to change, but that a convoy system earlier in the war could not have been effectively employed in the Atlantic without impairing strength elsewhere. In 1914–18 Britain faced the menace of a powerful German battle fleet close to her own coasts, which was not the case in World War II. Politically, too, there were certain arguments from the Foreign Office side against a convoy system in the Atlantic while U.S.A. was still neutral. U.S.A. was then extremely touchy on the subject of the freedom of the seas, and it was Germany's final error that she failed to respect this national touchiness and eventually brought America into the war against her.

On this subject Lloyd George was undoubtedly right and the Admiralty experts wrong, while the Foreign Office regard for the niceties of diplomacy did not take into account the fact that the U-boat campaign threatened to achieve by sea a victory that was impossible on land. This was a subject on which Ll. G. was able to bring to bear his imagination, his genius for improvisation and drive. Even these qualities were not enough: it required his talent for downright rudeness and defiant abuse before he broke down the Service chiefs at the Admiralty. The latter allied themselves with the Foreign Office against the Prime Minister and found excuse after excuse for taking no action. If on military matters Lloyd George can frequently be criticised, full credit must be given to him for the programme he devised for beating the submarine menace. He more than any man helped to end the U-boat menace, and it was perhaps his greatest achievement of the war.

He roundly denounced the timidity of the Admiralty and insisted that it ill-behoved the Mistress of the Seas to fail to take offensive action against the U-boats.

Admiral Sir Guy Gaunt, British naval attaché in Washington, wrote in his diary: "Up to the end of January, 1917, it was touch and go whether the U-boat campaign would do more harm than the whole of the German Army. More than 300,000 tons of British shipping had been sunk by submarine. Our intelligence experts are agreed that Germany can starve us out by midsummer if this rate of destruction is maintained.

"Hall [Admiral Hall of the N.I.D] has done his best to make this clear to the Admiralty, but they don't seem to listen. All now depends on the P.M., who is putting up a magnificent fight for a proper convoy system. He is the one man who has listened to our intelligence reports and has asked Hankey to work out a plan.

"Am told that Ll. G. horrified the Admirals by suggesting warships could escort merchantmen across the Atlantic. 'Unheard of,' said Jellicoe, 'tramps and merchantmen have no idea of discipline. They would never keep in station.' Ll. G.'s reply to this was: 'The Royal Navy aren't the only seamen in the world, you know. In the name of Nelson where's your offensive spirit? Are you afraid of presenting a target to the enemy? Isn't your job to draw him out and sink him?'"

Jellicoe's obstinacy persisted, but Admiral Beatty was finally won over to support the idea for giving Ll. G.'s plans a trial. In April,

P.A.-Reuter Photos

Camping with his wife in the Welsh mountains as Moel Heboz.

Lloyd George with
Col. Sir Maurice Hankey.

The coalition Prime
Minister cracking a joke
with Marshal Foch and
Aristide Briand.

Topix Picture Service

1917, the convoy system was generally adopted and a "Grow More Food at Home" campaign was launched on the Premier's instructions. Here, without question, was an instance of Ll. G.'s drive and imagination, his restless, critical mind destroying official inertia, even to the extent of descending personally on the Admiralty and challenging their figures not only on the availability of warships but of the total number of merchantmen requiring protection. It proved the turning point in the war at sea.

* * * * *

In May, 1917, the Prime Minister actually went to Paris to press for a continuation of the fight on the Western front. For once even he had no new ideas for waging war.

But his lack of respect for officialdom and experts in contrast to Asquith's deference to them, while giving him occasional triumphs when the experts were wrong, was always liable to be a serious defect. His quicksilver mind was not so much apparent in the sense of constructive mental fertility, but in being able to switch from one policy to its opposite without any inhibitions. Soon he was to change his mind again, consequently having an unsettling effect not only on the generals but on the troops. So often did Ll. G.'s mind dart off at a tangent on some fantasy of amateur strategy that, wrote Major-General Sir Frederick Maurice, "At least 20 per cent of the time of the General Staff at the War Office was occupied in explaining either verbally or in writing that the alternative projects put forward were either strategically unsound or wholly impracticable."

Lloyd George rushed to Rapallo at the height of the crisis on the Italian front solely because he wanted to institute the Supreme War Council, which he saw as a medium for giving him still greater powers. He insisted that the British military representative on this Council should be entirely independent of the C.I.G.S. and should give his advice direct to the War Cabinet.

In theory the setting up of such a Council seemed a wise move towards unity, especially as America had now joined the Allies. In practice its machinery was far too cumbersome and its effectiveness destroyed by the conflicting interests of the powers forming it. The most disturbing feature was that the British military representative chosen by Lloyd George was Sir Henry Wilson, who was opposed to the views of the C.I.G.S. Thus at a time when Britain's voice should have been of the utmost importance in the counsels of this body, it was weakened by the obvious divergence of views between Wilson and the C.I.G.S. All the other powers composing the Council were represented by their Chiefs of Staff, or the latter's spokesmen.

All the time, of course, Ll. G.'s tactics were directed as much against Haig as Robertson. The previous March, Haig had noted in his diary:

"Apparently the last thing the War Cabinet would like would be that I should resign. Ll. G., in Wigram's opinion, would then appeal to the country and might come back as a dictator." Two days later he commented: "The King was most pleased to see me and stated that he would support me through thick and thin, but I must be careful not to resign because Ll. G. would then appeal to the country for support and would probably come back with a great majority."

Such a statement clearly implies that Lloyd George had a majority of the nation behind him, and at that time there is little doubt that he had. His allies in the Press had ensured that: the pall of silence and propaganda over Britain had effectively obscured from the people the truth about Nivelle's disastrous campaign, the widespread mutinies in the French Army and the futile bloodshed of Passchendaele which achieved far less than the slaughter on the Somme the previous year. In his *War Memoirs*, Ll. G. posed the question: "Who and what was responsible for the delay that wrecked the chance of success?" It was, he argued, due to the workings of a divided command. "As it was, the armies were never given a decent chance. The stubborn mind of Haig was transfixed on the Somme . . . it took him a long time to extricate his mental top-boots from the Somme mud."

To this attack Lord Trenchard, Sir Noel Birch and Sir John Davidson made a joint reply in 1936, dealing with an allegation by Lloyd George that Haig had overlooked able men and that his military appointments were governed by favouritism. "Mr. Lloyd George says that Lord Haig appointed Sir Herbert Lawrence as Chief of Staff and implies that this appointment was governed by favouritism. But General Lawrence was not appointed by Earl Haig. He actually wanted to appoint someone else."

Volume IV of the *War Memoirs*, which dealt with Passchendaele—it would be more accurate to describe this campaign as the Third Battle of Ypres—created a furore all over the world. From General Sir Alexander Godley in Wellington, New Zealand, came the statement that "Passchendaele was forced on the British command by circumstances. The French had suffered so sorely that somebody had to fight and the duty devolved upon the British. The attack on Lord Haig is wholly unwarranted."

Nor was the defence of Haig at this time merely a matter of the generals and ex-generals ganging up against Lloyd George. The attack on Haig brought thousands of letters from ex-rankers to newspapers and military organisations. A challenge to Lloyd George to repeat on a public platform in Wales the allegations against Haig was made at a meeting of the Vale of Glamorgan District Committee of the British Legion at Cardiff. Nearly thirty branches were represented and they passed a resolution deprecating Ll. G.'s criticism that Haig sacrificed 400,000 lives for the sake of personal vanity.

Lloyd George tried to bolster his case by misquoting from the jottings in Sir Henry Wilson's diary. His own version of a meeting between Wilson and Foch was that the latter "wanted to know who it was who wanted Haig to go on a duck's march through the inundations to Ostend and Zeebrugge. He thinks the whole thing futile, fantastic and dangerous". In a reply in a letter to *The Times*, General Sir Frederick Maurice claimed:

"Mr. Lloyd George has misinterpreted Sir H. Wilson's diary. In 1928, shortly after the publication of the diary, Marshal Foch came to England . . . I showed him the passage in Sir Henry's diary and asked him what the reference to the 'duck's march' meant. I took down his reply:

"'I had just come to Paris to be Chief of the General Staff and had heard that Haig wished to relieve the French detachment at Nieuport, on the Belgian coast. When Wilson came to see me I asked him what this meant. Did Haig mean to go with the Belgians on a duck's march through the inundations? I did not then know of Haig's plan for a landing on the Belgian coast.'"

This trivial detail about a "duck's march" is significant in that the inundations made by the Belgians were far to the north of Haig's proposed attack by land. The preparations for the landing were made with great secrecy.

Mr. Herbert Russell, a war correspondent who, in his own words, was "through the Passchendaele show from the first day to the last", can perhaps be relied upon to give an independent view of the affair. Mr. Russell wrote to *The Times*: "Nivelle had launched his long-proclaimed offensive and failed disastrously. The French had their tails down. Haig was told that he must 'do something' or they would throw their hand in.

"Where else could Haig have 'done something'? Mr. Lloyd George says that Pétain wanted him to deliver a heavy attack on the Italian front. Haig could not afford to denude his own front with Pétain incessantly asking the British to take over still more of the line.

"Strategically, the Passchendaele scheme was perfectly sound. As originally planned the Navy was to have delivered a simultaneous attack, but this was abandoned. What killed the operations was the weather. The ceaseless, pitiless downpour of rain, day after day, was almost unbelievable. The ground became one vast bog.

"As to the conduct of the operations; I was permitted to attend the daily conferences of the Chief of Staff to the Second Army, General Sir Charles Harington, and . . . I have no hesitation in saying that never throughout the whole of the world struggle was there finer staff work displayed. . . . The routing of movements was a marvel of efficiency.

"Mr. Lloyd George makes allusions to misleading bulletins 'which turned defeat into victory'. It fell to my lot to send more dispatches than any other single individual and this allegation is too untrue to even arouse a glow of resentment.

"Mr. Lloyd George asks us to believe that so little did the Passchendaele offensive really trouble the Germans that they were able to detach troops for the capture of Riga. Anybody with knowledge of the situation at that time knows that these German troops were set free by the Russian revolution."

In the *Official History of the 1914–18 War* is this statement: "On July 28, 1938, Mr. Lloyd George told Brigadier-General Sir James Edmonds, with whom he was then on very friendly terms, being of the same age, that he felt he might have misjudged Haig and Robertson, that he had kept no diary or notes and had relied for the material of the Passchendaele chapter and other technical matters on a well-known publicist on military matters who had assisted him."

As a final comment on this bitter controversy two statements by Lloyd George make a contradictory epitaph. One was made when Haig died in 1928: "Earl Haig was a man of unfailing courage and tenacity of purpose. My personal relations with him were always of the very best. He behaved not merely like a great patriot, but like a great gentleman."

But in 1936 Ll. G. wrote: "Haig gambled on the chance that the Germans would break rather than face the dread alternative of a confession of failure to the politicians, who had deposed Lord French for a less stupendous error of judgment at Loos. Whilst hundreds of thousands were being destroyed in the insane egotism of Passchendaele, every message or memorandum from Haig was full of these insistences on the importance of sending him more and more to replace those he had sent to die in the mud."

The answer to this, in part at least, is the fact that during this period Lloyd George had signally failed to develop British military resources to the full. It took six months for a measure affecting manpower to produce the requisite additional soldiers for the Western front.

No one was more deeply grieved than Haig when the casualty figures came in; he was not insensitive to the appalling slaughter. No British commander ever had a harder choice to make, but it is certain that any wavering on his part would have meant even bloodier battles and even greater losses in the face of German forces who had had time to re-group and re-deploy.

* * * * *

By May, 1917, Nivelle had been dismissed. But those who thought that Ll. G. had learned his lesson about using too small forces on the Western front were swiftly disillusioned. The following month the Premier was again thinking up new diversions, and Sir William

Robertson was warning Haig: "There is trouble in the land just now. The War Cabinet, under the influence of Lloyd George, have started quite among themselves, plus Smuts, to review the whole policy and strategy of the war. . . . The Lloyd George idea is to settle the war from Italy and today the railway people have been asked for figures regarding the rapid transfer of twelve divisions and 300 heavy guns to Italy! They will never go while I am C.I.G.S., but all that will come later."

These were prophetic words. Lloyd George was making his last attempt to get rid of Robertson and Haig.

Meanwhile the Prime Minister, in the face of keen resistance by the Tories, brought Churchill back into the Government as Minister of Munitions in July, 1917. It required considerable political courage to do this, for Bonar Law, the Deputy Prime Minister, was strongly opposed to such a move, while the Conservative rank and file most unjustly considered Churchill responsible for the Dardanelles disaster. It would be unfair to suggest that Ll. G. merely wanted Churchill as an ally of the Government instead of a possible critic on the Asquithian benches, though such a thought must have crossed his mind. Churchill had a tremendously high regard for Asquith, though he admired and was fascinated by Lloyd George. The latter was equally fascinated by Churchill's energy and drive, and for many years he retained for him an affection which outlasted almost any other political friendship in his life.

In October, Robertson, who had just seen various members of the Government, wrote to Haig: "He (Ll. G.) is out for my blood very much these days. Milner, Curzon, Carson, Cecil and Balfour have each in turn expressly spoken to me separately about his intolerable conduct during the last week or two. I am sick of this d—d life. I can't help thinking he has got Painlevé and Co. here in his rushing way so as to carry me off my feet. But I have got big feet."

The situation on the Western front was becoming steadily worse. The collapse on the Russian front had enabled the Germans to bring extra divisions into Belgium and France. To counter this new threat the General Staff urged that Britain should merely act defensively in all secondary theatres of war and bring back to France as many troops as could be spared. There were at least 1,200,000 troops scattered elsewhere and a large number of these could have been sent to the Western front.

But Lloyd George was adamant. He denounced any suggestion of caution in the east and insisted that the only way to victory now lay through a new attack in that theatre of operations. For this reason he told Allenby to drive the Turks out of Palestine and forbade the transfer of any of the 100,000 troops in that area, despite the most vehement opposition from the French.

Thus the Western front was rendered extremely vulnerable for the

Allies. Nor was the compromise eventually arrived at between the "Easterners" and the "Westerners" in any way satisfactory. It merely meant that Allenby was to attack with the proviso that he could have no reinforcements from the west. Sir William Robertson protested against this plan and warned that it could only lead to disaster. He was over-ruled and removed from the post of C.I.G.S., his place being taken by Sir Henry Wilson.

Early in 1918 there was real consternation on the Western front. Haig knew that the attack would come against his Third and Fifth Armies: he repeatedly warned the Cabinet of this. The previous November he had to send five divisions to Italy and had received no replacements, notwithstanding his losses at Passchendaele, the depletion of the French armies and the longer front which he had taken over. If he had permitted any further troops to go to Palestine, it is almost certain that Ludendorff's attack would have succeeded in the spring, the British armies would have been crushed and the Channel ports captured.

The Supreme War Council was put to the supreme test and found wanting. Its only chance of influencing events before the Germans launched their next assault would have been to create a strategic reserve of troops. But as long as the tug-of-war between "Easterners" and "Westerners" continued none of the generals on the Western front was prepared to part with troops for such a reserve. It is significant of the doubts which the politicians must have felt that none of them tried to coerce the generals into contributing to such a reserve.

Lloyd George insisted throughout his *War Memoirs* that Haig "viciously resisted" the idea of unity of command. Yet it was Haig not Lloyd George who pressed for Foch to be made Generalissimo. The two men's conception of unity of command differed; the soldier wished for unity in the field, the politician for unity and complete power in a Supreme Council which would coerce the generals into absolute submission to the politicians.

The Prime Minister seems at this time to have had only one main aim—to prevent further action on any major scale on the Western front, despite the spate of intelligence reports which showed the enemy was planning a vast new attack. The voluble and conspiratorial Sir Henry Wilson was the chief instrument in achieving this by his replacement of the chief of the "Westerners", Robertson. A second and even more deplorable factor was the deliberate withholding of troops from Haig so that he could not possibly mount another offensive. It may seem incredible that any statesman claiming to be a patriot could devise such a tortuous and frustrating policy which, in effect, meant endangering the lives of whole battalions of British soldiers and risking, even courting, defeat. The Prime Minister had neither heeded the warnings of the military, nor those of his own more far-sighted colleagues.

Winston Churchill, who was back as Minister of Munitions, wrote in *World Crisis*: "The Prime Minister and his colleagues in the War Cabinet were adamant. They were definitely opposed to any renewal of the British offensive in France. They wished to keep a tight control over their remaining manpower until the arrival of the American millions offered the prospect of decisive success." But Churchill was not providing Lloyd George with the excuse that there was wisdom in waiting for the Americans. He went on to say: "They were fully informed of the growing German concentration against Haig and repeatedly discussed it. Haig was accordingly left to face the spring with an army whose 56 infantry divisions were reduced from a 13 to 10 battalion basis and with three instead of five cavalry divisions."

Yet the Prime Minister smoothly talked of the Western front being "over-insured".

The Germans started their great new offensive on March 21, 1918. Three days later Haig realised that in relying on Pétain, the general who became the arch-defeatist and apologist of 1940, he had made a fatal error. For once Sir Henry Wilson had been right: he had advised Haig that "he would have to live on Pétain's charity and he would find that very cold charity". Now, to his dismay, Haig learned that Pétain, far from putting all his efforts into preserving the link between the British and French armies in front of Amiens, was anxious to fall back to cover Paris. Pétain was already showing his innate pessimism and defeatism; he even urged the British to fall back and defend the Channel ports. It was then that Haig, in desperation, telegraphed to London for Foch to be named as generalissimo. Haig, the man whose mental top-boots were supposed to be sunk deep in the Somme mud, devised the one formula which eventually proved the right combination. What Ll. G. had tried to achieve by intrigue and devious methods —to unify the direction of the Allied war effort—was actually the work of his detested Commander-in-Chief.

Two men eventually sought to penetrate the curtain of silence which surrounded all these moves. They were Colonel Repington, who had left *The Times* to become military correspondent of the *Morning Post*, and Major-General Sir Frederick Maurice.

Colonel Repington, a somewhat conceited, but on the whole objective, observer, wrote an article attacking the Versailles Committee. On the face of it this was a direct challenge to Lloyd George and a defence of all that Haig and Robertson stood for. The Prime Minister, always swift to counter-attack, immediately decided to prosecute Repington under the Defence of the Realm Act for revealing military secrets. On February 21, 1918, at Bow Street, Repington and the editor of the *Morning Post* were each fined £1,000.

In his article Repington had written: "Newspapers have been strictly enjoined not to refer to one of the chief results of the Council.

In this way it is hoped that criticism will be burked. But there are times when we must take courage in both hands and risk consequences. One of the decisions taken is against all sound principles and can only breed confusion in a defensive campaign such as that to which we are restricted at present. . . ."

The chief point of the article was that while it was the duty of the Commander of the General Staff to issue orders of the War Cabinet to the Allies, there was now interposed the "Versailles soldiers under the presidency of General Foch, and the British general on this body is not apparently under the War Office, nor was he appointed by them. He owes his elevation to Mr. Lloyd George's favour alone".

In a reference to this incident in his *War Memoirs*, Lloyd George stated that he knew "nothing comparable to this betrayal in the whole of our history". He claimed that it was immediately "appreciated" in Germany and that Professor Delbruck, the famous authority on military questions, expressed his thanks for it in his magazine of February 24, 1918. "Repington's betrayal might and ought to have decided the war."

Presumably Ll. G. was trying to shift at least some of the blame for the losses inflicted by the German attack of 1918. It makes a useful if untenable alibi for the grim tale of Allied defeats during this period.

In January, 1918, the Government had decided that 100,000 additional men would meet the needs of the Army, but in April, when all hell was let loose on the Western front, 400,000 more were provided. Yet Robertson had asked for 500,000 the previous July. The men were in Britain: they could have been sent. Lloyd George alone refused to dispatch them.

It was the Prime Minister's attempt to cover up this manpower shortage which led to the unexpected broadside launched by Sir Frederick Maurice. On April 9, 1918, on introducing the measure to extend the age of military service to 51, the Prime Minister stated that our armies in France were stronger than they had been the previous year and denied that forces which might have been kept in France had been sent elsewhere.

This date is important. On April 9 the German advance was hammering home a devastating attack in the neighbourhood of Armentières. The Portuguese were running away through the British lines, taking their guns with them. Foch had on the same day declined to take over any part of the British line. It is not surprising that Lloyd George was anxious to put the best possible complexion on a situation which reeked of catastrophe.

General Maurice was in France when he first heard of the Premier's statement. Among officers and men it had aroused great indignation not merely because of its palpable falsity, but by the implication that Haig was to blame for not making the best possible use of his forces.

Having just handed over his post at the War Office—he was awaiting a new appointment in France—General Maurice was in a position to know how false this statement was. He immediately wrote to the C.I.G.S., drawing his attention to it and stressing the adverse impression it had made among the troops.

Hearing nothing from the War Office, Maurice risked his whole future career for what he believed to be his duty to the country. For it was Maurice who, in his capacity of Director of Military Operations at the War Office, had supplied the Prime Minister with the figures giving the strength of the Allied armies on the Western front early in 1918. He wrote a letter to the Press, denouncing the Prime Minister's statement.

"The facts are beyond dispute," he wrote. "The total strength of the Army in France on January 1, 1917, was 1,299,000 and on January 1, 1918, was 1,570,000. But in 1918 there were included in this total strength 300,000 unarmed British labourers and Chinese coolies who did not appear in the 1917 figures, while the fighting troops in 1918 were more than 100,000 weaker. Between January 1 and March 21, when the Germans attacked, Haig had to disband 140 battalions for lack of men to replace the losses we had suffered. In Palestine and Egypt there were at the beginning of March 213,600 white troops and 37,300 native troops. The extension of the front of the Fifth Army was undertaken because of the pressure which M. Clemenceau brought to bear on our Government."

If the public could not grasp the academic niceties of the pros and cons of the Versailles Committee, as expounded by Colonel Repington, they could at least understand this positive exposition of facts and figures. The curtain of silence had been pierced; the Maurice Letter produced an immediate sensation. At last Asquith made a real attack on the Government, feeling that the issues were too serious for further forbearance towards the ministry of the day. He asked Bonar Law what steps the Government proposed to take to examine the allegations contained in the letter. Tories as well as Liberals swarmed to the attack, and the postbags of M.P.s were filled with angry and anguished letters from parents of soldiers.

As soon as it was apparent that the Government was in serious trouble Bonar Law, more or less off-the-cuff, promised that the Government would appoint two judges to inquire into the charges. Then, between the making of this promise and the Parliamentary debate on the Maurice Letter, the Government changed their minds and sought for excuses to withdraw the promise of an inquiry.

Lloyd George, who loved a political fight, decided—wisely, as it happened, from his own point of view—to make the issue one of confidence in the Government. He answered Maurice's criticism in what was a remarkably adroit and sophistical parliamentary performance by claiming: "The figures that I gave were taken from the official records of the War Office, for which I sent before I made the statement. If they were incorrect, General Maurice was as responsible as anyone else. But they were not incorrect."

It was easy for Lloyd George to juggle with figures and, from his position as Prime Minister, to refute the allegations. Who was to gainsay him? Robertson had gone and the new C.I.G.S. was unlikely to quarrel with the man who had given him this post. Despite the fact that Maurice, a man of great integrity, had risked his professional reputation by implying that the Prime Minister had deliberately used figures he knew to be false in order to mislead the House of Commons and the country, the invoking of the vote of confidence had the effect of silencing most of the doubters. Only 106 had the courage to vote for a select committee to inquire into the general's allegations. The Government easily won the day. Nevertheless a hostile vote of 106 against a Government engaged in war was an unprecedented rebuff.

General Maurice was placed on half-pay. No one dared to suggest a court-martial, and the Prime Minister probably realised he was lucky to get away with his vote of confidence without risking even more damaging disclosures.

Hankey in his own memoirs has preserved a discreet silence on this question, which suggests that he personally was ignorant of the figures on which Ll. G. was working. Yet Hankey went out of his way to imply that Lloyd George, a year earlier, when he became Premier, was right in questioning the alleged superiority of Allied manpower over the Germans. On this occasion Ll. G. was anxious to show that the previous administration had lagged behind in the provision of manpower and, in justifying his own "dark estimate" of the situation, proving that it would be unwise to launch the agreed new drive against the harassed Germans. The War Office had then estimated that the Allies had a superiority of one million men, whereas Sir John French put the figure at 530,000. Ll. G. should have known that French always underestimated his own strength; no general ever clamoured louder for more troops. But, says Hankey, Ll. G. seized on this point, scoffing that soldiers must be ignorant of simple arithmetic. After searching criticisms and a reassessment of the figures with McDonogh, the Prime Minister announced that the original estimate had been prepared before Christmas when the German ranks had been depleted by heavy fighting and that since then large drafts had arrived to increase their strength. His deduction was that it was not safe to count on a total Allied superiority of more than 100,000 men. By that time it was the end of January, 1917. Three vital months had been lost.

So twice Lloyd George juggled with figures in this war; once to halt an offensive, the second time to bluff when an offensive was mounted against his country.

It is necessary to take further chronological liberties in order to follow this issue to its logical conclusion. In 1922 General Maurice wrote a letter to Lloyd George, challenging him to substantiate or withdraw his allegations that Maurice "was as responsible as anyone else" for the figures he had been given.

"I have waited patiently for the time to come for me to challenge that statement," wrote the general. "The facts are that in January, 1918, when there was still time to apply remedies, my department warned Ministers of the danger which our diminishing strength on the Western front constituted. On May 9 you said: 'When you talk about fighting strength, who are the combatants and who are the non-combatants? Are the combatants these men who stopped the advance of the German Army to Amiens? They are, if you begin to make a distinction between combatants and non-combatants. I am speaking of General Carey's force—they would not be treated as combatants.'

"Now I have before me the composition of Carey's forces and all the men in that force, with the possible exception of a few stragglers, were included in the fighting strength of our armies in France, which, as the returns at your disposal at the time showed, had been diminished on January 1, 1918, as compared with January 1, 1917. You made that statement because these same returns showed that, though the fighting strength had been diminished, the non-fighting strength had been increased by 410,897, of whom 190,197 were unarmed native labourers, and you wished to prove that the non-fighting strength was available for fighting.

"In your speech you went on: 'But I will leave that. Take the ordinary technical distinction between combatants and non-combatants.'

"You then quoted a note which had been prepared in the Directorate of Military Operations in reply to a question put by Sir Godfrey Baring on April 18 as justifying your statement of April 9—i.e., nine days before.

"That note, which you read to the House, ran:

"'From the statement included it will be seen that the combatant strength of the British Army was greater on January 1, 1918, than on January 1, 1917.'

"On this you based the assertion that I had supplied you with the figures from which you made your statement of April 9. You said that when you had at your disposal returns showing the diminution of the fighting strength of the Army in France on January 1, 1918.

"Now the facts with regard to the answer given to Sir Godfrey Baring on April 18 are:

"(1) My successor as Director of Military Operations arrived in the War Office on April 11. On Sunday the 14th I went to France with

Lord Milner and returned to London late on April 17. On the 18th, the day the answer was given, I was engaged in formally handing over to my successor and I knew nothing either of the question or of the answer until I read your speech on May 9.

"(2) I have since learned, and this the Duke of Northumberland is ready to confirm, that the answer was required in a hurry by Mr. MacPherson, then Parliamentary Secretary at the War Office. In the hurry a mistake was made in the answer and the whole strength of our Army in Italy was included in the strength of our Armies in France. With the addition of all these troops, a slight increase in the fighting strength on January 1, 1918, as compared with January 1, 1917, was shown, and the note you read was drafted accordingly.

"The mistake was discovered shortly afterwards and was reported to your principal private secretary, Mr. Philip Kerr, and later to Mr. MacPherson.

"The fact is, then, that you used on May 9 an accidentally incorrect return made on April 18, to justify what you said on April 9, though you had at your disposal a return showing that the note of April 18 was incorrect. You will, I understand, find records of all this in the War Office.

"Now I am prepared to believe that, in the hurry of preparing your speech on May 9, you did not verify all the facts: that you were not aware that Carey's force was almost wholly composed of combatants, and that you were not informed of the circumstances which led to the answer given on April 18 to Sir Godfrey Baring. If that is so, the hurry was due to the fact that you decided to refuse the inquiry for which I asked and to make an *ex parte* statement to the House."

The Duke of Northumberland, who was in 1918 the head of one of the sections of the Military Operations Directorate, sent a letter to Maurice stating:

"The Prime Minister's conduct in making his statement on May 9 and in declining to withdraw the imputation that you have supplied him with incorrect information is the more outrageous in that the Military Operations Directorate had repeatedly drawn his attention to the decline of the fighting strength of the Allies in France and to the steady increase of the enemy's forces on the Western front. These figures were continually challenged by Mr. Lloyd George, who insisted that the Allied strength was greater than was represented.

"The figures showing the increase of the German forces in the months preceding the great attack of March 21 were given weekly in the summary of operations circulated to Ministers, and in the same document during the same period the decline in our fighting strength was more than once stressed.

"The Prime Minister knew the figures sent by the Operations Directorate and, with this knowledge fresh in his mind, made the utterly false statement of April 9, and one month later actually pretended that if a too-favourable estimate had been given, the fault lay with the Military Operations Directorate, whose warnings he had consistently disregarded."

While Sir Frederick Maurice's letter was scrupulously fair, and even tried to provide the Prime Minister with a loophole for a graceful apology, without too much loss of face, the Duke of Northumberland's blunt and categorical statement leaves little doubt that the Prime Minister deliberately lied. On this evidence it seems obvious that Lloyd George had for his own ends deceived both the House of Commons and the country.

But he showed no signs of contrition. His only reply to Maurice was made through his private secretary, then Mr. E. W. M. Grigg (later Lord Altrincham). Mr. Grigg wrote:

"The Prime Minister has received your letter of the 15th and directs me to acknowledge it. What he said in 1918 he said in good faith and upon the information supplied to him; and he does not think it will be injurious to the public interest or unjust to you if he leaves your criticism, like much more of the same character, to the unprejudiced judgment of posterity.

"As regards your threat to publish, he would refer you with all courtesy to a short observation made in similar circumstances by the Duke of Wellington."

This cryptic observation shows that a Prime Minister who had already tried on Napoleon's hat in Paris and was delighted to find it fitted, now imagined he was as capable of safely flaunting public opinion as was the Iron Duke when the latter entered politics. Presumably it refers to a riposte by the Duke to his former mistress, Harriette Wilson, when she asked him through her publisher how much he would pay to be omitted from her autobiography. Wellington is said to have replied: "Publish and be damned!"

These letters were eventually published.

In his book *Men and Power: 1917–18*, Lord Beaverbrook quotes from the diary of Lady Lloyd-George (who in this period was Miss Frances Stevenson, the Prime Minister's secretary). She wrote: "Having been reading up the events connected with the Maurice debate in order to help Ll. G. . . . am uneasy in my mind about an incident which occurred at the time and which is only known to J. T. Davies (the Prime Minister's confidant) and myself.

"I was in J. T. Davies's room a few days after the statement (i.e. the Prime Minister's statement in the Commons) and J.T. was sorting out red dispatch boxes to be returned to the departments. Pulling out a W.O. box, he found in it, to his great astonishment, a paper from the D.M.O. containing modifications and corrections of the first figures they had sent. . . . J.T. and I examined it in dismay and then

J.T. put it in the fire, remarking, 'Only you and I, Frances, know of the existence of this paper.'"

Had Lloyd George seen this paper? And how is it the matter was never satisfactorily cleared up in view of the men whose honour and reputation were affected by the Maurice debate? Lady Lloyd-George's final diary comment was: "And as the official statistics since compiled seem to justify Ll. G.'s statement at the time, it were better perhaps to let sleeping dogs lie."

After the publication of the Beaverbrook book Lady Lloyd-George declared in a letter to *The Spectator* that the War Office message was not discovered until some time after the Commons debate on General Maurice's charges. But Miss Nancy Maurice, the general's daughter, commented to the author, "I think Lady Lloyd-George's memory has let her down, which would be natural when she is writing about what happened so many years ago. What she says now contradicts what she wrote in her 1934 diary which Lord Beaverbrook quotes in his book. She wrote then that Davies burned the paper 'a few days after April 9', and the Maurice debate was a month later on May 9."

11

FANDANGO OF VICTORY

"What is our task? To make Britain a fit country for heroes to live in."

Speech by Lloyd George at Wolverhampton on November 24, 1918

If Britain was lulled into complaisance by a smooth-talker in the gloomy spring of 1918, fortunately France was heartened by the presence of a formidable old man with Mongolian features who might well have presided over the tumbrills of the French Revolution.

Clemenceau the ferocious, the incomparable, had re-appeared to terrorise the fainthearts into a show of action and to take control at the very moment of crisis. Nor did he seek to hide the dangers from the people.

"I will fight in front of Paris. I will fight in Paris. I will fight behind Paris," he told the deputies of the French Parliament. Is it one of those providential episodes of history that Clemenceau rehearsed these very words to Winston Churchill, who was in Paris at the time, before he made them in public? Could it be that Clemenceau in 1918 not only carved victory out of thin air by his bellicose utterances, but that he directly inspired Churchill for his famous "fight on the beaches" speech which proved the moral turning point in World War II?

The Allied retreat before superior German forces continued; now it was swift and, in places, disorderly. Before dawn on March 21 the Germans had opened up with the most devastating bombardment of the war, at the same time enveloping the British lines and gun positions with poison gas. To make matters worse the attack began in a fog of great density which favoured the enemy, while neutralising the effect of the British rifle fire and making machine-gun defence useless.

H. G. Wells, with that glibness with which he was wont to talk about military affairs, wrote of "General Gough's unfortunate collapse" as being "more honourable to our hearts than our heads". But General Gough and the Fifth Army did not collapse. Their ranks were shattered, they fell, they died, but there still remained a gallant, indomitable fighting minority which forced the Germans to a standstill. Their gallantry, not the arrival of the Americans, turned the situation from disaster into hope and prevented the enemy's headlong drive for victory.

What was most remarkable in this battle was that many of the troops were half-trained men of doubtful stamina and often stunted growth; in physical fitness they were not to be compared with the Eighth Army of World War II or the highly trained, technically skilled and superbly fit body of men who formed the spearhead of the Normandy invasion in 1944. Yet the men of the Fifth Army fought above themselves. Many of them went for forty-eight hours without food or drink. Some battalions fought two German divisions in a single day, while others were reduced to mere skeleton forces of anything from 200 to twenty men. On one occasion only two machine-guns out of forty-eight were left in action.

But General Gough, leader of the Fifth Army, had been sacked on Lloyd George's personal instructions; here was a new scapegoat for another failure. The first man to give the British public some inkling that a great wrong had been done was Robert Blatchford. Writing in the *Illustrated Sunday Herald* of October 13, 1918, seven months afterwards, Blatchford was able to let in a little light and truth.

"I may at last venture to attempt some account of a glorious and tragic epoch of the war hitherto obscured by an invidious fog of official mystery," he said. "The story of this retreat has never been given to the country. Instead we have had vague speeches, dubious hints and ominous silences, and it is not too much to say that there has accumulated in the public mind an indefinite but dark suspicion that our generals or our armies failed before the German attacks in March and that our Fifth Army, under General Gough, was badly and ingloriously defeated.

"The March retreat, so far from being discreditable to our soldiers, was more arduous and more brilliant than the famous retreat from Mons. It was a retreat during which the Fifth Army contested every bit of ground against almost overwhelming odds and in which the bulk of our regiments fought without rest or sleep for seven days and nights."

The story of this valiant, rearguard action should have been revealed to the people months before. It was an epic in military history and human endurance; never in the annals of war, ancient or modern, had the human spirit endured so much as in that spring of 1918. The Fifth Army was on badly defended ground, it had no reserves and no strongly fortified line in the rear. The enemy had eighty divisions against Britain's fifteen.

Blatchford wrote: "Officers and men were worn out and yellow from want of sleep. Staff officers fainted while delivering their reports, men fired and loaded and advanced and retired, moving like somnambulists, gunners fought their guns in a kind of horrid dream.

Bassano & Vandyk

Field-Marshal Earl Haig.

Trebitsch Lincoln.

Topix Picture Service

Philip Kerr, Marquis of Lothian.

Press Portrait Bureau Limited London

"But there is one thing which is not easy to explain. How was it that with such odds the Germans failed to break our line and get to Amiens? How did our men, faint with fatigue, cut down to a mere fringe of their original strength, wet, muddy, hungry and blind for lack of sleep—how did they succeed in holding and stopping what was meant to be an overwhelming and triumphant advance?

"There is only one explanation with any claim to plausibility. It is that the Germans were fought to a standstill. On the Ancre they were stopped, and though they snatched Villers-Bretonneux for a few hours in early April from the thin British garrison, they never got beyond it."

At a conference in Beauvais on April 3, 1918, Haig wrote of Lloyd George: "The Prime Minister looked as if he had been thoroughly frightened and he seemed still in a funk. . . . And he appears to me to be a thorough impostor."

It was at this conference that the Prime Minister was nervously searching for a scapegoat for the retreat. "Gough is unworthy of further employment," he raged.

"I cannot condemn an officer unheard," replied Haig. "If you wish to suspend him, you must send an order to that effect."

Ll. G. consulted Lord Derby, then Secretary of State for War, who next day telegraphed Haig, saying: "It is quite clear to me that his troops have lost confidence in Gough, and, before seeing you, the Prime Minister had consulted me as to his retention in command of an army, and, with my full concurrence, notified to you yesterday that, pending report in detail with regard to recent operations, it was necessary that he should vacate his command of the Fifth Army and return home."

General Gough's own account of these incidents is as follows:

"That little ——, Henry Wilson, was Chief of the General Staff with the ear of Lloyd George. He hated me. I'd clashed with him over Ulster years ago. Then, when he was under me in the 1914–18 war for a time, I'd had to tick him off for writing political letters instead of attending to his duty. He never forgave me."

General Gough's own view was that if any general should have been disgraced at this time it was Pétain. "Wouldn't fight. In 1918 he sent me reserves armed with only twenty rounds of ammunition apiece. They blazed away and then beat it back to Verdun or somewhere where Pétain was sitting on his bottom."

Haig had the painful task of telling Gough, whom he admired, that he was sacked. Gough made no protest. All he said was: "Very well, Douglas, you'll have a busy time. I'll say no more. Goodbye and good luck."

At the comparatively early age of forty-eight, Gough found himself "disgraced" after a lifetime spent in the Army. He was ordered home, placed on half-pay and told by Lord Derby that an inquiry would be held into the circumstances of the battle. Gough believed that such an inquiry would exonerate him and lead to his reinstatement. Twice he wrote to the War Office, asking for the date of the inquiry. At length he was informed that no inquiry was to be held and that he had been "mistaken in thinking that a promise to that effect had been made".

In the House of Commons, Lloyd George made several statements which placed blame for the disaster on the Fifth Army in general and Gough in particular. The Prime Minister inferred that the Fifth Army was retreating precipitately while the Third Army held on. He claimed that Brigadier-General Carey's force of signalmen, engineers and labour battalions held up the German Army and closed the gap in the route to Amiens for about six days. But General Carey did nothing of the kind. He was not responsible for the formation of this force. He was away on leave in England when the force was formed and posted and did not take command until it had been in position for two days. This force, which Lloyd George eulogised, was one of several corps formed and posted under General Gough's direction.

It was a combination of Lloyd George, Lord Milner, Lord Derby and Sir Henry Wilson which got rid of Gough, but the evidence is indisputable that the primary responsibility was the Prime Minister's. The general had to wait nineteen years before he was finally and completely vindicated. First to open the defence of Gough was Lord Birkenhead, a Cabinet colleague of Ll. G. In his book, *Turning Points of History*, Birkenhead claimed: "If one soldier more than another was directly responsible for our victory in that year, that soldier was General Gough. When the attack came, the British front was driven back thirty-eight miles, but the Germans were stopped. Amiens was saved, so was Paris, so were the Channel ports; so was England. Whereupon Gough was recalled in disgrace. It is known that G.H.Q. neither recommended nor approved this action, which was due wholly to pressure from England, where only the apparent success and not the real failure of the German advance was as yet understood."

Lord Birkenhead disposed of the War Office statement to Gough that no inquiry had been promised: he said that both Ll. G. and Lord Curzon promised there should be an inquiry into the battle.

By the time Lloyd George came to write his own account of the battle in his *War Memoirs*, it was obvious even to his stubborn mind that he dare not ignore the serious implications of his stand against Gough. Either he must stand by what he had said and done and face a storm of criticism, or he must make some sort of apology and silence further and possibly more damaging evidence in Gough's favour. So on April 30, 1936, he wrote to General Gough, saying:

"I have written my first draft of the 21st March battle and the events preceding it. I promised to let you have a look at it before it was published. . . . I need hardly say that the facts which have come to my knowledge since the war have completely changed my mind as to the responsibility for this defeat. You were completely let down and no general could have won that battle under the conditions in which you were placed."

Ll. G. did not say by whom Gough had been "completely let down". Nor did he explain why he had not ascertained the facts at the time.

This guarded statement was very far from being a thorough vindication. A year later on the anniversary of the battle Lloyd George was to have attended a reunion dinner of the Fifth Army Old Comrades' Association in London. He declined on the grounds that he had a cold. But in a letter read at the dinner by his secretary, Mr. A. J. Sylvester, Ll. G. completed his public vindication of Gough:

"The refusal of the Fifth Army to run away even when it was broken was the direct cause of the failure of the great German offensive in 1918. I have *the best German authority* for that statement."

The italics are the author's. Lloyd George implied indirectly that he was not given the true facts by the War Office or the generals, but only learned them afterwards from the Germans. He admitted that the Allied forces were so distributed at the time of the battle that at the point of attack they were weaker in numbers, in artillery and reserves than at any point of the whole British line. "That was not the fault of General Gough. He warned G.H.Q. in time that the enemy were accumulating immense forces opposite the Fifth Army. The obsession of Passchendaele still held its grip on G.H.Q., and the neglected Fifth Army was left in the lurch. Why, then, punish General Gough?"

The cool impertinence of the last two sentences and the rhetorical question in particular are typical of Lloyd George's audacity when cornered. "It is, therefore, a matter of honour and of fair dealing," he continued, "that an opportunity should be afforded to a distinguished officer, who is resting under unjustifiable aspersion, to vindicate himself in the eyes of the country for which he fought."

Yet this admission was only wrung from an unwilling Lloyd George as a result of further elucidation of the circumstances of Gough's dismissal in an article published in the previous month's issue of the *Journal of the Royal United Services Institution* by Brigadier-General Sir James Edmonds, the official historian of the war. This article produced a mass of evidence—in the main a repetition of what has been told in this chapter—to vindicate Gough and blame Lloyd George.

Later that same year the story had a happy ending. In the summer of 1937 General Gough saw King George VI alone. As he handed him the package which contained the G.C.B., the King said simply: "I suppose you can take this as a recognition of the gratitude of your country."

* * * * *

Lloyd George's conditions of peace had been published when negotiations in Switzerland were proceeding. They included the restoration of independence to Belgium, Rumania and Serbia, as well as payment of compensation, the evacuation of all Allied territories occupied by the enemy and the return of Alsace-Lorraine to France. There was a vague mention of a new "international authority" to guard the peace, but on the whole it was an uninspiring document, offering no blueprint for prosperity and security in peacetime.

Dr. Thomas Jones told us that in 1918 "Lloyd George was not wanting in courage, but it never fell lower than in these months. He was restless, capricious, agitated, wishing to close down the campaign in Flanders, haunted by the mounting casualties, harassed by domestic politics and Press criticism." On January 9, 1918, Lord Derby had bet the Prime Minister one hundred cigars to one hundred cigarettes that the war would be over by next New Year's Day. Ll. G. disagreed; he had made up his mind that nothing decisive could be achieved before the spring of 1919.

Those close to Lloyd George, including his own staff, were shocked by his undisguised fear during air raids. Sir Harold Nicolson has declared that: "So far as physical courage goes, he may have been a coward, though he certainly had moral courage. I've seen him trembling and ashen at the sound of an air-raid siren in World War I, when the risks were pretty remote after all." One of his staff related how he "scuttled into the basement of the Foreign Office when there were raids and sang Welsh hymns to keep up his nerve, beads of perspiration pouring from his face". Even Dr. Jones told how "Lloyd George had not Churchill's reckless, physical courage, or should one say he showed greater prudence in danger? During the first world war he hurried instantly from Downing Street to the Foreign Office basement at the sound of the siren and during the second he built himself at Churt a de luxe underground shelter: the military camp at Aldershot was not far away and he feared he might be one of the enemy's targets."

When the holocaust broke and the German divisions exterminated the slender British columns on the Western front, Lloyd George relied on the elasticity of his mind to cope with the crisis. For the first and only time in his wartime Premiership he acted promptly and resolutely. He did what should obviously have been done months before, ordering the dispatch of a division from Italy and two more from Palestine to the Western front. It was once said of a French Premier that he mistook "movement for action"; it could equally be said of Lloyd George that the agility of his mind and the swiftness of his mental processes gave the impression of action even when it was lacking. Nevertheless, this time he acted purposefully. He not only seemed to be in command after the rout of March–April, 1918, but he ruthlessly and effectively took command. Here, belatedly, it is true, was positive proof of the resilience of the man, of his uncanny intellectual intuition, his gift of disengaging himself from one problem to tackle another, of his astonishing knack of throwing off a pessimism that had appeared as a pathological defect one day and suddenly becoming gaily, confidently aggressive. It was one of the Merlinesque characteristics of Lloyd George that he became gloomy when all around him were optimistic and yet drew forth reserves of moral courage from other people's lack of it. Surround Ll. G. with defeatists and prophets of doom and he perversely gloried in trying to prove that the situation was the opposite to what they thought. Sometimes in these periods it was. As some of the Cabinet showed unmistakable signs of gloom and panic, inertness and lack of phlegm, so he inspired them with a buoyant optimism which they never previously believed he possessed.

So out of the March 21 disaster he induced the conference at Doullens and, as the situation improved, as at last it was realised that the Germans had made their last supreme effort, so, as was his adolescently egotistical habit, the Prime Minister claimed much credit for the outcome of events. Because he had fought for so long for a unified, superior direction of the Allied cause, he attributed final victory to that factor, ignoring that Haig had ultimately recommended Foch for the job of Supreme Commander.

One Cabinet colleague at least was gratified by and almost in awe of Lloyd George's performance in these dark days. Churchill has gone on record as saying that "nobody who wasn't with the little man (*he always called Ll. G. this*) in March, 1918, has any right to criticise him. He alone displayed courage when everybody else was knocking at the knees." Churchill even went so far as to say that Lloyd George "ran the first world war better than I ran the second". History is unlikely to agree with so modest an assessment, for Lloyd George's failure to inspire trust was always a dangerous defect for a wartime leader, but it is not difficult to understand what Churchill saw in Ll. G.: he sensed the genius for dominating a situation which Ll. G. had in flashes, but which Churchill over the years developed into a consistently fine art. But it took Churchill far longer to achieve this mastery of events and he may well have envied the personality of his elder in the process.

Yet, when that unified direction of the Allied command was achieved, it did not come in the way Lloyd George had anticipated, and it was exercised by two men, working in close co-operation, Foch and Haig, whose ideas on strategy were the opposite to his own. In the end all was saved. But at what cost. Despite the clever propaganda of the "Easterners", the war was won on the Western front. The fact that everything had to be thrown in on this front to force the issue did not prevent, or even delay, the defeat of the Turks and Bulgars. Victory was achieved at the cost of wisdom after the event, at the cost of

300,000 casualties within five weeks—70,000 more than those suffered in the fourteen weeks of the battle of Passchendaele.

So there was the extraordinary enigma of a Premier who almost flippantly brushed aside pessimism in his Cabinet, even feigning elated optimism when the battle seemed to be going badly, and yet displayed the most marked disbelief as soon as his military advisers talked of victory.

The constant theme of his memoranda of this last period of the war was that Haig was "too optimistic". Between February and August, 1918, Lloyd George's emotional pendulum swung in unrhythmic fashion from chirpy confidence of "over-insuring" the Western front in the early spring to stark fright at the end of March, then over again to blithe optimism in April when the experts were nervously adding up their losses and, finally, to sheer disbelief in the dawning prospect of victory in the summer. Haig, like Churchill in 1940, like Prince Charles Edward Stuart on his march to England in 1745, believed in optimism as a policy—the optimism of the old-fashioned, religiously-minded general. It has invariably been optimism opposed to logic which has won Britain her ultimate military victories, while sustaining grievous defeats in the painful process.

As late as August 21, 1918, when Haig insisted that "we ought to do our utmost to get a decision this autumn", Ll. G. and his lackey, Sir Henry Wilson, both argued that the decisive period of the war could not arrive until the following July. Even when the tide had turned, the Prime Minister continually probed and quizzed for peace through negotiation. There had been the secretive visit of the mysterious "Mr. Coleyn" of Holland in May, 1918, the full purpose of which was never revealed, but on which Admiral Sir Guy Gaunt reported that "Admiral Sir Reginald Hall managed to side-track this ridiculous intervention of Lloyd George's own secret service". Ludendorff wrote in his *Kriegfihrung*: "England began to talk about peace at the Hague in June, 1918." The British intelligence services were always on the watch for some Lloyd Georgian peace manœuvre that would be launched without their being informed.

The war situation in August, 1918, can be compared with that in August, 1944, in World War II. On both occasions victory was within sight. In 1918 the military were full of optimism and wanted to take full advantage of the situation to gain a quick victory; the politicians, especially Lloyd George, demurred. In 1944 the situation was reversed: the politicians, including Churchill, saw the value of the quick cut to victory by a thrust to the north, while the military under Eisenhower and, to a lesser extent, an ultra-cautious British Admiralty, wanted to consolidate before moving on.

Haig, so often lambasted by Lloyd George in his *War Memoirs* as being obstinate, lacking imagination and incapable of appreciating any situation as a whole, saw clearly that Germany was hardly capable of any further resistance if really pushed. "If we allow the enemy a period of quiet," he wrote, "he will recover. The Third Army is halting today. I cannot think this is necessary. I accordingly issued an order directing the offensive to be resumed at the earliest moment possible."

But for Haig the great chance of a quick decision might easily have been lost and the war could have dragged on until late in the following year with the probability of revolution in France and serious industrial discontent in Britain. The French were so war-weary that they were not anxious to attack again, while the Americans, under Pershing, were still thinking in terms of victory in August, 1919.

Haig had the greatest difficulty in persuading the Prime Minister to agree to an attack on the Hindenburg Line. Eventually Lloyd George concurred, safeguarding himself, however, against its possible failure by getting Sir Henry Wilson to send the following telegram to the Commander-in-Chief:

"H.W. PERSONAL. Just a word of caution in regard to incurring heavy losses in attacks on the Hindenburg Line as opposed to losses when driving the enemy back to that line. I do not mean to say you have incurred such losses, but I know the War Cabinet would become anxious if we received heavy punishment in attacking the Hindenburg Line without success."

Such a telegram, of course, should never have been marked "personal". Either an order should have been sent, or nothing at all. It was an incredibly unbusiness-like method of briefing a Commander-in-Chief, while at the same time seeming to say: "If things go wrong, be it on your own head."

A lesser man than Haig might have compromised and made a half-hearted attack. "What a wretched lot of weaklings we have in high places at the present time!" was his summing-up of the situation.

The attack was launched and all went according to Haig's plan. News came through that the enemy was not only exhausted but cracking up mentally and morally. By October 6, Marshal Foch was able to vindicate the Haig policy by declaring that the Allies now had "the immediate result of the British piercing the Hindenburg Line: the enemy has asked for an armistice".

When Austria and Turkey abandoned Germany and the Kaiser abdicated, all was over. The most appalling war in history ended when Marshal Foch met the German delegates in the Forest of Compiegne on November 11, and at five o'clock in the morning signed the terms of Armistice. Opinion will probably always be divided as to whether this war could have been won without such wholesale carnage, but it remains mainly an academic question. None of the critics of the generals has suggested how a less bloody victory could have been achieved. Events were too overpowering for the men on either side to cope with them. Modern war had reduced generals and politicians to the status of intellectual pigmies. It is impossible to say that either on land or sea the war threw up a genius in the strategical sense, and consequently militarism was dealt a devastating blow which naturally and rightly produced a wave of pacifism. World War I was won not so much by brains as by character, not so much by strategy as by courage. History may reveal that some French generals showed more flair and *panache* than their British counterparts, but it also clearly reveals that in character and courage leaders like Haig and Gough had more durable and viable assets.

* * * * *

Few commanders-in-chief after a victorious campaign have been so shabbily treated as was Haig by Lloyd George in 1918. True, eight days after the Armistice he received a telegram from his Prime Minister informing him that "His Majesty *on my recommendation* has been pleased to approve that the dignity of a Viscountcy be conferred upon you." But when the King came over to France a week later he told Haig that he personally had "told the Prime Minister to offer you a peerage".

Haig's first reaction was to decline this honour until adequate grants for the British war disabled had been made. He wrote to Wilson saying he felt very strongly about "the manner in which our disabled had been disregarded and that until the British Government gave me an assurance that the disabled, widows and children would be adequately provided for, I could not accept a reward of any kind."

The Government had not given a hint as to what they proposed to do for those unfortunate victims of war. All that followed in the feverish, victory-flushed weeks of November was a great deal of pie-crust oratory. Such talk can be summed up in the fandango-of-victory oration which Lloyd George delivered at Wolverhampton on November 24: "What is our task? To make Britain a fit country for heroes to live in." This pre-election tub-thumping was quickly to lose its coinage. A few years later it was being parodied by Davy Burnaby's Co-Optimists concert party as "a country fit for pierrots to live in".

But the unkindest blow to Haig was a telephone call from the C.I.G.S's private secretary with a message from the Prime Minister that the latter wished the Field-Marshal to come to London to take part in a ceremonial drive with Foch, Clemenceau and Orlando (Italian Premier), intimating that Haig was to be in the fifth carriage along with General Sir Henry Wilson. The architect of victory on the Western front, the man who had triumphed despite the constant sniping of the politicians at home, was, in his hour of triumph, to be relegated to the fifth carriage.

For Haig it was the crowning insult from a man who was now

boasting that the war had been won through his foresight. "The real truth," wrote Haig that day, "which history will show, is that the British Army has won the war in France in spite of Lloyd George, and I have no intention of taking part in any triumphal drive in order to add to Lloyd George's importance and help him in his election campaign."

So Haig told the War Office he would not come to London unless ordered to do so by the Army Council. Ll. G., with the utmost cynicism, had decided that a snap election right away in the first flush of enthusiasm for the Armistice was his only chance of winning success at the polls. His popularity was at its zenith and there was a widespread belief among the masses, fed for so long on newspaper fiction, that he had indeed won the war himself. His colleagues—especially the Tories—were only too glad to bask in this reflected glory. And Ll. G. saw the victory parade as a wonderful chance for propaganda for himself—the more so because the King was out of the country, visiting his troops in France, and therefore the Prime Minister would be the central figure in the whole affair.

The first Lord Birkenhead said that: "The man who enters into real and fierce controversy with Mr. Lloyd George must think clearly, think deeply and think ahead. Otherwise he will think too late!" Haig could think remarkably clearly, if not deeply; he could also look ahead with much greater prescience than many of the politicians, but he could not match the mental agility and speed of speech of Lloyd George when it came to a conference. On paper Haig could express himself with lucidity and logic, but in his speech, according to Lloyd George, he was "devoid of the gift of intelligible and coherent expression". It was one of Lloyd George's failings that he had a contempt for men who were tongue-tied, however admirable their characters or intellect. If a man talked well and brilliantly, whether it was Birkenhead, Nivelle or Trebitsch Lincoln, he could overlook almost all his other defects.

"I am not writing history as a historian," Ll. G. told Herbert Fisher, "but as a solicitor in possession of the documents." But it is not the documents which he used to lash the generals, but his own deep-rooted, personal animosity to them. The *Memoirs* are rarely dispassionate, the judgment anything but statesmanlike; instead there is the monotonous theme of the one infallible man of war—the author.

Equally childishly treated by Lloyd George were the First Sea Lord, Admiral Wester Wemyss, and Admiral Hall. According to Lady Wester Wemyss, Lloyd George was furious with her husband because after Wemyss signed the Armistice agreement with Marshal Foch he telephoned the tidings to the King. "The Prime Minister had apparently planned a spectacular announcement of the Armistice in the House of Commons on the afternoon of the 11th, the news being meanwhile kept secret. This proved impossible after Wemyss's telephone call to the King."

Alone among all the war leaders Wemyss was neither thanked nor honoured. As to that backroom sailor whose keen political sense had welded the Naval Intelligence Department into a brilliant organisation which played a notable part in winning the war, Admiral Hall was completely ignored. President Wilson once said that "Britain's naval intelligence was the astutest in the world and a powerful factor in the final victory." Certainly but for Hall's skilful work at the Admiralty, America might not have entered the war so soon or so smoothly, for the political problems of President Wilson were appreciated far more at the Admiralty than at No. 10 Downing Street. Hall clashed several times with Ll. G. and regarded him not merely on personal judgment, but on the strength of intelligence reports, as "the last man in the world to be trusted with top-secret information".[1]

Lloyd George, on his part, never forgave Hall for the D.N.I.'s refusal to pass on all information he received. Hall had expected to attend the Peace Conference as head of the intelligence bureau, but Lloyd George intimated that he had "no intention of taking Hall to Paris". Nor was Hall included in the honours list for his invaluable efforts in building up what had become one of the finest intelligence organisations in the world.

* * * * *

Within a fortnight of the Armistice being signed Parliament was dissolved. Polling was fixed to take place on December 14. Had the Prime Minister delayed the dissolution for another three months the results might have been vastly different. He took advantage of a snap election at a time when his personal popularity was great, when the troops were absent abroad and war hysteria rampant. In 1918 there was no education bureau to set vital social problems before the forces, and the true picture of how victory had been achieved was clear neither to the ordinary soldier nor the man-in-the-street. A new electorate based on the recently passed Electoral Reform Act, which provided for universal male suffrage and extended the vote to women over thirty, was not only politically inexperienced, but completely bewildered by the complex Party line-up for this election. One image alone was clear—the image, cleverly built up in the Press, of a great statesman who by his dynamic personality had produced the final drive to victory. That was, by and large, the view of Lloyd George held by the great mass of floating, unpolitically-educated voters. But this transient mood of the electorate was also welded into landslide proportions by Ll. G.'s lively speeches which told the people what they wanted, if not what they ought, to hear. He was without question

[1] From a letter to Admiral Sir Guy Gaunt.

the most consummate demagogue of modern times, and the lively, simple imagery, the pungent wit of his speeches, and the charm of that lilting Welsh accent were intoxicating ingredients in the days which followed victory. All this was allied to a modernity of approach to problems and a speed of thought and action hitherto unknown in British political life so that they made Ll. G. seem a Titan astride the affairs of state. His real greatness in this period lay mainly in his adaptable mental equipment for the merry-go-round style of government which had succeeded the staid and leisurely coach of state of Edwardian days, leaving so many names famous in that decade strewn like flapping fish on a dry beach, politicians who had neither the temperament, nor the impetus to cope with the rag-time tempo of the Coalition machine.

Where Lloyd George can be criticised for acting like a demagogue and abusing democratic processes was in his attempt to turn the election issue into a personal vote of confidence for himself with what amounted to a blank cheque for further political action. This move for a snap election cannot be compared with Churchill's appeal in 1945. Churchill had not wanted a snap election; he had hoped for a continuation of the National Government until the war against Japan was ended. When that was impossible Churchill fought the election on Party lines and made his policy clear. But Lloyd George wanted the Coalition to continue in what was almost an attempt at one-Party government. It was cleverly disguised dictatorship, aided and abetted by the Tories. Even more undemocratic was his use of blackmail tactics by issuing "coupons" to his supporters. The result was to give the country one of the least creditable Parliaments in its whole history.

The campaign had been cleverly organised. The idea was to present Lloyd George as the saviour of his country and to show that he, and he alone, was strong enough and had sufficient experience to negotiate peace terms. Therefore a vote against Ll. G. was an act of sabotage against the state. Sir William Sutherland, the Prime Minister's Press agent, had first launched this campaign at the height of the German onslaught of March, 1918, partly to detract attention from the Allied losses, but equally to safeguard his master's position in the event of the Western Powers having to come to terms with Germany. At that time, though he kept his fears to himself and chided his colleagues for showing pessimism, Lloyd George believed he might have to seek terms from Germany and, if this happened, he wished to make sure of retaining the Premiership.

The Tories, who had spent the war sniping at the Liberals rather than getting on with the supreme task, knew how deep were the rifts in their own Party and, though they mistrusted the Prime Minister, feared the rise of Socialism above all else. So they were quite prepared to cut their immaculate clothes according to the tawdry cloth available and to snuggle under the mantle of the Welsh Wizard. Ll. G. and Bonar Law had already made an appraisal of the candidates upon whose support they could count, and the two men decided to go to the country as a Tory-Liberal Coalition.

But promises of support were not considered enough. Lloyd George instituted the unprecedented device of issuing a certificate, signed by himself and Bonar Law, to be given to whatever candidate they deemed reliable. The Tories, in the main, were only too eager to accept the certificate as a magic password to victory, but for the Liberals this device was nothing more or less than a form of moral blackmail. Either they repudiated their own leader, Asquith, and promised Lloyd George blind support, or they were damned as men who had deliberately opposed the effective prosecution of the war. Thus the Asquithian Liberals were in effect proscribed, and everybody who voted against the Government in the Maurice debate was singled out as unworthy of a certificate. The "wait and see" canard was once again nailed to the masthead of the Government's propaganda.

Having set the pace for the election and introduced methods that would have been more in keeping with a totalitarian state, Lloyd George proceeded to allow the election campaign to descend to depths unknown in modern times. The so-called Liberals far outstripped the Tories in political "verminism". Asquith dubbed it the "Coupon Election".

It has been suggested in Mr. Malcolm Thomson's biography that Ll. G. tried for reconciliation with the orthodox Liberals and that he offered Asquith the Lord Chancellorship. Asquith has put it on record that no such offer was made to him, and that when he himself raised the subject of his going to Versailles with Ll. G., the Prime Minister ignored the proposition.

As for the suggestion that Ll. G. tried for reconciliation, the facts belie it. Prior to the election three important deputations of Liberals—from Manchester and from the National Liberal Federation and the Scottish Liberal Federation—called upon both Asquith and Lloyd George with the object of securing a *rapprochement* between the two factions. In each case they failed to achieve their purpose. The reason for this failure was provided by Sir George Younger, the Conservative Chief Whip. He revealed that Ll. G. "kept the seats he could contest" and asked him (Younger) to provide candidates for the remaining Liberal seats—i.e., where free Liberals had been chosen by the local organisations.

Did Lloyd George disclose to any of these deputations that he had already asked Younger to put up candidates against a large number of Liberals? One must assume that he did not, for, when he addressed his Liberal followers on November 12, he said: "I have done nothing in the few years in which I have been First Minister of the Crown which makes me ashamed to meet my fellow-Liberals. Please God, I am determined that I never shall."

When he made this statement his bargain with Sir George Younger was not only signed and sealed, but being carried out.

The main themes for the election were, first, "the land for heroes" (in which Ll. G. indulged in such clichés as "the rosy future" and "the dawn of better things"), the need for a "tough man" to negotiate "a tough peace" and the absolute necessity of "hanging the Kaiser". Privately, Lloyd George seems to have been in doubt from the very day of the Armistice as to whether Germany could pay colossal sums in reparations. In his book, *The Truth About the Peace Treaties*, he refuted the idea that in his public utterances he deliberately misled the people into believing that Germany could be made to pay phenomenal amounts in reparations. He quoted from a speech he made at Bristol during an election campaign, in which he said that Treasury officials were doubtful whether "we could expect every penny" of the cost of the war to be paid by Germany.

But this statement was only part of a speech which, taken in its entirety, conveyed a very different impression. In fact he mentioned the Treasury view that the Central Powers could pay £1,200,000,000 a year as interest on the total cost of the war to the Allies (£24,000,000,000) only to cast doubt on its soundness and to imply that he would go one better. He informed his audience that he proposed "to demand the whole cost of the war from Germany at once".

Then there was the demand that the Kaiser must be hanged. In later life Lloyd George repeatedly denied that he used the phrase "hang the Kaiser", but there is plenty of evidence that he did. In an aside, in answer to a question from a crowded meeting at Bristol, he actually said: "I am in favour of hanging the Kaiser." On two occasions in North Wales he declared: "The Kaiser must be brought to the White Tower of the Tower of London and I have little doubt that justice will see that he is hanged there." In an article entitled *Le Diable aux Yeux Bleus*, by S. Lauzanne, it was noted by a French observer that he referred to "hanging the Kaiser" in twenty public speeches. Sir Winston Churchill himself has declared: "Mr. Lloyd George, himself an actor although a man of action, would, if he had had his way . . . in order to gratify the passions of victorious crowds . . . have redraped this melancholy exile (the Kaiser) in the sombre robes of more than mortal guilt and of human responsibility and led him forth to a scaffold of vicarious expiation."

A few days after the Armistice the Cabinet decided to apply to Holland for the extradition of the Kaiser. F. E. Smith (Lord Birkenhead) had just appointed Professor J. H. Morgan, K.C., as vice-chairman of the British Committee of Inquiry into German Breaches of the Laws of War. Smith told Morgan that the Kaiser should be charged with "high crimes and misdemeanours". "I think," he said, "that banishment will be a sufficient punishment. We don't want to make him a martyr, but Lloyd George wants to hang him."

President Wilson was disgusted and angered by this indecorous fandango and made his views known to Lloyd George in no uncertain terms. Then, in a moment of extreme intoxication with his own power, the Prime Minister talked to the French of "trying the Kaiser in London". That outraged even the bitterest enemies of Germany in France. Briand, after the election, asked Lloyd George with biting sarcasm: "When are you going to try the Kaiser in London?"

"Oh, that," replied Ll. G. airily, "that was purely an election stunt."

While it had been expected that the Coalition Government would be returned to power, few expected such a landslide as indeed occurred. Five hundred and twenty-six Coalitionists were elected and the Independent Liberals were reduced to twenty-six, Asquith himself being defeated at East Fife. Demagogy had triumphed over fair play.

Thus did Lloyd George deal the death blow to the one British political party which had been in the vanguard of progress and reform for more than seventy years. Into second place stepped the Labour Party with sixty-three members. The Tories never intended to lose their identity in any centre Party, except perhaps for one or two of their leaders. They were determined that if anyone was to lose his identity, it must be Lloyd George.

It may seem an interesting comparison in assessing the two wartime leaders of Britain in this century that Lloyd George swept the country in the "Coupon Election" of 1918, while Churchill was heavily defeated when he staged his victory election in 1945. It may well be that the older members of the electorate in 1945 had learned a lesson from 1918. Certain it is that the younger electorate in 1945 was tired and disgusted of a "Rump" Parliament and they registered a protest vote against a discredited Tory Party who had for so long neglected urgent reforms. In 1918 the name of Lloyd George alone was sufficient to have ensured victory for any combination at which he stood at the head. Such was his hold on the majority of his countrymen at that time.

12

THE "TICKET-HOLDERS" GOVERNMENT

"England does not love Coalitions."
Benjamin Disraeli

"Hard-faced men who looked as though they had done well out of the war," was how Stanley Baldwin described the newcomers to Westminster on the Coalition side.

They were a motley assortment of war-time officers, business men and opportunists far more concerned with their own vested interests than with the traditions of a British Parliament. To glance at a list of those M.P.s today is to run through a catalogue of names long since forgotten, of men who entered politics merely by the purchase of a Lloyd George "ticket". They were faceless men in every sense of that modern idiom, lacking political principles and beliefs, groping for a career as drowning men might clutch at a floating log. To them might well be applied that satirical speech of Churchill's when attacking the Balfour Government on the fiscal issue:

". . . Their patriotic duty compels them to remain, although they have no opinions to offer, holding their opinions undecided and unflinching, like George II at the Battle of Dettingen, *sans peur et sans avis.*"

There never has been a Parliament before or since in modern times in which charlatans and adventurers have formed so large a number on the back benches. Asquith's biographers state that "to the end of his life" Asquith "continued to say it was the worst House of Commons he had ever known".

All the former Coalition Cabinet had held their seats, but in the rout of the Independent Liberals out had gone Simon, Samuel, McKenna and Runciman. Forty-two Coalition Unionists and twenty-seven Coalition Liberals had been returned unopposed. A typical slogan of one of the Coalition Unionists had been, "Vote for Hall and hang the Kaiser."

The Government was predominantly Tory in the worst sense of that word; it reflected not the conservatism of Lansdowne and Walter Long, or the inbred statecraft of the Cecils, but the uncouth, gangster tactics and sharp practice of the self-made business man. The "Ticket-

Holders"—as those who had bribed, flattered, blackmailed or even bought their way into getting the Lloyd George coupon were known—were a bunch of feckless intriguers of extremely limited intellectual ability whose knowledge of political problems was in many instances almost non-existent. Collective responsibility was a myth.

Lord Northcliffe realised too late that he had backed Lloyd George too long. After the election he wrote to Dawson, editor of *The Times*: "Never again will I allow myself to be over-ruled in a matter like that. I am very willing to be led in matters that I do not understand, but I do understand character. The Welsh are illusive, cunning and ingrate."

This was government by a mixture of coercion and capitulation in its approach to the problems of the day. Its performance was as vague and erratic as had been Ll. G.'s pre-election speeches. It was never even clear whether this was a Free Trade or a Protectionist administration, and the Prime Minister on more than one occasion toyed with the idea of Imperial Preference. He certainly showed the Tories far greater consideration than he did his much smaller band of pseudo-Liberals. He was seldom in the House, for the simple reason that whereas in wartime he could ride roughshod over Parliament and threaten the Opposition that if they attacked him he would regard them "as traitors, throwing up their hands and shouting *Kamerad*", in peacetime it was difficult to avoid direct answers to awkward questions and there was no Defence of the Realm Act to fall back on.

"History has yet to reveal—perhaps it will never fully reveal—the measure of corruption which Lloyd George permitted to enter politics during his six years as Prime Minister," wrote Robert Blake in *The Baldwin Age*. "There was an obverse side to that brilliant sparkle."

In the war years that corruption was mainly confined to the chicaneries of the Prime Minister, but in the "Ticket-Holders" Government it infected Parliament as a whole and extended its tentacles deep into Whitehall, into the hitherto incorruptible Civil Service to which Ll. G. recruited his own chosen agents. The story of this Government from now on is a series of chapters which show only too clearly how power corrupts, how money bought candidatures and honours and, above all, how Lloyd George himself undermined the moral structure of British public life and touched off the moral degeneration which is the greatest political problem of the present day. How long this rot, or rather the effects of the rot, have lasted is not easily apparent. Baldwin did his best to eliminate the worst excesses of those days and to some extent to cleanse the Tory stables, but the moral rot has been visible from time to time in both the Labour and Liberal Parties. In 1945 many opportunists jumped aboard the Labour band wagon and weakened the Socialists with their misdemeanours; fortunately Attlee, unlike Lloyd George, openly purged his ranks. Only in the nineteen-sixties have the small band of Liberals succeeded in putting their own house in order and creating a new image for themselves. But the curse which Lloyd George put on British Party politics was the curse of me-tooism, the pretence of each major Party that it had the virtues of the others. In this way Conservatism has become more and more indeterminate and incomprehensible, while Socialism has frequently shown its weakness for facing both ways, thus losing its radical appeal and trying to look respectable, while more often appearing anti-British and the Party of class hatred.

* * * * *

Those ministers who answered for Lloyd George in the Commons rarely knew what the Prime Minister really thought on any subject, as his mind changed so rapidly, so they were evasive and incoherent in their replies.

The Peace Conference was a subject on which the Prime Minister was most quixotic in his policy. From the first he was determined to try to dominate that conference and to brook no interference from any member of the Cabinet. Lord Beaverbrook has written: "Lloyd George was now the most powerful man in Europe. . . . When Lloyd George arrived in Paris for the Peace Conference he at once took control. He really dominated the French Prime Minister. He had immense authority with President Wilson. He was the arbiter of all Europe."[1]

This is exactly what a *Daily Express* leader writer might have said in 1919. But the portrait is, to say the least, overdrawn. Lloyd George disliked the idea of holding the Peace Conference in Paris, arguing that it was unwise to meet in the "excited atmosphere of a belligerent nation". The truth was, however, that the Prime Minister had become violently anti-French now that his honeymoon with the French generals was over, and he preferred Geneva as the venue for the conference in order to push France into the background. Whether tempers would have cooled more easily in Geneva than in Paris is a matter for conjecture, but Clemenceau over-ruled Lloyd George. "The Tiger" insisted that as France had suffered most from the war she had a right to see peace made on her own soil.

President Wilson's Secretary of State, Robert Lansing, said in his book, *The Peace Negotiations*, that Lloyd George was "vague as to general principles", his judgment was "fluid", but that he considered certain election pledges binding. "Of these," added Lansing, "Germany's payment of the cost of the war and the public trial of the Kaiser attracted the most attention. He was very insistent . . . although he must have known that the first was impossible and the second unwise as well as in defiance of all legal precepts."

What perplexed the other Allied leaders was the slow realisation—as expressed by Poincaré—that "Britain now has two Foreign Offices, Lord

[1] *Men and Power:* 1917–18.

Curzon's and the one in which Lloyd George from his Downing Street offices plans to confound Curzon and trick France". It became clear that Lloyd George was determined that Curzon should be Foreign Minister in little more than name, a fatal tendency in a Prime Minister which repeated itself disastrously under Chamberlain, unhappily under Eden and, to a lesser extent, though with more reason, during the first Macmillan Ministry.

Mr. A. J. P. Taylor, studying the *Documents on British Foreign Policy* 1919–39, says that all that keeps these records "alive is the personality of Lloyd George. They present a wonderful picture of Lloyd George in action, the statesman of infinite resource . . . but himself always unmoved. In 1920 Lloyd George was at the height of his power. He ran foreign policy almost alone. Curzon, the Foreign Secretary, trailing after him like a humble Foreign Office clerk. . . . He strove at one international gathering after another to produce reconciliation from his conjurer's hat."

Curzon was angered at the manner in which his authority was undermined, but there was little he could do about it except resign, and Curzon, with his eye firmly fixed on the Premiership which one day he felt would surely be his, had no intention of committing political suicide by resignation. Curzon discovered that Lloyd George had nominated one of his own men to the Foreign Office for the sole purpose of spying on Curzon and sending confidential reports to Downing Street. Meanwhile, the key people in Ll. G.'s own "Shadow Foreign Office" were Philip Kerr, who had marked prejudices against France, Eric Drummond, Lionel Curtis, William Sutherland and J. T. Davies, a strange combination of starry-eyed Imperialists, wire-pullers and unorthodox civil servants.

During the Peace Conference in Paris the French had Lloyd George's telephone wires to London tapped by intelligence agents. To defeat this move Ll. G. used to speak in Welsh to his secretaries, Tom Jones, J. T. Davies and Ernie Evans. The French were seriously concerned that the British Premier was consistently sabotaging the work of his own Foreign Minister.

In a letter to his wife in 1921 Curzon gave vent to his frustration in these pathetic words: "Girlie I am getting very tired of working with that man. He wants his Forn. Sec. to be a valet, almost a drudge."[1]

The atmosphere at the Peace Conference was anything but pacific. Stephen Bonsal told a story in *Unfinished Business* of an occasion when President Wilson intervened to prevent Lloyd George from "doubling his fists and squaring off against Clemenceau. Mr. Wilson was compelled to intervene to prevent fisticuffs. As he returned to his corner the little Welshman said: 'Well, I shall expect an apology for this outrageous conduct.'

[1] *The Decline and Fall of Lloyd George* (Lord Beaverbrook).

"'You shall wait for it as long as you wait for the pacification of Ireland,' was the hot reply."

Clemenceau's recorded comment on the incident was: "There was little George doubling up his fists and squaring off. If Wilson hadn't intervened, I would have given him a clip on the chin with a *savatte* stroke."

So this was the *Peace* Conference! Further evidence of the antagonism between the two Premiers was provided in Mr. Wickham Steed's book, *Through Thirty Years*. He wrote that M. Clemenceau "accused Lloyd George so flatly of repeated inaccuracies of statement that Lloyd George seized him by the collar and demanded an apology and that after President Wilson had separated them Clemenceau offered Lloyd George reparation with pistols or swords."

Madame Gauthier, a relative of Clemenceau, commenting on these reports, said: "Both stories are substantially correct. Mr. Bonsal was a member of the American delegation and was present at the time. M. Clemenceau was infuriated when he found that Lloyd George had been consistently tricking him. When challenged, Mr. Lloyd George was very insulting to my great-uncle and called him an 'old fool'. Though he was a very old man then, M. Clemenceau was never afraid. He challenged Lloyd George to a duel, knowing that he was a physical coward who would never dare accept the challenge."

It is said that Ll. G. sought the intervention of Sir Basil Zaharoff to placate Clemenceau on this occasion. There is this to be said in Ll. G.'s favour: he was never scared of standing up to Clemenceau verbally in the conference chamber, a virtue which few of the other war leaders possessed. Indomitable and inspiring in a war crisis, Clemenceau was too old, his prejudices too deeply engrained to give him the elasticity of outlook so necessary for a conference on the future of Europe and the world. From him stemmed that inflexibility which successive French leaders adopted in subsequent conferences, though, as time showed, the fear behind that inflexibility was justified in the long run. Germany was caged, but not cured of her lust for aggression.

It was his swift change of mood, his switch from one attitude to another, the apparent lack of fixed principles in his dealings with statesmen that fanned the fires of suspicion of Ll. G. He, of course, would excuse himself by explaining that rigidity was the thing to avoid at all costs, that flexibility and conciliation were more useful in settling the future of Europe. But one can understand why he insisted on a careful recording being taken at all these meetings. Otherwise he would never have remembered what he had said from one day to the next.

Sir Harold Nicolson, who served under Curzon at the Foreign Office in this period, has described Lloyd George as being the most "interesting—fantastically interesting man" he had ever known in politics. "He really was a wizard. His power was his charm. His physical manner was engaging. When you entered a room he would come bounding up to you, lead you in, throw his arms about as he spoke, give a great impression of friendliness, exuberance and simplicity. The other method of charming you was by flattery. He was a great one for paying compliments. Particularly to junior people. As well as charm he had the great politician's gift for knowing what was going on in people's minds. . . . When the effects of the flattery had worn off and one's eyes had opened . . . he was dishonest and unscrupulous; you couldn't trust him. You could never be sure if what he was telling you was the truth."

In his dealings with foreign statesmen Ll. G. would alternate between flattery and banter, a peculiarly Welsh form of banter, which had an unpleasant edge to it. Frequently he would employ these bantering tactics as a cloak for his own ignorance of their problems. He made two fatal blunders at the outset of the Versailles Conference: he alienated Clemenceau and at the same time failed to give full support to Wilson, with the result that at no time was he able to reconcile France and U.S.A. The Middle East was his chief preoccupation after the war. The crooked, turbulent intrigues, the atmosphere of mystery and adventure, the turgid imbroglios at cosmopolitan dinner parties . . . these were the political ingredients he loved, and he entered wholeheartedly and gaily into the game of power politics. He had a genius for the snap decision on an occasion when a lesser man would have wanted time to think, but, not surprisingly, those decisions were not often right. Quick, makeshift agreements, gaining a point here and giving a point there, by-passing the Foreign Office, dealing direct through Venizelos or Zaharoff, or some secret agent, keeping an ear open for rumours, never hesitating to accept a bright idea from some unimportant intermediary who appealed to him: these were the Lloyd George methods of tackling Middle East problems. His own Cabinet were kept in the dark as to many of his manœuvres, and Middle East ambassadors had an impossible task keeping up with the changes of front.

It was on Middle East policy that he first fell out with Clemenceau. Almost his every act had the effect of poisoning Anglo-French relations and spoiling the carefully built-up Entente. He hated to play second string to anyone, and he deliberately set out to clip the wings of the dominant power in Europe in 1919—France. The obvious way to do this was to check French influence in the Middle East; this became a permanent objective of his foreign policy. It was a policy which was joyfully welcomed in Berlin, where already they saw the ultimate chance of separating Britain and France, a chance they seized eagerly in 1940. There was a distinct link between 1919 and 1940, for Lloyd

George's tactics in 1919 created a wave of Anglophobia in France, the first consequences of which were the anti-British tirades of Maurras, the advent of Fascist and neo-Royalist parties, and the final results of this could be seen in the emergence in 1940 of the old guard in France, the men whose dislike of Britain dated back to those days.

To thwart France, Lloyd George made it his aim to win back the oil market for Britain and to control Mosul oil. When Clemenceau was driving through London with Ll. G. after the war—before the two men had quarrelled—"The Tiger" turned to Lloyd George and asked: "What do you specially want from the French?"

It was one of the rare occasions when Clemenceau made a tactical error in negotiating with a foreign statesman.

Ll. G. promptly seized the initiative. Smiling, he replied: "I want Mosul attached to Iraq and Palestine from Dan to Beersheba under British control."

This was Clemenceau's own version of the incident. French official sources confirm that he put this query to Ll. G., but suggest that the British Premier's reply was not quite so brutally phrased as Clemenceau implied and that he had been vague on the subject of Mosul. In Paris, when Clemenceau returned, M. Poincaré rightly commented that "the stink of oil makes an unpleasant background to discussion of the problems of peace". There were grave doubts as to just what had resulted from the informal talks between Lloyd George and Clemenceau. Herr Hoffman, of the School of Politics in Berlin, a skilled observer of the European political scene, later claimed: "According to the secret minutes of the 'Big Four', Lloyd George had as early as December, 1918, got Clemenceau to consent to the handing over of Palestine to Britain and to the political renunciation of Mosul. In compensation France was to get a share of the oil plunder and a free hand in Germany."

It seems incredible that "The Tiger" could have been tricked in this way, for at no time did Lloyd George intend to allow France a free hand in Germany. But in December, 1918, with a General Election pending, with the clamour for "getting tough with Germany", he may have found it suited his purpose to appear to support France on this issue. No one can be quite sure what passed between the two men in private and their bargaining remained as secret as the prolonged fight for Mosul. One reason for Clemenceau's duel challenge to Ll. G. was the latter's denial of ever having promised to back France in using tough measures against Germany, even to the extent of threatening Clemenceau that "in certain circumstances I should have no hesitation in making Germany a close ally of Britain, especially if I thought France wanted to dominate Europe".

All this, however unpleasant in its double-talk to an old ally, might have made some sense if Lloyd George had intended to give full support to the League of Nations project. But Ll. G. ignored Wilson's appeal to humanity and liberalism throughout the world, and even when he wrote his book on the Peace Treaties summarily dismissed Wilson with the comment: "He did not make the same appeal to the combative instincts of the British as did Clemenceau and Foch."

Such inconsistency of thought must have left his contemporaries frequently gasping with astonishment. But, as Dr. Thomas Jones pointed out, "there are other than combative instincts even in the British", and the fact that Wilson made a very great appeal to the British people is amply borne out by the tremendous influence which the League of Nations Union had in Britain right up to 1935.

So the Versailles Conference lacked a guiding mind and a truly international figure who could bridge the gap between Wilson's idealism and Europe's need for security, one who could set the problems of peace in the objective perspective of the historian. Ludendorff, who in many ways was the forerunner of Adolf Hitler, saw this clearly and declared: "Versailles has shown that there is no unity among the Allies. In ten years Germany will have risen again and, providing she keeps the Allied camp split and wins over one or two nations to her side, she can win back all she has lost." How right he was.

Wilson, admittedly, showed poor strategy in standing out against the French plan for annexing the Rhineland and the Saar Valley. Had he concentrated on the League of Nations plan and compromised on other points, the gap between him and Clemenceau might have been bridged. Clemenceau was always doubtful about the League, but was prepared to support a plan which would "give the League teeth". France and Britain could have provided these teeth. In private Clemenceau urged Lloyd George to agree to a plan for limited conscription in all countries which were members of the League so that it should have the force to back up its decisions. Ll. G., with one ear cocked to his chances of survival at home, demurred. "The League," he told the French Premier, "would make conscription unnecessary in any country. Disarmament is the way to peace."

"You will rue that decision," "The Tiger" bluntly told him.

In his Fontainebleau Memorandum the British Premier pleaded for "a peace based on justice" for Germany. "We cannot cripple her *and* expect her to pay." It was a very different tune from that played by the Welsh Piper at Bristol and his "demand the whole cost of the war from Germany" talk during the election campaign. The French reply to this memorandum struck the right balance between the old and the new: "Mr. Lloyd George's note lays stress—and the French Government is in agreement with it—on the necessity of making peace which will appear to Germany to be a just peace. . . . In view of German mentality, it is not certain that the Germans have the same conception of justice as have the Allies."

Some of the wilder men in the new Coalition Government were enraged that Lloyd George should now coo like a dove about Germany whereas before he had roared like a lion for retribution. They protested verbally and in writing. Ll. G. could hardly complain, for he had set the pace for such wild talk.

From being the most virulent of the "squeeze the Germans" protagonists he swung over to the other extreme. Ll. G. wanted the Peace Treaty signed quickly, he wanted all the ends tied up in a neat package so that he could bask in the triumph of being personally responsible for a settlement.

Yet all these twists of policy, all these evasions and fondness for speedy action should not obscure the fact that Lloyd George worked with tremendous energy and skill to force diametrically opposed forces to come to terms. History cannot and will not easily reveal these gifts of his, gifts which, had they been allied to higher principles and more humility, might have brought richer harvests in the political field. Only those who saw him in action can conjure up for us the picture of so remarkable a negotiator. When faced with intransigence he could be the apostle of sweet reason, if in the mood, as he showed on the subject of how far Poland should be encouraged to refuse peace. At the Spa Conference he exuded sympathy for French grievances and demands, while telling the Germans behind the backs of the French how unreasonable he really thought the latter were. He played the one against the other, flattering the French and scaring the Germans that he agreed with an occupation of the Ruhr. Then, with France and Germany each despairing of any agreement, he used his histrionic talents in a dramatic last-moment bid. With forefinger dramatically poised in the air, with eyes cast down on his watch, he stressed that there was little time to be lost. "You have no further suggestions, gentlemen; you have talked all day and made no progress. Let me show you what can be done, despite all our difficulties."

In the end he was spontaneously dictating an agreement, which both sides accepted silently, each wondering which of them had been cheated. It was magnificent political play-making, but it was not statesmanship.

Lloyd George was even prepared to welcome Germany into the League of Nations within a few months. "Have you forgotten who started the war?" asked Clemenceau with a fierce sarcasm. "It is not for us to ask pardon for our victory."

Britain's first and greatest error was her refusal to guarantee France's security in a concise, unequivocal and adequate form in 1919. After the attempted assassination of Clemenceau by an anarchist the British Premier recognised his mistake and clumsily tried to correct it at the Cannes Conference, a meeting which he largely arranged himself to deal with some of the European problems which the Peace Conference had failed to settle.

The Great Post-War Myth, fathered by Maynard Keynes and twisted and transformed by every pontificating anti-Bolshevik, do-gooder and Francophobe, was that the policy of Nazi Germany was forced upon that country as a result of a long series of betrayals by the Allied Powers.

There is, of course, some excuse for Keynes, whose *Economic Consequences of the Peace* became the economic Bible of the enlightened but incredibly muddled thinkers of the post-war generation. Economically the Versailles Treaty was certainly unsound. But though Germany at the end of the war may have been in a state of moral disintegration and financial chaos, she was not so conscious of the fact that she had been defeated. The war had not been carried deep into the heart of Germany; Berlin, Hamburg, Bremen and Dusseldorf had not been hammered into submission. The people felt cheated by their own rulers, but not beaten by the Allies.

It has been said that the French at this time could not "think straight because of fears amounting to paromania"; in fact, the cooler-headed of the French—Briand and Poincaré among them—took an extremely realistic view of the European situation. Germany's domination of Europe was ended after fifty years of nightmare for France, and this in the French view offered a chance for building up, if not a United Europe, at least a *Pax Gallus*.

"We may be victorious," Poincaré, then Foreign Secretary, told Lloyd George, "but we must stay that way. And how can we stay that way unless the Allies establish a permanent front against Germany and unless we have order and not chaos in Russia? Russia used to be France's ally. Now we have in that country the Bolshevik vacuum, and who shall say that either Germany or the New Russia will not exploit that situation one day?"

Prophetic words, however diehard they may have sounded in 1919. Poincaré was perhaps one of the least charming of Frenchmen, but he had a singularly clear mind and a passion for detail; he never arrived at conclusions without making a detailed analysis of every aspect of the world situation. Yet this was the man whom Lloyd George talked of as "a greedy, grasping, suspicious Frenchman" and to whom he once likened a sour orange—"full of pips, like Poincaré."

* * * * *

"The Peace Conference," said Lloyd George in a rashly confident mood, "will settle the destiny of nations and the course of human life for God knows how many ages."

Yet his approach to European problems was often astonishingly flippant for one who pretended such settlements could last for infinity. In urging the creation of small new states, he practically ensured the eventual break-up of Europe into rival power blocs. A "United States of Europe", which was Briand's ideal, made no appeal to him, nor did a federal system guaranteed by the League of Nations.

To use the word flippant of Lloyd George's approach to these problems may seem hyperbolical, but if ever there was an example of such flippancy carried to the point of zaniness, it was in his scheme for the future of Albania. It was typified by that half-joking cynicism in which he was accustomed, when all else failed, to set about employing the tactics of an estate agent to rebuild the New Europe. For years Albania had been the problem child of the Balkans. Two warring tribes based their hatred of one another on a family feud which had developed into two power blocs, with the Slavs supporting one side and the Italians the other.

The Albanian throne had been vacant ever since Prince William of Wied, who as reigning monarch held the title of the Mpret, found his position untenable and fled to Germany in 1914.

After World War I, the Albanians felt the time had come to restore the monarchy. There was even a suggestion that the title of Mpret should be offered to a wealthy American, Harry Sinclair, the oil magnate and owner of Zec. Meanwhile the Albanian police had been trained by a British officer, Brigadier Charrington, and the activities of the Anglo-Persian Oil Company gave Britain a stake in the country.

Lloyd George discussed Albania with Venizelos who, having appreciated that the British Premier was susceptible to comparisons between foreign countries and areas of the British Isles, casually remarked that "Northern Albania could become the Wales of Serbia, but Southern Albania could become the Cornwall of Greece."

This was just the sort of simple analogy which appealed to Ll. G. and he seized on it with alacrity. Very few people, even in the British Foreign Office, knew much about Albania, but an ex-officer, J. S. Barnes, by spending long hours in the British Museum and elsewhere searching for information on that country, had persuaded the Foreign Office to give him a job in its South-Eastern European Section. Barnes advised Lloyd George on the subject, impressing on him that the two rival groups in Albania were based on a system of society which closely resembled the clan system in Scotland.

"This is a Balkanised version of Scotland," Lloyd George told Curzon. "We must make the country work on a clan basis. What they want is a king and what could be better than a king who has a personal knowledge of the Scottish clan system. I know the very man —Atholl."

"Personally," replied Curzon, "I should rather be the Duke of Atholl than King of Albania."

"The comparison between the two countries is too marked not to take advantage of the fact," retorted Ll. G. "The tribes are just like clans, and those distinguishing patterns of their white wool jackets are on the same principle as tartans."

The Duke of Atholl, who had commanded the Scottish Horse during the war, at first seemed amenable to the idea, but he did not want to be the Mpret, but merely to accept an interim Regency, provided he was granted an adequate civil list. Lloyd George seemed anxious to carve up this territory into spheres of influence as suggested by Venizelos, though there was never a real case for Greece annexing Southern Albania where there were no Greek Christians. The people in the plains were mostly Moslems and the majority of the mountain dwellers were Roman Catholics. But the British Premier hankered after the idea of a British-sponsored "king" and even suggested advertising the post. Whether he was optimistic enough to think there was any prospect of swelling his political funds by the sale of this "kingship" one cannot tell, but it is significant that, through Sir William Sutherland, he called in Maundy Gregory, that bizarre figure who lurked in the shadows of the Coalition Government, and asked him to look for suitable candidates. More than seventy applications for the throne were received, mostly from London and the suburbs.

Maundy Gregory's true place belongs to another chapter and it is unnecessary to digress on him at this stage, but the story of this quest for a "king" is such a fantasy that, if only as an aside on Lloyd George's re-planning of Europe, it deserves the tolerance of a mention. One of the applicants from Streatham stated:

"I am not a country gentleman myself, but I come from country gentleman's stock on my mother's side. I stand six feet two inches in my socks and measure forty-four inches round the chest. I take the greatest interest in the welfare of the working classes. I accordingly believe I would do very well by you."

In the possession of a peer who is still living is a letter from Gregory, dated April 6, 1919. It states: "Dear ——, I am requested to submit to you a proposal of a highly confidential nature. As you are doubtless aware, the future of Albania has for some time been a problem which has occupied a great deal of the Prime Minister's time. He is both anxious that this country should have a monarch and that the links which have been established between Albania and the United Kingdom should be maintained. I am therefore authorised to ask you whether you would kindly consider accepting the dignity of kingship for Albania.

"You will appreciate that it is not possible to go into full details in a letter as this matter is extremely delicate and must remain strictly secret. I should greatly appreciate a chance of meeting you in London during the next week to discuss things.

"I am well known to ——, with whom it is safe to mention this project."

How many people Gregory approached on this subject is not known, but the peer in question emphatically turned down the proposal when he met Gregory. For the price Gregory asked for the kingship of Albania was £250,000!

The first Lord Inchcape was also asked whether he would consider "accepting the dignity of kingship of Albania". There is no indication as to who approached him on the matter, but he wrote to the agent, saying:

"My dear ——, I duly received your letter of the 29th ult. and am sorry I have been so long replying. It is a great compliment to be offered the Crown of Albania, but it is not in my line. Yours sincerely, Inchcape."

Later some Albanians took the initiative in seeking a monarch; this particular group wanted both "an English nobleman and a Moslem". Sir Charles Watkin Hamilton and Lord Headley were approached. Both were of the Moslem faith and Lord Headley was President of the British Moslem Society and had made a pilgrimage to Mecca. Each declined the offer.

Ultimately Zog, who was backed by the Italians, became king. In the spring of 1939, the Italians treacherously turned on him, forced him off the throne and occupied Albania. It is perhaps hardly surprising that at the end of World War II a country which was so cynically treated by Britain, Italy and Greece should accept with apparent zest a Communist régime—an ultra-Communist régime at that.

* * * * *

J. S. Barnes, the Foreign Office official who later became an Italian citizen, gives an illuminating account of the cynicism of the "Big Four" during the peace talks in his book, *Half a Life Left*.

Describing a meeting in Lloyd George's apartment between the British Premier, Clemenceau and Orlando—"lying on their tummies over a large map of Albania"—he wrote: "Lloyd George, with his face in his hands, gave a summary of the plan (for dividing Turkey between the Powers). It was a very bad one. Nicolson (Sir Harold) blinked when he was asked for his advice.

"'Well, sir,' he said at length, 'I don't like it. It is indefensible on the grounds of morality.'

"At these words Lloyd George, then Clemenceau, then Orlando rolled off their tummies on to their backs. There they allowed themselves to be convulsed with laughter, kicking their legs as I have seen babies do.

"'Come, come, Nicolson,' said Lloyd George. 'Can't you give us a better reason than that?'"

13

LLOYD GEORGE AND RUSSIA

"That the sunshine of England is pale,
And the breezes of England are stale,
An' there's something gone small with the lot."
Rudyard Kipling

When the *élan vital* which war creates dissolves in the junketings of peace, there is a natural tendency to seek security above all else.

Thus it was at the end of 1918; war weariness brought with it little inclination to make the building of peace an adventure, and the mood of the country was aptly summed up by Kipling's "English Irregular Discharged".

There was a demand for swift demobilisation that resulted in various petty but ugly mutinies. Horatio Bottomley was sent to Dover to placate the troops when protests were made at the rest camps. At Kinmel Camp in North Wales troops awaiting demobilisation mutinied and five men were killed and twenty-one men and two officers injured in the rioting that ensued. American soldiers fought the police in the Aldwych and outgoing drafts sang the "Red Flag".

Workers' councils talked of "direct action" and opposed the sending of troops to Russia to fight the Bolsheviks. Electrical engineers threatened to plunge the City of London into darkness unless their demands were met. The Police Union balloted in favour of a strike.

"February, 1919," wrote Sir Basil Thomson, "was the high-water mark of revolutionary danger in Great Britain. Everything was in favour of the revolutionaries. Many of the soldiers were impatient at the delay in demobilisation. Russia had shown how apparently easy it was for a determined minority, with a body of discontented soldiers behind them, to seize the reins of power." There were attempts to form the Soldiers' and Workers' Councils on the Soviet model in Britain. Revolutionary leaflets were distributed in the Army, and the Sailors', Soldiers' and Airmen's Union was set up as a revolutionary body in close touch with workers' committees. At the same time Edward Soermus, a Russian violinist, toured the country, attracting to his concerts large numbers of working men and women, most of whom came to hear his revolutionary speeches rather than his music.

A feverish political *malaise* had infected a vast section of the people;

the symptoms were not those of healthy and normal political curiosity about new ideas, but of intoxication with the ideas. The real meaning of Marxist-Leninist philosophy was lost on the masses, but they were excited at the idea that the underdog could seize power. In many industrial centres riots broke out; an attempt was made to seize Glasgow City Hall.

This was the sudden death of Liberal England, and it resulted in a security-searching flight to the left or the right in politics, according to whether people believed there was safety with the Tories, or Utopia with the Socialists. Some Cabinet Ministers were largely responsible for exaggerating the situation and alleging a Bolshevist purpose in this talk of "direct action". The workers, the unemployed and the demobilised Servicemen were conscious of the ostentatious display of wealth around them; in the House of Commons of this period it is said that more champagne was drunk than at any time in its history. The people were disillusioned by the unfulfilled promises of the Coalition Government. As a contemporary book, *Just the Other Day*, summed it up: "Strikes expressed the vanity of the skilled workmen swollen by the flattery of Lloyd George in his wartime appeals for increased production."

Sir Basil Thomson, in his capacity as anti-saboteur chief at Scotland Yard, had to tackle the problem of Bolshevism in Britain and advise the Cabinet on it. Thomson and Lloyd George did not always see eye to eye on how to tackle this menace. Thomson, who by now was one of the most powerful men in Britain, favoured tough measures and demanded wider powers. Lloyd George was anxious to avoid provoking trouble through giving the impression of being "tough" towards the workers.

Early in 1919 the Special Police Branch was formed into a separate organisation under Thomson's control to deal with Bolshevik attempts to spread their doctrines in Britain. Lloyd George, in the early days at least, took singularly little interest in the Bolshevik problem either in Russia or Britain. "Don't worry, Thomson, the drought will end soon and once it rains and drives the people indoors there will be less opportunity for the agitators. Besides, the last thing we want is to let Churchill know that there are Bolshevists in the Police Force. He's already got Reds on the brain and wants to crusade against them all the way from Glasgow to Archangel."

Thomson, like Admiral Hall, brought to this problem of Communist agitation the mentality of the intelligence officer. This was the beginning of a long period in the doldrums for all the British intelligence services. From 1918 onwards the Secret Service tended to become so obsessed with Communism that it grew more pro-German and more anti-Russian, and the whole system was geared to an anti-Bolshevik machine. Thus it tended to collect information that proved Russian intrigues, but to ignore a great deal that pointed to Germany's determination to recover what she had lost.

Yet at the same time it is probably true to say that neither before nor since—not even during the height of Soviet popularity in Britain during the latter part of World War II—was the United Kingdom nearer to becoming indoctrinated with Communism than in 1919.

The Council of the Third International was so confident of the success of its organisation in Britain that it forecast "a revolution in the United Kingdom within six months". In France and Italy the extreme left was expected to seize power even sooner, while it was confidently assumed when the Comintern was founded in March, 1919, that a Communist dictatorship would be set up in Germany. A sardonic note of defiance was struck in Glasgow, where Mr. John MacLean grimly announced that Lenin had appointed him as the first President of the Soviet Republic of Great Britain. Such hollow and unrealistic gestures as these did not help the Communist cause, but it was as much luck as judgment that averted serious trouble, and Basil Thomson maintained to the end of his days that Lloyd George took an appalling risk in hiding from the Cabinet the true facts about Communist infiltration in Britain.

There were, of course, two separate problems—that of Bolshevism in Britain and what Britain's attitude should be to the new Soviet Government. The first problem required greater vigilance than Lloyd George thought necessary, but less prejudice than the Secret Service agencies brought to bear on it. Much of the trouble could have been alleviated if the Government had done something to discourage the flaunting of wealth by the large number of war profiteers.

The second problem was more difficult in that, though quite a distinct issue from the first, the method of tackling it inevitably had repercussions on the influence of Communism in Britain. Lloyd George was at first indifferent to Russia, whether White or Red. Curzon, as Foreign Secretary, was frankly hostile to any idea of a deal with the Bolsheviks; Bonar Law was, as usual, ultra-cautious, disliking any new foreign commitments and inclined to be anti-interventionist, while Churchill was almost tearing at the leash to launch an attack on the Soviet. The language used about the new Russian leaders by the rank and file of the Coalition Government was Blimpish in the extreme. It provoked almost equally extravagant words by their opponents. At the 1918 election Lieut.-Colonel Cecil L'Estrange Malone was elected Liberal Coalition member for East Leyton. He quickly became disillusioned with the conduct of his fellow Coalitionists and in 1920 caused a sensation by supporting the Russian Revolution at a meeting at the Albert Hall. He hoped it would "soon be followed by a British revolution. What are a few Churchills and Curzons on the lampposts compared to the massacre of thousands of human beings?"

Sentenced to six months' imprisonment on a charge of sedition, Malone later joined the Labour Party and sat as M.P. for Northampton from 1928–31. An honest, patriotic, if on the isolated occasion referred to, an indiscreet man, he was sufficiently highly thought of for his services to be accepted in the Royal Navy from 1943–45.

In one sense Lieut.-Colonel Malone was absolutely right; a campaign against Bolshevism involving the loss of thousands of British lives to put back the old Czarist régime would have been an act of madness. Whatever doubts the Russian masses may have had about their new masters, there was no question at all that they detested the old régime and all it stood for. But Lloyd George vacillated between two extremes in his attitude to Russia, tactics, admittedly, largely dictated by the differences of opinion within the Cabinet on how to handle the situation. Thus he increased the mistrust among the Communists as to Britain's real intentions, while leaving her allies, the White Russians, at the mercy of the Bolshevik butchers. Ll. G. had in the early days of the revolution sent a message to the head of the Provisional Government in Petrograd, expressing the "sentiments of profound satisfaction" with which the peoples of Great Britain and the British dominions had "welcomed the adoption by Russia of responsible government", and he went on to describe the revolution as "the greatest service that the Russian people have yet made to the cause for which the Allies are fighting". This in itself was a most ambiguous message, open to a variety of interpretations. Its enthusiasm can only be forgiven by appreciating that then nobody knew that Lenin would shortly take over from Kerensky's liberal-minded government.

Certainly the Kerensky revolution was hailed with such approval in Britain that in Russia there was a disposition to believe that the whole affair had been engineered by British diplomacy. This belief hardened in Czarist circles when it was learned that there was no desire to give the Czar and his family asylum in Britain. It was from the Provisional Government that the first request came that the Imperial Russian family should be removed to Britain. The tale that followed was a sad and not particularly creditable one. At first the British Government issued a formal invitation for the Russian royal family to come to Britain; this invitation was not immediately accepted on the grounds that one of the Czar's children was ill. Then left-wing prejudice against the Czar and his family was whipped up in Britain and, finally, the British Government completely refused to receive the Czar on the grounds that, according to Sir Harold Nicolson, "The presence of the Imperial family in Britain would be exploited to our detriment by the extremists as well as by the German agents in Russia." Shortly afterwards the Czar and his family were murdered by the Bolsheviks in a cellar at Ekaterinburg.

All this was sadly against the best traditions of British sympathy for foreigners desiring asylum. For more than fifty years Britain alone had given sanctuary to scores of revolutionaries from Russia when they were barred in the rest of Europe. Now that same sanctuary was not even to be extended to the head of an Allied country.

It was indeed the moral duty of the Allies to stand by their comrades in arms in Russia, those valiant men who had scorned the Bolshevik surrender to Germany and carried on the fight. It was morally as indefensible to leave these men to their fate as it would have been to force unwilling Free Polish soldiers back to Communist Poland after 1945. Yet, while allowing for this moral duty on the part of the Allies, the majority view of most historians of the period is that the tide of Communism could not then have been held back, that on military and economic grounds aid to the White Russians was never a practical proposition.

One can accept this majority view, but with reservations. Seemingly more impossible tasks have been attempted successfully, and on the grounds of international morality there was a case for Britain doing more than she attempted. At the same time it must be conceded that in the first seven months of 1919 more than £100 million was spent by Britain in aid to the White Russians and that, in making Churchill his War Minister, Lloyd George in the early part of that year came down more positively on the side of the interventionists than against them. It was Churchill who coined the phrase, "the foul baboonery of Bolshevism"; it was Churchill who believed that resolute action by all the Allied powers could defeat the Communist menace.

Czarism had ended; there was never any question of aiding the White Russians to restore the old régime. All that Admiral Kolchak wanted was to destroy the Bolsheviks, to restore Russia to the Western Entente and to give his country a democratic form of government. A stalwart champion in his early forties, Kolchak had, on the outbreak of the revolution, been advised by the Provisional Government to seek refuge in Japan. He was, wrote Churchill, "honest, loyal and incorruptible. His outlook and temperament were autocratic, but he tried hard to be liberal and progressive". It was a fair judgment.

But the White Russians should not be judged on Kolchak alone. Nor on Kornilov, nor Denikin. If there is any doubt as to the new spirit which actuated this "Free Russia", one has only to study the character of Boris Savinkov, who became its accredited head. Savinkov, the life-long revolutionary, the implacable opponent of Czarism. "I am astonished to be working with him," said the Czar's former Foreign Minister, M. de Sazonov, "but he is a man most competent, full of resource and resolution. No one is so good."

Savinkov was in the Nihilist tradition. His whole life had been spent as a revolutionary, plotting against Czarism, using violence and sabotage. He was devoted with impressive single-mindedness to one ideal: the freedom of the Russian people and the creation of a democratic system of government. When Lenin replaced the Czar as the symbol of Russian tyranny, he uncompromisingly and loyally stood by the White Russians and made his terms with them.

To which side, then, could the Allies look for reasonableness and fair-dealing, for co-operation in rebuilding Europe and upholding a genuine League of Nations? From the German-sponsored Soviet Government with its trappings of mass assassinations and police rule, or from the strange combination of ex-Czarist generals and admirals, liberals and revolutionaries, banded together through fate and hardship against the new dictatorship? On moral grounds there is no doubt what the answer ought to have been, but Lloyd George's instinct was to establish relations with the forces of Communism, to gain the ear of their leaders while still playing along with the White Russians. He cared nothing about the moral issue, but saw such relations as a bargaining counter in the game of power politics. Perhaps from the strict standpoint of expediency he was right, for Communism could never have then been overthrown unless all the Allied powers had thrown their weight into the cause and it became increasingly evident that some of them were dragging their feet. There was certainly no hope of a quick victory, and a prolonged war could have created industrial unrest at home. While Lloyd George believed that Basil Thomson exaggerated the Communist threat inside Britain, he never doubted that an unpopular and ineffective war against the Soviet could bring organised labour into a formidable front against him. On the Russian question he was to a marked degree the prisoner of the Tories, and to that extent he had to appear to favour intervention against the Bolsheviks. He may, at times, have shared Churchill's view that intervention could succeed, but his speeches and memoranda show that he was never happy about the outcome of the Russian campaign and he constantly warned Churchill of the terrible cost of aid to White Russia and the danger of believing other Allies would give sufficient additional aid to make intervention worth while: the French, he averred, were biased by the enormous number of small investors who put their money into Russian loans and would like "to see us pull the chestnuts out of the fire for them". It was an accurate assessment in that the French politicians never backed their own military commanders in the Russian campaign when it came to finding more cash and it was amply borne out when Ll. G. asked Clemenceau what aid he was proposing to make to the White Russians and back came the answer "None!"

In his speeches on the Bolshevik régime Ll. G. constantly changed his tune. "It is impossible to make peace with the Bolsheviks because we are committed to Admiral Kolchak and General Denikin," he said at a time when 18,400 British troops were in North Russia.

"Bolshevism is rapidly on the wane," he declared on another occasion. "We cannot interfere and impose any form of government on another people however bad we may consider their present government to be," he stated later on. No one had suggested we should "impose" any government; once order had been restored the White Russians could have handled the situation. Before the Cannes Conference, which he convened largely to straighten out the unsolved problems of Versailles, Ll. G. told Briand: "It would be a very good thing if we could meet the heads of the Russian Government. It might be possible even for Lenin to attend. I am prepared to go anywhere for such a conference."

This was the worst possible manner in which to arrive at any satisfactory solution with any kind of Russian government. The evasions, the switches of policy and the half-heartedness of British strategy in dealing with this situation paved the way to that mistrust of Britain which has lasted more than forty years. Such expediency might possibly be excused by the fact that the French were often equally indeterminate in their policy-making, but there is little doubt that more resolution by Britain would have produced better results in Paris.

Churchill alone had the historic sense to seize on the crux of the whole complicated problem. The new Russia of the Soviets was not a natural upsurge among the people for a liberal régime; it was not the child of Savinkov and other liberal revolutionaries; it was a grotesque, barbaric, hybrid export from Germany. And Churchill saw clearly the danger of Germany and Russia coming together as a new menace to Europe, as they did in 1939. It is wrong to portray the Churchill of this period as an impracticable reactionary; he had intense sympathy with the sufferings of the Russian people and no desire to restore Czarist despotism. Yet his counsels were ignored just as they were in 1934–39.

The mistake of the Secret Service and all its branches, of the Conservative Party and of such politicians as Lothian, Chamberlain and Halifax was that they sought to build up Germany as an ally against Soviet Russia. The mistake of the extreme left-wing was that they saw Soviet Russia as a reliable bulwark against Fascism, dictatorship and extreme Conservatism and an ally of liberal democracy. Had all the Allies wholeheartedly backed the White Russians, these alternative and extreme viewpoints need never have been posed. In the circumstances it was perhaps fortunate that Lloyd George was the prisoner of the Tories in his policy-making towards Russia, for the pro-Soviet line to which he originally leaned would have split Britain and France and Germany and Russia might have drawn closer together, with the ironic result that a German-Soviet Pact might have come about much sooner.

Bolshevik Russia was an ally of militaristic Germany and a political alliance between these two nations was even then her fixed policy. A document found in the files of the German Ministry of Foreign Affairs, now in the custody of the British authorities, reveals the relations between the Imperial German Government and the Russian Bolshevik Party. The message, dated December 3, 1917, was addressed by the Minister of Foreign Affairs, Baron R. von Kühlmann, to an official who was to communicate its contents to the Kaiser. It states:

"The disruption of the Entente and the subsequent creation of political combinations agreeable to us constitute the most important war aim of our diplomacy. Russia appeared to be the weakest link in the enemy's chain. The task was gradually to loosen it and, when possible, remove it.

"This was the purpose of the subversive activity we caused to be carried out in Russia behind the front—in the first place promotion of separatist tendencies and support of the Bolsheviki. It was not until the Bolsheviki had received from us a steady flow of funds through various channels and under varying labels that they were in a position to be able to build up their main organ, *Pravda*, to conduct energetic propaganda. . . .

"The Bolsheviki have now come into power . . . it is entirely in our interest that we should exploit the period while they are in power, in order to attain, firstly an armistice and then, if possible, peace. . . . Once cast off by her former Allies and abandoned financially, Russia will be forced to seek our support.

"We shall be able to provide help for Russia in various ways; firstly in the rehabilitation of the railways; I have in mind a German-Russian Railways Commission—*under our control*—which would undertake the rational and co-ordinated exploitation of the railway lines so as to ensure speedy resumption of freight movement, then the provision of a substantial loan. . . . Austria-Hungary will regard the rapprochement with distrust and not without apprehension."

Here is proof that at no time did the Bolshevik Party adhere strictly to the principles of revolutionary ethics which they professed in common with other Russian revolutionaries. B. V. Nikitine, a counter-espionage agent in the Provisional Government in Petrograd, stated that legal proceedings were started against the Bolshevik leaders on the grounds that Lenin and others were German agents. Later, at the request of the Bolsheviks, the Central Committee of the Soviets set up its own commission for the investigation of the case of Lenin and others. It was only while this commission was leisurely pursuing its inquiries that the view gained ground that the suspicions against Lenin were the basis of a counter-revolutionary plot.

Lloyd George complained afterwards that "Mr. Churchill very adroitly seized the opportunity created by the absence of President

Wilson and myself to go over to Paris and urge his plans (armed intervention against the Bolsheviks) with regard to Russia upon the consideration of the French". Ll. G. told Lord Riddell that this would "cause a revolution in Britain".

From Churchill alone did the French military experts who wanted to carry out a punitive war against the Soviets get any real backing inside the British Government. To Churchill went a telegram from Ll. G. saying: "Am very alarmed at your second telegram about planning war against the Bolsheviks. The Cabinet have never authorised such a proposal."

Churchill's retort was that Lloyd George had himself admitted Britain was at war with the Bolsheviks. Bonar Law and Balfour were frightened of intervention on anything like a big scale. These two men, like a majority of the Tories after the cost of the war had dawned on them, were far more afraid of the bogy of Bolshevism inside Britain than in Russia. Lloyd George swiftly realised that the Tory mood was changing and decided to remain personally uncommitted as far as possible: he neither killed the plan to help Admiral Kolchak, put forward in January, 1919, nor gave it any worth-while support. He procrastinated, doubtless waiting to see how Kolchak got on.

From this point onwards it is difficult to criticise the Prime Minister's handling of a situation in which he had little room to manœuvre. If he had been the prisoner of the Tories when they were baying for Bolshevik blood, he was equally now hampered by the canniness of Bonar Law and the reluctance of Balfour, not to mention the failure of the French effectively to implement their military experts' proposals. Intervention had been too slow, too small and too ambiguously offered to give the White Russians any real chance.

In March, 1919, Churchill wrote to the Prime Minister, saying: "The four months which have passed since the Armistice was signed have been disastrous almost without relief for the anti-Bolshevik forces. This is not due to any great increase in the Bolshevik strength, though there has been a certain augmentation. It is due to the lack of any policy on the part of our Allies, or of any genuine or effective support put into the operations which are going on against the Bolsheviks at different points of Russia."

Whether the French, with their frequently changing Governments, were as willing to provide the policy Churchill wanted is open to some doubt, but the fact remains that they mistrusted Lloyd George and suspected him of being anti-interventionist at heart.

By June, 1919, some further aid to Kolchak in the form of munitions, supplies and food was promised. "If this far-reaching and openly proclaimed decision (he was referring to the Allied promise to help Kolchak and his forces establish themselves as the Government of Russia) was wise in June, would it not have been wiser in January?"

wrote Churchill in his *World Crisis*. "No arguments existed in June not obvious in January, and half the power available in January was gone by June. Six months of degeneration and uncertainty had chilled the Siberian armies and wasted the slender authority of the Omsk Government. . . . The moment chosen by the Supreme Council for their declaration was almost exactly the moment when that declaration was certainly too late."

This delay settled matters; by July, Kolchak was in full retreat. The Bolsheviks pressed remorselessly on, setting up their dictatorships in each village, pillaging, killing and replacing the Cheka by the O.G.P.U.

Churchill did not, as has often been suggested, consort with the reactionary forces of Czarism; in Paris he met Savinkov, the former anarchist, knowing that, whatever the stormy past of this revolutionary, he had always been loyal to the Allied cause and an inveterate enemy of German militarism. Savinkov had fought valiantly, he had produced armies on Polish soil without equipment or funds. When resistance inside Russia seemed doomed, he organised guerrillas all over Soviet territory.

Shortly before the collapse of the White Russians, Churchill brought Savinkov to Chequers to meet Lloyd George. It was a last effort, a desperate bid to make the Premier see the perils ahead. In *Great Contemporaries*, Churchill described what took place at Chequers. ". . . We had our talk. I recall only one of its episodes. The Prime Minister argued that revolutions like disease run a regular course, that the worst was already over in Russia, that the Bolshevik leaders, confronted with the responsibilities of actual government, would quit their Communistic theories or that they would quarrel among themselves and fall like Robespierre and St. Just, that others weaker or more moderate would succeed them and that by successive convulsions a more tolerable régime would be established.

"'Mr. Prime Minister,' said Savinkov in his formal way. 'You will permit me the honour of observing that after the fall of the Roman Empire there ensued the Dark Ages.'"

* * * * *

At Cannes Lloyd George sought to placate the bloodthirsty tyrants of the Bolshevik Revolution. Aristide Briand was now the French Premier; he and Ll. G. had much in common, and for a very brief period it seemed that Lloyd George might get along better with the French. This, however, soon proved to be an illusion, as it became apparent at Cannes that Lloyd George's aim was to keep Briand away from the conference atmosphere as much as possible and to prevent him from being influenced by anyone else. To carry this out Ll. G. conceived the idea of inviting Briand, Bonomi, the Italian,

Riddell, Bonar Law and Edward Grigg to play golf with him and to continue the talks on the links. But neither Briand nor Bonomi knew anything about the game which developed into sheer buffoonery. Lloyd George had tipped off a photographer to take a picture of a British Prime Minister teaching golf to the French and Italians. It has been said that when the French Press published these pictures it meant the end of Briand's premiership. The truth was that the French military intelligence reported back to Paris that Ll. G. was plotting to appease the Bolsheviks at the expense of France. The report was highly coloured, exaggerated and inaccurate in many details, but it was sufficient to cause the defeat of Briand in the National Assembly and the accession of Poincaré to the premiership.

In 1919 world revolution had seemed a matter of months and early in 1920 a question of weeks. But the triumphant progress of the Communists was halted in August, 1920, when the Red Army collapsed before Warsaw, and subsequently the invaders were driven back on to Russian soil and Poland, thanks to aid from France, compelled the Russians to sign a peace treaty of advantageous terms to the Poles. "Now," said Trotsky, "world revolution is perhaps a question of years."

Meanwhile, the trade union movement in Britain was angered by the renaissance of what they, not inaccurately, regarded as a military junta in Poland. All sections of the trade union movement combined to form a Council of Action to watch developments in this sphere of operation and on August 10, 1920, a deputation of seventeen leaders went to see Lloyd George.

Mr. Trevor Evans writes in his biography of Ernest Bevin that "Bevin bluntly told Lloyd George that the resolution of the conference which had sent them there was not merely one in opposition to direct military action—the use of soldiers and sailors in actual fighting—but it was a declaration in opposition to an indirect war, either by blockade, or by the supplying of munitions, or by assisting the forces that were now at war against Russia. 'The resolution,' Bevin added, 'expressed the feeling of the overwhelming majority of six million trade unionists in the country.'"

Lloyd George asked whether this meant that, if the independence of Poland was really menaced, and if Bolshevist Russia did for Poland what their Czarist predecessors did a century and a half before, that "we cannot send a single pair of boots there, otherwise Labour will strike".

It was a strong point, but Bevin insisted that the independence of Poland was not at stake.

By this time organised labour was bent on sabotaging any aid to Poland, and when dockers refused to load the *Jolly Roger* in London docks, a general strike seemed a possibility. The Government appeared to condone this threat: no real effort was made to appeal to the public against what was undoubtedly an act of sabotage against the state. Gradually the Russians, though defeated by the Poles, stabilised their relations with Britain. Lloyd George was determined not to have industrial trouble on his hands, and an important trade agreement was reached between the Soviets and the British Government, carrying with it *de facto* recognition and diplomatic relations. Meanwhile Ll. G. spent his time preaching to the French that the "Bolsheviks are not so bad. They are learning to be good Europeans". Another attempt at reconciliation at the Genoa Conference was ruined by the news that Dr. Rathenau of Germany and the Russian delegate, M. Chicherin, had signed a separate and secret agreement, by which they accorded each other *de jure* recognition and renounced reparations. Thus the Germans gave full warning of their future intentions: the ill-fated Weimar Republic, no less than Hitler and von Paulus afterwards, was prepared to make a deal with the Devil, if it would further Germany's own interests.

Yet the next moment Lloyd George would be off at a tangent again, talking of the "menace of Bolshevism" and the need to save Germany from it. He openly insulted M. Klotz, the French Minister of Finance, by mocking at his Jewish looks and calling him, "Shylock with the money bags, who won't send food or gold to Germany to save them from starving." This was a sudden change of front, for Ll. G. had deliberately ignored warnings from his own generals in Germany that food must be sent to avert public disorder.

A few months after the trade agreement was signed between Britain and the Soviets it was reported that the Russians were directing policy in Britain through the *Daily Herald* and supporting it by subsidies. On September 10, 1920, the *Herald* asked its readers: "Shall we take £75,000 of Russian money?" then, a few days later, decided not to accept the offer.

Lloyd George said Lev Kamenev, the visiting Russian trade commissar, had broken an undertaking not to engage in propaganda while in Britain. Kamenev, he said, had "taken steps to subsidise a newspaper sowing strife between classes. . . . I have no hesitation in saying that this is a gross breach of faith . . . the Soviet Government . . . have sent an emissary here under an obligation not to interfere in our internal affairs and they have instructed that agent to break his word. It is quite impossible to have dealings with a Government until at any rate it can conform to the ordinary obligations of honour which are applicable to dealings between nations and individuals. If Mr. Kamenev had not been leaving tomorrow, it would have been our business to ask him to leave."

Bolshevik Communism was a Teutonic product, patented by Marx and Engels and brought to fruition by Lenin as a German agent. The aim of the New Russia was to make Germany and Russia into one vast Soviet Empire. Indeed it is worth recording for the benefit of those dishonest intellectuals of the left-wing who are only interested in facts when they fit their theories, that Moscow was only intended by the Comintern as a temporary headquarters of the revolution. When suspicious delegates from Asia and Central Europe talked of shifting the centre from Moscow, they were told by a Soviet delegation: "We are only waiting to move into Soviet Berlin."

It will, perhaps, always remain an enigma as to what would have been the best course for the Allies to have adopted towards Russia in 1919. The possibility, which to the fainthearts was always a probability, was that armed intervention on a large scale would have failed and paved the way to further revolutions, yet surely what happened in Poland, when there was resolute action, is to some extent the answer to such a theory. On the other hand a massive victory for the White Russians might have led ultimately to a less progressive régime than Churchill believed possible. Even that, however, might have been better than the first thirty-five years of Communist tyranny. But it must be admitted that, in face of the conflicting interests of the time and the fluctuations in the ebb and flow of Communism, Lloyd George had a difficult path to tread. Where Churchill would have courageously, if rashly, secured a mandate for firm action against the Soviets, Lloyd George, by instinct, chose a more devious route. Britain lost her rôle as a leader of world opinion by this cautious expediency. Churchill's backing of full intervention, however powerful morally, was not enough to thwart the lethargy of Law and Balfour. Law was always insular in his outlook, and a restraining influence on all foreign adventures into which Britain might be tempted. Teeth for the League of Nations could have killed the Bolshevik despotism and created a genuine international army to keep the peace. That was the one way out, the only method of intervention which might have overcome the prejudices of trade unionists and Socialists. Instead the Bolsheviks were allowed to consolidate and turn the whole of Russia into a vacuum of sealed-off and spiritually starved humanity, utterly isolated from any European influences.

14

COERCION FROM DOWNING STREET

"God has chosen little nations as the vessels by which he carries His choicest wines to the lips of humanity to rejoice their hearts, to exalt their vision, to stimulate and strengthen their faith."

David Lloyd George

Not the least of Lloyd George's feats of political acrobatics was his somersault on the Irish question between 1910 and 1919. The young man who had backed Home Rule for Ireland because he hoped to win Irish support for a similar measure for Wales swiftly, ruthlessly and pitilessly turned on the Irish nation with a savagery and venom unparalleled since the days of that other dictator of Welsh descent, Oliver Cromwell.

But to those who knew him well, it was no surprise, especially, as we have seen, in that he regarded Irish Home Rule as being largely the prerogative of the Catholics. Lloyd George could speak lovingly of "God's chosen little nations" when it suited him, but, as any intelligent Belgian must have known, it all depended upon the circumstances of the hour. As Dr. Thomas Jones has said, he "Never was, as Gladstone was, a crusader for Home Rule".

The American Ambassador in London, Dr. Walter Page, warned the Prime Minister that if the Government did not find a solution for the Irish problem, it would have serious repercussions in America, where Irish-American opinion was extremely vocal. "If you fail in Ireland, then the American people will regard the League of Nations as an instrument of hypocrisy and power politics," said Page.

In April, 1918, in a moment of panic after the German push into France, Lloyd George had extended conscription to Ireland: "One of the most foolish experiments ever attempted in that country," declared Lord Middleton. King George V, with far more foresight than his ministers, pleaded with Ll. G. that, whatever the generals or politicians might say, "Conscription in Ireland was bound to have the direst consequences in the near future. It could mean the end of Ireland as part of the British Empire."

Until this moment the Coalition Government had had loyal backing in the prosecution of the war from the Irish Nationalists, except for a handful of extremists. When, quite naturally, they opposed conscription, Lloyd George quarrelled with them. No Coalition "coupon" was given to any Nationalist candidate in the 1918 election and the Sinn Feiners captured 73 seats, ousting the Nationalists from constituencies which had long been theirs traditionally. The Sinn Feiners were for an absolute and sovereign Irish Republic and refused to take their seats at Westminster.

Conscription in Ireland was a dismal failure, as the King had prophesied. After two months the experiment had to be abandoned. This confession of blundering by the Government encouraged the Sinn Feiners to organise a conspiracy against law and order. They knew that if the Nationalists, by constitutional methods and co-operation in the war effort, could not influence the Government to grant Home Rule, only open revolt would obtain results.

So, as peace came in Europe, civil war and bloodshed spread across Ireland. There was open guerrilla warfare between the Irish Republican Army, organised by Sinn Fein, and the police, or Royal Irish Constabulary. Arthur Griffith, dour and taciturn and a student of the tactics of European nationalist movements, saw Sinn Fein as a means of establishing an alternative government.

So he set up a judicature, a "police force" and a system of Parliamentary revenue. In its origins Sinn Fein ("For ourselves alone") was devoted to the principles of passive resistance, but when Lloyd George proscribed the Dail these methods were discarded in favour of violence.

Neither the R.I.C. nor the troops poured in from Britain proved to have a satisfactory answer to this revolt. A wag painted on a wall in Dublin, "Join the R.I.C. and see the next world." The constant fear of seeing that other world by the agency of a stray bullet caused many members of the R.I.C. to resign. They preferred to lose their pensions, not their lives.

Frank Ryan, one of the I.R.A. leaders who later broke away from the terrorists, told the author in 1936, shortly after De Valera had proscribed the I.R.A., that "we had an agent in Ian Macpherson's[1] office who secured for us a verbatim account of what Macpherson told Basil Thomson about Lloyd George's desire for a new drive against the I.R.A. It was because of this report that the Sinn Fein launched the terrorist campaign before the Black-and-Tans got going."

This report cannot be regarded as conclusive evidence with which to indict the British Government, but as it supports the view that the excesses of the Black-and-Tans were sponsored by that Government, it may usefully be quoted. Ryan claimed that Ll. G. had told Macpherson: "We have got to meet terrorism with terrorism. The military are far too mealy-mouthed and soft for this sort of job. There must be immediate recruitment in London of a new police force that is

[1] Minister responsible for Irish affairs.

tough and not squeamish, and it would be a good plan if we introduced into its numbers some ex-officers who have a reputation for toughness. We do not want ex-Regulars, but men who can be relied upon to apply unorthodox tactics. Doubtless Basil Thomson can recommend some of his men who can wage war without looking too closely at the rule book."

Ian Macpherson resigned in April, 1920, and was succeeded by the tough and ruthless Sir Hamar Greenwood. In 1936 Greenwood (then Lord Greenwood) declined to make any comment on Ryan's statement, but Sir Basil Thomson and General Crozier both concurred that it represented the general idea of Lloyd George's instructions. Sir Basil even claimed to know who was the agent of the I.R.A. in Macpherson's office. "The whole affair got out of hand," he added. "I was prevented from having any real control over the recruitment in the way I wished. It would have saved many lives, if, instead of a force of thugs, a disciplined counter-espionage unit had been organised and moved to Dublin. That was what Macpherson wanted and one reason why he was forced to resign."

Nicknamed the Black-and-Tans because of their black tunics and caps and khaki trousers, the auxiliary force were paid £1 a day (good money in 1919). The majority of them were not police, but the scum of the Army, ex-officers with bad reputations who had been punished for brutality and lack of discipline, men with convictions for assault, loot and rape, even men awaiting trial were freed from jail to join the new force.

If such a state of affairs sounds incredible under a modern British Government, here is confirmation from a source that is undeniably sober and unlikely to be coloured by emotion or prejudice. The late Lord Simon (then Sir John Simon) wrote in his memoirs: "The continuing failure of the Government to put down insurrection had led them to form and arm an auxiliary force which was so imperfectly disciplined that its members were carrying on, by way of reprisal, nothing less than a competition with the Sinn Feiners. Time and again these auxiliaries matched some specific outrage by indiscriminate vengeance, setting fire to a whole village, or to a row of buildings without any ground for thinking that the victims had anything to do with the guilty parties. They indulged not infrequently in shootings which had no object but to terrorise the countryside. . . . It became clear that shocking things were being done by Crown servants in a desperate attempt to force the Irish into subjection, and that, to say the least of it, they were winked at by their superiors."

Asquith, who won a by-election at Paisley in 1920, boldly declared that the solution of the Irish problem must be found in complete "Dominion Home Rule". What was the reply of the former Home Ruler, Lloyd George, to this statesmanlike proposal? It was, in effect, contained in one word: "lunacy". "The idea of complete Home Rule for Ireland was ridiculous," replied Lloyd George. "If they decided to have conscription there, why, you would have to have it here. And what about submarines? And mines? Our ports in Ireland were the sea gateway of Great Britain. Complete Home Rule? Was there ever such lunacy proposed by anybody!"

In a speech at Caernarvon the Prime Minister jeered that Asquith had given "a bone to the dog that bit him in the leg and chased him out of Downing Street", an oblique reference to the fact that Asquith had written a letter on the subject to Lord Northcliffe's *The Times*. Ll. G. defended the policy of reprisals as "the necessary way of dealing with Irish murder".

For once the mild-mannered Asquith hit back with a speech that must go on record as one of his most forthright and angriest utterances. "On the tone and taste of the Prime Minister's latest speech I don't think it worth while to dwell, but all its flippancies and vulgarities have not diverted, and cannot divert, attention from the outstanding fact that it is a naked confession of political bankruptcy. Mr. Lloyd George says that you cannot have a one-sided war. The vast majority of the cases are in no sense acts of self-defence. They are acts of blind and indiscriminate vengeance. In not a few instances these so-called reprisals were deliberately aimed at the destruction of local industries. The policy of the Government can only fitly be described as a policy of despair."

With Edward Carson, the cosh-boy of the Tory Party on his side, Lloyd George felt he could win over the right-wing from the intrigues of the party's "cabin-boy", as Lord Birkenhead later designated Sir George Younger. But he must have been uneasy at the shock to public opinion which the activities of the Black-and-Tans caused. A "Peace with Ireland Council" was formed and Dr. Garbett (later Archbishop of York) and G. K. Chesterton spoke at a protest meeting against the conduct of the auxiliaries.

Not even the Germans in Belgium perpetrated such outrages on a civilian population as the Black-and-Tans in this darkest and starkest chapter of British imperialism. Armed with revolvers, they entered private houses, stripped the women and raped them. It was claimed that the Irish women were in the habit of hiding their menfolk's guns inside their dresses, but how this excused rape is less easy to understand. The auxiliaries were a shameless, befuddled and lawless band who smashed up shops, looted and in some cases destroyed whole hamlets. In a Dublin suburb they stripped all the women in one street and paraded them in their nakedness to a communal wash-house, where they were locked up and left for some hours before their clothes were returned to them.

Near Bandon, County Cork, auxiliaries murdered a priest and a boy who was walking with him. A British officer, a Captain Prendergast, who had praised the behaviour of Irish soldiers during the war, was manhandled by Black-and-Tans, frogmarched to the River Blackwater, thrown in and drowned. Nobody was punished. Arson and looting were systematic tactics: in one session at Clare County Court the judge (a Crown official, be it noted) awarded compensation amounting to £187,046 19*s*. 6*d*. for damage to property committed by British forces. But, to add insult to injury, this sum was only recovered by making it a charge on the rates.

Naturally the Irish rebels hit back and ambushed British soldiers and police. Atrocity was matched by atrocity. Martial law was proclaimed and in Dublin there was a curfew. When the I.R.A. shot a policeman outside Cork, auxiliaries with masked faces and disguised as Sinn Feiners broke into the house of the Lord Mayor, Thomas McCurtain, and shot him dead—simply and solely as a reprisal. He had nothing whatever to do with the shooting of the policeman.

Brigadier-General Frank Crozier, in recalling his experiences of the Auxiliary Royal Irish Constabulary, of which he was commandant, stated in a book he wrote afterwards (*Ireland For Ever*): "In 1920 and 1921 the whole Cabinet should have been marched to the Tower in company with the Chief of Imperial General Staff (Sir Henry Wilson) and there shot, on account of what they permitted to be done in the King's name and by the authority of his uniform in Ireland."

But the signal for ferocity which would match that of the Black-and-Tans came when Michael Collins was tipped off by one of his agents that Field-Marshal Wilson had instituted a policy of "shooting by roster" in Ireland. Collins, the most fascinating and romantic figure in the I.R.A. movement, was Director of Intelligence for the Sinn Feiners. With a price of £10,000 on his head, this cheerful, disarmingly charming character, without any attempt at disguise, bicycled all over Dublin to keep his appointments with fellow agents, often calling in at public houses to have a drink right under the noses of the police. Behind his mask of nonchalance he hid an implacable purpose. When he received this tip he called a meeting at a secret hide-out in the Dublin suburb of Clontarf. But what finally convinced Collins that terror must be met by even bloodier terror was that in September, 1920, when a Black-and-Tan had been shot dead in a tavern argument at Balbriggan, lorry-loads of auxiliaries were rushed to the small town to "beat it up". The Black-and-Tans fired through the windows of houses as they drove through the town. They placed lorries, armed with machine-guns, at strategic points around Balbriggan and set about destroying the place. Furniture was burnt or flung into the streets, shops were looted and fired, men, women and children were dragged from their beds, thrown into the street and in some instances bayoneted. Families, left homeless, who escaped the cordon of lorries, fled into the open country to sleep in woods and ditches.

This incident led directly to "Bloody Sunday" on November 21, 1920. On Collins's instructions immediate reprisals on British officers were ordered to be carried out. Fourteen officers were murdered in their billets that Sunday morning, some in the presence of their wives and children. It was an outrage that shocked both nations. That afternoon British troops and Black-and-Tans drove up to Croke Park, Dublin, where a football match was taking place, ostensibly to search for arms among the crowd. A saner precaution would have been to cancel the match rather than risk the inevitable disorder which this clumsy search was bound to entail. But authority seemed bent on being provocative, and the Black-and-Tans mounted the fences round the ground, opened fire on the vast crowd, killing twelve, wounding nearly a hundred people, while hundreds more were badly injured in the riot that followed.

General Crozier later accused Sir Henry Wilson of organising a murder gang in Dublin and asserted that the British officers who were killed in their billets were "commissioned assassins" with a bad record of arson and murder. Three distinct bodies were operating on behalf of the British Government in Ireland at that time—the Army, the Black-and-Tans and a Secret Service force which was reputedly independent of Dublin Castle H.Q., and responsible to someone in London. Bowen, a former officer with a distinguished war record, who was one of these Secret Service agents, had become disgusted with the tactics of his colleagues. According to General Crozier, he "foolishly told his superior he would cross to England and tell David Davies, the influential Welshman, about the irregular way the Service was being run. . . . He was threatened he would be put away."

Sometime later a dead body was pulled out of the Liffey; it was identified as that of Bowen.

Early in 1921 Brigadier-General Crozier resigned from his post as Commandant of the Auxiliary Division of the R.I.C. as a result of a disagreement with General Tudor, Chief of Police, over the dismissal of twenty-six cadets.

General Tudor sent a long telegram to Sir Hamar Greenwood on this subject which was read in the House of Commons as "a satisfactory explanation of the whole affair". Crozier suggested that the telegram had been written in order "to produce a false impression". General Tudor claimed in the telegram that on receipt of a complaint that a party of the Auxiliary Division had been guilty of looting, he had directed that the Commandant should make an immediate inquiry. Crozier said this was untrue: "I received no directions and acted entirely off my own bat."

The telegram said that on arrival in England the cadets protested to the Chief of Police at the Irish Office that they had been dismissed without trial. But they were not "dismissed without trial" for looting or any other offence. Their services were dispensed with "for failing to answer questions and give evidence as policemen". On his return to Dublin, General Tudor directed that the dismissed cadets be recalled without prejudice to any future disciplinary action if found guilty. This was the purest humbug, because there was no question of the cadets being tried.

But Brigadier-General Crozier had in his possession a letter from General Tudor which completely contradicted all the implications of the telegram read in the House of Commons. This stated:

"Dear Crozier, I think it will be best for you to keep these T/C.s suspended until I come back. I want to discuss it with the Chief Secretary. He gets all the bother. My main point is that it is an unfortunate time to do anything that looks panicky. I think also these T/C.s will have a distinct grievance if the platoon commanders and section leaders are acquitted. Tell them that they are suspended, pending my return, or, if you prefer it, keep them back by not completing their accounts till I come back."

This letter is surely unequalled in the annals of modern military and police administration. The men were in effect to be detained by withholding their pay. This affair can be summed up as follows: General Tudor had urged General Crozier on the telephone to reconsider his decision about the cadets; Crozier refused and Tudor's letter to Crozier followed by the Irish mail-boat twenty-four hours later. What caused General Tudor to reverse his decision? The letter would seem to imply that the order came from high up. Crozier believed that it was on the joint instructions of Lloyd George and Hamar Greenwood: it was for this reason that he resigned his post in disgust.

By the summer of 1921 it was clear that the Government must either end the policy of reprisals and seek a negotiated peace with Ireland, or send more troops and subdue the country by force. In *The World Crisis* Winston Churchill gave the lie to any suggestion that Ll. G. was the prisoner of the Tories in his Irish policy by stating that the Prime Minister was "markedly disposed to fight it out at all costs". For days the Premier toyed with the idea of sending a vast force to Ireland to "crush murder for all time". He thought an additional 60,000 troops would "do the trick", as though the Irish question was a game of cards and not a serious problem in human relationships. Appealing to the military for their view of how many men would be required, he was told, "At least 100,000, and the task will take at least two years."

It was an appalling thought. After the "war to end wars" were 100,000 British citizens to be poured into a conflict which was directed not at the British people, but at the politicians who by neglect, treachery, betrayal and incompetence had made a civil war inevitable? Lloyd George told Hamar Greenwood that he was "prepared to take the risk". Greenwood agreed to send secret instructions to unofficial agents in Ireland to organise the seizure of I.R.A. sectional leaders in Dublin, Cork and other centres.

Then, suddenly, when the die seemed to have been cast for increased bloodshed, Lloyd George changed his mind again. Negotiations with the Irish began, secretly at first and then by an open proposal by the Premier for a conference with the rebel leaders. Thus Asquith's plan for "Dominion Home Rule for Ireland", which Lloyd George had condemned as "lunacy", was in the end adopted as the one possible way out of the dilemma.

What brought about the change of front? In August, 1921, the British people read the following sensational headlines quoted from the *New York Times*:

"IRISH PEACE OFFER ORDERED BY KING
Told Premier, Editor says, 'I cannot have my people killed in this manner.'"

Mr. Wickham Steed, then editor of *The Times*, had gone to New York with Lord Northcliffe and, while there, had agreed to make a "personal statement" on the critical Irish situation to the *New York Times*. Having received authority from Lord Northcliffe, he was alleged to have dictated a statement giving an account of differences between King George and Lloyd George.

"Are you going to shoot all the people in Ireland?" the King was said to have asked.

"No," replied the Prime Minister.

"Then you must come to some agreement with them. I cannot have my people killed in this manner."

The statement was given as coming from Northcliffe. It was published in the *New York Times* and reached the office of the London *Times* for publication under Lord Northcliffe's name. In spite of this it was suppressed, but the Irish edition of the *Daily Mail* published the story as an interview with Lord Northcliffe and not with Steed.

According to Steed, "In what must have been a moment of mental aberration, Northcliffe had told Bullock's assistant in New York to cable to London, as having been said by him, everything published in his name or in mine." On learning what a sensation it made in London, Northcliffe disowned the story in a cable to the King. But both he and Steed were belated in denying the interview. How was it that neither of them took any steps to make a correction between the Monday, when the interview was published, and the Friday, when it was denounced in the House of Commons? By that time the story had worked effectively against Lloyd George and the tardy denial mattered little one way or another.

But the main questions are: were such statements made by the King to Lloyd George and, if so, were they passed on to the *New York Times* by Wickham Steed? Steed admitted that "I chatted informally with the reporter as I might have chatted with any honourable journalist. I said nothing of a conversation between King George V and the Prime Minister for the simple reason that I had never heard of it."

That seems categorical enough. But the "rectification"—Steed's own word—which the *New York Times* gave told a different story. It stated: "The interview with Mr. Wickham Steed published in *The Times* was written by a trustworthy reporter who believes he reported accurately what Steed said. Steed has since told *The Times* it contained matter that should not have been published. Steed did not have an opportunity to revise the interview. As re-printed in England it appears the interview was incorrectly attributed to Lord Northcliffe himself. Northcliffe has not given, nor has *The Times* reported him as giving, any statement of a purported conversation between the King and Lloyd George."

There is no denial that Steed told this story. Therefore was the interview "bogus" as *The History of the Times* suggests? Steed claimed that neither he nor Northcliffe heard anything of the sequel to the "interview" until "the following Friday in Washington". This seems hard to believe, for Northcliffe kept in the closest possible touch by telephone, radio and cable with his London staffs: it is impossible to accept the suggestion that so keen a newspaperman as Northcliffe would fail to realise that this story would create a first-class political sensation.

Steed's last words on this affair, published in a letter to the *Evening Standard* of London on June 20, 1952, are as follows: "It transpires that a telegram from Paris to an American news agency mentioned an acrimonious conversation between the King and Lloyd George shortly before I reached New York, and the reporter saddled me with this story, though his paper had not published the telegram."

The King was displeased with Lloyd George's Irish policy and held strong views on the subject. The previous month Lord Stamfordham, the King's Secretary, had written to Hamar Greenwood: "The King does ask himself, and he asks you, if this policy of reprisals is to be continued and, if so, where it will lead Ireland and us all? It seems to His Majesty that in punishing the guilty we are inflicting punishment no less severe upon the innocent."

Did someone in Buckingham Palace deliberately leak the information that the King had spoken on these lines to Lloyd George? If so, was this done with the King's authority? Mr. A. M. Murray, at this time correspondent for the *New York World* in Paris, assured the author that "the information about the King's argument with Lloyd George was passed through top-secret diplomatic channels from London and released in Paris so that it should not seem to have come from London."

The publication of the story in the *New York Times* not only worried Lloyd George, but had had an effect on those leaders of the Tory Party who were diehards on the Irish question. There was an uneasy feeling in their minds that the King might have said something of the sort to Ll. G. It was even whispered that Lord Stamfordham and Curzon had plotted this between them and that Curzon had revelled in the change of revenging himself of Ll. G. for the latter's interference at the Foreign Office.

Terrorism on the Irish side had been stepped up. Cathal Brugha, Sinn Fein Defence Minister, had ordered reprisals in England. Warehouses were destroyed in Liverpool, and Field-Marshal Wilson was assassinated in London. In desperation Lloyd George used his Secret Service agents to seek out I.R.A. leaders for a basis for negotiation. Sir Alfred Cope, Assistant Under-Secretary for Ireland, was the Prime Minister's secret intermediary with the Sinn Feiners. Ll. G. exchanged letters and telegrams with De Valera. Meanwhile the King had shown great personal courage in insisting on going to Belfast to open the first Parliament of Northern Ireland. "The eyes of the whole Empire are on Ireland today," said the King. "I speak from a full heart when I pray that my coming to Ireland today may prove to be the first step towards the end of strife amongst my people. . . . I appeal to all Irishmen to pause, to stretch out the hand of forbearance and conciliation, to forgive and forget, and to join in making for the land they love a new era of peace, contentment and goodwill."

From that moment the Prime Minister speeded up his negotiations with De Valera. Even so, he handled this difficult man with incredibly bad judgment, trying first to charm, then to bully. It was not until the end of September that De Valera at last agreed to send delegates to London "to explore every possibility of settlement". Still not trusting the British Government, De Valera, who had escaped once from Lincoln Prison, did not intend to risk capture again. He remained in Dublin. The Irish delegation included such contrasting types as the gloomy Arthur Griffith, the volatile and voluable Michael Collins and Erskine Childers, an ex-public schoolboy and former British officer.

The talks dragged on and failure seemed inevitable until on December 5, 1921, according to Dr. Thomas Jones, "Lloyd George awoke at five and in less than twenty-four hours he had completely transformed the situation and had shaken hands with the Irish delegates over a signed peace treaty which Griffith later declared should end the conflict of centuries."

In fact much of the credit for this agreement must go to Dr. Jones himself. He it was who saw and coaxed Michael Collins, who only the previous day had declined to go to Downing Street. It was Dr. Jones who gave Collins new assurances about the Boundary Commission which would meet the point of view of the Southern Irish. But it was touch and go right up to the moment when the pens were put to paper. Thomas Jones's proposal to delimit the frontier line between North and South Ireland in accordance with the wishes of the inhabitants certainly swayed the delegates: it meant the gain of the best part of two and a great deal of three other counties to the South. On the other hand Collins maintained that Lloyd George's threat to resign if agreement were not arrived at decided the issue. At two o'clock the following morning the Irish Treaty was signed in the Cabinet Room.

For Lloyd George the Treaty meant a brief triumph. For the Irishmen it was, as Collins had said, "signing our own death warrant". Griffith died at St. Vincent's Hospital, Dublin, from a cerebral haemorrhage, Erskine Childers and Collins were shot. Duffy alone escaped by fleeing to Rome. To the fanatics of the I.R.A. the signing of the Treaty was an act of betrayal. De Valera, who had wisely kept out of the talks, immediately denounced the Treaty as such, even though a small majority of the Dail accepted it.

The break-up of the British Empire, as the King had anticipated, dated from the era of repression: the signing of the Irish Treaty merely confirmed the trend. But after this orgy of coercion and terrorism Britain could hardly fail to suffer a serious loss in moral prestige within the Empire and Commonwealth. The Tories in 1921 were as blind to realities as they had been in opposition when they did their utmost to obstruct Liberal proposals for Home Rule which would have left Ireland an indisputable part of the Empire. They still believed that the settlement of 1921 would keep Eire within the Empire. Lloyd George cunningly concealed from them the full implications of the Irish Treaty. This laid down that the Irish Free State "shall have the same constitution and status in the Commonwealth of Nations and Empire as the dominion of Canada. . . ." But, when challenged, Lloyd George refrained from answering the question, "What does dominion status mean?" He preferred, he said, to speak of the dangers of definition and rigidity in these matters.

This was, of course, mere evasion of a vital issue. A different and more statesmanlike view was taken by General Smuts, who urged the Governments of the Commonwealth that: ". . . Unless dominion status was quickly solved in a way that would satisfy the aspirations of these young nations, separatist movements were to be expected in the Commonwealth. . . . The only way to meet such movements is . . . to anticipate them and make them impossible by the most generous concessions of the dominion's nationhood and existence as a state."

Just as Lloyd George was too slow in conceding that, in the case of

Eire at least, a more precise definition of dominion status was needed, so in his dealings with the Irish he was too impatient. "Was Mr. Lloyd George, however prolonged the Treaty negotiations, however slow the Irish delegation to reach firm conclusions, wise in the end to impose a settlement by a threat of war?" asked Dr. Nicholas Mansergh in his *Survey of British Commonwealth Affairs*. "It is a fact that the threat, however veiled or diluted, was a stigma from which the dominion settlement of 1921 never escaped."[1]

A definition of dominion status in 1921 and a promise to re-examine the Ulster question after a period of five years might have meant the retention of Eire as a permanent partner in the Commonwealth, but it was left to a Tory administration to introduce the legal instrument which finally took Eire out of the Empire. Lloyd George had encouraged the dominion Premiers to believe that Britain could concede more rights to them. The Statute of Westminster of 1931 authorised a dominion to change its constitution even though this involved repudiation of a treaty. This was the second step towards the break-up of the Empire and it is worth noting that each step was taken during predominantly Tory administration. Thus the door to the full aspirations of the Southern Irish was left open and, by the Ireland Act of 1949, the Republic of Eire was eventually recognised, free from any allegiances to the Crown.

[1] It must have been a very veiled threat, as Ll. G. could hardly have threatened his own resignation and renewed warfare at the same time. He may have implied that following his resignation renewed warfare was a possibility.

15

GO-BETWEENS IN THE SHADOWS

> "The world is governed by go-betweens. These go-betweens influence the persons with whom they carry on intercourse by stating their sense to each of them as the sense of the other; and thus they reciprocally master both sides."
>
> *Edmund Burke*

The pages of British history are littered with confusing examples of disreputable, squalid characters who have acquired power and influence over their rulers out of all proportion to their positions in the community. The ante-rooms, boudoirs and kitchens of the royal palaces have been happy hunting grounds for historians steeped in the Whig and Puritan tradition.

Yet while this type of historian conscientiously rummages among the faded love letters of royal mistresses, or ponders on the idiosyncrasies of a Highland ghillie, there has been a singularly marked reluctance on his part to reveal the equally shadowy figures who have surrounded mere politicians. One learns authoritatively who were the homosexual paramours of James I; every schoolboy realises he was the "wisest fool in Christendom", yet is barely cognisant of the debt he owes this monarch for the heritage of a new and enriched Bible.

Some psychological quirk among historians causes them to treat British Prime Ministers with greater respect and far more inhibitions than a Sovereign. Frequently the historian seeks deliberately to pinpoint the aberrations, frailties and defects of a Sovereign, to describe in detail the lesser personages around him; it is part of the Whig philosophy of denying the divine, hereditary right of kings and, without doubt, it is a wise, if sometimes overdeveloped technique. Yet, with Prime Ministers, there is a tendency to disregard the "go-betweens" in the shadows, to whom Burke so aptly referred. In analysing and sifting the facts of Lloyd George's premiership it is impossible even to grasp the complexities of his career, and indeed of the whole political life of the nation, without taking a close look at those aides, go-betweens and advisers who gathered in the shadows of No. 10, Downing Street, and in that secret rendezvous nicknamed the "Garden Suburb".

No Prime Minister has ever before or since assembled around him quite such an incongruous, almost bizarre and even sinister band of figures, some of whom might have stepped from the pages of a spy-thriller story. Often the lesser characters provide more clues to the mystery of Lloyd George's mental make-up than the more sedate of his civil servants, and even with the latter Ll. G. preferred unorthodoxy.

Most of these evil genii of the Magician from Llanystumdwy have long since been forgotten; they are names which evoke an occasional question mark, a hint of some faded scandal and nothing more. Yet their influence on events in this period was far greater than that of some of his Cabinet colleagues.

Lloyd George was the first modern Premier to set up what is now loosely called a brains trust. It was something much more informal than the teams of specialists set up by Franklin Roosevelt and President Kennedy. Fortunately for the country there were in his secretariat and entourage some men of high moral character and outstanding ability. In the background was the figure of Maurice Hankey, head of the Cabinet secretariat, who has been described as a "powerful and catalytic agent in reducing to order the multitude of meetings and consultations". In the secretariat during the war were Dr. Thomas Jones, Professor W. G. S. Adams, Waldorf Astor, David Davies, Philip Kerr and J. T. Davies.

To Dr. Jones, Ll. G. owed an immense debt for much wise advice on relations with labour and his ability, as we have already seen in the Irish conference, in skilful negotiations behind the scenes. Starting life as a timekeeper and wages clerk in a Monmouthshire ironworks at the age of fourteen, Thomas Jones eventually became a university professor and deputy-secretary to the Cabinet. It was a most remarkable achievement. "Perpetual Motion" Jones they called him in Whitehall; later when he rose to second-in-command in the War Cabinet secretariat there were jealous murmurings among some of his colleagues about the "little Bolshevik" who had acquired such success and influence.

It was a grossly inaccurate description. Thomas Jones was a man with no personal ambitions; he might best be described as slightly to the left of Liberalism, with a keen appreciation of the lessons of Fabianism and the need for closer and better relations between Government and organised labour.

Lloyd George did not always heed this advice. David Davies was the man who filled the rôle of Cassius to Ll. G.'s Brutus. He was forever the whisperer at the elbow, the slightly sanctimonious tale-teller who was ominously hinting in profusive letters and memoranda at the weaknesses and misdoings of others. In short, he was the chief spy of the actions and conduct of the other members of the Ll. G. team. Edward Grigg, as private secretary, had a genius for composing evasive replies to awkward letters, and the Prime Minister relied heavily on his talent for taking avoiding action.

Of the other members of the brains trust two men were particularly influential with the Premier—Philip Kerr and Lionel Curtis. Kerr and Curtis were the mainspring of whatever inspiration Lloyd George had for the Empire and Commonwealth, and the former was regarded as a valued adviser on foreign policy. But both Kerr and Curtis were imperialist mystics whose approach to the problems of Empire was almost metaphysical. Kerr's odd background of a Roman Catholic upbringing combined with a passion for Christian Science made a dangerous basis for imperial re-thinking. He and Curtis had founded a grave and austere magazine named *The Round Table* to express their views, and it was natural that Edward Grigg, another Round Tabler and a former assistant editor of the magazine, should link up with them.

These three men made incongruous associates for Lloyd George the empiricist. Mentally they were much closer to Lord Milner, but their skill at drafting agreements attracted them to a Prime Minister who liked to have his own ideas etched in detail by someone else's hand. The main theme of the Round Tablers was to change the Empire gradually into a Commonwealth—not a body of peoples dominated by one group, but an association of free peoples. Indian reform, the independence of Egypt and the creation of the Irish Free State were all Round Table conceptions and, though never men of action, Kerr and Curtis managed to carry out a revolution in political thinking almost without the Prime Minister being aware of it. They saved him from the worst aberrations of his Irish policy and produced a new blueprint for the Commonwealth.

Kerr and Curtis, both great admirers of the United States, pretended that Europe could do in a few years what the various states of America have achieved in less than a century. They insisted that France and Germany could live together in amity and concord. Such talk from two rather pretentious intellectuals was to the French just another example of British humbug; what seemed to Kerr and Curtis as a mere exercise in Christian science was to the French a betrayal of their cause. Thus Kerr, especially, and Curtis, to a lesser extent, helped, however unwittingly, to make Anglo-French accord difficult. In their ideas about the Empire the Round Tablers were undoubtedly right, if not always practicable, but their conception of Europe, with its bland assumption of the mystical power of a superior morality peculiar to Anglo-Saxons, was disastrous.

Of a totally different character was J. T. Davies,[1] another of the Welshmen at No. 10, who claimed most of the Prime Minister's time and nearly always got it. Davies's shifts and shuffles in policy and impatience with academic thought endeared him to a Prime Minister

[1] Later Sir J. T. Davies; private secretary to Ll. G. 1912–22.

who preferred quick thinkers to "professors", as he somewhat contemptuously called intellectuals. When J. T. Davies was appointed a director of the Suez Canal Company by Lloyd George, Lord Curzon said: "It is the greatest piece of nepotism since Caligula appointed his horse to be a Consul."

Lloyd George used intellectuals as drafters and, in the last resort, as a subtle check on any hastily improvised policy of his own which went wrong. If he did not acknowledge a mistake, he was quick to see it was rectified. Thus, when he realised the hopeless impasse into which his Irish policy had precipitated the Government, he turned to Kerr and Curtis. But he was never a man to rely on a few advisers of proved ability and integrity. Diversity of advice and novelty of ideas were what he thrived on and he preferred brilliant rogues to honest plodders who too often provided a douche of caution, or a reminder that moral principles were more important than expediency.

No Prime Minister made himself so accessible to people who had new ideas to offer. During his Premiership there was a steady flow of callers to No. 10 Downing Street, not only through the front door but by the back door and to the discreetly sheltered hut which he ordered to be built in the garden, the "Garden Suburb". Some of the callers found themselves made civil servants at a moment's notice.

Lloyd George had a flair for talent-spotting which amounted to real genius. Though many of the leading figures behind the scenes at No. 10 were charlatans, all had vigour, drive and immense capacity for tilting against the windmills their master put up for them. But there was frequently a lack of co-ordination. A reshuffle in one ministry might improve it beyond recognition, but it often led to chaos in its relations with other ministries. The picture presented by some biographers of a presiding genius over a brilliant staff is not borne out by the men who were closest to him.

Mr. A. J. Sylvester, a member of the secretariat, had this to say about his chief: "The plain unvarnished truth is that, left alone, Lloyd George was a most unholy muddler . . . left to himself he could not even dress himself without upsetting everything in the room and losing half his clothing. . . . His staff were always in arrears with work because of his slipshod methods. The fact that he was causing people inconvenience didn't worry him in the slightest. . . . Temperamental and impulsive, he often would give an order and cancel it a few minutes later."

Others among Ll. G.'s staff have testified to his wild rages and unhappy trait of bullying those under him. To avoid making a decision he would upset a telephone on the floor, or throw files across the room and leave his staff to work things out. If their decision did not prove to be right in the circumstances, he would have no hesitation in blaming them.

* * * * *

There is not a single reference to Sir Basil Zaharoff in Lloyd George's *War Memoirs* and Ll. G.'s biographers completely ignore him. Yet the two men were closely associated throughout World War I and during the whole period of the 1918–22 Coalition Government. It is curious that objective biographers should have ignored this enigmatic figure who, as much as anyone, was responsible for the events which caused Lloyd George's fall from power.

"Chief Munitions Agent for the Allied Powers" is how Zaharoff has been described, but he was not merely a munitions agent, but a deliberate fomenter of wars. Not content to harvest his gains, he re-invested them in newspapers which urged the need for rearmament, in carefully calculated bribes and payments to unscrupulous agents who would spread confusion, doubt and lies across three continents. Like Lloyd George himself, he had a fondness for destroying incriminating evidence so that even his origins are still obscure. In 1873 he testified in court that he was born in the Tatavla quarter of Constantinople and was twenty-two years of age. In 1892 he produced a birth certificate which told a different story—that "Zacharie Vasiliou Zacharoff or Zacharoff Basile was born in Mouchliou on October 6, 1849, the legitimate son of Vassiliou and Helene Zacharoff". So closely did he keep his secrets that neither his closest friends nor his biographers, who spent years collecting information about him, had any idea that he married an Englishwoman. Up to the age of 74, when he married the Duchess de Villafranca de los Caballeros, the world believed him to be a confirmed bachelor. But the document proving his marriage is in the register of a London church, showing that on October 14, 1872, he married Emily Ann Burrows at the Church of All Saints, Knightsbridge, under the assumed name of Prince Basilius Gortzacoff.

Two months later, again under the assumed name, he was charged at the Mansion House Police Court with having stolen merchandise and securities worth in all about £8,000. Later at the Old Bailey he was found guilty, bound over and eventually set free.

Through his influence with Skuludis, the Greek Premier, he joined the Anglo-Swedish arms firm of Nordenfelt. Summing up those early days of his career, Zaharoff told Rosita Forbes: "I made my first hundreds out of gun-running for savages. I made wars so that I could sell arms to both sides. As a very young man I realise there is always a woman behind the public personage. I got introduced to her, sent her flowers or jewels, courted her and eventually sold whatever I wanted to her husband or lover."

When Nordenfelt produced a submarine he sold one to Greece, then told the Turks and immediately persuaded them to buy two. He negotiated a merger between Nordenfelt and Maxim and, in 1897, brought off the biggest coup of all, a deal between Vickers, the British armaments combine, and the Maxim-Nordenfelt Guns and Ammunition

Company. Thus he became Vickers's chief agent with a roving commission to go where he liked and sell arms wherever he could on a percentage commission basis. He was one of the principal fomenters of the armaments scare which, by exaggerating the extent of German naval construction, sought to force Britain into a dreadnought building race.

Lloyd George had been one of the most caustic critics of the people who stirred up this armaments scare, and his opposition to increased naval building was partly based on this. Shortly afterwards Zaharoff made the acquaintance of Lloyd George, whom he had long regarded as a potentially dangerous enemy with too close an interest in his machinations. He took steps to find out all about Lloyd George, his weaknesses and secrets, and the man he employed to do this was none other than Arthur Maundy Gregory, the honours tout. Gregory had long been closely associated with Sir Basil Thomson on counter-espionage work and, according to Thomson, Gregory informed him that he had discovered that sometime during the early nineties Lloyd George had had a brief liaison with Zaharoff's English wife. To what extent Zaharoff used this uncorroborated information to gain influence with Ll. G. is not clear, but he seems to have decided that, while Lloyd George could be a dangerous enemy, it would be preferable to come to terms with him. He may even have lured Lloyd George into erroneously believing that he had left-wing sympathies, for Zaharoff had as many friends on the left as on the right in politics. In this connection Sir Basil once made a highly significant remark to Sir Robert (now Lord) Boothby: "Begin on the left in politics," he advised, "and then, if necessary, work over to the right. Remember it is sometimes necessary to kick off the ladder those who have helped you to climb it."[1]

Zaharoff could make such outrageous statements and get away with them. He spoke with the assurance and autocratic authority of a Hapsburg, looking more like a king than most monarchs. By sheer force of personality and will he had obliterated the mannerisms and foibles of the brothel tout he once was just as he had removed police dossiers and secret reports from half the Chancelleries of Europe.

When World War I broke out Zaharoff was at the height of his power and his plans were well laid. In France he had his headquarters, in Britain his agents, while he was on the closest terms with the Russian Imperial family. His fortune at one time totalled more than £40 million. His relations with Lloyd George at the Ministry of Munitions have already been mentioned. "As a representative of Vickers, Zaharoff was the confidant of Lloyd George, Minister of Munitions, and this personal relationship continued when the latter became Prime

[1] *I Fight to Live*, by Sir Robert Boothby.

Minister," wrote Richard Lewinsohn. "In England his best friend was Lloyd George," claimed Guilles Davenport.

When the name of Zaharoff loomed large and scandalously in the hearings of the Senate Munitions Investigation Commission in Washington in 1934, Mr. Alkin E. Johnson expounded on the theme in the French review *La Lumière*: "Someone belonging to Lloyd George's more intimate circle" told him that "we use Sir Basil Zaharoff as a kind of super-spy in high society and influential circles. At the same time we have him watched by two or three of our best police agents."

It would be interesting to know who this intimate of Lloyd George's was. But, though this is hearsay, it fits into the picture of this scheming arms merchant and his various missions for Ll. G. That he was of paramount importance to the Allies there is little doubt, though it is equally clear that, in the first year of the war, he was still fulfilling arms orders for the enemy. The Turkish guns served by German artillerymen at the Dardanelles were delivered by Zaharoff.

Because Lloyd George was an "Easterner" in strategy he appealed strongly to Zaharoff. Here was the chance the munitions agent was looking for—a Western statesman who could be persuaded to extend the war in the East and give to Greece the future which Zaharoff in his rare sentimental moments saw for her, that of a modern empire in every way the twentieth-century counterpart of that of Alexander. Zaharoff provided large sums of money for Allied propaganda in Greece and led the drive against the activities of Baron von Schenck, the German agent.

During his wartime premiership Lloyd George always kept open the door for any peace envoy from whatever quarter of the enemy's camp he might come. His publicly declared policy was one of "war to the bitter end", but his private intrigues all too frequently implied peace at somebody else's price. Both military and naval intelligence organisations were kept in the dark about the Prime Minister's circuitous methods of probing peace possibilities. Zaharoff not only kept him closely informed on the Balkans, but, at Ll. G.'s request, carried out many unofficial missions for him in Central Europe. The relationship of these two men was of particular significance in March, 1917, when Zaharoff tipped off the Premier about a secret letter written by the Emperor of Austria to his brother-in-law, Prince Sixte de Bourbon, an officer in the Belgian Army. This letter was intended for the French, but Zaharoff was determined that Ll. G. should hear of it first. Lloyd George had several interviews with Prince Sixte in London and Paris. It was suggested that Austria should agree not to send large forces against the Allies on the Western front in return for support by Britain for the reactionary Austro-Hungarian régime. Zaharoff's plan was not to bring the war to an end—that would not have suited his purposes as an armaments merchant—but to take advantage of any lull on the Western front to stir up trouble in the Middle East and the Balkans, thus finding new customers for armaments and bringing Greece into the war. Such a plan obviously fitted in perfectly with the strategy of Lloyd George, who persisted in advocating the project even after it was opposed by France and Italy.

M. Paul Cambon, the French Ambassador in London, warned Prince Sixte about the British Premier: "He is a Welshman, not an Englishman. An Englishman never goes back on what he has once said: Lloyd George is apt to perform evolutions, his words have not always the same weight as Balfour's."

Naturally the financial world took a keen interest in these talks, and Zaharoff was consulted by a group of Allied bankers in Paris. Lord Bertie, the British Ambassador in the French capital, reported: "Basil Zaharoff is all for continuing the war *jusqu'au bout.*"

During the war Zaharoff was sent on various secret missions by Lloyd George, and these activities certainly substantiate the claim made by Mr. Alkin Johnson. Once the passenger steamer in which he was travelling had been tracked down by the German naval authorities who had even obtained the number of his cabin. A German submarine halted the ship on the high seas and demanded the handing over of "Herr Zaharoff from Cabin 24". But Zaharoff was prepared for this eventuality. Indeed, it is said that he knew about the Germans' plans to capture him and that he had deliberately travelled with a "double" who could impersonate him. The German sailors went to Cabin 24 and arrested a man whom they took aboard the submarine. It was not until they arrived back in Germany that the man was found to be not Basil Zaharoff but his secretary.

Zaharoff's home in Paris during the war was more like that of a monarch than a private individual. The "Big Three"—Wilson, Lloyd George and Clemenceau—met there once or twice to discuss some major peace problem, and during the last two years of the war Zaharoff was frequently consulted on policy-making. T. P. O'Connor once stated, "Allied statesmen and leaders were obliged to consult him before planning any great attack." That may merely have been Zaharoff's own version of his influence, but he certainly received deferential treatment from all the Allied leaders.

On one occasion Zaharoff went to Germany, on Lloyd George's personal instructions, disguised in the uniform of a Bulgarian Army doctor. He was not a man to risk his skin unnecessarily and it says much for Lloyd George's powers of persuasion that he could entice the most powerful man in Europe to play the rôle of a common spy. The story of this mission, though not its details, is confirmed by the Quai d'Orsay, though French authorities declare it was carried out without their prior knowledge. According to Clemenceau, "the information which Zaharoff secured in Germany for Lloyd

George was the most important piece of intelligence of the whole war".

A lengthy search of available records has produced no reliable answer as to what that information was, but French sources are inclined to believe that Zaharoff reported German fears of a Bolshevik uprising in Eastern Germany and Hungary. A Soviet diplomatic dispatch to the Russian representative in Athens in the midsummer of 1918 stated categorically: "M. Zaharoff, the agent of the British firm of Vickers and the man who financed the Putiloff works, has urged the Allies to make peace before the end of the year as he fears that if the war continues it will upset his plans for provoking war between Greece and Turkey and that by early next year the Bolshevik Revolution will have completed its second phase and extended the Socialist Republics to the banks of the Rhine."

Insisting that not a word that he uttered was to be published until after his death, Zaharoff in 1933 gave an interview to Rosita Forbes, the author, which included his own version of this incident. This account stated that Zaharoff "during the war . . . went to Germany to discover certain things that Lloyd George wanted to know, in the uniform of a Bulgarian doctor". He described how he was met by Clemenceau on his arrival back in Paris and told by the French Premier to report to Lloyd George at once. "I went to London by the next train to be greeted by Mr. Lloyd George with the G.C.B. in his pocket. They say that the information I brought ended the war."

This is probably a typical example of Zaharoffian exaggeration. The decoration could not have been the Grand Cross of the Order of the Bath, which was not conferred on him until 1921. This is a detail which Zaharoff, with his multifarious awards, may pardonably have overlooked. He was, however, awarded the G.B.E. in 1918, which was the year in which the events described took place.

But one mission which Zaharoff undertook for Lloyd George and of which the details are known casts a new light on the extent to which the politicians were often outwitted by the international armaments wire-pullers in World War I. At the end of 1916, shortly after he became Premier, Lloyd George asked Zaharoff what were the chances of obtaining unofficially from the enemy a token withdrawal of troops on both sides in selected areas of the Western front on New Year's Day. This approach was made at a time when the Allied conference at Chantilly had recommended an intensified drive against the enemy, but while Ll. G. was secretly considering German peace feelers.

Zaharoff, however, had other ideas. He was seriously perturbed because at this very time M. Albert Thomas, French Minister of Munitions, was demanding the bombardment of Briey, close to the German frontier where, before the war, a system of blast furnaces had been created by the French *Comité des Forges*.[1] In August, 1914, no

[1] Zaharoff had close associations with this company.

attempt had been made to defend Briey and French forces were immediately withdrawn to a distance of twenty-two kilometres behind the frontier, leaving this valuable industrial plant intact in German hands. Throughout the war no offensive action was taken by the Allies against either Briey or nearby Thionville, a German industrial area which was vital to the German army for mineral supplies.

The proposed bombardment of an arms plant in which he had an interest naturally disturbed Zaharoff who immediately sought to distort Lloyd George's plea into a plan for a mutual agreement between the Allies and the Central Powers to desist from attacking each other's arms factories. He consulted armament agents on both sides, as a result of which orders to bombard Briey were cancelled.

Years afterwards M. Thomas declared: "The Minister of War repeatedly said that he had given orders for the bombardment of Briey, but that these orders were not in fact carried out. . . . The reasons given were the inadequacy of the number and power of the aircraft, to which we replied that if there were enough aeroplanes for the open towns, there were enough for Briey as well."

More enlightening was the testimony of M. Barthe in the French Parliament on January 24, 1919: "I declare that, either owing to the international solidarity of heavy industry, or in order to safeguard private interests, orders were given to our military commanders not to bombard the factories of the basin of Briey exploited by the enemy during the war."

M. Barthe compiled a dossier on this sordid episode of the war. It was suppressed by the French authorities. This dossier revealed the story of negotiations between Zaharoff and Lloyd George, commenting: "Lloyd George finally concurred with Zaharoff's viewpoints and agreed it would be senseless to destroy industrial plant and to end up the war with derelict factories and mass unemployment. Lloyd George was in favour of anything that would slow down the tempo of the war on the Western front, and it was better to have the means of supplying arms to the theatre of war which really mattered to him—vital salients of the *Moyen Orient*."

On October 10, 1917, the German newspaper *Leipzige Neueste Nachrichten* stated: "If, in the first days of the war, the French had penetrated to the depth of a dozen kilometres in Lorraine, the war would have ended in six months by the defeat of Germany."

Zaharoff himself put this even more bluntly in a letter to M. Venizelos: "You can sum up our war position to the fainthearts in Athens as follows: the Western Powers must win this war. They alone have the war potential to carry them through. Only incredible stupidity could give the Central Powers victory. Germany was far more vulnerable in 1914 than she or the West realised. I could have shown the Allies three points at which, had they struck, the enemy's armament potential could have been utterly destroyed. But that would have ruined the business built up over more than a century and nothing would have been settled. The world would have been ripe for revolution. Our policy is to contain the Central Powers, then to achieve victory without permitting industrial chaos in Europe."

In other words, victory for the armament firms. When a French pilot, M. Bossoutrot, lost his way in a storm and found himself over Briey, he dropped his bombs on installations there. But there was no decoration for him; instead he was punished on orders of the General Staff.

* * * * *

Investigation of the extent of Soviet activities in Britain after the war were conducted by Sir Basil Thomson, chief of the Special Branch of Scotland Yard. Thomson, son of an Archbishop of York, had, after an education at Eton and Oxford, entered the Colonial Service. His remarkable career had embraced such diverse activities as Prime Minister of Tonga, authorship of novels and plays, prison governor and Assistant Commissioner of the Metropolitan Police. But it was as a brilliant, if ruthless, intelligence officer that he proved his real genius. Due to his foresight a clean sweep of German agents in Britain was made in August, 1914.

To maintain the necessary executive power vested in the police by law, the Government decided that Thomson should continue in his office as Assistant Commissioner, but be responsible only to the Home Secretary. For more than a year this organisation, anomalous though it may have been in certain respects, worked admirably, and Thomson came to be regarded as an adviser to the Cabinet over a wide field of subjects. But Lloyd George, who looked upon Thomson almost as a personal adviser on intelligence matters; was apt to use the police chief's information for himself alone.

At this time the police forces were seething with discontent and rife with corruption. Matters came to a head when the Police Union balloted in favour of a strike. The real trouble was that many of the police leaders at this time were themselves inefficient and corrupt. Blackmail, graft and bribery existed at all levels in the London police and were not wiped out until the arrival of Lord Trenchard years later.

The Commissioner of the Metropolitan Police was General Horwood, an unfortunate choice, for he was either unwilling or unable to stamp out corruption. Thomson, who was a violent and outspoken critic of Horwood and barely on speaking terms with his chief, insisted on raising the whole question of police control with Lloyd George. He pointed out that the Police Union was riddled with Bolshevik agents, that its immediate aim was to approach members of the Triple Alliance unions in the hope of forcing joint strike action for the reinstatement of a police constable who had been dismissed for circulating strike propaganda among his comrades. Lloyd George urged Thomson not to worry about "these trivial things".

Without warning, in November, 1921, the Home Secretary, Mr. Shortt, sent for Thomson and told him that if he did not retire *voluntarily*, he would receive a less generous pension and be summarily dismissed. When he demanded a reason for such peremptory action and asked to see the Prime Minister, he was told that no useful purpose could be served by granting either request.

The manner of Thomson's dismissal angered his old intelligence colleagues and in a debate in the House of Commons a storm raged around the Home Secretary. Mr. Shortt was as uncommunicative as possible. He refused to answer questions as to whether the resignation had been preceded by consideration of the subject by the whole Cabinet, nor would he say whether he had himself received instructions from the Prime Minister to call for the resignation. The suggestion was made in the House that Sir Basil Thomson had been sacrificed to placate Labour opinion.

Thomson himself in his book, *The Scene Changes*, told how four young Irishmen chalked up on the summer-house of Chequers, while Ll. G. was in residence, the words "Up Sinn Fein". They were arrested and brought before Thomson, who, satisfied that this was nothing more than a skylark, ticked them off and let them go. But Horwood, who was responsible for the Prime Minister's safety, objected to this leniency and reported the matter to Ll. G. This, he thought, provided the excuse that Lloyd George wanted for getting rid of Thomson. It is true that the Premier regarded Thomson's weekly reports on the subversive activities of certain Labour leaders as exaggerated and he was anxious to placate the Labour benches. But the real reason for wanting Thomson out of the way was that, as Thomson himself afterwards asserted, he knew too much.

Sir Basil in the course of his probes into Bolshevik activities had discovered documents which incriminated servants of the Crown as secret agents of Sir Basil Zaharoff *with the knowledge of Lloyd George*. Thomson had certain suspects followed, and then learned that Zaharoff, the man who had lavished presents on the Czar and his family, had established links with the Bolsheviks. It was purely a temporary arrangement by which Zaharoff sought to divert munitions supplies intended for the White Russians so that they could be delivered to Greece and certain Balkan countries for ultimate use against the Turks. Zaharoff had by devious means done his utmost both in London and Paris to call off the campaign against the Bolsheviks. Not, of course, that he was pro-Communist, but simply that he wanted the arms to carve an empire for Greece in the Balkans. Zaharoff knew that if the White Russians won, they might agitate for Constantinople,

Wide World Photos
A. Maundy Gregory.

Topix Picture Service
Sir William Sutherland.

Central Press Photos Ltd.

Lloyd George at 10 Downing Street in 1918 with (on his right) Marshal Foch and Georges Clemenceau.

as promised to them in the Sykes-Picot Agreement. He wanted Constantinople for Greece and he had received an assurance from the Bolsheviks that they would make no claim for this city.

* * * * *

During his sojourn at the Board of Trade, Lloyd George discovered a promising young civil servant whose combination of bluntness and subtlety appealed to him. His name was William Sutherland, a Scot with a big voice, uncouth manners and a passion for outsize cigars and good living.

Eyebrows were raised when Ll. G. took Sutherland with him as secretary to the Cabinet Committee on Supplies and Munitions in 1915. To the staider Liberals, Sutherland's name was anathema, but Lloyd George insisted on his protégé's outstanding ability and, as his private secretary in 1917, Sutherland was made responsible for the Prime Minister's relations with the Press and for political propaganda on the domestic front.

"Bronco Bill", as Sutherland was known at Westminster, had no scruples about putting out the most scurrilous rumours about Lloyd George's enemies, these being disseminated not through the Press, but by word of mouth through private agents in West End clubs. The disgraceful stories about Asquith, Haig and Sir William Robertson were largely engineered and invented by Sutherland.

As a manipulator of the Press he was the first of his kind and extremely successful. One of his innovations was the broadsheet *Future*, which was issued from the Press Bureau at No. 10. In the *Daily Mail* at a time when the Northcliffe-Lloyd George honeymoon had ended in 1919, a correspondent described in satirical vein how Sutherland worked. "Each year he seeks to improve his methods of leg-pulling the Press. This is rendered necessary by the fact that the business of advertising the Premier becomes ever more difficult.

"Sir William's (by then Sutherland was a knight) *modus vivendi* is simplicity itself, which partly accounts for his success. He receives all Press callers . . . these divide themselves into three categories: representatives of the sycophantic and willingly gullible Press; the friendly Press and the critical Press.

"In regard to the third lot he adopts the rôle of candid friend. At the same time he appealingly points out the tremendous difficulties with which the Premier is meeting and endeavours to draw for the editors the picture of a good and guileless man struggling bravely with adversity.

"Such is the insidious influence of this well-trained propagandist's conversation that members of the third category have constantly to be on their guard lest they fall an easy prey. Even the toughest-skinned journalist has been known to have his leg pulled by Sutherland."

Whenever Ll. G. was in difficulties he always sent for Sutherland. Once he urgently required his presence in Paris during the Peace Conference, and the Prime Minister's Press agent had to sort out the bad impression which Lloyd George had made on American and French newspapermen.

Often there was complete confusion among correspondents as to which was the predominant mind in some of the extraordinary stories that came from Downing Street. The hand behind them might be that of Lloyd George, but the nuances and phrasing were undoubtedly those of Sutherland. As Ll. G. changed his mind several times a day Sutherland often had to do some furious somersaulting. He would put out a rumour in the morning and blandly be the first to deny it when it was published that evening. Yet, "At a fair computation," said the *Daily Mail*, "Sir William Sutherland is worth £10,000 a year to his master"—which, at this time, would have been double the Premier's own salary.

Sutherland was the master-mind of all the Prime Minister's "go-betweens", the chief channel of information from all quarters. He had informants inside the Metropolitan Police and had a great deal to do with the building up of the notorious Lloyd George Personal Fund. Sutherland, as will be shown later, was the direct intermediary between Lloyd George and Maundy Gregory in connection with the latter's rôle as pedlar of honours.

In 1919 Sutherland was created a K.C.B. and also a Commander of the Order of Leopold, the latter being a sign of Gregory's intervention in the honours field: it was a decoration which he unfailingly obtained for his friends. At the "Coupon Election" Sutherland was given a candidature for Argyllshire, a seat which he held as Coalition Liberal M.P. until October, 1924. From 1920 to 1922 he was a Privy Councillor and Chancellor of the Duchy of Lancaster. At Westminster, where for a time he was Coalition Whip, he used his influence in the field of honours with remarkable effect for the Lloyd George Fund.

* * * * *

Another "go-between", but one who never accepted a Coalition "coupon", was Horatio Bottomley, M.P. Bottomley was in many ways symbolical of the Lloyd Georgian era; all the attributes and defects of this period were exemplified in this podgy, paunchy man with his mixture of demagogy and crooked finance, of bombastic, hollow patriotism and cynical disregard for the decencies of democratic government.

Lloyd George had, wrote Thomas Jones, "an insatiable curiosity for charlatans like Jabez Balfour and Horatio Bottomley", and Bottomley's biographer, Julian Symons, tells us: "Lloyd George respected his (Bottomley's) quick wit and liked his impudence." If Lloyd George wanted a particularly obnoxious story about the defects of some Liberal minister published and nobody else would print it, it was to Bottomley he turned.

When there was trouble at a munitions factory Lloyd George would always say: "Send for Bottomley. He'll talk them out of trouble." The relationship of these two men, though not close and conducted by go-betweens, dated back to about 1910 when Bottomley was M.P. for South Hackney. Even as early as 1912 Bottomley asserted in his magazine, *John Bull*, that Asquith would go to the House of Lords and that Lloyd George would become Premier. Each man saw in the other a glimpse of his own devious character.

Lloyd George regarded Bottomley as a dangerous enemy but a useful ally. When mutiny occurred in sections of the Army in 1919, Bottomley was the only man to whom the troops would listen. But his big chance was missed early in 1918 when he was invited to Downing Street to meet Lloyd George and Carson. Bottomley had a new plan for beating the Germans, a propaganda gambit with some merits. But he overplayed his hand: he demanded that Ll. G. should make him Director of War Propaganda. That was an error of judgment which made Ll. G. pause. He had been about to offer Bottomley an Under-Secretaryship, but he changed his mind in the face of the latter's demand.

After the war Bottomley conceived the idea of forming a club so that the "little man and the little woman" could share in the Victory Bonds scheme by subscribing smaller sums than the bond value of £4 5*s*. and with the accumulated amount Bottomley would buy Victory Bonds. The outcome for the "little man and woman" was disastrous, and in 1922 Bottomley was convicted of the fraudulent conversion of more than £250,000 of moneys received by him from the public for investment in the Government Victory Loan.

16

"FOR GREEKS A BLUSH, FOR GREECE A TEAR"

"'Tis something in the dearth of fame,
Though link'd among a fetter'd race,
To feel at least a patriot's shame,
Even as I sing, suffuse my face;
For what is left the poet here?
For Greeks a blush—for Greece a tear."

Lord Byron

Byron, who had sufficient detachment to turn the waxen-hot material of romantic love into cool, classic columns of marble verse, became a stuttering, love-sick swain where Greece was concerned. He symbolised that uncritical passion for Hellenic ideals which spasmodically during the past 150 years has coloured and permeated the British political outlook towards Greece.

Yeats once said that the Irish problem could "be solved tomorrow, if only the English would believe in fairies". Yet the Celtic pixies were rejected as a sign of Irish immaturity, while the Hellenic fairies were raised to the status of goddesses. The classicists of England have not been content to inspire a deep sense of gratitude for Hellenism, but have sought to mislead us into viewing an unstable nation of merchant adventurers and political buccaneers as the arbiters and defenders of liberal democracy. When Liberalism followed the pipes of Pan, and Gladstone's love of Homer made him the greatest Hellenist of them all, that hard-headed school of Mancunian Liberals began to realise there was sound commercial sense in pursuing a pro-Greek policy. This, coming from the greatest power of the nineteenth century, not unnaturally flattered Greece into believing she had an imperialist future as well as a past.

So the aesthetes and classicists joined forces with the cotton and corn exporters. Thanks to this and to the wars between the great powers between 1776 and 1815 the Greeks had become the chief merchandise carriers of the Mediterranean and even monopolised the Black Sea trade. Achieving financial dominance out of all proportion to her status as a nation, Greece nevertheless kept her people on the lowest standard of living in the whole of Europe. She became a prime example of how private economic adventuring cannot provide national prosperity.

The tentacles of the Greek merchants and bankers extended to Britain, France, Italy, Austria, Turkey and Russia. Italian shipping was largely in Greek hands, Athens had a virtual monopoly of the grain trade in the Black Sea. Cobden's pro-Hellenism can be traced to his interest in the exchange of calico for corn; the mid-nineteenth century Liberals backed Greek nationalism largely in the interests of the Baltic Corn Exchange. There was a commercial alliance of the Gladstones of Liverpool, the Rallis of Chios, the Benachis and Rodocanachis of the Nile Valley cotton fields.

It can be argued that British policy towards Greece brought great practical results between 1900 and 1914. The Greeks played a useful part in bringing about the Entente Cordiale. But the Entente's only lasting monument was the Franco-British alliance, and in 1919–22 this was seriously impaired by the pro-Greek policy of the Lloyd George Government.

Greece, or rather the group of merchant adventurers who represented her, was clearly working for a form of economic imperialism a hundred years ago. As long as Greece remained a vassal to Western European capitalism, Greek nationalism was not mentioned as such, but the domination of the Balkans was the ultimate aim. The position at the beginning of the First World War was that Greece, despite the prosperity of her merchant-bankers, was short of funds. She had been exhausted by a series of wars, even though Zaharoff was said to have subsidised the Greek Government to the extent of £20,000 a month when he was equipping the Balkan armies for their onslaught against the Ottoman Empire. But neither Venizelos, the architect of Greek nationalism, nor his ally, Zaharoff, lost sight of the chance that World War I offered them eventually a chance to recoup their losses and win even greater domination.

> "The isles of Greece, the isles of Greece,
> Where burning Sappho loved and sung,
> Where grew the arts of war and peace,
> Where Delos rose and Phoebus sprung!
> Eternal summer gilds them yet,
> But all, except their sun, is set."

The sun might have set, but Greece from 1910–22 remained the *enfant terrible* of the Near East, the beguiler of the West and the bedeviller of international politics.

* * * * *

The British Foreign Office never trusted Venizelos, whom they regarded as sly, crafty and self-seeking, whereas Lloyd George developed a real affection for the Cretan. In the beginning Lloyd George's feelings about Greece were purely sentimental and based on the prospect of a small and mountainous country wishing to be united with its brethren across the borders. He had an affinity for mountain races like the Greeks and Albanians. But more personal influences were to carry greater weight in his policy towards Greece. His interest in that country had been stimulated by Zaharoff and by Domini, Lady Crosfield, the Greek wife of Sir Arthur Crosfield, Liberal M.P. for Warrington. He admired the business acumen of the cotton merchants whom he regarded as Britain's best allies in Egypt, and his high opinion of Venizelos may be judged by the fact that he once described that statesman as the "Lloyd George of Greece".

At the end of the war Venizelos and Zaharoff were united in one aim—the spread of Greek influence in Europe and Asia and the creation of a Greek empire in the Near East. In *Zaharoff: the Armaments King*, Robert Neumann wrote: "Through Lloyd George, Zaharoff had the same influence with the British Government as he used to have with the French." This was a theme constantly echoed in the French Press in the early twenties: "France once again has become the shield of Islam. And if England has reckoned up the price which it will have to pay from India to Egypt for a policy of Zaharoff, it will no doubt realise that it must again conclude peace with Islam. Then it can count on our good services."[1]

At a secret meeting in his Paris house during the Peace Conference, Zaharoff told Lloyd George he had made preliminary arrangements for valuable concessions in the Middle East to British firms. The first of these was for industrial development in Rumania, which Sir Basil, as representative of Vickers and a close friend of Queen Marie, had obtained. The second was a concession granted to the Anglo-Persian Oil Company to exploit petroleum wells in Greek Macedonia.

Well might M. Poincaré have talked about "the stink of oil". Lloyd George was delighted with the news Zaharoff gave him and extracted a further promise that British firms should receive preferential treatment from King Constantine's Government in and around the "free" town of Smyrna. By this means Zaharoff won from Lloyd George a promise of full backing for any claims Greece might wish to make: it amounted to a blank cheque for the armaments agent.

Once he was embroiled with Zaharoff, Lloyd George was automatically in trouble with the French, with whom the arms magnate was now on the worst possible terms largely through his own double-dealing. One of the British Premier's first aims was to sabotage the Sykes-Picot plan, to which Zaharoff, as we have seen, strongly objected, by provoking a rupture with France. This secret agreement of May,

[1] Senator Henri de Jouvenel in *Le Mabin.*

1916, shared out the territories of the then unconquered Turks among the powers of the Entente. Russia was to have the Dardanelles, Constantinople and a large area around Erzerum and Trebizond. Britain was to have the vilayets of Basra and Baghdad; France was to have Cicilia, a large part of Upper Mesopotamia and the coastal regions of Syria, including Alexandretta, down to a point near Acre, with Mosul included. Italy—and not Greece—was to have Smyrna and some of Southern Anatolia. Palestine was to be a condominium of Britain, France and Russia. The concessions to the Italians were added later because the original agreement had been concluded without their knowledge which, not unnaturally, drew from them angry protests. Nothing was promised to Belgium, Montenegro or Serbia.

It was the Bolsheviks who upset this secret "package" agreement by publishing details of it after they had discovered a copy of the terms in the archives of the Czarist Government. The Sykes-Picot Agreement has been severely criticised as an example of the trouble caused for posterity by secret diplomacy. It is easy to find fault with what was a wartime expedient, but at least it had the merits of aiming chiefly to preserve intact the façade of the Triple Alliance, while the proposal for condominium over Palestine showed more foresight than any similar plan advocated after the war.

Lord Curzon, Foreign Secretary in the Coalition Government of 1918–22, described the Sykes-Picot Agreement as "A sort of fancy sketch to suit a situation that had not arisen and which it was thought extremely unlikely would ever arise." Those who knew the language Curzon normally used could hardly doubt that the Foreign Secretary was hastily improvising an alibi for his Prime Minister. For Lloyd George's purpose, which his Foreign Secretary's statement was meant to obscure, was to put the blame on the Liberal Foreign Secretary, Grey, who authorised the agreement, and to seek some means of avoiding condominium in Palestine. In other words, Ll. G. wanted to keep Palestine for Britain. Sweet words for Jewry were merely meant to disguise this intention, or, to put the best construction on them, to win Jewish approval. Yet J. T. Davies insisted on hailing Ll. G. as a "twentieth-century Good Samaritan championing the Zionist cause".

Asquith, in his *Memories and Reflections*, summed up the position by saying that Lloyd George, "who did not care a damn for the Jews, or their past or their future, felt it would be an outrage to let the Holy Places pass into the possession or under the protectorate of agnostic, atheistic France". Ll. G., though he had several Jewish friends, had often been known to express anti-Semitic views and had no real interest in a National Home for Jewry. Indeed the Prime Minister's Jewish friends were mainly those who were anti-Zionist, like Sir Charles Henry and Mr. Lionel de Rothschild. Lord Beaverbrook records that Sir Charles

Henry "reported that in an interview the Prime Minister had given his assent to the anti-Zionist view," that is, those opposed to the idea of a National Home for the Jews.

It was Sir Herbert Samuel who, first of all, argued the case for Britain taking over Palestine as a protectorate. But Samuel was not a fanatical Zionist and he did not intend his idea to be developed in quite the manner that Balfour, a converted pro-Zionist, conceived in his famous Declaration of 1917. Condominium for Palestine might well have been the best temporary solution for that territory if Russia had still been a member of the Entente. In any event, there was a strong argument for setting up an interim Anglo-French condominium. But Lloyd George, intent on preventing any risk of such a move, had urged Allenby to advance on Damascus and Aleppo, militarily a rash idea before the Hejaz railway forces had been put down.

So from the autumn of 1918, through the various stages of the Peace Conference, and later at Genoa, Lloyd George's Middle and Near East policy developed piecemeal. First, to thwart the French and keep them out of Palestine; second, to gain control of Middle East oil; third, to support Greek merchant adventurers; and fourth, to create new dominions for Britain in the Arab territories.

The Arabian adventure was complementary to the Greek adventure; indeed, Lloyd George believed that the latter would indirectly assist the furtherance of the former. Just as Zaharoff was the all-important figure in the Greek policy, so T. E. Lawrence, the leader of the Arab revolt against the Turks, was the pawn in his schemes for aggrandisement in Arabia. The relations between Ll. G. and Lawrence are of special interest in that they serve as an example of the insincerity and vanity of both men. Each possessed the devious propensities of a certain type of Welsh mind; each had in his make-up an element of humbug. Lloyd George saw the defects of Lawrence much more quickly than the easily flattered Lawrence realised those of the Premier. What Ll. G. appreciated was the possibility of exploiting the romantic legend which had been built up around Lawrence's name, largely, of course, by Lawrence. He was anxious for the Government to gain some kudos from this legend and to project this self-appointed crusader as an instrument of policy in the Arab territories. So each man fawned on the other, Ll. G. praising Lawrence's "clear gifts of exposition", while Lawrence was shrewd enough to flatter the Premier by telling him exactly what he thought he wanted to know.

Nobody could be a bigger liar than Lawrence when it suited his purpose. He knew that Lloyd George was a Francophobe, and he played on this by discrediting the French, and assured the Prime Minister that France was plotting to destroy British influence in the Middle East. This was a little too much even for Lloyd George to swallow; he told Lawrence that he very much doubted if France would dare to do this, but encouraged him to back Feisal in his claim to Syria—"just to throw a spanner in the French works".

Lawrence vacillated between vague plans for imperialist expansion and equally obscure proposals for bettering the life of the Arabs. The Prime Minister was anxious to take advantage of any ideas that offered Britain scope for expansion. He seized on a phrase of Lawrence's as a news editor will whip a sentence out of a message and make it a headline—"Britain's first brown dominions." Here was an imaginative proposal, thought the Premier, to show the British public that the Coalition Government was really boosting British prestige in the Middle East. Here was the chance to add to the Empire, to build a British bloc in the vital oil areas and keep down French influence. By cunningly implying that some of these areas would have dominion status he could throw a sop to those who talked about the self-determination of native peoples.

No time was to be lost. First, the minor intelligence agent must be built up into a national myth. "Give Lawrence the maximum of publicity," he told Sutherland. Lawrence's massacres of sleeping Turks by his gangs of Bedouin killers must be represented as gallant epics of war. Lawrence needed little bidding to play the part. As a virulent Turkophobe he fitted in perfectly with Ll. G.'s plans for supporting the Greeks; as a pro-Arabist and anti-French agitator he was exactly the man the Prime Minister required. Lloyd George gave enthusiastic support to Lowell Thomas's lectures on Lawrence and the Arab revolt.

Statesmen do not take infinite pains over so pathetic a crank as Lawrence unless there are good reasons to fear him. When Lawrence, always masochistically-minded, secretly enlisted in the ranks of the R.A.F. under another name, he was protected by all manner of instructions from on high. His machinations against the French during Lloyd George's régime did immense harm to Anglo-French relations, and for years he was able to exercise a degree of influence in high circles in Britain out of all proportion to his status, even threatening authority with impunity. Somewhere a corpse was buried and Lawrence knew what it was: the full story of the anti-French intrigues and double-dealings with the Arabs.

With the utmost cynicism Lloyd George agreed to set up a commission of inquiry into the questions of Palestine, Iraq and Syria. The Commission was packed with the type of person who could hardly fail to give the British Premier the answers he wanted: it included two anti-French British missionaries and was accompanied by Allenby's military secretary. The mission did not even visit Baghdad and Mosul; it confined itself to finding excuses for not granting a French mandate for Syria. Many of the findings of the Commission were irrelevant, but the irrelevancies were intended to show up the French in the worst possible light. "French education," stated their report, was "superficial" and "inferior in character-building to the Anglo-Saxon". French education led to knowledge of "that kind of French literature which is irreligious and immoral".

Mrs. Grundy might well have written this report which reeked of hypocrisy and puritanism. It is obvious that the Moslem witnesses were asked leading questions with the object of getting them to make replies unfavourable to the French. Thus one learns that when Moslem women receive a French education, "they tend to become uncontrollable"—whether that meant sexually, or from the viewpoint of their lords and masters, was not made clear.

Lloyd George threw the blame for failure to deal promptly with the Syrian question on Milner, whom, he said, was "in a state of nervous lassitude". When Milner went to Paris to discuss Syria he was mysteriously recalled to London "on urgent colonial business" before the talks started. Did Ll. G. recall Milner on some flimsy pretext merely to keep him out of the way, knowing that Milner did not see eye to eye with him in his dealings with the French? Milner may have had his faults; he was not a bold executive, but he was a thoroughly capable administrator. As to the allegations of "nervous lassitude", he later dealt in a most competent fashion with a revolt against the British in Egypt.

It is illuminating to see what Milner himself wrote on March 8, 1919. "Although I am aware that I have almost every other Government authority, military or diplomatic, against me, I am totally opposed to the idea of trying to diddle the French out of Syria." Lloyd George coolly quoted this damning comment in *The Truth About the Peace Treaties*, and brushed it airily aside. He merely argued that there was no intrigue against the French in Syria.

* * * * *

Many Tories were becoming acutely distressed at the growing estrangement between Britain and France. They noted that whereas Lloyd George had produced no coherent economic policy and had allowed a boom year in 1919 to turn into a slump and mass unemployment, in France, under the orthodox but brilliant financial leadership of M. Poincaré, stability was returning.

Lloyd George, who had become so impressed by Venizelos, failed to notice the outstanding leadership of Mustapha Kemal Pasha over the Turkish Nationalists. Had he sought Kemal Pasha as an ally, British influence not only in the Middle East but throughout the Moslem world might have been greater. The pro-Greek policy in no way helped to forge the bonds of Empire to which he paid lip service.

The British Premier was, in fact, "going it alone". Alone with Zaharoff and Venizelos. Curzon had the gravest doubts about his chief's policy and at times was actually aiming at coming to a settlement with the Turks. Even Sir Henry Wilson, some little time before he was assassinated, warned his old ally of the war days: "Mr. Lloyd George has put his money on the wrong horse. We shall never get peace in Palestine or Mesopotamia, or Egypt or India, until we make love to the Turks. It may be very immoral, or it may not. It is a fact. Can anyone tell me why Mr. Lloyd George backed the Greeks? I know it was not upon the advice of Curzon, or the British Ambassador in Constantinople, or Lord Reading. I was at the Quai d'Orsay when Lloyd George gave Smyrna to the Greeks and I had to arrange for troops to go there. Why did Lloyd George back them? Was it to please Zaharoff, or was it because Venizelos told him that the Greeks were so prolific that they would rebuild the Near East in two or three years?"

Meanwhile Zaharoff recklessly pursued his ideal of a Greek Empire. He backed the Anglo-Persian Oil Company, with which, in the Middle East, he worked in close conjunction, and disputed American claims to the market in this area. The road was wide open for a free-for-all scramble by British capitalist enterprises. The British Trade Corporation took over the National Bank of Turkey and set up the Levant Company to develop trade in the area. The Federation of British Industries, a body which in the thirties was to show marked favouritism to Hitler Germany, spread its tentacles far and wide, nominating its first trade commissioner to Athens. It is not surprising that after 1945 U.S. oil interests determined to get their own back and thwart the British in the Middle East.

The worst features of Britain's failure to make peace with Turkey was that it exacerbated Moslem feelings throughout the Empire. In India it produced something that could scarcely have happened before —an alliance of Hindus and Moslems in a civil disobedience campaign.

"Almost the only support on the side of the victors that Turkey could muster was Indian," wrote the late Aga Khan in his *Memoirs*. "The greater part of Muslim interest in India in the fate of Turkey was natural and spontaneous and there was a considerable element of sincere non-Muslim agitation, the object of which, apart from the natural revolt of any organised Asiatic body against the idea of European imperialism, was further to consolidate and strengthen Indian nationalism in its struggle against the British."

Gandhi, wily politician that he was beneath his mask of piety, immediately capitalised this feeling and made Lloyd George's anti-Turkish policy an excuse for a campaign of agitation that swept across the whole of India. Edwin Montagu, then Secretary of State for India, saw the danger signals and made an emphatic protest against the plans for partitioning Turkey. It is interesting to note that Arthur Balfour, the fastidious Gentile aristocrat, was devoted to Zionism and violently anti-Turk, while Edwin Montagu, a Jew, was warmly sympathetic to the Islamic cause. Of such incongruities is history made.

Indeed Montagu felt so strongly on this question that, without Cabinet authority, he published a telegram from the Viceroy, Lord Reading, recommending the evacuation of Constantinople, and, in effect, a pro-Turkish policy. Montagu was immediately sacked and censured by the Prime Minister for ignoring the doctrine of Cabinet responsibility.

"Cabinet responsibility is a joke," said Montagu. "Having connived at its disappearance, the Prime Minister now brings it out at a convenient moment and makes me its victim."

The Aga Khan went as member of an Indian delegation to see Lloyd George. "But we realised our mission was doomed to failure," he wrote, "for meanwhile the Turkish Treaty was being prepared, with strangely little regard for the realities which, within a few years, were to shape the Near East anew. The unfortunate Sultan was under rigorous supervision, a solitary and helpless prisoner in Constantinople. Turkish, Arab and Greek deputations were hurrying backwards and forwards between the Mediterranean and London. Sometimes their arguments were listened to; often they were not. The Treaty of Sèvres was to be an imposed not a negotiated treaty."

By this time Lloyd George was one hundred per cent committed to Zaharoff's reckless plans. At one moment he promised Constantinople to the Greeks; then he retracted. But Zaharoff would not let him retreat too far; he had bargained for Britain and won favours for British capitalists and he was determined to demand something in return from Britain. He told Lloyd George:

"I want a free hand to direct matters in the Middle East. The crisis is near. I want you to support every Greek move against the Turks from now on."

Then one day Lloyd George came to see him. "They tell me it is your birthday today," said Ll. G. casually. "I should like to give you a present that will make you really happy. So go along and tell your friend Venizelos that I make you a present of Asia Minor."

It was probably one of the happiest days of Zaharoff's life, but it was a birthday present that was to cost Greece a hundred thousand lives and Zaharoff himself a loss of some millions of pounds.

Even at this juncture Zaharoff was not entirely satisfied. He reminded Ll. G. that despite the fact that Greece had rejected the offer of Cyprus by Britain early in World War I, Greek aspirations still extended to this island. Zaharoff had pressed Lloyd George for some few years on this subject, but so far all he had obtained from him was a guarded statement by the British Premier in a letter to the Archbishop of Cyprus in November, 1919, that "the wishes of the inhabitants of Cyprus for union with Greece will be taken into a most careful and sympathetic consideration by the Government when they consider its future". Without consulting his colleagues, Ll. G. agreed to cede

Cyprus "as soon as the Turkish business was settled and at the same time that Italy ceded Rhodes to Greece".

This fatal promise marked the beginning of the long and bitter Enosis campaign for the cession of Cyprus and which, on the basis of Lloyd George's promise, was vigorously renewed in 1947 when Greece and Italy made peace with the cession of Rhodes as part of the bargain. The Prime Minister's colleagues vigorously disagreed with the assurance he had made of his own accord, and the next Government took advantage of Turkey's cession of all rights to the island by making it a Crown colony.

The gift of Asia Minor to Greece made Italy the potential enemy of Britain for the first time in modern history. In May, 1919, the Greeks occupied Smyrna with the tacit approval of the "Big Four". For once Lloyd George bulldozed through French, American and Italian opposition, ruthlessly forcing his own decisions without a thought for the diplomatic consequences, and, against the advice of British and French military experts, drew up a treaty which put Smyrna and Eastern Thrace under Greek control and internationalised Constantinople and the Straits.

"You will live to regret this crazy blunder," Poincaré warned Ll. G. "When you incorporated this plan in the Treaty of Sèvres you made certain that you had built something as fragile as Sèvres porcelain. Within a few years it will be smashed to little pieces."

17

THE END OF THE COALITION

"The garlands wither on your brow;
Then boast no more your mighty deeds."
J. Shirley

The European situation changed swiftly when Poincaré became Premier of France after the fall of Briand. Poincaré was a naturally suspicious man; it was perhaps his major defect and due to an insularity of outlook which, while not preventing him from being remarkably far-sighted in his summing-up of foreign problems, impeded seriously his dealings with the statesmen of other nations. Poincaré was insistent that the Treaty of Versailles must be enforced to the last full stop and against any concessions to Germany or Russia, appreciating more than Lloyd George the dangers of a remilitarized Germany unless the Allies stood firmly together.

Two men more different in temperament and mental processes than Lloyd George and Poincaré would have been hard to find in political circles. Each was so much the antithesis of the other that a mutual antagonism and irritation was inevitable. Ll. G. had charm, whereas Poincaré was to many people so lacking in that quality that he appeared repulsive. By now the British Prime Minister realised that he could not continue to carry on diplomacy by a mixture of charm and bullying. Charm alone carried no weight at all with Poincaré: if anything it repelled him. Nevertheless, realising the seriousness of the rift with France, Ll. G. went to Paris to try to win over the French Premier, making him an offer of full naval and military support to France in the event of any future aggression by Germany. "You make this suggestion rather late in the day," snapped Poincaré. "Why could it not have been made eighteen months ago? I am not convinced that this proposal is made in good faith. Have you discussed it with your Cabinet colleagues?"

The atmosphere of the talks was stormy from the outset. Poincaré was foolishly hostile and unyielding and he made no secret of his mistrust of Lloyd George personally. Ll. G., on the other hand, seems to have made a real effort at last to dispel the tension between the two countries. He tried to suggest to Poincaré that this offer had been "agreed in principle a year before", but that there had been so much other work to occupy his mind in the meantime.

"More important work than Anglo-French solidarity?" asked the Frenchman. "My information is that you have not discussed it with your Cabinet. How can I take you seriously on so serious a matter as this when you do not trust your judgment to submit it to your colleagues?"

The talks continued in this acrimonious vein. The offer of a pact, argued the French Premier, must be clear and detailed. Where were the details? He insisted that there must be a Military Convention with specific undertakings about the number of troops, divisions and equipment which Britain would furnish in such an emergency. Britain had not even got conscription; how could she underwrite such flimsy proposals?

Ll. G. had made a verbal offer of a security pact with France, guaranteeing that Britain would come to her aid, during Briand's premiership, but Briand had been defeated shortly afterwards. Now he repeated this offer, but Poincaré demanded it should be "in writing, in detail and with complete sets of figures". But Ll. G. was not prepared to agree to a Military Convention with precise details: how could he when, on the evidence of Dr. Thomas Jones, he was acting in advance of Cabinet approval already, evidence which justified Poincaré's taunt.

Poincaré's caution amounted to an exasperating aberration to foreigners when subjects concerning the security of France were under discussion. His orderly mind irritated Lloyd George. It was the battle of the unbriefed, fiery advocate, prepared to compromise, against the lawyer who disliked oratory and stuck rigidly to his brief. If Poincaré lacked the wit and sparkle of the Welshman, he made up for it by devastating repartee and a grasp of facts and figures that were the product of a mind resembling a filing cabinet.

Somewhat pompously, Mr. Malcolm Thomson, Lloyd George's official biographer, commented on these discussions: "The British do not measure out their military contributions by the pennyworth when their word is pledged, or their honour and national interests are involved in a struggle. The offer of a guarantee lapsed."

But the offer should never have been allowed to lapse. Poincaré certainly exacerbated the situation by his intransigence, but he was acting in the true, if rather narrow, interests of his country. A vaguely worded guarantee to France would have been the worst possible result for both nations. In any event why did not Lloyd George agree to consult his Cabinet colleagues and put forward a new and more detailed plan? Was the answer that some of his colleagues—particularly the provincially insular Bonar Law, with a phobia about any kind of commitment and a dislike of making up his own mind—would not have agreed to anything so precise? Wickham Steed wrote at the time that Lloyd George had informed M. Barthou, the French Foreign

Minister, that "British opinion was hostile to France and his advisers, especially Lord Birkenhead, had been constantly advising him to break with France". This statement was repudiated by the Prime Minister and by Sir Austen Chamberlain, and Mr. Frank Owen explains that Wickham Steed's "informants had mixed up two interviews, one between Lloyd George and Barthou and another between him and Philippe Millet, a French journalist . . . though the general sense of what Lloyd George said was perhaps not so very far different from Steed's version". Here, at least, appears powerful confirmation of the irresponsibility of Lloyd George in his interview to foreign Press men and that anti-French attitude which continually ruined relations with Paris and made him so deeply mistrusted there.

After World War II, Britain very nearly made the same mistake again until, in the face of far worse difficulties in France than in 1919–22, Sir Anthony Eden made his famous categorical pledge to maintain British troops on the Continent for fifty years at the Conference of London in 1954.

The Treaty of Versailles was, perhaps, the best compromise that could be reached in so short a time after the war. But it need not and should not have been rushed through so quickly. Had it been carried out to the letter, as the French wanted, had Britain given something more than lip service to the League of Nations, it might have formed the basis for a more comprehensive treaty later on. Lloyd George was right in his belated demand that Russia and Germany should not be treated as outsiders, but France was also right in insisting that they should not be admitted into the counsels of nations until adequate guarantees had been worked out. The divergence of views among the Allies when the Treaty of Versailles was signed must inevitably have forced it to be replaced by something more durable unless chaos was to intervene. After World War I the French insisted that the placating of American opinion was relatively unimportant as they were convinced that the Americans would discard Wilson and repudiate the League. The view was realistic as it happened, but the attitude was short-sighted. What was more serious was the rift between France and Britain caused by a remorseless logic and a deep mistrust on the part of France, and a fickle policy on the part of her neighbour across the Channel for trying to be all things to all nations. Thus was the good work of Lansdowne and Grey ruined, enabling later on such poisoners of Anglo-French relations as Laval, Darlan and Déat to rise to power.

Maynard Keynes, witty, skittish, donnish and quixotic, became the symbol of that power without responsibility which has been the curse of modern economists. Already headlong in pursuit of his dream to make inflation respectable and to cure unemployment by an orgy of spending, he drew a grossly exaggerated picture of the economic consequences of the peace. His criticisms of the Treaty's financial aspects

The Irish rebellion: a street barricade in Dublin.

Topix Picture Service

Michael Collins addressing a meeting.

Radio Times Hulton Picture Library

Keystone

A typical oratorical pose.

—right as far as they went—were extended into a general attack on the whole settlement. His arguments were used by the banker-industrialists to pump funds into German industry and so bring about a new armaments race, while the pacifist-economists and politicians distorted them into a plea for excusing German rearmament by blaming it on Versailles.

Versailles provided a glimmer of hope, it showed far away a torch of reason and justice, but none grasped the chance to reach it because in truth the statesmen knew, even though they did not admit it, that World War I was never finished off. For Germany it was a war that need never have been lost and therefore one to be started again as soon as possible; for France there was the deep and abiding fear of yet another holocaust, a belief that Europe would continue in a state of war unless she put a ring of satellite states around Germany; in Italy there was disillusionment and a feeling that she had lost as a victor where the neutrals had gained much; in Russia there was an unmistakable desire to seize every opportunity to weaken the hated capitalist nations of the West. At Versailles, Cannes and Genoa enough was said and done by cynical statesmen to ensure that war would flare up again. No single statesman, except Wilson, gave a lead in mobilising the widespread pacifist sentiment into a tremendous moral force which, through the League, could have spoken "nation unto nation" far more effectively than the self-appointed doyens of the clenched fist.

* * * * *

Only politically immature Soviet Russia seems to have shown any real foresight or diplomatic skill during this period. Russia, by Marxist tactics in her foreign policy, achieved an accord with the Germans to the anger of the Allies. Czarist Russia, with unconcealed expansionist aims, had claimed Constantinople as her prize when victory came. Soviet Russia, having withdrawn from the war, could not, of course, possibly make any such claim. So she did better: she wisely and categorically renounced it. It is sometimes assumed that Turkey and Russia are natural enemies and must always be so, yet on three occasions in the nineteenth century events forced them into alliance—in 1800, against Napoleon, in 1833, against Mohamed Ali, and in 1849, when the two countries jointly occupied the Danubian principalities.

In 1921 France realised what Lloyd George ignored—the intrinsically Western character of Turkish civilisation. As results showed, the Europeanisation of Turkey by Kemal was really the culmination of a long-cherished national aspiration. So the French decided to answer British chicanery with an even more ruthless chicanery of their own. It was understandable. Double-crossed for the past three years, thwarted in almost every move she made, threatened with the prospect of a new war in the Middle and Near East, France had little alternative but to fight Lloyd George in the only manner which he seemed to understand. France had powerful interests, commercial and financial, in Turkey, which she was determined not to lose. Turkey, argued France, must stay strong and stable, so secretly she came to an agreement which led to her selling arms to the Turks and confirming that Constantinople should be left in Turkish hands. This French secret intervention on the Turkish side coincided with the handing over to Greece of most of Turkey-in-Europe except Constantinople and Western Asia Minor. But the Treaty of Sèvres was never ratified. Poincaré's prophecy came true.

Kemal Ataturk proved himself a statesman as well as a general of no ordinary calibre. He had set up a provisional capital at Angora (now Ankara) and reformed and re-equipped the Turkish army, while a secret understanding with Russia enabled him confidently to face the future without a threat from that direction.

Venizelos's hour of triumph was brief. He was defeated in his country's General Election in November, 1920. Back into power came King Constantine who continued the campaign in Anatolia with Lloyd George's secret encouragement. When the Greeks were defeated at the Battle of Sakbaria, the ultimate issue was not in doubt. On August 26, 1922, Mustapha Kemal attacked and destroyed their columns. The Greek army dissolved into rebellious mobs with the Turkish cavalry hard at their heels. By September 9, Mustapha Kemal occupied Smyrna and drove the Greeks across the Straits into Europe. The town was enveloped in flames.

There have been many accounts of these actions, many of which have portrayed the raping, looting Turks pursuing the Greeks in a frenzy of blood lust. It is therefore worth noting that a close associate of Lloyd George, Viscount St. Davids, delivered a striking indictment of Greek conduct at this time. Speaking at the half-yearly meeting of the Ottoman Railway Company, which ran from Smyrna to Aidin, he said that the Greeks "burned every Turkish village they saw. They robbed individual Turks, and when these resisted they killed them, and they did all this nowhere near the front and without military necessity. They did it out of sheer malice. Our reports are that it was done systematically by regular troops under orders.

"The Greeks took from Smyrna a number of leading Turks and deported them to Athens. I do not know whether it was done to squeeze money out of them, or to hold them as hostages. King Constantine's servants are very bad at fighting, but they are first class at robbery, arson and murder."

Unlucky King Constantine, so badly served by his advisers, was hounded out of Greece with insult and mockery. In Athens there was a great upheaval and six ministers, condemned for high treason, were dealt with by a firing squad.

Three months later Constantine died in exile at Palermo.

* * * * *

The machinations of Zaharoff and his relations with Lloyd George not only aroused the deepest suspicions of pacifists in the Labour ranks, to whom the arms magnate was a black-hearted, bloody villain, but disturbed many orthodox Conservatives. Labour regarded Zaharoff as a malevolent figure who pulled the strings of international finance and stirred up strife with the object of selling more armaments. For Lloyd George, the erstwhile pacifist, to associate with such a man was to them the basest treachery. The Conservatives were concerned because they saw that Britain's Greek policy was not only drawing the country into a new and disastrous war, but alienating Moslem opinion in the Empire.[1]

In the House of Commons on July 17, 1922, Lieut.-Colonel the Hon. Aubrey Herbert said: "I do not want to mention names, but there is one name I shall mention, and that is the name of a very great financier, who is reputed to be the richest man in the world—Sir Basil Zaharoff—it is said that his very great wealth is derived from this source: that he has owned munition factories in many countries.

"He has been one of the strong supporters of the Greek policy. The result of that Greek policy has been that the whole of the East is in chaos, and that Great Britain has made enemies throughout the entire East. Sir Basil Zaharoff is reputed to have paid £4 millions out of his own pocket for the upkeep of the Greek invading force in Asia Minor."

In the House of Commons and in the country the campaign against Lloyd George and Zaharoff was stepped up. Lord Rothermere, who now had charge of the *Daily Mail*, said that "the Levantine Zaharoff must be taught that the British nation was master in its own house". Lord Beaverbrook's *Daily Express* demanded that the doors of Government offices should be shut to Sir Basil and his agents. Beaverbrook, who had helped to bring Lloyd George to power, was now convinced that the Prime Minister was set on a course that could only bring hardship and disaster to the Empire.

The persistent Lieut.-Colonel Herbert asked: "If Sir Basil was consulted before the Greek landing at Smyrna by the Foreign Office or the Prime Minister." No satisfactory answer was ever given. Officially, of course, Zaharoff was never called into the Coalition Government's counsels, nor was he ever received at the Foreign Office during this period. His sole dealings were with Lloyd George

[1] There has always been a powerful, yet informal and unorganised pro-Moslem "lobby" in the Tory ranks.

in private. His agents were in constant touch with officials at No. 10, at the Board of Trade and prominent in the counsels of the Prime Minister's notorious "Shadow Foreign Office".

Mr. Walter Guinness in a scathing speech declared that "the voice behind the Prime Minister was probably that of Sir Basil Zaharoff", and added that if it was necessary for Ll. G. to have advisers at all in foreign affairs, these should be English.

These criticisms were fairly easily muted because Zaharoff had then covered his machinations too well. He had even wisely safeguarded his finances against a possible set-back to the extent of founding in March, 1920, when war with Turkey seemed imminent, a new bank, the *Banque Commerciale de la Mediterranée*, which was housed in the same building as that of the former *Deutsche Orientbank* in Constantinople.

From the sun-baked rocks of Anatolia Mustapha Kemal conjured an improvised but efficient fighting machine and drove the Greek troops, financed by Zaharoff and armed by Britain, out of Smyrna with weapons provided by France. The policy of "keeping the French down" had completely boomeranged. It meant the end of Greek imperialist ambitions and the renaissance of Turkey. It struck a blow at Britain's prestige in the Middle East from which she has never since recovered.

Lloyd George's reaction was one of panic. He imagined that Kemal would chase the Greeks into Europe and set the Balkans ablaze with a curtain of fire. Now he turned to the hand he had bitten and begged aid from France. To Italy and all the British dominions he went, almost abjectedly, pleading for aid against Turkey. The Allied Commander-in-Chief, Sir Charles Harington, was ordered to defend the neutral zones.

The replies from France and Italy were swift: each nation ordered its forces to be withdrawn. The British dominions viewed the situation with dismay and showed no desire to be drawn into "Lloyd George's war". The Canadian Premier objected publicly, the Australian privately; only New Zealand and Newfoundland offered help.

It has been argued that, in standing firm, Lloyd George saved the situation from developing into a major Balkan war. His action in making an isolated stand is said to have stayed the advance of Kemal. Had Kemal desired to press on, nothing could have stopped him. In fact there is no evidence that he had any intention of pushing into the Balkans. When an armistice was concluded at Madania in October, 1922, it was largely due to the common sense and statesmanship of the soldier on the spot, Sir Charles Harington, and Kemal's calculating moderation. Yet these last acts of the Coalition Government have been hailed as a moral victory for Lloyd George. Dr. Thomas Jones wrote: "Lloyd George's promptitude prevented war, his desire to deliver Asia Minor from the Turkish yoke was defeated, but the Arab world—Iraq, Arabia, Palestine and Syria—was set free. Turkey and Britain were reconciled and their friendship endured throughout the second world war."

Friendship with Turkey, in fact, only developed later and then mainly through the close personal relationship which the British Ambassador, Sir George Clarke, established with Kemal. Even so, Turkey remained neutral in World War II. As for the setting free of the Arab world, this really meant a veneer of freedom beneath which all these territories were exploited by capitalism in the place of imperialism.

* * * * *

The Turkish adventure caused the Tory back-benchers to exert more pressure on their leaders to withdraw from the Government, and discipline in the Coalition ranks collapsed. But the rot had set in long before this: the Greek-Turkish conflict was merely the last nail in a coffin which should long before have been laid to rest. In an effort to placate the Tories some time before this, Ll. G. had completely antagonised his left-wing supporters by his treatment of Dr. Addison. Addison had been mainly responsible for the Housing and Town Planning Act designed to provide the homes "fit for heroes", but in setting about his task with tremendous enthusiasm, neglected to provide adequate stocks of materials. Prices for building materials which were in short supply rocketed to unprecedented levels and the Government declined to introduce any controls even as a temporary measure. Lloyd George decided to appease the Tories rather than to come to the aid of his old friend Addison by taking such measures, cynically revealing his intention in this cruel letter to Austen Chamberlain:

"I will send for Addison. . . . He does not in the least realise his position. He regards himself as a martyr to the cause of public health. . . . Men in this condition of exaltation are very difficult to deal with and I am not looking forward to a very pleasant conversation with him."

Addison never knew of this letter. He was forced, according to Carson, by "a disgusting intrigue" to resign. It was one of the worst political betrayals of an era of betrayals and Addison always insisted that, if he had been allowed to carry on, he would "have abolished the slums". Later he was to stage a magnificent come-back, taking office in two Labour Governments and eventually being made a peer, Labour leader in the House of Lords and the first Knight of the Garter in the Socialist ranks.

"If Lloyd George was a political Samson," wrote Mr. Malcolm Thomson, "Greece had unwittingly been cast for his Delilah, and delivered him bound into the hands of the Tory Philistines." Conservatives meeting at the Carlton Club decided by a vote of 186 to 87 that there must be an appeal to the country at once and that the Tory

Party should act independently and with "no understanding" with Lloyd George. Austen Chamberlain, Balfour and Birkenhead among the Tories remained loyal to Ll. G. to the last; Bonar Law, whom he had trusted, hesitantly capitulated to the Tory Party machine. The Tory Ministers left the Government and Lloyd George tendered his resignation to the King. The worst Parliament in modern history had ended its career.

Bonar Law formed a Conservative Government and immediately went to the country, the Tories gaining a majority of seventy-two seats over all other parties, the Socialists moving into second place, with the Independent and National Liberals coming third and fourth.

18

WORSHIPPING THE MOLTEN CALF

"And he . . . fashioned it with a graving tool, after he had made it a molten calf; and they said, 'These be thy gods, O Israel, which brought thee up out of the land of Egypt.'"

Exodus, c. XXXII, v. 4

When a Prime Minister deliberately sets out to create for himself a vast personal fund with which he can dominate, blackmail and destroy the very existence of a political Party, the foundations of even an ancient and well-tested democracy are threatened. Out of the instrument of a political fund Lloyd George fashioned a molten calf which proved to be the undoing of the great Liberal Party to which he belonged.

Perhaps the quickest and most cutting retort to which he was ever subjected in the House of Commons was made by Mr. Wedgwood Benn. The Labour Government of 1929–30 had promised dominion status for India. Ll. G., with his fondness for Biblical metaphor, described how Mr. Benn, then Secretary of State for India, had smashed the "tables of the Covenant and substituted new ones of his own".

"This pocket edition of Moses," was his description of Mr. Benn.

"But I never worshipped the Golden Calf," retorted the Secretary of State, misquoting from Exodus.

It was a rebuke which reduced Lloyd George to an unaccustomed silence.

The earliest financial scandal in which Lloyd George was involved was the Marconi Affair. In his early days, no doubt due to the exhortations of Uncle Richard, he had shown on many occasions a disregard for wealth, the Boer War being a prime example of this. But, as promotion succeeded promotion, as he drew nearer to the coveted Premiership, so his heart hardened and he became more conscious of the power which the possession of wealth could bring. Early in 1912 rumours in the City alleged that Liberal ministers were speculating in shares as a result of their knowledge of negotiations on behalf of the British Government with the English Marconi Company for a network of wireless stations which the Committee of Imperial Defence had insisted on being set up. The Postmaster-General, Sir Herbert Samuel (now Lord Samuel) had negotiated with the Marconi Company for the work, and on March 7, 1912, accepted their tender subject to parliamentary approval. The chairman of the English company was Godfrey Isaacs, brother of Sir Rufus Isaacs, a member of the Liberal Government. The following month the American Marconi Company, which had no financial connections with the British company of the same name, made an issue of new shares and Godfrey Isaacs agreed to place a block of these on the British market.

Godfrey Isaacs offered his brother Rufus some of the shares, but the Attorney-General at first declined them, only subsequently making a purchase of 10,000 shares when he learned that the American company was quite independent of the British concern. Lloyd George was at this time very friendly with Rufus Isaacs and, on the latter's suggestion, he and the Master of Elibank bought from him 1,000 shares each. The shares rose two days later when dealings opened on the London Stock Exchange and Ll. G. sold half his holding for a profit of £743, buying a further 1,500 shares a month afterwards as an investment.

Rumours of these dealings, some of them ventilated in the Press, led to the setting up of a select committee to inquire into the matter. This committee opined that there was no foundation for charges of corruption and "no ground for any reflection upon the honour of the Ministers concerned". This verdict was accepted, but Lloyd George's frank admission that he regretted the purchases had been made and that he had been indiscreet did not convince the House, a vote of censure being lost by only 346 votes to 268. Lloyd George's biographers have already given much space to the Marconi Scandal and for that reason it seems out of place to reiterate here what has been well documented elsewhere, more especially as, in fairness to Lloyd George, his part in the whole affair, though indiscreet in the light of the publicity accorded it, was far less serious than that of the Attorney-General, Sir Rufus Isaacs. The point of mentioning this incident and taking it out of chronological order in this chapter is not to indict Lloyd George, but to show how in his middle and later years he gradually took a shrewder interest in pecuniary gain. Mr. Frank Owen states that Ll. G. "offered the Prime Minister his resignation, but Asquith had stood by him loyally". Certainly Asquith regarded the political uproar about the deals as distasteful and out of proportion and it was generally conceded at the time that Lloyd George owed him much in escaping the full consequences of this escapade. Equally loyal at this time was Winston Churchill, who even went to the extent of persuading Northcliffe to handle the story in a friendly way.

But the Marconi Scandal pales into insignificance in comparison with the story of a Prime Minister who sought to build up a financial war chest over which he could have supreme control.

Lloyd George, having tasted the sweets of office, had no desire to sustain himself on the strictly rationed fare of a secondary figure in the

Liberal Party, nor did the prospect of an old-fashioned Tory menu appeal to him even if he were appointed head waiter of the "club" he had spent so many years berating. His chances of success, as he saw them, consisted either of forming a new Centre Party through which he could weaken the main Parties by drawing support from Liberals and Tories and bolstering it up with non-Party businessmen, or maintaining a Coalition Government for an indefinite period on the grounds that the national interest required it.

To achieve either object he needed funds. As a free-lance Prime Minister with no Party machine behind him he was at a disadvantage. Therefore, while on the count of Party loyalty he can be condemned for acting in a manner calculated to destroy the Party to which he belonged and to upset the political equilibrium of the nation, he was within his rights in seeking to give himself both a Party machine and funds to maintain it. That is the right of any political leader in any democratic country. But the manner in which he built up his fund and his despotic control over it are quite different matters. In effect he issued not one, but several false prospectuses—verbally, of course, and not in writing or print—to lure people to contribute to the fund. These lures were all so different that they often contradicted each other and no one could be sure whether the purpose for which he had contributed was valid in Lloyd George's eyes.

During the war Lloyd George's income from investments increased considerably. Lord Riddell had purchased a house for him at Walton Heath, and in 1919 Carnegie endowed him with a life pension of £2,000. Nevertheless, Lloyd George, though comfortably off, had not yet achieved the great wealth of his later days and he insisted on maintaining the strictest personal control over his political fund.

His simple life of earlier days had given way to a more spacious and opulent mode of living. Though no spendthrift—in many ways the reverse—he acquired a love of luxury and he was continually seeking alternative methods of making an income should he ever decide to quit politics. Towards the end of World War I he had been very anxious to obtain control of a newspaper for furthering his own interests. He secured an interest in the *Daily Chronicle* and *Lloyds Sunday News* through the agency of Lord Dalziel; he also acquired a controlling interest in the *Edinburgh Evening News* and the *Yorkshire Evening News*. When Lloyd George took an active interest in the *Daily Chronicle* he developed a profound dislike for the editor, Sir Robert Donald, and sacked him. Eventually he sold the *Daily Chronicle* at a substantial profit and always claimed that his fund benefited from this.

Less well known is Lloyd George's attempt to buy *The Times* in 1922 shortly before the fall of his Government. He was anxious to have control of the most influential newspaper in the country during an expected period in opposition. Northcliffe had died the previous

August and Ll. G. sounded out various friends with a view to making an offer. One of these friends was David Davies, the coal-owner, who was promised the office of senior trustee of the paper. Yet even in his efforts to bring off this deal Lloyd George could not refrain from double-crossing his friends; he promised the post of editor to Lionel Curtis, yet told David Davies that he himself would be managing editor and that he would "give up my connection with the House of Commons". It is believed that Davies himself extracted this promise from Ll. G., though it seems equally certain that Ll. G. would never have agreed to leave politics permanently.

There was at the time a rumour, never substantiated, that he had approached Zaharoff for funds for *The Times*. It is known that Zaharoff was anxious to obtain an interest in a British newspaper and that he had sometimes selected *Times* correspondents in the Balkans as sub-agents for Vickers. Sir Basil, according to his obituary in *The Times*, also had newspaper interests in Britain, though it was never clearly divulged what these were.[1]

But the very whisper of such a plan for Lloyd George to acquire control of *The Times* was enough to bring powerful forces to bear, and these made quite sure that this paper would never fall into his hands. The Lloyd Georgian bid for *The Times* resulted in that newspaper being converted into a trust permanently safe from the intrigues of a single individual.

Some contributions to the Lloyd George Fund were genuine gifts from personal admirers, possibly given without any qualifications. Others came from businessmen who were anxious to be on the Coalition band-wagon, or as payment for the privilege of being given office in the Government, or key posts in the Civil Service. Thus the principle was established of buying one's way into political power and into the Civil Service, often over the heads of competent professional servants of the state, who had the frustrating experience of seeing untrained self-seekers promoted over their heads. But by far the worst feature of the fund was its subsidising by the sale of honours and titles. It was in this sphere that Sir William Sutherland—in the early stages at least—and the notorious Maundy Gregory were touts-in-chief for the Lloyd George war chest, and the latter succeeded not only in enhancing Lloyd George's power, but, by deducting commissions for services rendered, in substantially enriching himself.

Arthur Maundy Gregory, like Zaharoff, had a genius for obliterating vital clues for anyone trying to probe his past. The son of a vicar of Southampton, he was for a time an actor-producer and, after 1909, he claimed that he ran a private detective agency on the strength of

[1] The *Sunday Express* stated in 1922 that Zaharoff was part owner of a prominent Coalition newspaper which was assumed at the time to refer to the *Daily Chronicle*, though this was denied.

which he was able to offer his talents to the Secret Service when war broke out. Certain it is that he worked closely with Sir Basil Thomson and Sir Vernon Kell, the head of M.I.5. This, however, does not explain the extraordinary influence which Gregory came to have in the years immediately after the war, nor does it account for his apparent wealth, nor his close association with King George of Greece, King Alfonso of Spain and the Montenegrin royal family. It was Sir William Sutherland who introduced Lloyd George to Gregory, and he was the principal intermediary for exchanges between them. Sometimes there were telephone calls between No. 10 and Gregory's offices in Parliament Street, but more often the Prime Minister discussed business through Sutherland, "Freddie" Guest, his Chief Whip, and Sir Warden Chilcott, a close friend of the Prime Minister and Coalition M.P. for a Liverpool constituency. A plump, middle-sized man who always wore a rose or an orchid in his buttonhole, a bon viveur and lavish host, Gregory flitted in the wings of the Coalition stage like a gilded butterfly, waiting, watching, scheming, enriching himself and others.

There were precedents for raising political funds by the sale of honours. The purchase of titles was practised by the Stuart kings; Charles II and his ministers bribed M.P.s with pensions and subsidies. Walpole was a notorious trafficker in honours, while Lord Bute as Prime Minister in 1762 was reputed to have paid £25,000 for securing a majority for the Peace of Paris.[1]

But in Victoria's day the practice was condemned. Lord Palmerston bluntly told an honours tout: "The throne is a fount of honour. It is not a pump, nor am I the pump handle." To confirm this generally accepted thesis Lord Selborne proposed a resolution in the House of Lords in February, 1914, urging that a contribution to Party funds should not be considered justification when honours were being given and that all Parties should adhere to this rule. This perhaps is some indication that there were still breaches of the unwritten rule on this subject and that rich men who contributed to Party funds somehow found themselves recommended for honours. The fact that the initiative for the donation of honours had through the centuries been passed from Monarch to Prime Minister had not been an adequate safeguard against the abuse of this prerogative. While King George II could, by the kind of brilliant inspiration that comes to kings more easily than politicians, bestow a knighthood on a dragoon who had cut his way through the French cavalry, two centuries later Raymond Asquith was bitterly complaining in World War II that, when it came to decorations, it was always found that the Dukes were the bravest men and after them the Marquises.

Yet there was no public outcry, no major criticism on the subject of honours won through contributing to Party funds until the Coalition

[1] Stanhope's *History of England: 1713–83*.

era. Lloyd George, who had boasted of his cottage ancestry and had been the most vehement critic of privilege, took a closer interest in the subject of honours than any other Prime Minister of this century, or indeed, of the previous hundred years. This was the measure of the extent to which power had corrupted him and almost corroded the idealism of his youth. It might possibly be said in extenuation that, because he detested privilege and honours, he cynically set out to ridicule the honours racket by what he did and that his exploitation of them were indirectly an indictment of the whole system. Yet the fact remains that he put back the clock to the days of the Stuarts and Georges, disregarding the Victorians and Lord Selborne who took a wiser view of such abuses.

Sir Harold Nicolson tells us that Sir George Younger, the Unionist Chief Whip, did not "appreciate the Prime Minister's distribution of honours, or the accumulation under his personal control of large election funds. The King himself questioned the suitability of some of those whom the Prime Minister recommended for high distinction. Mr. Lloyd George insisted, and the King with explicit reluctance was obliged to give his assent."

In the State Papers at Windsor Castle there is some very acrimonious correspondence on the subject of honours, but Lloyd George always refused to put his views on honours in writing to the King.

There was constant bickering between Lloyd George's representatives and Sir George Younger on honours. It is certain that Younger's views were tinged with jealousy of the Ll. G. fund. Bitterly he complained: "These damned rascals come to me demanding to be made knights and, when I refuse, go straight round to Lloyd George's Whip's office and get what they want from him."

To what extent the Tories also dabbled in the sale of titles at this time is uncertain, but it was never on the same scale as the Lloyd Georgians. Mr. Robert Blake in his biography of Bonar Law, *The Unknown Prime Minister*, throws some light on Tory dealings with Ll. G. in this connection. He quotes Lord Edmund Talbot as saying about Lord Farquhar (the Conservative Party treasurer): "I have a strong suspicion that he has handed sums—perhaps large sums—to Ll. G. for his Party, while acting as our treasurer."

Lord Farquhar, who had received an earldom from Lloyd George, had been involved in a row about some Tory funds which, Farquhar claimed, belonged to the Coalition Fund and not the Conservative Party. Presumably by "Coalition" he meant the Lloyd George fund.

Mr. Blake also revealed that Hicks, the Conservative Party accountant, was told by Farquhar that the latter had "given no money to Ll. G. except £80,000 from Astor". This referred to Lord Astor who had died in 1919. Farquhar insisted that Lord Astor had given him £200,000 to dispose of as he saw fit and that he had given £40,000 to a charity in which the King was interested and divided the rest between the Tory funds and the Lloyd George fund.

"But no money was handed over to me," replied Talbot. The mystery of what happened to the balance of the £200,000 remains unsolved, but it would seem that a great deal of it went to the Ll. G. fund.[1]

Maundy Gregory, who was also an associate of Lord Riddell, saw illimitable possibilities for making money out of his association with Lloyd George. From the latter's viewpoint Gregory had one positive asset: he had no political affiliations, yet, being on closer terms with the Tories than the Liberals, he was able to lure Tories into the Coalition camp as well as sell them honours. At the end of the war there was an enormous surplus of wealth, swollen by profiteering, in the hands of a number of very rich men. Businessmen purchased titles as they would a yacht or a piece of land. Lloyd George, with a combination of cynicism and flattery, encouraged the practice of selling honours until his personal fund was past the £3,000,000 mark. There are some people who put the total higher and say that at least another million went to the Prime Minister's own pocket.

A fluctuating tariff for titles met both the seniority of the honour and the pocket of the recipient. The top price for a peerage is known to have exceeded £150,000 and baronies were considered cheap at £80,000. A baronetcy cost as much as £50,000 and ordinary knighthoods round about £12,000. Lesser honours, though costing hundreds instead of thousands, were so prolific that they produced a considerable aggregate. In 1917, on his own initiative and on the advice of Sir William Sutherland, probably with some prompting from Maundy Gregory, Lloyd George created the Order of the British Empire.

This title, which rapidly became a music-hall joke because of the lavish way in which it was dispensed, soon brought opprobrium rather than respect to its recipients. No fewer than 25,000 O.B.E.s were distributed during Lloyd George's ministries and afterwards the Bonar Law Government altered the Order's statutes to limit its future membership. In Britain O.B.E. was contemptuously referred to as "Order of the Bad Egg" on account of the many "bad eggs" among its members, while in France the *chansoniers* of the cabarets called it the *Ordre Britannique Embusqué*.

Viscountcies, baronies, baronetcies and knighthoods were stepped up at a rate which not only infuriated hereditary members of the House of Lords, but worried King George V, whose responsibility it was to confirm the honours lists submitted to him. Between 1916 and 1923 Ll. G. nominated ninety-one new peers, double the average of

[1] Lord Beaverbrook gives more details of this chicanery in *The Decline and Fall of Lloyd George*, Only after he had been made an Earl was it discovered that Farquhar was an undisclosed bankrupt who had been secretly diverting the huge sums the Tories had acquired through the Honours system into Lloyd George's political fund.

new peerages created either by Asquith or Campbell-Bannerman during an exceptional period when it was politically necessary to increase the Liberal representation in the Lords.

Prior to 1918, pointed out the Duke of Northumberland in 1922, "Only two or three honours were conferred upon journalists every year, but you will find that the number of this profession who have been appointed Privy Councillors, peers, baronets and knights since amounts to no fewer than forty-nine, and that number does not include C.M.G.s and other unconsidered trifles of that kind."

This reference to journalists also includes newspaper proprietors upon whom Lloyd George relied heavily for support. There never was an era when the Press of the nation had such an unhealthy and wholly unwarranted influence in Downing Street, though long before 1922 Northcliffe had become disenchanted with Ll. G, and Lord Beaverbrook, though a great admirer of the man and to a large extent his supporter, was sufficiently independent to come out strongly against the machinations of Zaharoff and the Greek adventure. But in other sections of the Press sycophancy could be detected. At a later period two such diverse figures as Stanley Baldwin and Aneurin Bevan equated sections of the British Press with "harlotry" and "prostitution": "Power without responsibility, the prerogative of the harlot throughout the ages," was Baldwin's comment; "The most prostituted Press in the world," was Bevan's. But in Coalition days those who went a-whoring in the newspaper world usually found that Ll. G. was the whoremaster and not the whore.

While all honours are in constitutional theory conferred by the Sovereign, in practice, of course, the Sovereign only confirms the recommendations of his or her ministers. The Prime Minister is responsible for advising the monarch on all awards except for those of the Services, the Orders of the Garter, Merit, St. Michael and St. George and the Royal Victorian Order. The Chief Whip of the political Party in power always has the major say in the award of political honours, and this was where Sutherland's influence made itself felt. Where the scope for corruption occurs most easily in the field of honours is in its allegedly democratic tradition that any person or recognised body of persons can recommend anyone for an honour.

It is remarkable that Lloyd George, who always had his ear to the ground for the first rumblings of public discontent, should have contemptuously ignored the growing criticism of his lavish and indiscriminate distribution of honours. He first of all excused himself on the grounds that an increase in awards was necessary in order to recognise services rendered during the war. But in the last eighteen months of his period of office he was still handing out titles as though they were handbills—26 peerages, 74 baronetcies and 294 knighthoods.

The lists between 1916 and 1923 contain countless examples of a flagrant disregard for the principles governing the conferring of awards. Zaharoff's embezzlement of funds did not prevent his receiving a knighthood. There was the peerage of Sir William Vestey, who, during the war, had moved his business to Argentina to avoid taxation, throwing some 5,000 men into unemployment as a consequence. The citation said he had "rendered immense services to his country" by providing "gratuitously the cold storage accommodation required for war purposes at Havre, Boulogne and Dunkirk". Yet it transpired that, while no payment had been made to Sir William for cold storage, payments had been made to the Union Cold Storage Company of which he was chairman.

Scores of businessmen were similarly honoured for "services" which were either non-existent or a distortion of the real facts. It was not surprising that the Prime Minister was asked in the House of Commons on June 20, 1922: "How much do you give for a baronetcy and what is the price of a knighthood?"

"Why is it," asked a Socialist member, "that only the very rich men seem to get the honours?"

A man who had been created a baronet one year and a Privy Councillor soon afterwards was later proved to have traded with the enemy. Another who had made his living by writing pornographic songs, which he sold secretly on the continent, was recommended for a knighthood. Fortunately someone at Buckingham Palace drew attention to the matter and the recommendation was speedily withdrawn. A man convicted of food hoarding was also knighted and another who had been found guilty of homosexual practices with young boys was awarded the C.B.E.

The Banker, a non-political journal of high standing, declared: "Many [referring to the latest honours list] are gross, illiterate profiteers, doubtful in their reputations, vulgar in their lives. . . . Mr. Lloyd George's funds are the wages of their over-gorged vanity."

Twenty-five distinguished persons wrote to *The Times* making a plea for greater care in selecting candidates for honours. Slowly the Press was shaking off its temporary sycophancy. Then on July 3, 1922, the King wrote to Lloyd George on the subject. In Sir Harold Nicolson's *King George V: His Life and Reign* this letter is published:

"My dear Prime Minister, I cannot conceal from you my profound concern at the very disagreeable situation which has arisen on the question of honours.

"The peerages which I was advised to confer upon Sir —— and Sir —— have brought things rather to a climax, though for some time there have been evident signs of growing public dissatisfaction on account of the excessive number of Honours conferred; the personality of some of the recipients and the questionable circumstances under which the Honours in certain circumstances have been granted.

"You will remember that both in conversation and in written communications I have deprecated the ever-increasing number of those submitted for the half-yearly Honours Gazette and in recent years there have been instances in which Honours have been bestowed where subsequent information has betrayed a lack of care in the enquiries made as to the fitness of the persons selected for recognition.

"The case of Sir —— must be regarded as little less than an insult to the Crown and to the House of Lords and may, I fear, work injury to the Prerogative in the public mind at home and even more in South Africa."

This last paragraph referred to the proposal to give a peerage to Sir Joseph Robinson. In the House of Lords the Lord Chancellor, Lord Birkenhead, admitted that no dominion citizen should have an honour conferred upon him without the approval of the Government of that dominion. But neither the Governor-General of the Union of South Africa nor the South African Premier had recommended Robinson. The last-named, who had been ordered by the Chief Justice of South Africa to pay £500,000 in compensation for making an "illicit profit" which he concealed from the shareholders of the Randfontein Estates Company, took fright at the furore raised in Parliament. He wrote, begging to "decline the proposal".

The citation announcing the award of a barony to Sir Joseph Robinson described him as "chairman of the South African National Banking Company". In fact this company had been liquidated seventeen years before!

Well might King George be concerned at the effect on public opinion in the dominions by the creation of such titles. In Canada, Parliament passed a resolution that no titles were to be conferred upon persons resident in Canada and that any such titles already conferred should be cancelled. A "no honours" motion was put forward in the South African Parliament.

One candidate for a peerage was asked by Maundy Gregory for the "fee" for obtaining this in advance of the honour being conferred. This cautious aspirant made out a cheque, post-dated it and then signed it by the title he proposed to take. Lord Rhondda, quoting the case of a South Wales peer, said he "Was paying for his honour on the hire-purchase system, but died before finishing the instalments. The executors refused to conclude the payments, saying they had no further use for the title."

Critics in both the Lords and the Commons forced the Government to take the subject of the abuse of titles seriously. A motion urging the appointment of a committee of inquiry, tabled by Mr. Locker-Lampson, supported by 180 members, finally forced a debate which was made the subject of a vote of confidence. But, as a last attempt to stave off a full-scale inquiry, Lloyd George proposed the appointment of a committee of three Privy Councillors to consider the question.

During the past six years, he claimed, there had been an exceptionally heavy honours list because of the war and these had included the names of more than 400 Servicemen.

This figure was challenged by Lieut.-Colonel Malone, who said there had only been twenty-four awards to Servicemen. The discrepancy between the two sets of figures can be explained by the familiar Lloyd Georgian technique with awkward statistics employed with the same dishonesty as in the Maurice debate. Lloyd George was referring to naval and military decorations as well in his total of more than 400 and these awards had no connection with the Prime Minister's department, whereas Lieut.-Colonel Malone showed that the number of peerages, baronetcies and knighthoods given to Servicemen were a paltry twenty-four compared with 173 honours of those categories to businessmen.

J. R. Clynes, from the Labour benches, quoted a devastating statement by Lord Carson, until recently a Cabinet Minister: "I have had more than once in my chambers to advise on cases in which I have examined long correspondence which showed there was a brokerage for the purpose of obtaining honours."

Proof of the sales of titles came from all quarters. The Duke of Northumberland in the House of Lords on July 17, 1922, told how "a gentleman who held a position of great civic importance in the north of England" had been informed by a certain M.P.[1] that to make sure of an honour he must contribute to Party funds. He declined to give any money and his name was not included in the next honours list. The Duke quoted from a letter sent by an honours tout to two distinguished men. The letter merely stated: "I am requested to place before you a matter of a very confidential nature which it is thought may be of interest to you. Will you kindly let me know whether you can suggest a meeting within the next few days in London or elsewhere. I cannot put more in a letter."

That letter, said the Duke, had emanated from 10, Downing Street, according to evidence he had received, and the recipient was told at a subsequent interview that he would have to pay £40,000 if he wanted a baronetcy. The man who received the second letter interviewed the writer and was told: "The Government would not last very long and that when Lloyd George went to the country he wanted funds to contest certain seats."

The Duke of Northumberland also gave details of a letter from another honours tout, a Mr. Robert Wells, who made an appointment with a prospective "victim". When asked the name of the person to whom the money was to be paid, Wells was quoted as saying: "It was formerly Sir William Sutherland. I don't know exactly who it will be this time, but probably Mr. McCurdy."

[1] Sir William Sutherland.

Charles McCurdy was Coalition Liberal Chief Whip at the time and was later on the committee of management of the Lloyd George fund.

Eventually the Prime Minister agreed to the appointment of a Royal Commission of Inquiry into the question of honours. Its terms of reference were obviously designed to avoid delving too deeply into the subject. The Commission had no power to compel the attendance of witnesses or to take evidence on oath, which ensured that the inquiry would be restricted. The terms of reference laid emphasis on the future, not the past: "To advise on the procedure to be adopted in future to assist the Prime Minister in making recommendations to His Majesty of the names of persons deserving special honours."

The Commission did not begin its meetings until after the Lloyd George Government had resigned. Its findings evaded the real issue. The recommendation that in future there should be a committee of three Privy Councillors, appointed by the Prime Minister, to whom he should submit his final honours list for scrutiny, was a piece of political eye-wash, even though it specifically stated that the Privy Councillors should not be members of the Government. The only really important recommendation was the proposal for an act imposing penalties on any person offering to become instrumental in securing an honour for another person in respect of a money payment.

The Commission's report was signed by all members except Mr. Arthur Henderson, who said:

"I am of opinion that the Commission might with advantage have made a more searching inquiry than they have done. I regret that though the Commissioners were in possession of the names of persons who are conveniently and appropriately described as 'touts', none of them has been invited to give evidence. Nor was any person who had been approached by 'touts' called to give evidence before us, though the names of such persons were also before the Commission. . . . The proposals contained in the report of my colleagues would not, if put into operation, be sufficient, in my opinion, to prevent abuses or to allay the suspicion which undoubtedly exists in the public mind."

In a final flurry to boost his political fund and knowing that responsibility would be his no longer, Ll. G. cynically announced forty-five names in his Resignation Honours List of 1922, nearly three times the number submitted by Asquith in 1916. Was it a mere coincidence that this list was published not officially from Buckingham Palace, as was customary, but from an official of the National Liberal Party headquarters.[1]

Echoes of the honours racket linking it with the Lloyd George fund continued for some years afterwards. At a meeting of creditors in con-

[1] It should be made clear that in this narrative any mention of "National Liberal" or "Coalition Liberal" whether to individuals or Parties refers strictly and only to Lloyd Georgian Liberals not to the official Liberal party.

nection with the sequestration proceedings concerning the estate of the late Sir John H. Stewart in July, 1924, it was stated that Sir John made a contribution to Party funds of £50,000. In December, 1922, he was in serious financial straits and in order to avoid bankruptcy asked for repayment of this sum.

The report of the case in *The Times* added:

"It was repaid to the deceased in December, 1922, and was distributed amongst his creditors who were then pressing him.

"Mr. Ralston (representing Mr. William Rowland): 'Was that £50,000 paid to Mr. Lloyd George?'

"The Trustee: 'I have not the slightest idea.'

"Mr. Ralston: 'But you have access to information. You must know something about its destination.'

"The Trustee: 'I would just say once and for all that this statement was prepared and I am not prepared to add anything to it or take anything away from it.'"

Later in the inquiry Mr. Ralston said he did not believe that £50,000 was "the utmost paid for that baronetcy. It was more likely that £150,000 was paid and he did not believe the money was repaid".

A few days later the Press Association was informed by one of Lloyd George's secretariat that the ex-Prime Minister "had no knowledge of any such transaction" as the payment of £50,000 to Party funds for a baronetcy.

* * * * *

Because the Lloyd George fund became a private trust, and therefore detailed disclosures about it did not have to be made by law, its exact origins and, more important, its precise purpose remain shrouded in mystery. Yet, private or otherwise, the fund was a matter of public interest not on the narrow political issue of which Party, or section of a Party, was entitled to draw upon it, but on the grounds of what policies it was scheduled to support.

Captain Guest, who had, as Coalition Chief Whip, played a leading part in collecting money for the fund, claimed that it was "anti-Socialist in its aim" and intended to help both Tories and Liberals to "fight Bolshevism".

Sir Montagu Webb, who gave full details in a letter to the *Morning Post* of November 23, 1922, of an offer made to him during the Coalition period, wrote: "The Party officials who in 1921 offered to sell me a baronetcy stated quite explicitly that the money was wanted 'to help Lloyd George to fight the Bolshies'."

As far as can be ascertained, the fund was never used for anything of the sort; certainly Lloyd George's Russian policy made no pretence to "fight Bolshevism", but it is easy to see how touts could conjure money from the pockets of frightened capitalists by the suggestion that it could be used in this way. Maundy Gregory set himself up as the arch-priest in the fight against Communism and Bolshevism. He whispered to influential friends in West End clubs that he needed vast sums to conduct Secret Service operations against the "Communist enemy". In his journal the *Whitehall Gazette*, he devoted much space to anti-Communist articles, to denigrating the achievements of the Soviets and to supporting all opponents of the Communist régime, including Mussolini and the Finnish war lords. Gregory, as has been mentioned before, was an associate of Zaharoff, and it is interesting to note what a former secretary of Zaharoff, Mr. Archie de Bear, had to say on this subject: "Even British honours were bestowed occasionally through his (Zaharoff's) external instrumentality when it pleased him to select this means of rewarding a colleague for services rendered.

"The honours traffic, indeed, as directed from Paris in those days, was brought to a fine art. And it was not always a one-way traffic. Sometimes, that is to say, the purchase price went more or less openly to Party funds; sometimes it went by rather more devious channels to private funds."

In the dossiers of both the Quai d'Orsay and the Turkish Foreign Office there is evidence that Sir Basil Zaharoff was involved in the purchase of honours during Lloyd George's premiership. Zaharoff, stated a report compiled by M. Barthe, "purchased the support of Britain for Greece by disimbursements to the Lloyd George fund".

The proposals of the Royal Commission did not prevent further abuses in the granting of honours, even though Bonar Law, Baldwin and Ramsay MacDonald reduced the size of honours lists. The Honours (Prevention of Abuses) Act of 1925, which followed the recommendations of the Royal Commission, resulted in the prosecution of Maundy Gregory in 1933. A retired naval officer, Lieut.-Commander E. W. B. Leake, reported to the police that Gregory had suggested he should pay £10,000 for a baronetcy or knighthood, claiming he was able to "pull strings in the right places".

The Maundy Gregory case caused much alarm both at Tory Party H.Q. and among Lloyd George's own political associates. Gregory at first entered a plea of "not guilty", changing this to "guilty" when the case was resumed. Meanwhile he had induced a number of his friends to lend him money on the understanding that he would keep their names out of the case. Gregory had been severely hit by the decline in the honours traffic and his means had dwindled accordingly.

The case was speedily disposed of; Gregory was convicted, fined £50 and sentenced to two months' imprisonment. His bankruptcy swiftly followed. While he was in jail Scotland Yard began investigating the circumstances of the death of a close friend of Gregory's, a Mrs. Rosse, who had died in his house, leaving him all her money. An exhumation order was issued and Mrs. Rosse's remains were removed from a riverside churchyard in Berkshire. Despite the fact that a subpoena had been served for his attendance, Gregory, who had completed his prison sentence, failed to attend the inquest, having left for France. An open verdict was recorded by the coroner and two damning revelations were made—first, that the details as given on the death certificate were wrong, secondly, that a post-mortem failed to reveal the cause of death, the coroner remarking that certain drugs decompose when a body has been buried in waterlogged soil.

Whether Gregory was guilty of murder remains a mystery. There seems to have been no excuse for officialdom allowing him to escape from the country when he had been subpoenaed. He spent the remaining years of his life in various parts of France, impudently arrogating to himself the bogus title of "Sir Arthur Gregory". Despite his bankruptcy and the fact that he had no job, he lived in the Hotel Vendôme in Paris and spent freely on himself and his friends, telling them he was "in receipt of a Government pension and that he had been victimised in the case brought against him, having taken the blame on behalf of friends in high positions".

Mr. Gerald MacMillan, in his book *Honours for Sale*, tracked down Gregory's movements until the latter's death in the Val de Grace Hospital in Paris in 1941. Mr. MacMillan writes: "Party managers of one or more political Parties might well have thought it worth their while to pay Gregory to remain abroad. In fact, it has been said that, when the summons under the Honours Act was issued, he was offered a pension of £1,000 a year from the funds of one Party, if he would plead guilty and then go abroad and stay there; and that Gregory held out for £2,000 and got it."

M. Emil Lachat, a waiter who was a valet to Gregory in France, told the author: "I overheard Gregory say that he had an income of £2,000 a year, but I am quite certain his income was far in excess of this. He was able to hire a yacht for cruises whenever he wanted. He had a friend called Pierre[1] who arranged the remittance of money to him from London for a while, but he also had funds sent to two different Paris banks. I understand that Sir William Sutherland was one of his influential friends who sent him a pension. He also boasted that he was in receipt of a pension from Mr. Lloyd George. Whether or not this was true, I cannot say, but he certainly had a meeting with Lloyd George in Paris shortly before World War II. I was the only other person present at that interview, though not in the room all the time."

[1] Presumably this was Peter Mazzina of the Ambassadors Club in London, a close associate of Gregory and a friend of Mussolini.

19

NOW RIGHT, NOW LEFT

"When gracious Anne became our Queen,
The Church of England's glory,
Another face of things was seen,
And I became a Tory.

"When George in pudding-time came o'er
And moderate men looked big, sir,
I turned a cat-in-pan once more,
And so became a Whig, sir."

From "The Vicar of Bray"

After the fall of the Coalition Government, Lloyd George sought in an American tour to maintain his reputation as a leading statesman. Fêted, lionised and cheered by large crowds, he handled his susceptible audiences with a skilful and sympathetic touch that was a refreshing contrast to the usual chilly artificialities of visiting British politicians. "It is natural for you to boast," he told the people. "It is your right. In this country you never saw the Dark Ages. The Middle Ages passed you by."

Describing Europe as "a ragged man standing in front of the plate-glass windows of a well-stocked shop, but unable to buy food or clothes because he cannot pay for them", he originated the legend that later was to become such an obsession with some Americans—the vision of Europe as a sick, incompetent and feckless beggar.

But if his immediate aim was to obtain American co-operation in the settlement of a desperate Europe, the rôle of apologist for Europe as a whole and his grim picture of "currency gone, confidence gone and hatreds still left" were not the way to set about achieving it. While Lloyd George won a great deal of personal popularity—one newspaper said: "He is the most popular Briton to visit U.S. since Charles Dickens"—his speeches strengthened the hands of the Isolationists.

Before he returned to Britain there was speculation about the possibility of another political somersault by which Lloyd George would support a protectionist programme. That idea was promptly scotched by Stanley Baldwin, who had succeeded Bonar Law after the latter's brief Premiership. Baldwin forestalled Ll. G. by announcing that to conquer unemployment he would need to protect the home market. That forced Lloyd George to a decision. Sensing acutely that any move by the Tories to seek a mandate for protection would be fatal to the Party's interests, he ceased his flirtation with tariffs and arrived home to assure the nation that he was "an unswerving Free Trader".

Baldwin's version of this affair was given in his pamphlet, *A Memoir*. "I had information that he (Ll. G.) was going protectionist and I had to get in quick. I got the Cabinet into line. But for this move Lloyd George would have got Austen Chamberlain with Birkenhead and there would have been an end of the Tory Party as we know it."

Baldwin was almost certainly exaggerating the dangers to the Tory Party, but, as a politician, he was always more than a match for Ll. G. True, Baldwin failed to get his mandate from the electorate, but he won something far more valuable for the Tories. He finished the election with the Conservatives still the strongest Party and a one hundred per cent united Party at that. A Labour Government took office for the first time with a minority of 192 members; the Liberals had 160. The Liberal Party was in desperate straits financially, but Lloyd George remained aloof and declined to give it assistance. Behind the scenes he still hankered after a new Centre Party to include Austen Chamberlain, Birkenhead and Churchill, and such shifty tactics made the uneasy alliance of Asquithian and Lloyd Georgian Liberals a doubtful proposition for the electorate.

Lloyd George also had to face the fact that Labour was now the stronger challenger as alternative to the Tories and, when the Labour Cabinet was photographed with the King, its image in the country became more respectable. Asquith, who was still leader of the Liberal Party, was not only of the opinion that Labour ought to be given a chance to show it was capable of responsible government, but that there could hardly be a more propitious moment for such a risk to be taken safely, with Labour governing mainly through the courtesy of Liberal votes.

Various accounts have been given of the wrangles between Lloyd George and the Liberal Party over the Ll. G. fund. They have been mostly pro-Lloyd Georgian versions and omit many vital facts. Lloyd George insisted that "my fund does not represent gifts made to any Party. It started with donations made through my Whip to me when I was a non-Party Premier to be used for such political purposes as I thought desirable to spend upon them".

He refused absolutely to let the fund out of his personal control. Asquith objected on principle to the existence of such a fund in the hands of an individual in the Liberal Party when traditionally it should have been vested in the Chief Whip.

Mr. Vivian Phillipps, who was Chief Liberal Whip during the 1923–24 Parliament, was the man responsible for direct negotiations with Lloyd George regarding the fund. A man of the greatest integrity, a meticulously accurate recorder of events and possessed of clarity and impartiality of mind, Mr. Phillipps's observations on this matter are of considerable importance. These are set out in various papers, letters and diaries and also in a book, *My Days and Ways*, which Mr. Phillipps had printed for private circulation only, intending that it should provide documentary evidence for a later generation. He wrote:

"The cascade of baronetcies and knighthoods, and indeed a spate of peerages, conferred during Ll. G.'s régime had resulted in the accumulation of a vast political fund amounting to something like £3,000,000 (this figure was never subsequently challenged by Ll. G.), and on the break-up of the Coalition Lloyd George walked off with this huge fund and set up a headquarters of his own with an elaborate personal staff at No. 16, Abingdon Street, three doors from our Central Office.

"During the first Parliament after the fall of the Coalition, when it was uncertain whether Ll. G. would decide to ally his group with the Tories or to rejoin the Liberals, the question of his 'personal fund' remained in abeyance. When reunion with the Liberal Party came in 1923, it was expected that there would be a pooling of funds between him and Liberal headquarters, but this did not happen. Ll. G. continued his separate headquarters and kept control of his fund in his own hands. The position was far from comfortable, with a prominent leader of the Party sitting aloof from the Central Office and controlling a large fund which he was free to use for any political adventures.

"More than once when a constituency organisation had recommended as their chosen candidate in a by-election Mr. X, an intimation would come from Ll. G.'s headquarters that they did not approve of Mr. X and preferred Mr. Y, with a hint that if we endorsed the constituency's choice of Mr. X, they might provide Mr. Y's election expenses 'in order to give the constituency a free choice between X and Y', which, of course, would mean splitting the Liberal vote and the loss of the seat."

When the Labour Government resigned and a general election was imminent, Donald Maclean and Vivian Phillipps went to state the urgency of the position regarding funds. To Maclean's amazement Lloyd George merely remarked: "Why should we have more than 300 candidates?"

Vivian Phillipps recorded: "I told him (Ll. G.) we had 280 candidates, whereas with adequate funds it could well have been nearer 400. He said to me:

"'You do not want more than 300.'

"I replied: 'Why, that is ruin.'

"He said: 'Oh no, this election does not count.'"

At the last moment Ll. G. agreed to contribute £50,000. "We managed to add some sixty-odd candidates to the 280, but the Party had been assassinated and the electors had no use for this corpse," wrote Vivian Phillipps.

The Liberal strength was reduced to 42, while the Conservatives were returned to power with 415 seats.

* * * * *

In foreign policy Lloyd George pursued his vendetta against the French. He described the Geneva Protocol of 1924, which provided for the outlawing of war and compulsory arbitration supported by sanctions against an aggressor, as "a booby trap for the British". Would the French refer disarmament and the evacuation of the Rhineland to arbitration, he sneered. He even went so far in mischievous speech-making to hint that history would regard Locarno as "slobbering melodrama". There were passages in some of his speeches which were almost an incitement for Germany to march into the Rhineland.

His articles in the Press, which were syndicated all over the world, were, wrote Dr. Thomas Jones, "inspired by such animosity to France that he and Riddell quarrelled over them and were estranged for some time".

Meanwhile he used every opportunity to snipe at the leadership of the Liberal Party and to criticise the competence of Party H.Q. Sir Robert Hudson, who was treasurer of the National Liberal Federation, attended a private Party meeting and demanded bluntly of Lloyd George: "How much money have you got? Where did you get it from? What do you propose to do with it?"

Lloyd George declined to answer any of these posers. In the *Life of Sir Robert Hudson* one learns: "The Lloyd George fund hung over the 'Million Fund' (the appeal launched by the Liberal Party in 1925) and finally extinguished it. The small subscribers ear-marked their subscriptions for their local associations; the bigger ones wanted to know more of the facts before they gave freely."

The failure of the Million Fund drew from Lord Rosebery a letter to *The Times* referring to the Lloyd George fund and asking: "What is this sum, how was it obtained? It surely cannot be the sale of the Royal Honours. If that were so, there would be nothing in the worst times of Charles II and Sir Robert Walpole to equal it."

The reply from Lloyd George's office was: "We do not think it necessary to comment on Lord Rosebery's letter further than to say that the fund which Mr. Lloyd George controls was raised in a way that does not differ from that followed by the Conservative Party or by the Liberal Party in the days before the Coalition, and that all along it has been devoted to legitimate Party purposes."

This is a distinct change from the original suggestion that it was raised for "fighting Bolshevism".

It is not denied that on various occasions Lloyd George subsidised the Liberal Party from the fund. But the manner of doing this was arbitrary and autocratic. During negotiations with Mr. Vivian Phillipps, Ll. G. said he regarded the fund as "at his own disposal, to be given to or withheld from the Central Office of the Party, upon such conditions as he saw fit to impose".

Not only did Ll. G. dictate terms upon which he would contribute to the Million Fund, but he obstructed the fund in every possible way. "No doubt it was as obvious to Ll. G. as to everyone else that the greater the success of the Million Fund, the less would be the dependence of our Central Office upon financial help from him," wrote Vivian Phillipps. ". . . He assured me that I need not trouble about Wales, as he would be responsible for looking after the fund in the Welsh constituencies. From that moment, so far as Wales was concerned, the fund became a fiasco, and it soon began to look as if Ll. G.'s method of 'looking after the fund in Wales' was to block every attempt from London to make it a success."

On July 13, 1925, Vivian Phillipps had an interview with Ll. G., who told him that he "had consulted his Trustees and that he was prepared to subscribe £20,000 a year for the next three years to the (Liberal Party) Organisation. . . . There was, he said, one difficulty which he felt must be satisfactorily cleared up and that was the matter of the new Land Policy. He disclaimed any idea of desiring to force the Land Policy upon the Party, but he said he felt it would be a ridiculous position for him, if he had bound himself to subscribe £20,000 a year to the Liberal Organisation and then found that the Headquarters Organisation was not merely giving no hand to the Land Policy, but might actually be opposing it."

Phillipps's reply was that he personally could not accept a contribution of that kind save with the assent of the Administrative Committee of the Million Fund. "He (Ll. G.) did not raise any objection to this, but suggested that the £20,000 a year might be subdivided in three or four lesser divisions under initials in the public list of the fund.

"I said I thought I should have to tell the Administrative Committee that he had made this offer, as they would naturally wonder where these large donations came from, and, at the same time, they might well be under the impression that he was doing nothing to help.

"He went on to say that in addition to the £20,000 a year, he was prepared to bear the whole expense of the Land Policy campaign."

Plans were made for a Party conference to consider the Land Policy, and Phillipps called on Ll. G. and reminded him of the arrangement which he had suggested, and which Asquith had accepted, that provided the Shadow Cabinet were prepared to hold such a conference, he would instruct his "Trustees" to send a letter binding themselves to implement his offer of £20,000 towards the expenses of Headquarters for the current year.

"To my astonishment he repudiated any knowledge of any such agreement," wrote Phillipps. "He would make no contribution to Party funds until he knew what the conference might have decided about his Land Policy."

Then Lloyd George, in breach of his unofficial undertaking to Party H.Q., announced in his own newspaper, the *Daily Chronicle*, the launching of a "Great Land Campaign" under a new organisation styled the "Land and Nation League", with himself as its president. Protests poured into Liberal Party H.Q. against the launching by the leader of the Parliamentary Party of a policy which had not yet received the official approval of a Party conference. Subscribers to the Million Fund wrote in withdrawing their support.

Phillipps summed up the situation as follows: Lloyd George "had ignored Asquith's appeal to him; he had gone back on his promise to me of help for Headquarters; he had repudiated the agreement, to which he himself had been a party, to avoid public propaganda for the Land proposals until they had been approved by the conference and he was now threatening the Party with a refusal of any financial help unless it undertook to make his Land proposals an integral part of its official policy."

There was marked opposition to that part of Ll. G.'s policy which aimed at "nationalising" the land, undoubtedly a proposal aimed at winning left-wing support. But though Runciman and other right-wing Liberals regarded the Land Policy as involving nationalisation, Asquith did not take this view and was sincerely anxious to thrash out an agreed and detailed policy. Some of the best brains in the country were employed in working out Ll. G.'s Land Policy which, despite certain financial problems which it posed, could have prevented the agricultural depression of the thirties and certainly would have avoided the evils of the present system of subsidies. Ll. G. had, with that inborn pessimism that was never far from the surface, convinced himself that Britain's industrial supremacy had gone for ever and that her people must grow more food on their own soil. His idea was that the state should take possession of agricultural lands, paying off existing landlords, but giving them security of tenure at fixed rents, providing they kept their land properly cultivated and, more important, developed it, using more modern methods. By this scheme, in theory at least, production would be increased, and profits raised without rents being increased.

Yet even as late as 1925 Lloyd George was still dickering with the possibility of an alliance with the Tories. When Baldwin announced that the Government had decided to grant a subsidy to the coal mines in order to give time for the owners and miners to come together on the question of hours and wages, Ll. G. caused surprise by what appeared to be an appeal for a Tory revolt against Baldwin's leadership. He taunted Churchill (now back in the Tory ranks) as one "who had been very eager to fight the Reds on the Volga, but had run away from them on the Thames, leaving his purse behind". He inferred that he would have no truck with the demand of the miners for a subsidy in aid of wages.

In view of Lloyd George's irresponsible attitude during the General Strike of 1926 this is an important point to bear in mind. Vivian Phillipps wrote to William Pringle, a back-bench Liberal of the "Wee Free" persuasion:

"If he (Ll. G.) could manœuvre a combination with some of the Tories for 'No surrender to Communism' or some similar cry, he might down Baldwin and Ramsay at one blow."

At the same time J. L. Garvin was suggesting in the *Observer* that men like J. H. Thomas and Lloyd George "would not be averse to a policy of construction, production and communication throughout the Empire". While Ll. G. was negotiating with the Liberals about his Land Policy, he was scheming with Garvin to revive a Centre Party. The *Observer* fulfilled the compact between them by stating that "Mr. Lloyd George's gifts for national leadership may be urgently wanted".

But once it was clear that Baldwin's position was not being undermined and that any idea of a Centre Party could not be revived, Lloyd George turned smartly to the left. He felt that MacDonald's leadership of the Labour Party could not be long maintained, not merely because MacDonald was causing increasing dissatisfaction to his left-wing supporters, but by reason of his sudden liking for the drawing-rooms of Mayfair.

Lloyd George's succession to Asquith, now in the Lords as the Earl of Oxford and Asquith, as Parliamentary leader had done nothing to improve the fortunes of the Liberal Party, at least half of whose members mistrusted him. But the final show-down which led to his absolute rejection by millions who had previously voted for him came when he revealed his attitude to the General Strike of May, 1926. To keep this story in its proper perspective it is important to recall that when the Sankey Coal Commission in June, 1919, recommended by nine votes to five the nationalisation of the mines, Ll. G. had rejected the plan. He slammed the door hard on the one enlightened proposal which might have avoided the bitterness, the recriminations and the anarchical attitude which besetted and besotted the problems of Britain's coal for so many years.

By this single act he inevitably paved the way for the General Strike of 1926. His rejection hardened the hearts of the miners who resolved to challenge the nation at the first opportunity.

In fact, it says much for Baldwin's handling of his Government's relations with organised labour that a show-down did not come earlier than 1926. There is some evidence that Baldwin foresaw the risks of a general strike, played for time by not aggravating labour relations and worked feverishly behind the scenes to build up a "shadow" organisation which would ensure the strike's failure when it came. It is hard to imagine the placid Baldwin working feverishly at any time, but he certainly showed more foresight on the home than on the foreign front. Matters came to a head when the Royal Commission of Inquiry, under Sir Herbert Samuel, recommended some immediate reduction in miners' wages, for which the coal owners had been pressing, and urged the acquisition by the state of the ownership of coal, but not the nationalisation of the industry. This was a somewhat provocative and two-faced recommendation, and it added insult to injury by suggesting that the coal subsidy should not be renewed. Indeed the whole report was unhelpful, unrealistic and, in a sense, an incitement to direct action. The miners had had a very bad deal over a long period and the threat of a cut in wages with no prospect of any real amelioration of conditions gave them a strong case.

But, when the Council of the T.U.C. proposed a general strike, if the Government "failed to make any acceptable proposals", and in effect held the nation to ransom, a very different situation arose.

The Liberal Shadow Cabinet decided to condemn the strike and support the Government in resisting it. Lord Oxford suggested the Government should facilitate an accommodation with the miners and that the coal subsidy should be continued pending the reaching of an agreement.

The sequence of events clearly shows what was in Lloyd George's mind. On May 7 he had an interview with MacDonald, Clynes and Snowden. He told them he was compelled to make an appearance of "contesting" against the General Strike, but that his sympathies were really with the T.U.C. He was prepared to attack the Government, but he realised that if he did so it would cause a serious breach in the Liberal front.

What would their attitude be, he asked, if he decided to attack the Government and possibly march boldly into the Labour camp. Then he reminded his listeners that he had the residue of a large political fund which, in the present state of trade union finance, would be useful to them if a general election should suddenly be fought upon this issue.

MacDonald, Clynes and Snowden refused to commit themselves, but promised to "sound out" other Labour members. That these "soundings" were made is quite clear from an article by Josiah Wedgwood, M.P., in an article in the *Evening Standard* of June 27, 1926. Wedgwood declared: "The Labour members of the House of Commons had been asked as to what their views would be if Ll. G. desired to join them."

J. H. Thomas confirmed that approaches were made by Ll. G. and he personally seemed in favour of them But the *Sunday Worker*, a left-wing Labour newspaper, emphatically rejected the plan in an article which was headed: "We won't touch him with a barge pole," and added: "We warn any politician in the Labour Party who thinks of bringing this man in that he will be flung out of the window first."

When the Liberal Shadow Cabinet met on May 10, a letter was received from Ll. G., declining to attend. He attacked the Shadow Cabinet for refraining from criticising the Government. Afterwards he said the action of the Government was "precipitate, unwarrantable and mischievous".

This marked the final cleavage between Lloyd George and Lord Oxford. To make matters worse Ll. G. wrote an article for the American Press in which he had nothing to say against the stoppage of work and even suggested it would be of long duration. His policy at this time was to hinder and obstruct the Government, to make personal capital out of the whole issue and to leave himself uncommitted in the hope that the strike would last long enough to bring about the downfall of the Government and pave the way to a Coalition of Lloyd Georgian Liberals and Labour.

There were even secret negotiations between Lloyd George and A. J. Cook, one of the fieriest of the miners' leaders, and it was from this source that Ll. G. seems to have been assured that the strike would last for a few months. In accepting this assurance he made a faulty judgment, for after nine days the strike was unconditionally called off by the T.U.C., a decision described by Baldwin as "a victory for common sense".

Meanwhile, at a Sunday service in a Welsh Baptist chapel in London, Lloyd George had told his congregation that "if Jesus Christ had been one of the Liberal leaders at the time of the General Strike, He, probably, would have been excluded from the Shadow Cabinet".

Neither Lord Oxford, nor his leading colleagues, would accept the olive branch which Ll. G. proferred after the strike. Lord Oxford wrote to him: "I have refrained from writing to you until the strike was over and the life of the country had resumed its normal course. I should not be doing my duty as Leader of the Liberal Party, if I did not convey to you my regret at the course which you pursued in the greatest domestic crisis which the country has had to confront in your time or mine."

Lord Oxford referred to Ll. G.'s article in the American Press: "It contains a despondent, though highly coloured picture of our national traits. It predicts a long duration of a conflict and the ultimate wearing down on the steadfastness of our people through 'worry about their vanishing trade'. I cannot but deplore that such a presentation of the case should have been offered to the outside world on the authority of an ex-Prime Minister of Great Britain and the chairman of the Liberal Parliamentary Party."

In reply Lloyd George talked scornfully of "the privilege of being a Liberal Shadow" and reproached the "official gang" of the Party with having "allowed Labour to capture the old Ark of the Covenant, which for over three centuries had been resting in the Liberal Temple".

* * * * *

After more than four months during which he had refused to co-operate with his old Liberal colleagues, Lloyd George offered to provide the election expenses of some 300 Liberal candidates in the rural constituencies. Mr. Vivian Phillipps circulated to members of the Liberal Shadow Cabinet a memorandum of which the following is an extract:

"The position is that Lloyd George is now offering to make a substantial contribution to the next general election fund, at a moment when the difficulties he created in May last are still unresolved and the resources of Liberal Headquarters are precarious and dwindling. If the position taken up by Lord Oxford and his Shadow Cabinet colleagues in May last remains unaltered, how can this offer be accepted? . . . The acceptance of the offer will mean that well over half of the candidates at the next election will be financed by Lloyd George and, because of this, chosen by him."

This offer was a barely veiled ultimatum: Lord Oxford could retain the leadership of the Party only at the price of making his peace with Ll. G. and accepting a "dole" from the latter's fund. Lord Oxford, worn out with ill-health and his mind set against further wrangling, resigned from the leadership of the Party in September, 1926.

With Lord Oxford out of the way Lloyd George increased and improved his offer to include the financing of urban as well as rural candidates. Mr. Phillipps in his papers made the remarkable revelation that Charles Hobhouse, one of the leading lights of the N.L.F., represented to the Party's Administrative Committee that "if they accepted Ll. G.'s proposal, the whole of his 'personal fund' would be handed over to Liberal official headquarters."

This bait was undoubtedly laid with the full knowledge of Ll. G., who was closely associated with Hobhouse, but it is equally certain that Lloyd George never had any intention of parting with the whole of his fund. Shortly afterwards a meeting of the Administrative Committee was packed with Ll. G. supporters—at least a dozen of whom had never previously troubled to attend a meeting—and, on their motion, carried by a majority of four, Vivian Phillipps was called upon to resign from the chairmanship. This was the price demanded before Ll. G. would fulfil his promise of financial aid to the Party.

The *Morning Post* commented: "The money is paid over and the body of Mr. Vivian Phillipps is thrown out of the committee-room door! Never since the head of John the Baptist was delivered on a charger has there been a transaction more crudely and cruelly direct, and in such circumstances the use of words like 'trust' and 'honour' seem singularly out of place."

There is an illuminating passage on these events in a note made by Vivian Phillipps of a conversation he had with Sir Robert Hutchison, Lloyd George's Whip.

"He (Hutchison) said that Lloyd George was 'all over the shop'. Hutchison had asked Ll. G. whether Herbert Samuel would be acceptable to him as my successor. Ll. G. was not at all favourable.

"Hutchison then said: 'Well, what about Charles Hobhouse?'

"Ll. G. said: 'Hobhouse! He isn't fit to run a whelk stall.'"

Hutchison told Phillipps: "If all the decent men in the Party will have nothing to do with him, he (Ll. G.) is finished, and the money won't save him. My dear Vivian, I don't understand how you have borne it."

* * * * *

By the time Lloyd George became leader of the Liberal Party suspicion of him among the chief figures of Liberalism was so marked and mistrust of his tactics so acute that he had little hope of maintaining a united front. The management of his personal fund had passed to a committee on which were two ex-Whips, Charles McCurdy and William Edge. Later there was a new and enlarged committee, of which Lord St. Davids was chairman.

A good deal of money from the fund was expended on drawing up a plan for curing unemployment. Lloyd George enlisted the support of some of the most brilliant economists of the day, men like Walter (later Lord) Layton, Maynard Keynes and H. D. Henderson. Ideas flowed from these fertile minds, brilliant pamphlets were poured out of the presses, but they were little more than the blueprints of economists living in their ivory towers surrounded by statistics. Nothing short of *dirigisme* and a planned economy could have made them practicable, and in this direction Lloyd George and his planners were ultra-timid in their approach.

Added to this was Lloyd George's extravagant claim that if the Liberals were returned to power, he would reduce the number of unemployed by 50 per cent. Apart from Ll. G., no one in the Party knew how it was proposed to do this. It would have meant finding work for 700,000 at a time when unemployment was still increasing.

In 1929 six per cent of the population of Britain had been unemployed for eight years. The Welsh valleys were doomed; their population dwindling. In the Rhondda alone the population had dropped by 35,000 in ten years. In the distressed areas of the north, the midlands and South Wales there were whole streets of empty shops, and property which had brought good rents in 1919 was now derelict. To rescue the nation from the apathy and dejection into which it had sunk it required something far more dynamic either than Stanley Baldwin's electoral slogan of "Safety First", or the theorising of Lloyd George's team of academicians.

Can Lloyd George Do It? was the title of a book which aimed at giving the public the economic facts of life in simple terms. It was a competent little pamphlet written by Keynes and Henderson; an apter title would have been *Can Maynard Keynes Do It?* for the central theme was the familiar Keynsian thesis that in times of depression and unemployment vast sums must be spent on public works. A decade later these methods were being put into practice effectively through the stimulus which rearmament and redistribution of wealth through full employment gave nations in wartime.

The Lloyd Georgian-Keynsian case was that since 1921 a sum of £500 millions had been paid out in unemployment relief: this was enough to build a million houses. Lloyd George's calculation of the development programme suggested by the authors of the pamphlet was that £100 millions a year would bring back 500,000 men into employment.

The programme on which Lloyd George went to the polls in 1929 was a technocrat's blueprint without the positive co-ordination of state and private enterprise measures for putting it into action. It relied too much on the co-operation of Government and private enterprise; its implementation would have called for much more drastic measures than were suggested: for example, the nationalisation of transport and the mines, the establishment of development corporations. Lloyd George was not prepared to commit himself to such controls. Yet, with all its limitations, the Liberal programme was the best of any in this election, and very similar policies were adopted a few years later by President Roosevelt to enable America to recover from the slump. Certainly the economic policy of the Liberals ill deserved the sneers of the Tories—"relief work" was how Churchill termed it. "We are opposed to such a system especially when directly conducted by the state," was the reply of Chancellor of the Exchequer Churchill, now a high priest returned to the Tory temple.

During the election Churchill complained that the Lloyd George fund, which was "Raised for the express and avowed purpose of enabling Conservatives and Liberals to make common fight against Socialism, is now being used for the purpose of securing the return of as large a number of Socialists as possible. It is an unjustifiable action, a breach of moral faith."

This was one of the few occasions on which Churchill spoke really harshly against Ll. G. The allegation, of course, was not strictly correct as far as Lloyd George's intentions were concerned, but in effect the Liberals helped in many constituencies to put Labour in and put the Tories out. The people were not dazzled by the election posters of a white-haired Lloyd George in white armour on a white charger slaying the Dragon Unemployment. They rejected this prospect as emphatically as they turned down Baldwin's "Safety First" plea. The election gave Labour 289 seats, the Tories 260 and the Liberals a mere 58, despite their poll of twenty-three per cent of the votes cast.

Labour showed itself as irresolute, incapable and fearful of tackling the unemployment problem as it did in facing up to the rapidly deteriorating economic crisis. Unemployment rose alarmingly as the effects of the Wall Street crash in the autumn of 1929 were felt in Britain. Inevitably talk of coalition was in the air.

Lloyd George leaned a little further left. In March, 1931, at a meeting of Liberal candidates at Caxton Hall, he declared: "In the working of the three-Party system, unless common action between the two Parties (Labour and Liberal) is obtainable, the democratic system for which Liberalism has fought is utterly doomed. A defeat of the Government on a major issue today, with trade and unemployment as now, would mean that we should have a protectionist majority."

But if there was some measure of agreement between Liberals and Labour on the issues outlined by Lloyd George—unemployment, disarmament, an Indian Settlement and Free Trade—the right wing of the Liberal Party, headed by Sir John Simon, firmly opposed Labour's complicated and ambiguous Trade Union Bill and the proposed tax of a penny in the £ on land values. Lloyd George supported the latter under a mistaken impression that it was based on the principles of land taxation embodied in his own Budget of 1909. In effect the new plan meant that landowners who were already taxed under Schedule A would be taxed twice over, a grossly inequitable proposition.

Towards the end of July, 1931, Lloyd George had to undergo a serious operation—inconvenient at the time for him, but a remarkably opportune moment for Baldwin. The Conservative leader immediately got in touch with Simon. Despite the prospects of an unbalanced Budget, Ll. G. refused to regard the approaching crisis as anything more than a bankers' ramp and he confidently believed he could form an alliance with Labour on terms of equality with Ramsay MacDonald.

His intuition about a bankers' ramp was nearer the mark than was conceded at the time, but in his hopes of making a deal with MacDonald he was being unduly optimistic. MacDonald found himself increasingly alienated from some of his colleagues and was dismayed by their refusal to take unpopular measures to check the flight from the pound. To what extent the rôle played by King George V exceeded the bounds of strict constitutional procedure may be a matter of conjecture for many years to come. The King encouraged the formation of a National Government and laid himself open to the charge of a "Buckingham Palace plot" by failing to consult other Labour leaders. Thus when the Labour Cabinet broke up and a National Government was formed, with MacDonald at the helm and Baldwin, Simon and Samuel as his chief colleagues, it appeared as though the King had connived at a plot hatched during the recess.

The phrase "National" Government was a misnomer; this was essentially a Tory Government with MacDonald its outwitted prisoner. It went far beyond its immediate mandate, which was to check the flight from the pound, and made the financial situation the excuse for exaggerated economies. It was bad enough to cut the salaries of state employees, but it was indefensible to slash unemployment benefit by ten per cent. Lloyd George's first inclination, once the new Government was a *fait accompli*, was to veer round towards agreeing for the need for it. But when it became known that MacDonald would appeal to the country he regarded this—and rightly so—as a Tory plot to gain a majority. He was angered at MacDonald allowing himself to be inveigled into an election which he dubbed as "a partisan intrigue under the guise of patriotic appeal".

Baldwin was shocked out of his usual imperturbability when he heard Lloyd George had suggested from his sick bed that he should be taken to Buckingham Palace in an ambulance to confer with the King, MacDonald and the Tory leader. Had such a meeting taken place the whole situation might have been transformed; it is certain that Lloyd George would have argued against an election. But the ambulance trip never took place and Baldwin recovered his equilibrium.

Speculation as to whether Lloyd George would join the Labour Party was again aroused when a secret meeting was held at Churt between Arthur Henderson and the Liberal leader. At this meeting it was agreed that no Labour candidate should oppose any member of the Lloyd George family at the forthcoming election.

Ll. G. told the *Daily Herald* correspondent, W. N. Ewer, "Where there is no genuine Free Trade Liberal candidate and a Labour Free Trader opposes a Tory Protectionist, I would vote Labour without the slightest hesitation. The return of Mr. MacDonald and his Tory friends to power would be disastrous to all progress. It would put the clock back over eighty years."

Ll. G. took no part in the election. The battle was fought in his own constituency by his family, friends and gramophone records of the master's voice. The election, which was waged by methods almost as discreditable as those of the "Coupon Election" of 1918, produced a stampede towards Toryism. The National Government, having told the electorate that Labour proposed to confiscate Post Office savings —a dastardly lie, brazenly propounded by, of all people, Philip Snowden, the Socialist Chancellor of the Exchequer—was returned with 554 seats, 471 of them going to the Tories. Ll. G., his son Gwilym, his daughter Megan and a relative by marriage, Major Goronwy Owen, all won their contests to form a tiny and ineffective group in the new Parliament.

In prophesying that a victory for Toryism would put the clock back eighty years, Lloyd George may have been exaggerating, but he was certainly near to the truth. The National Governments of 1931 and 1935 dawdled through the economic crisis with the negative policy of deflation, neglected to conquer unemployment and failed lamentably to give the nation adequate defences, reducing Britain to the status of a feeble and arthritic power which swiftly became the chief target for impudent political attacks by Germany and Italy. This Government of uneasy compromise declined to invest in the Commonwealth and neglected to utilise the vast sums of unused capital on deposit. It connived at the disintegration of the League of Nations, encouraged every aggressor from Tokyo to Berlin, dismayed its allies and evoked the contempt of its enemies. Not a man in those two Governments could match Lloyd George for ability or drive, but, alas, the political Titan of the past had tarnished his reputation by the corruption which power had brought to his soul.

* * * * *

"The view of the Lloyd George fund as a trust rather than a Party chest accords with a Deed signed on May 5, 1925, by D. Lloyd George, J. T. Davies, C. A. McCurdy, W. Edge and H. Fildes," wrote Frank Owen in *Tempestuous Journey*. Yet Lloyd George had declined to reveal the names of the trustees to Vivian Phillipps. Later Lord St. Davids told Sir Herbert Samuel that the fund stood at £765,000 and about the same time Ll. G. was writing a letter to the Marquis of Reading, claiming that it was "not a Party fund at all".

After 1931 the name of the fund was changed from "National Liberal Political Fund" to "Lloyd George Fund". In 1937 there was an extraordinary suggestion that Dr. Addison, now a Labour M.P., should serve as a trustee, but this idea appears to have been scotched by Lord St. Davids. It would seem that at that time Lloyd George was again toying with the idea of giving some kind of financial assistance to Labour, for by this time the idea of a Popular Front of Labour,

Liberals and Communists against Fascist aggression was being built up. Labour stamped on the idea by expelling Sir Stafford Cripps from the Party when he openly advocated it.

Then in 1939 the Liberal leaders set up a private inquiry into the fund to see whether any money could be claimed from it. They took this step because two of the trustees had died within three days of one another. One of Davies' executors tried to prevent the fund being transferred back to Lloyd George. But Sir Wilfrid Greene (later Lord Greene) gave it as his opinion that the fund was indisputably Lloyd George's and that he could, if he wished, "gamble it away at Monte Carlo".

Figures produced at the time of the Liberal Party inquiry showed that a sum of £1,375,000 had been spent out of the fund between 1918 and 1935 on expenses for general elections, contributions to the Liberal Party fund, etc. This would suggest that the estimate of a £3 millions fund at some time or other was fairly accurate. But do these figures tell the whole story? Dr. Thomas Jones stated that Lord St. Davids "destroyed" the papers relating to the fund. Why were they destroyed and what secrets did they contain? Was it desired that later trustees should not learn the exact details of how the fund was built up, or even the original total of the fund?

The Trust Law of this country is extremely complicated. *Wharton's Law Lexicon* says a "Trust is simply a confidence reposed either expressly or impliedly in a person for the benefit of another. Since it is not necessary that a Trust be declared in writing, but only so manifested and proved, no form is requisite either as regards the nature of the instrument or the language; the Statute will be satisfied if the Trust can be established by any subsequent acknowledgment of the Trustee, however informally or indirectly made, as by letter under his hand, or by a recital in a deed, provided it relate to the subject matter and the precise nature and object of the Trust can be ascertained."

But the precise nature and object of the trust of the Lloyd George fund remained even more baffling after the technically accurate, but frivolously expressed observation of Sir Wilfrid Greene. After Lloyd George's death the Inland Revenue authorities made inquiries about the fund, but were satisfied it was a private trust, which, by law, need not make disclosures. So public curiosity as to the exact amount of the fund and the purposes for which it existed remained unsatisfied. One important question has been answered since and biographers of Lloyd George have not referred to it. When Lloyd George died many Liberals believed that the bulk of the fund would pass to the Party funds. This belief caused some people to withhold subscriptions from the Liberal Party until the position could be cleared up. An official approach was made by the Liberals to the trustees. The reply was polite but firm: the Liberals could expect no payment from the fund.

Yet in 1931 Lloyd George had laid down terms, approved by the trustees, that grants should be made from the fund for "political purposes which would advance Liberalism in this country".

The Lloyd George fund is but one example of the undemocratic workings of such trusts and funds to which money may have been given under a misapprehension as to the purpose for which it could be used. In the past the Tory Party was dominated by the power of the brewers' purses, yet today trade unions' contributions to the Labour Party funds constitute a similarly unsatisfactory situation. It is highly desirable that Party funds should be raised as far as possible solely by membership subscriptions from individuals and not from commercial firms, honours' touts, pressure groups, business organisations and trade unions.

* * * * *

By 1934 Lloyd George was, temporarily, at any rate, turning right again. The Liberals were hopelessly split up into Simonite, Samuelite, Lloyd Georgian and even pro-Labour groups, all at war with one another. Lloyd George wrote to Sir Herbert Samuel saying that he was not a candidate for any office in the Liberal Parliamentary Party because he was at variance with the disastrous course into which the Party had recently been guided.

During 1934 he prepared another programme of "reconstruction", worked out in consultation with various agricultural and industrial experts. This time he spoke as an elder statesman, aiming at a non-Party appeal. But the prescription offered was not very different from that suggested in 1929. The project attracted favourable attention from some of the younger Conservatives, notably Harold Macmillan and Robert Boothby. But it placed far too much emphasis on agriculture and was ridiculously optimistic in its estimate of how many extra people could be settled on the land. Lloyd George was bemused by the belated success he had himself attained as a farmer, forgetting that he was a rich man who could afford to play with thousands of pounds before results were achieved.

Nevertheless he still clung to the idea that he might yet return to power, and overtures for a reconciliation with the Government were made at various levels. "During these months," wrote Dr. Thomas Jones, "Lloyd George thought it just possible that he might be asked to join a refashioned Cabinet. Baldwin, who became Prime Minister in June, 1935, was now believed to be not unwilling to welcome Ll. G." But three people resolutely opposed any arrangement of this nature —Mrs. Baldwin, who was reported to be adamant against such a suggestion, Simon and Neville Chamberlain, who hinted that he would resign if Ll. G. were included in the Cabinet.

As an antidote to political frustration, Lloyd George founded the Council of Action for Peace and Reconstruction, which not only attracted the interest of many non-Party people, but of some Tories who were promptly blacklisted by the Whips.

Reference has been made in earlier chapters to the evidence which Lloyd George gave to the Royal Commission on the Private Manufacture of and Trading in Armaments in 1936. It is indeed strange that biographers who have praised him so extravagantly for less praiseworthy actions should have disregarded his opinions on arms manufacture. For Lloyd George left the Commission in no doubt as to what his opinion now was: he emphatically supported a state monopoly for arms manufacture. As has already been shown, in many respects he contradicted views he had previously held, but in a written memorandum he made a cogent and forceful case against the private manufacture of armaments "to avoid the creation of powerful vested interests whose prosperity depends upon war". Rearmament, he argued, doubled the value of holdings of every shareholder in arms firms.

Here again was another example of those fascinating changes of front of which Lloyd George was capable. The man who had backed, intrigued with and honoured Zaharoff had never completely let go of the pacifist beliefs of his youth. Political expediency might call for deals with armament racketeers, but this was something apart from what one felt to the very core of one's convictions. Perhaps only a Welshman could think this way, perhaps, more probably, only a great individualist would be bold enough to admit it, but Lloyd George then proved—against majority opinion, against the Government, against his old subordinate, Hankey, and against that massive, materialistically-minded body of mediocre minds, the trade unionists of the right-wing, who lapped up rearmament as a means to fuller employment—that he was in the vanguard of progressive forces in a bid to take the cancer of private interest from the bowels of national defence.

20

KING'S CHAMPION

"And indeed he seems to me
Scarce other than my king's ideal knight,
Who reverenced his conscience as his king;
Whose glory was, redressing human wrong;
Who spake no slander, no, nor listen'd to it;
Who loved only one and who clave to her—
Her—over all whose realms to their last isle,
Commingled with the gloom of imminent war,
The shadow of his loss drew like eclipse,
Darkening the world. We have lost him; he is gone."

Lord Tennyson

Had anyone told Lloyd George during the Boer War that he would one day become the champion of a king whom Parliament had rejected, he would probably have laughed outright at the suggestion.

Yet, despite jibes at the monarchy in his youth and a dislike of Queen Victoria for her undisguised mistrust of Liberalism, he grew to have an affection for the Throne which was deep and abiding. With King George V he often clashed, but angry words from his Sovereign never dismayed or upset Lloyd George; he accepted them with equanimity and replied with all the charm at his command. There was a measure of Celtic mysticism behind Ll. G.'s regard for the monarchy. He *had* to believe that his Sovereign was King of Wales as well as of England, as indeed he was, but until George V's reign there was very little appreciation of this truth from the Throne itself. Yet Lloyd George felt that if Wales could not get Home Rule, at least she could be accorded a greater degree of recognition by the monarchy.

A story is told of one day, when he wandered through the streets of Caernarvon to the archway entrance to the ancient grey turrets where sat Mrs. Watkins-the-Castle, the stout, cheery saleswoman in the black straw mushroom hat, who kept a stall and sold picture postcards, and dolls in the Welsh costume of high hat, *shawlan bach*, check apron and red cloak.

"Good morning, Mrs. Watkins," he said in Welsh. "It's a pity now that those lovely dolls of yours aren't real. Charming Welsh girls they are and soon I suppose we shan't see their like again."

"Pity it is, too, Mr. George. Pity it is, too, that this old castle is dropping to pieces. Can't you do something about it now in London? High time it is we had a Prince of Wales come to see his true home. There's something you might see about as well, Mr. George."

This talk with Mrs. Watkins-the-Castle set Lloyd George thinking. He walked round the castle, climbed the stone stairs to the top of Eagle Tower and peered through the long arrow-slits in the masonry out across the Menai Straits. Looking down at Queen Eleanor's Gate from which, centuries before, there was shown to the Welsh people a babe, the infant son of an English King born in Caernarvon Castle, he pondered on whether this ancient piece of history could not be reconstructed in the form of a majestic pageant that would make the Welsh feel the monarchy belonged to them.

The picturesque ceremony of the investiture of the Prince of Wales at Caernarvon Castle had been neglected for three centuries. Lloyd George decided to press for its revival. In this he received the ardent support of his old antagonist, Bishop Edwards of St. Asaph, later to become the first Archbishop of Wales when the Welsh Church was disestablished under the Coalition Government. But in some quarters the idea was regarded as a betrayal of Home Rule principles. A Welsh Nationalist newspaper stated: "There has been talk here in Caernarvon of the visit of some Prince of Wales, but the truth is that no such Prince exists. The last Prince of Wales was Llewelyn . . . but as for the young, fair-haired boy who comes amongst us, let him knock at any cottage-door to ask for a drink of water and we would give him milk and a welcome."

The Prince of Wales was seventeen years old in 1911. "Surprisingly enough," wrote the Duke of Windsor in *A King's Story*, "Mr. Lloyd George, who only a few years before had shocked my family with his famous Limehouse speech attacking inherited privilege, decided that its revival (the investiture) would appeal to the national pride of his people. With an eye to what would please his constituents, Ll. G. proposed that the ceremony be transformed into a spectacular Welsh pageant. My father agreed."

King George told Ll. G.: "You had better take the Prince in hand. Teach him to speak Welsh." So the radical Welshman became the tutor of the Prince for a brief spell, and the Duke of Windsor still has in his possession some of the Welsh sentences he spoke at the investiture, copied out in Lloyd George's own handwriting.

"Out of these meetings," wrote the Duke, "despite the difference in our years—and, I might add, in politics—grew a friendship that lasted until his death."

For Lloyd George the investiture was a personal triumph in which he took the greatest delight. Caernarvon made the perfect backcloth for this superb piece of pageantry, with Snowdonia's peaks proudly holding up their heads to the July sky. The young Prince in his white satin breeches and purple mantle, edged with ermine, with a slender coronet cap on his fair hair, was not the only figure dressed specially for the occasion; Lloyd George himself was a resplendent principal in his uniform of Constable of Caernarvon Castle.

Yet if the occasion was pure symbolism, who knows what lasting impressions it may have made on the leading actors. There was King George V, who hinted gravely to his son that if he went through this ceremony satisfactorily it might help him in his dealings with the "difficult Mr. Lloyd George". The young Prince seems to have had a distaste for the pageantry and dressing up: "I decided things had gone too far . . . what would my Navy friends say if they saw me in this preposterous rig? . . . I made a painful discovery about myself. It was that, while I was prepared to fulfil my rôle in all this pomp and ritual, I recoiled from anything that tended to set me up as a person requiring homage." Was this a shadow of events to come? Was the act of abdication conceived subconsciously in the impressionable mind of a young Prince that day at Caernarvon?

And Churchill, too, who was present in the capacity of Home Secretary. He had rehearsed his part on the golf links with Lloyd George. Did this act of faith and pageantry inspired by Lloyd George bring him closer to the fiery radical? One can well believe that it contributed towards such a frame of mind.

From that day in July, 1911, Lloyd George always insisted on regarding the Prince as a Welshman. Here, he felt, was a future monarch who could bring the democratic touch to the throne, one who had at an early age shaken the dust of the Court from his feet and rubbed shoulders with ordinary people in the trenches. He set out to win over the Prince as an instrument through which he could modernise the conception of the monarchy and relate its message overseas.

"The Prime Minister also had ideas for my employment in the Empire beyond the seas. . . . He was anxious that before the ardour of wartime comradeship had wholly cooled, I should set forth at once upon a series of tours to thank the various countries of the British Commonwealth, on my father's behalf, for their contributions to the war. . . . As he once explained to me, the appearance of the popular Prince of Wales in far corners of the Empire might do more to calm the discord than half a dozen solemn Imperial Conferences."

In this decision Lloyd George was undoubtedly right and he acted with great imagination. Not since the days of the young Henry VIII had a scion of the British royal family so fascinated the ordinary people everywhere as Edward, Prince of Wales. The half-shy, half-wistful smile won the hearts of Australia and Canada as it had at home. The monarchy seemed about to enter a new and more glorious phase. But, as the Duke later ruefully admitted, Lloyd George "drove me hard".

The globe-trotting tours, the constant round of receptions, the foundation stone-laying, the planting of trees, the speech-making and civic functions were wearying in the extreme; the adulation, the hero-worshipping made it hard for a young Prince to settle down and live a normal life.

When, after a tour of nearly 41,000 miles, the Prince returned to Britain, Lloyd George, then Prime Minister, welcomed him back in this speech at the London Guildhall:

"Whatever our feeling for him was before he went to India, it is deeper today. It was a high act of statesmanship, carried through with inimitable gifts of grace, of tact and of a drawing attachment which is so very much his dominant characteristic. More than that, it was a high act of courage, carried through with faultless nerve.

"There were difficulties, there were menaces, there was an atmosphere which gave great concern to everyone. He went indomitably at the call of duty, and whatever the Empire owed him before, it owes to him a debt which it can never repay today."

"A debt which it can never repay." That was a phrase which was quickly forgotten in 1936. But Lloyd George, to his credit, did not forget. Whether his motives were disinterested, inspired by a desire to make political mischief, or actuated by his own personal feelings on the subject of love and duty, one cannot be sure. But he could claim with every justification that he became the King's Champion when almost every hand was against his monarch and when the people who had lauded him often hysterically a few years earlier now indulged in one of those occasionally disgusting exhibitions of moral humbug which make the British race so incomprehensible to foreigners. How could a French Catholic be made to understand why a nation, who had defied the Pope so that Henry VIII could get a divorce, should now make so much fuss merely because a modern king wanted to marry a divorced woman? Meanwhile the long knives were being sharpened by pompous parish priests and narrow-minded bishops; all the bitter gall of the Book of Ecclesiastes was being distilled in vitriolic sermons, and once again Lloyd George was the audacious, lonely and unorthodox campaigner fighting for a lost cause.

Ll. G. had welcomed the accession of King Edward VIII. His heart warmed to the monarch who defied protocol-worshipping Court officials by walking to his office in the rain, holding up an umbrella like any other citizen. He admired the new King's passionate desire to do something for the unemployed, chuckled when he learned that the monarch felt that the Baldwin Government was inert and inept in tackling this problem.

"The King will do what nobody else can do," Ll. G. told James Maxton. "He will get rid of this Government, not by unconstitutional methods, but simply by showing that he is more concerned about the unemployed than they are. Why, King Edward VIII is the Labour Party's greatest asset if they only knew it."

This remark, which was made in a loud voice in the lobby of the House of Commons, was repeated back to Stanley Baldwin. It was meant to be. Baldwin stirred himself from his usual lethargy to consider the problem of a King who, wittingly or otherwise, allowed himself to be associated in the popular mind with the underdog. To Baldwin and his Tory colleagues this was not "playing the game". Some, notably Chamberlain, wanted Baldwin to persuade the King to play down this rôle and avoid visits to the distressed areas.

Whatever the apologists for the Abdication may claim, there is little doubt that the King's independence of mind and his keen interest in social and economic problems with which the Government only temporised, tended to set ministers against him quite as much as his well-known friendship with Mrs. Simpson. When King Edward, accompanied by the Minister of Labour, Ernest Brown, toured the grim and jobless valleys of South Wales, he was moved to tears by the tragedy around him, a tragedy heightened not by resentful faces and sullen hatred, but by the friendliness, the gleam of hope in the gaunt, pinched faces and by the festooned Davy lamps which were the best the out-of-work miners could do in the way of decorations. The pathetic attempts at cheering by men and women with empty stomachs and the sad little smiles of bare-footed children brought a lump to the King's throat.

It was on this occasion that he made the simple, rather obvious, but nevertheless sincere utterance: "Something must be done."

That was a natural, innocuous human heart-cry, but in Government circles the word "must" was regarded as tactless and implying that the Government had done nothing.

Lloyd George knew all about the King's devotion to Mrs. Simpson and sympathised with his Sovereign's difficulty in resolving this problem of the heart. He had been kept closely informed of the matter and also of the anxiety of some ministers to force the King's hand. Nevertheless, it was hardly in keeping with his desire to help the King to pass the information on to William Randolph Hearst, the American newspaper proprietor, at whose British home, St. Donat's Castle, Ll. G. had often been entertained.

Lloyd George's view was that Baldwin acted far too dilatorily in the beginning and that in the end he forced the Sovereign into an impossible position. He also shared Lord Beaverbrook's opinion that underground and underhand forces in public life and in the Press deliberately paved the way for the Abdication. And he let it be known that if the King ever wanted "a champion against Baldwin and Company, I am prepared to fill that rôle".

Baldwin knew this and dreaded its consequences. It was, therefore, with relief that the Prime Minister learned that Ll. G. had gone to Jamaica on holiday. If he needed any prompting it was provided not by Geoffrey Dawson, the editor of *The Times*, but by Wickham Steed, an earlier editor and one who, as we have seen, was never well disposed towards Lloyd George. Steed told Baldwin: "There is not a moment to be lost. If this matter is to be settled without appalling dangers to the country, it must be settled now while Lloyd George is abroad. For I have information that Ll. G. intends to make a political issue of this. You will find he will try to create a King's Party."

Baldwin grunted non-committally, but he took notice all the same.

The mystery of the "King's Party" has never been completely solved, if indeed there ever was so foolish an organisation in anything other than the heads of a few misguided people. Those who had either been groomed for it, or who had groomed themselves for it, have since maintained an absolute silence. But Wickham Steed was wrong in thinking that Lloyd George would have created such a Party. He was far too wily a politician for that. What he would have done was to exploit such a Party. The British Union of Fascists, under Sir Oswald Mosley, was certainly in favour of a King's Party, but in fairness both to King Edward and Sir Oswald, the former had nothing to do with this and the latter had not the ulterior motives suggested by his adversaries. The late Sir George Sutton declared that "150 business-men and industrialists were willing and ready to form a King's Party, if the need arose". One can well imagine into what a hotchpotch of reaction and semi-Fascism any such combination might have developed.

There are indications that an attempt was made at government level to mislead Lloyd George at this time. "There had," wrote Mr. Malcolm Thomson, "been no indication of an imminent constitutional crisis when Lloyd George left for Jamaica. Ll. G. afterwards declared that he would never have left London, 'if I had not been deceived about the true situation'."

But once again Baldwin outwitted Ll. G. He had his plans well laid; his agents had made very sure of their ground. From the Labour leaders and from the new and Conservative-minded Liberal Party chief, Mr. Clement Davies, he had had unofficial promises of support. Me-tooism was rampant in all political circles. Speeches, Press leader articles and even sermons had been written weeks beforehand to wait for just such a moment as this. The signal was given for the silence barriers to be lifted, and Press, Bishops and minor clergy rushed to denounce the man whom for years they had idolised in the most extravagant terms.

Baldwin forced the issue: renounce Mrs. Simpson or go. To this the King replied, as one would expect from a man of honour: "I intend to marry Mrs. Simpson and I am prepared to go."

Lloyd George was "profoundly distressed" at the news. "He agreed that Mrs. Simpson could not become Queen," wrote Mr. Malcolm Thomson, "but he did not want to lose the King and would have been willing to allow a morganatic marriage by which she would be the King's wife, but not his Queen. He was out of touch with the currents of opinion in Britain which were mainly hostile to any such solution."

But were they "mainly hostile"? We shall never know for certain, because public opinion was given no time either to make itself felt, or to form an accurate judgment. It is certain that the Government would never have dared to take a referendum on this matter. The creation of a "King's Party" was also a possible, if not a serious risk. Lord Beaverbrook has said: "When Dawson set out to mobilise opinion against the King in the columns of *The Times* he deliberately suppressed all the letters which were in favour of the King."

The History of The Times stated: "Dawson organised an analysis of the vast mass of correspondence that had poured into Printing House Square—the largest ever received—in order to have the basis for the following day's leader. . . . None of these letters to the editor was ever published, but they were studied for the indication they gave of the progress of public opinion. The earliest letters, following the shock of the first newspaper comments, mainly reflected an unquestioning loyalty to the occupant of the throne."

It is beside the point that later letters "gradually wavered and gave way to a more critical approach". For by then the King's case had gone by default.

Lloyd George feverishly prepared to return to Britain to do battle for the King. He sent out messages, insisting on the King's right to marry whom he chose and was anxious to join with Churchill in an onslaught on the Government. But Baldwin refused a debate in the Commons and compelled the King to sign the instrument of Abdication before Lloyd George could return.

The Christmas after the Abdication, appalled by the attacks on the ex-King and the deplorable "they stand rebuked" tirade against the King's friends by the Archbishop of Canterbury, Lloyd George sent this cable to the newly created Duke of Windsor:

"Best Christmas greetings from an old Minister of the Crown who holds you in as high esteem as ever and regards you with deep and loyal affection, deplores the shabby and stupid treatment accorded to you, resents the mean and unchivalrous attacks upon you and regrets the loss sustained by the British Empire of a monarch who sympathised with the lowliest of his subjects."

This cable has often been criticised as a mischievous and unwarranted intervention. In fact, coming just after the unedifying spectacle of Christian prelates crucifying verbally a man who was down and out, it summed up the true feelings of the majority of the British people.

The unctuous Archbishop had done more to restore the ex-King in the people's favour than anyone else could have achieved: after Cosmo Gordon Lang's vituperation Lloyd George's message was a signal of returning sanity and sense of proportion. The Duke replied: "Very touched by your kind telegram and good wishes which I heartily reciprocate. *Cymru am byth.*"

Lloyd George always took the view, which he caused to be aired in the American Press, that the King had been partly dethroned because of his sympathy with "the lowliest of his subjects". It was a distortion of the facts, but it had an iota of truth in it all the same. His views on the Abdication, however, soon brought trouble on his head, this time, ironically enough, in Wales. Mr. Thomas Waterhouse, chairman of the North Wales Liberal Federation, said:

"I hold strong views on this matter and I am indeed surprised that Mr. Lloyd George should have thought fit to intervene, particularly as the North Wales Liberal Federation passed a resolution during the crisis expressing their determination to stand behind Mr. Baldwin and the Government to uphold the dignity, authority and integrity of the Throne."

Other prominent Liberals also criticised Ll. G. One comment was that he "had shocked the consciences of many Christian Welshmen from whom he drew votes at election time" . In Caernarvon Boroughs it was estimated that he had lost himself at least 2,000 votes.

Meanwhile, Ll. G. agreed to sit on the committee to frame the new King's Civil List, fixing the incomes of the Royal Family. He registered a protest against the fact that no State provision was to be made for an income for the Duke of Windsor. A year later, while holidaying at Cannes, he dined with the Duke and Duchess.

The lessons of this tragic chapter of British history do not seem to have been learned. The whole position regarding royal marriages remains obscure, archaic, unsatisfactory and inhuman. A similar, though far less serious, problem concerning a proposed royal marriage occurred again in the fifties. Future governments need to take warning from a letter which the Duke of Windsor received from a friend: "I must humbly express my intense admiration of your obvious and inflexible determination not to encourage a 'King's Party'. It was within your power to create Civil War and chaos. You had only to lift a finger, or even to come to London to show yourself, to arouse millions of your subjects to your support."

Another time such a situation might end in the overthrow of the monarchy. That was Lloyd George's firmly held view. In 1936 Britain was in a bewildered and fluctuating mood when confronted with a situation people had never dreamed could ever confront them. A King's Party would have been an act of absolute folly, drawing into its wake all the most irresponsible and reactionary elements of business, industry and politics, and the quasi-romantics with their impractical sentimentalism. It could have provoked an opposition equally irresponsible and ended in a bitter struggle between left and right.

Lloyd George summed up this problem when he told Lord Castlerosse: "An institution so pampered and panoplied as the British monarchy is bound to be changed into a hot-house plant and that is just what we have done with it. When Victoria was on the throne, awkward old devil that she was, at least the monarchy fended for itself and, though she was sheltered at Osborne and Windsor, she developed an uncanny instinct for symbolising the middle-class strength of Britain. Under Edward VII and George V that trend was slightly reversed even though Edward VII was more progressive in his outlook than Queen Victoria. It was reversed because the aristocracy, for whom the old Queen never had much time, now began to draw closer to the monarchy for protection from what they believed was an attack on their privileges by the Commons. But Edward VIII could have changed all this. He could have brought about a spring-cleaning of the monarchy, wiping away the cobwebs from its palaces."

All that Edward VIII unhappily succeeded in doing was to reveal the hitherto hidden truth that the Sovereign is as frail as any flower in the fields. The Abdication may have been right, but its cost was the stifling of the sure instincts of Sovereigns of modern times for paving the way for the right sort of changes. All such changes seem better when the impetus appears to come from the highest in the land. Self-effacement was the useful but negative virtue which George VI had to offer. But self-effacement, surrounded by panoply and mysticism, is not the ultimate answer.

21

VISIT TO HITLER

> "'You are old, Father William,' the young man said,
> 'And your hair has become very white;
> And yet you incessantly stand on your head—
> Do you think, at your age, it is right?'"
>
> *Lewis Carroll*

While Neville Chamberlain as Chancellor of the Exchequer was putting his faith in a cheap-money policy and Imperial Preference as the cure-all for Britain's economic ills, Adolf Hitler, one-time corporal and house-painter, was solving Germany's problems of poverty and unemployment with remarkable success.

This noisy demagogue of the Munich beer-halls had by personal magnetism, relentless political pressure and bloodcurdling denunciations of the "enemies" of Germany, made himself more powerful than the Kaiser had ever been. He was, wrote Churchill in 1933, "The child of the rage and grief of a mighty empire and race which had suffered overwhelming defeat in war."

By the mid-twenties Lloyd George had revived much of his early admiration for Germany and he continually urged that her claims to equality of status and fairer treatment were well founded. At Barmouth in September, 1932, he declared: "All the trouble that has arisen in Europe and in Germany in particular has come from a flagrant breach of the undertaking to disarm by all the victors but one, and the League of Nations' failure to enforce that pledge has destroyed its moral influence. If the Powers succeed in overthrowing Nazism in Germany, Communism will follow."

This was very much the Hitler theme, and one which was propounded by such misguided intellectuals as the Marquis of Lothian and Lord Allen of Hurtwood and by bankers and economists such as Montagu Norman and Josiah Stamp. Yet already Hitler had shown his hand by his ruthless suppression of opposition, his anti-Jewish pogroms and his contempt for liberal democracy. If ever there was a moment when Britain should firmly have announced her determination to stand by France this was it. Strangely, while tolerating Hitler, Lloyd George was harsh on Mussolini. He was not opposed to giving Germany back some of her former colonies "as a gesture", but he condemned Mussolini's march into Abyssinia. Even when

Hitler made a fool of the Western Powers by occupying the Rhineland and had the impertinence to back it up with the offer of a twenty-five-years' peace pact, Lloyd George thought this should "be taken seriously".

Undoubtedly Ll. G. was influenced by the views of his old friend, Philip Kerr, now Marquis of Lothian, who, while lecturing France in tones of moral indignation, proclaimed that Germany was inspired by a noble crusade against Bolshevism.

In Germany Lloyd George's views on the new régime were noted with approval and interest. When Hitler insisted that "we must not lose this unexpected and valuable ally of the German Reich", his Ambassador in London, Herr von Ribbentrop, formally invited Lloyd George to visit Germany. The Welshman willingly agreed, though he was cautious enough to announce that his visit was simply to see what Germany had accomplished in conquering unemployment. Lothian had hailed the trip joyfully and Professor Conwell-Evans, of Königsberg University, a Welshman who enthusiastically supported Hitler at that time, was requested to make the necessary arrangements and act as interpreter.

There have been various versions of the meeting between Lloyd George and Hitler on the Obersalzberg, near Berchtesgaden, on September 4, 1936. It lasted for four hours and was, wrote Dr. Thomas Jones, who accompanied Lloyd George's party, spent "in the friendliest fashion".

"For Hitler's National Socialism and his totalitarian system Lloyd George had no sympathy whatsoever," wrote Malcolm Thomson. This can hardly be reconciled with Ll. G.'s enthusiasm over his German visit, his extravagant praise of Hitler on his return, or by the evidence of those who overheard their talks.

When Hitler walked briskly down the steps to greet the white-haired British statesman, there was nothing of the arrogance and chilly contempt with which he later received Chamberlain. The Führer was in his sunniest and most charming mood.

"I am particularly glad," said Hitler as he shook hands with Lloyd George, "to greet in my house the man who always seemed to us to be the real victor in the world war."

"And I regard myself as lucky," replied Lloyd George, "to be able to meet the man who has gathered the whole German people behind him and who has helped his people rise again after defeat."

They sat together in the reception room of the Berghof, of which the most striking feature was the vast window which filled one side of the room and looked out on the Berchtesgaden countryside in the full glory of its September sunlight.

Details of their conversation can be pieced together from the statements both published and unpublished of various people who were present, including Dr. Thomas Jones, Mr. A. J. Sylvester and Dr. Paul Schmidt, chief interpreter of the German Foreign Office, who gave a very detailed account in his *Statist auf Diplomatischer Buehne*.

Lloyd George told Hitler that "alliances are always dangerous. In the last war they spread hostilities like a prairie fire. Without them the conflict might have been localised". This ill-chosen view, of course, coincided exactly with Hitler's insistence on the futility of collective security.

The two men also discussed German measures for solving unemployment, relief works and Nazi methods of teaching people how to use their leisure time. There appears to have been only one disappointment for Hitler: Ll. G. declined to accept an invitation to attend the Nazi Party meeting in Nuremberg. "I have not come to Germany for matters of politics," said Lloyd George in explanation. "I wanted to study your social institutions and above all your solution of the unemployment problem. If I went to Nuremberg, it might be misunderstood in Britain."

Next day the veteran British politician and the dictator of the German Reich met again for tea. Hitler presented his guest with a signed photograph of himself, to which Ll. G. replied: "I am honoured to receive this gift from the greatest living German. I shall place it beside my pictures of Marshal Foch and President Wilson."

Dr. Schmidt described how Lloyd George asked Hitler: "To which positions we had withdrawn, what moral effects the Allied counter-thrust had made on us, and interrogated me almost as carefully as the American interrogation officers in 1945.

"I had read in Clemenceau's memoirs of a dinner party which Clemenceau and Lloyd George attended on the eve of the Armistice. The future of Germany was discussed and Lloyd George was of a different opinion from his French colleagues.

"'What has happened to you?' Clemenceau asked gruffly. 'You have completely changed.'

"'Yes, don't you know that from today I am pro-German?' Ll. G. answered. Lloyd George assured me this story was true."

But if Hitler impressed Ll. G. the aged statesman charmed and delighted Hitler. Heinrich Hoffman, Hitler's photographer, said Hitler told him, "Lloyd George is the greatest visiting statesman I have met." Hoffman also mentioned a remark of Lloyd George's: "You can thank God you have such a man as your Führer."

Hitler's admiration for Ll. G. was not transitory. Even in 1942 he continued to speak in highly eulogistic terms of the man who visited him in 1936. Many of these remarks are recorded in Professor Trevor-Roper's book, *Hitler's Table Talk*.

"Churchill's pre-destined opponent was Lloyd George. Unfortunately he is twenty years too old."

Or this judgment: "The man who without doubt will find himself justified by history is Lloyd George. In a memorandum drafted at the time (the Peace Conference) Lloyd George declared that, if peace were made in the conditions foreseen, it would lead to the start of a new war. The Germans fought so heroically, he wrote, that this proud nation will never be content with such a peace. If Lloyd George had the necessary power he would certainly be the architect of German-English understanding."

Again in August, 1942, Hitler declared: "The Briton who made the deepest impression on me was Lloyd George. Eden speaks a repulsive, affected type of English, but Ll. G. is a pure orator and a man of tremendous breadth of vision. What he has written on the Versailles Treaty will endure for ever. He was the first man to declare that the Treaty would lead to another war.

"I asked Lloyd George why it was that he had failed to gain his point when negotiations for the Peace Treaty were in progress. He explained that Wilson opposed him from the beginning and that the French never ceased from their witch-hunt. It was not his fault and he had done all that was in his power to do."

Lloyd George reminded him that at the time "The British were hated by France. He also told me that he was surprised and taken aback when at the last minute the German delegation declared its readiness to sign. As they went out Clemenceau hissed in his ear: 'Voilà!'"

From these scraps of conversation and comment it is possible to gain a fairly accurate picture of the line which Lloyd George took with Hitler: criticism of the recently signed Franco-Soviet Treaty, stressing the bad points of the Versailles Treaty, while ignoring the prospects of collective security which it could have offered.

Evidence of the damaging admissions Lloyd George was prepared to make about his own country is provided by Heinz Linge, Hitler's valet. "I believe that it was not only Ribbentrop, but your own great statesman, Lloyd George, and other British visitors who helped to implant in Hitler's mind the idea that Britain hated the idea of war, and from this he drew the conclusion that Britain would put up with anything rather than fight again.

"After Lloyd George visited him at the Berghof, Hitler said to me: 'Lloyd George has just told me that for some time during the war Britain was on the point of surrender. I told him I believed the German mistake was that we surrendered at five minutes to twelve.

"'He agreed with me. I have told him that if there is ever another war between Germany and Britain, so long as I am the Führer, Germany will fight until five minutes past twelve.'

"It may be that the version he gave me of his meeting with Lloyd George was due to a mistranslation of what the British statesman really said. Maybe. But whether those words were actually used by Lloyd George or not, the impression was firmly implanted in Hitler's mind that they had been."

During his visit Lloyd George saw factories, reclamation schemes and even the labour camps of Robert Ley's *Arbeitsfront*. There can be no excuse that he did not know what was going on in Germany, for Dr. Schmidt has testified that Lloyd George "got to know Robert Ley's *Arbeitsfront* people quite well and was taken to see the 'social installations'". In other words he saw some of those camps bearing the sardonic motto *Arbeit Macht Frei* (Work Makes Free) over the entrance gates, but which were really concentration camps.

On his way home, according to Dr. Thomas Jones, Lloyd George was "so enthusiastic in praise of Hitler and all his works that the combined pressure of his fellow travellers had to be brought to bear upon him to tone down his superlatives". This was a reference to an article he was writing for the *Daily Express*.

"I have never seen a happier people than the Germans, and Hitler is one of the greatest of the many great men I have met," he told reporters on his arrival back in London. "I am fully convinced that the German people earnestly desire peace. . . . Undoubtedly Germany fears an attack by Russia, and in the same way Russia fears an attack by Germany. Germany, too, is very suspicious of the Franco-Russian Pact. It is quite natural that she should be suspicious, because you have two of the most powerfully armed countries in the world on her frontiers. This is really why Germany is re-occupying the Rhineland.

"We hear a great deal of the efforts that Germany is making in the direction of rearmament, but very little is said of the colossal schemes that are being pushed through for the development of the internal resources of the country and the improvement of their working population.

"They have reduced unemployment from six millions to one million in three and a half years . . . that in itself is a very great achievement."

But it was his *Daily Express* article that attracted most attention and which sent a shudder of horror through the ranks of orthodox Liberalism. It was a wildly extravagant tribute to Hitler: "One man has accomplished this miracle. He is a born leader of men. A magnetic, dynamic personality with a single-minded purpose, a resolute will and a dauntless heart. . . . The old trust him; the young idolise him. It is the worship of a national hero who has saved his country from utter despondency and degradation . . . not a word of criticism or disapproval have I heard of Hitler. He is the George Washington of Germany."

The George Washington of Germany: this recklessly eulogistic phrase was to re-echo mockingly round the world, syndicated for profit in a score of languages. But it was symbolic of an era summed up so well in Douglas Reed's *Insanity Fair* in which bishops told us the Nazis were stamping out immorality and Tory back-benchers were referring to Fascist Franco as "a gallant Christian gentleman".

A clue to the reason why Lloyd George detested Mussolini and yet lauded Hitler was provided in a letter he wrote to Professor Conwell-Evans at the end of 1937: "It looks as if the Führer has committed himself to Mussolini—that adds enormously to the obstacles in the path of a friendly accommodation of the troubles of Europe. Mussolini is temperamentally an aggressor. I have never thought that Herr Hitler was and I do not believe it now."

It was the vanity, the posturing and petty boastfulness of Mussolini which Ll. G. disliked, and he could not, or would not, believe that Hitler, who had achieved such power over a whole nation, could be other than a great statesman. It was partly wishful thinking: Hitler was for Lloyd George the sort of colossus he himself desired to be.

* * * * *

Meanwhile in Germany Lloyd George was marked down as a potential ally of the Third Reich in the same way that Hitler had already singled out Pierre Laval in France.

When Lloyd George sent his sympathetic cable to the Duke of Windsor its contents were duly noted in the Berghof, and Hitler decided that the ex-King and ex-Prime Minister would, in certain circumstances, be a formidable and useful combination. Ribbentrop also reported to the Führer that "the ideal team for us in Britain would have been King Edward and Lloyd George. Together they could have achieved through public opinion all that we could desire".

Hitler heartily agreed about this, and so an invitation to the Duke and Duchess of Windsor to visit Germany was sent from Berlin. The intermediary was Charles Eugene Bedaux, an American businessman who had become a member of the Windsors' intimate circle of friends. Bedaux was detested in America on account of his Fascist ideas on industrial and labour problems and his close links with Nazis and French Fascists. British friends, including Lord Beaverbrook, advised the Duke not to make the trip, but he ignored their warnings, sincerely believing this visit might help international relations. So in October, 1937, the trip, sponsored by Bedaux's friend, Dr. Ley, took place.

* * * * *

Working as a secretary in the archives of the Berghof was a young woman, Helga Stultz, who was an informer for the American intelligence. She had been secretly married to an aide of Captain Roehm, the head of the Stormtroopers who was purged in the blood bath of June 30, 1934. The secret of the marriage had been kept from Roehm because the aide had been a paramour of this notorious homosexual.

When the aide was summarily executed after Roehm's death it was still necessary for Stultz to hide her past, so she changed her name. Not unnaturally Helga Stultz had no reason to love the Nazis. She had come to spy for the Americans because they arranged for her to smuggle funds to Switzerland where she had a child.

Back to Washington went this report from Helga: "I have overheard a conversation between Hitler and Ley. They discussed the visit of the Duke of Windsor. Ley said he was keeping in close touch with the ex-English Prime Minister, Lloyd George, through the *Arbeitsfront*. Hitler was very excited. 'You must find a way of letting Lloyd George know that in my opinion the only hope of an understanding with Britain would be if he returned to power and the ex-King came back to the throne. That cannot happen unless there is a war. But, though the British don't want to fight and have no stomach for it, I believe they may blunder into war. If that happens, they will collapse within a year. We should have new rulers to deal with and I am certain Lloyd George would give us back our colonies without any fuss. He promised me he would agree to this.

"'Lloyd George's position is not easy. He has to pretend to work with the left-wing of his own Party and the ruling clique mistrust him. But I am not without hope that Lothian may play a part in removing the ruling clique's dislike of Ll. G.'"[1]

That message was transmitted to Washington by a free-lance American agent who happened to be on the staff of Admiral Canaris' intelligence service.

For a long time Washington refused to believe it.

Secret lists of possible supporters of the Nazi régime abroad were prepared in Berlin during the years 1937–39. These lists were frequently revised as intelligence reports constantly contradicted each other. The chief failing of the German Secret Service was its decentralisation, information being provided by some thirty competing agencies. Copies of the lists have been discovered from time to time since the war. Some are in private hands; others are in the hands of Allied Governments. Lloyd George's name appeared on a number of these lists. It was markedly prominent in 1936–37, it was demoted from "probable" to "possible" in 1938, when for a brief period Ll. G. attacked Chamberlain's appeasement policy, but it was presented in 1939–40 as follows:

"David Lloyd George, ex-Prime Minister of Great Britain 1916–22. Critic of the Versailles Treaty. Has worked for National Socialist co-operation with England. The only politician with sufficient authority and prestige to act as leader in the event of the downfall of the Chamberlain Government and to maintain order by creating a pro-German administration." A somewhat naïve footnote added: "Alternatively

[1] Wythe Williams (see bibliography).

might be made Gauleiter of Wales, if —— could be persuaded to become head of the British Government."

* * * * *

In March, 1938, Lloyd George paid a visit to Paris. He met Léon Blum, Paul Boncour, Herriot and Reynaud, but Daladier, the Prime Minister, refused to see him, recalling that, whatever his views about ending non-intervention in the Spanish Civil War which was then raging, Lloyd George was notoriously sympathetic towards the Sudeten Germans and that he had referred to Benes, of Czechoslovakia, as "that little French jackal". And for Daladier the imminent dangers of Germany's claims on Sudeten territory were of more importance than the Spanish Civil War.

For a while Lloyd George warned the Government that the policy of appeasement was leading to war, not pacification. "You have retreated so often before the dictators that they have come to the conclusion that there is no point at which you will stand. They are convinced you won't fight. So am I."

Yet, while winning cheap popularity by his attacks on one of the most unpopular and unconvincing Premiers Britain has ever had, he gave ample evidence that he was not prepared to carry his opposition to Chamberlain to the extent of defending every bastion of democracy in Europe. When the Czechoslovakian crisis came his sympathies were with the Sudetens and, privately, he agreed with Chamberlain that "Czechoslovakia was not worth a war".

Not even the British Premier's belated guarantees to Poland, Rumania and Greece impressed Berlin. Why should they when the countries selected for such guarantees were territories which Britain could not possibly defend? However defeatist Lloyd George's speech of May 8, 1939, may have sounded, he was being realistic when he declared:

"Without Russia these three guarantees to Poland, to Rumania and to Greece are the most reckless commitments that any country has ever entered into. They are demented pledges that cannot be redeemed with this enormous deficiency, this great gap between the forces arrayed on the other side and the forces which at the moment we can put in."

The only military advisers the so-called National Governments of 1931–40 were prepared to listen to were "yes-men". General Sir Leslie Hollis, who was secretary of the Joint Planning Committee of Imperial Defence during part of this period, has told how one draft of a plan providing against attack by Germany on Britain was received by the Cabinet. "It was rather a gloomy forecast . . . the first draft did not pull its punches. But our document by no means found favour with them. Mr. Baldwin in particular was extremely cross . . . Hankey gave me a severe dressing-down. My future in the Committee of Imperial Defence clearly hung by a thin thread."

Hankey's influence on the Cabinet in these years appears to have been quite the reverse of what it was in World War I. But the last straw in the edifice of defence without bricks was Chamberlain. By his obstinate, insensate folly he had changed the balance of power in Europe overnight. He had put even the most resolute opponents of the Nazi régime in an impossible position; the prospect of standing up to Hitler without an alliance with Russia was far more "midsummer madness" than the imposition of sanctions on Italy during the Abyssinian crisis. In condemning the guarantees to three near-Fascist powers with thoroughly corrupt governments, when we had failed to stand by the democracies of Czechoslovakia and Republican Spain, Lloyd George was, from any strategical conception, talking common sense.

The die was cast in August when it was revealed that Ribbentrop had brought off his biggest triumph—a German-Soviet Pact of non-aggression, largely if not entirely due to the fact that Chamberlain had never taken talks with Russia seriously and had, as Lloyd George aptly pointed out, only sent his "Foreign Office clerk"—Strang—to discuss the possibility of military co-operation between the two countries. Ll. G. lashed out at Chamberlain in bitter tones and stung the Prime Minister into promising that full details of the abortive negotiations with Russia would be published in a White Paper—a promise that was never fulfilled. Nine days later the invasion of Poland began. When, after two days' delay which shocked the nation, Chamberlain, in the accents of a political mouse, spoke to the British people, and announced that we were at war with Germany, Lloyd George said in the House of Commons: "The Government could do no other than what they have done. I am one of tens of millions in this country who will back any Government that is in power in fighting this struggle through."

It was the last time that he so positively and openly supported the war effort.

22

WORLD WAR II

> "Here lieth one, who did most truly prove
> That he could never die while he could move;
> So hung his destiny, never to rot
> While he might still jog on and keep his trot."
>
> *John Milton*

Lloyd George was convinced that Chamberlain would not last long as Premier. Because of this he continued to be a prophet of doom and gloom. When Germany announced the partition of Poland after her first victorious *blitzkrieg* and said that Britain and France could have peace if they desired it, he urged that this question should be considered in secret session of the House of Commons. He suggested a conference between Britain, Germany, Russia, Italy, France and the United States.

"I do not propose to do anything to weaken the hands of the Government, but I ask the House and the Government to pause and not to be in a hurry coming to a conclusion.

"In my judgment, if you had a conference, it would be a first-class mistake to enter into it unless you invited not merely Russia and Italy, but the United States as well, because there you have a great power whose interests are not European interests and which has not been involved in any of these disputes and quarrels.

"The fate of this war may depend not upon Britain and France and Germany, but upon the neutrals. Italy has proclaimed herself neutral.[1] The fate of this war may well depend upon the attitude of these three powers."

His speech was attacked. Duff Cooper "deplored and regretted it" as a "suggestion of surrender". Sir Henry Morris-Jones, Liberal-National (Simonite) member for Denbigh, declared that Lloyd George "had done a great disservice to this country. Wales would be ashamed of the words he uttered".

Chamberlain's refusal to consider a conference only made Lloyd George more determined to follow up this theme. At a special meeting of the Council of Action in London he proposed that Britain should invite Hitler to state his peace terms. On October 21, 1939, he told

[1] Italy did not enter the war until the following year.

people at Caernarvon that "we could be firm at a conference as on the battlefield". At the same time he developed the argument that, even if Germany were crushed, the next and more dangerous enemy might well be Russia. The tremendous interest which this meeting aroused—many of the 8,000 present came from as far afield as Liverpool and the midlands—was a tribute to the magic which Ll. G. still evoked.

"The international situation," he declared, "has fundamentally changed with the signing of the Russo-German pact, and our diplomacy should be based on the realisation of this fact. The reluctance to open large-scale hostilities reveals a desire for peace. . . . The Prime Minister has himself predicted that the war will last for three years. The Russo-German pact may well prolong that period, for it has appreciably diminished the chances of a blockade. I, therefore, think that if there were an opportunity of achieving our aims by peaceful means now it is better than running tremendous risks and incurring terrible sacrifices to achieve at the end terms which might not be better than those we have a chance of securing now, providing we obtain the presence and help at the conference of neutral states who are as anxious to avert the consequences of a prolonged war as we are. That is my proposal."

Lloyd George went on to condemn the "rash guarantee to Poland without even consulting Russia". It was, he pointed out, only after Britain had given her guarantee to Poland that negotiations with Russia were opened. "Two-fifths of Poland is not Polish at all. It is occupied by men of another race, language and religion who protested fiercely against this act of aggression by Poland and even fought against it. The Supreme Council of the Allies in Paris protested against it. The Versailles Treaty did not recognise it. Vilna was subsequently annexed by Polish forces in spite of the protest of the League of Nations. I am very glad to learn that the Russians have restored it to the Lithuanians, to whom it belonged. We guaranteed Poland without reference to these facts.

"We guaranteed Poland without even consulting our General Staff as to whether it was possible to make such a guarantee effective. I rose immediately in the House of Commons and said that you could not send a single battalion to the aid of Poland without first of all securing the help of Russia, and I described a guarantee without Russia's aid as an act of madness—walking into a trap. You must agree with me that what I said then has been completely justified by the event. We never sent a single tank or gun to Poland because it was impracticable. We might have relieved the pressure on Poland by our Air Force. We employed our aeroplanes to amuse the Germans with childish tracts."

Lloyd George had been the only politician ruthlessly and accurately to expose the futility of the guarantee to Poland without first obtaining the aid of Russia. His logic here was indisputable. One can criticise the wobbling policy which he pursued in these years, one can condemn the lack of principles and the ever-present desire to improvise policies according to the exigencies of the moment, the urge to have a foot in both camps. Yet it must be conceded that he pinpointed the dangers and sign-posted the errors and fatuities of the Government with much greater foresight, lucidity and imagination than any other critic of the Government at this time. It would be quite erroneous to suggest he was suffering from senile decay. He never had the unflagging patriotism of Churchill, and he regarded his old colleague's return to office at the Admiralty with some dismay. Ll. G. feared that Chamberlain might blunder to defeat through sheer incompetence, but he feared even more that Churchill might lead the nation to defeat by obstinately refusing to recognise that the combination against Britain was too formidable. By this time he realised that if Chamberlain had to go, Churchill was a natural candidate for the leadership on the strength of his pre-war warnings about Nazi Germany.

From September, 1939, until May, 1940, the war was looked upon by a majority of the British people with an apathy and calm indifference that seems incredible when one contrasts it with the Dunkirk mood of a few months later. Lloyd George probably misinterpreted this mood as meaning the British people had no heart for a long and hard war, whereas in reality what the people disliked was the uncertainty of the military position and the unreality of the "Phoney War" period. In Britain the fact that the Germans had refrained from attacking the Maginot Line and bombing open cities over here did not impinge on their nervous systems so much as was the case with the French, whose morale was undermined during the long lull in fighting during the winter months.

Lloyd George's mind was as flexible as ever early in 1940. One moment he would be talking in the accents of defeatism, the next he would be evolving novel ideas for surprising the enemy. In the *New York Journal* he complacently assessed the reasons why Germany was stronger than in 1914, saying "as the belligerent nations will be all equally tired of the costly futility of war which provides no spectacular appeals to national emotions, they will be in no mood to prolong a destructive conflict for the satisfaction of the ambitious schemes of their leaders".

Yet Lloyd George was one of the first to see tremendous possibilities in raising a force of Commandos. He even claimed to have originated the phrase when he told Admiral Sir Roger Keyes: "Don't let us copy what *we* did in the Boer War, let us copy the Boers. Don't launch whole armies on a big front, but send out surprise attacking parties of Commandos—like the Boers, at night, and where they are least expected." Whether Ll. G. really impressed this idea on the military initially one cannot tell, but Admiral Keyes's biographer records that Lloyd George had a long talk with Keyes, whom he greatly admired, more especially as Keyes was a stern critic of Chamberlain. The subject of this talk was Combined Operations, of which Keyes was eventually made Chief. Ll. G. believed that Commando operations on the South African model could be employed at relatively little cost of life to make surprise attacks during the stalemate on the Western front.

On March 14, 1940, Ll. G. conferred with Sumner Welles, President Roosevelt's "peace ambassador". Immediately afterwards there was a report in the American Press that Lloyd George might enter the Cabinet. He certainly confided to his friends that "my day will come yet" and continued to lead vigorous assaults on the toppling Chamberlain Government: "Don't turn yourselves into a bomb-proof shelter for an inept government." The Norway débâcle, when after a gallant naval action, the British were forced to retreat, made the Prime Minister's "Hitler has missed the bus" speech seem foolish in the extreme. Chamberlain made a further error when he talked about his "friends" saving him in the division lobby. Lloyd George had not intended to speak that day; he was in the smoking-room of the House of Commons when a friend reported to him what Chamberlain had said.

"*His friends?*" exclaimed Ll. G. in amazement. "He has dared in the face of this terrible fiasco to plead for his friends to support him? I never recall such a thing happening in Parliament before in a national crisis. I wasn't going to speak, but now I must."

Then, without time for preparation and completely off the cuff, Lloyd George tore into Chamberlain with a series of crushing retorts. He intended to break the Prime Minister and force his resignation, and his forthright denouncement must have made many Tories abstain from voting.

"It is not a question of who are the Prime Minister's friends," he stormed in the Commons, "but a far bigger issue. He has appealed for sacrifice. I say solemnly that the Prime Minister should give an example of that sacrifice, because there is nothing which can contribute more to victory than that he should sacrifice the seals of office."

Chamberlain won his vote of confidence by the narrow margin of eighty-one votes. There were some in the Cabinet who were weary of the war and believed that Chamberlain should stay on in office until France and Belgium fell and then make way for a government which would be prepared to sue for peace with Germany. Not all these intrigues were conducted by members of Parliament; powerful figures outside Parliament and close to the throne were even prepared to suggest to King George VI that, in the event of the fall of France, the King should send, not for Churchill, but for Lloyd George. In this event Lothian would probably have been recalled from Washington to become the new Foreign Secretary. There was still a powerful anti-Churchill clique who, while disliking Lloyd George, preferred him to Churchill.

As for George VI, his own biographer, John Wheeler-Bennett, has revealed that it would not have been Winston Churchill for whom the King would have sent if he could have avoided it. George VI was probably the worst-equipped and least politically knowledgeable monarch who could have sat upon the throne of Britain in such a crisis. Only the constitutional system saved him from precipitating an appalling blunder and then only by a political hair's breadth. The King at that time—though later they were to be on the best of terms—distrusted Churchill, partly because of his opposition to Chamberlain before he entered the Cabinet, but mainly because of the rôle he had played in supporting his brother, Edward VIII, at the time of the Abdication. The King wrote in his diary about his last interview with Chamberlain: "We then had an informal chat over his successor. I, of course, suggested Halifax, but he told me that H. was not enthusiastic, as being in the Lords he could only act as a shadow or a ghost in the Commons where all the real work took place. I was disappointed over this statement as I thought H. was the obvious man."[1]

The contrast between the commonsense political *nous* of his father and this new and naïve monarch shows how perilously the functions of the monarchy operated in this time of crisis. It does more than this: it reveals how uninformed and ill-briefed George VI must then have been on the political facts of life. Halifax was a peer, and ever since Curzon was turned down for the Premiership it had been generally accepted that the Prime Minister must be a Commoner. In addition, Halifax, though a man of great integrity and high principles, was far too closely linked with the policies of appeasement to be acceptable to the left.

Sir Harold Nicolson, giving his own views of the dangers of those dark days when a groping monarch was utterly at the mercy of bad advisers, has said: "If there had been no Winston, I rather think that Chamberlain would have gone on until we were pushed out of France. Then he would have resigned and the King would have sent for Lloyd George. Lloyd George was hopelessly pessimistic at the time of Dunkirk. I used to see him from time to time—he kept an office in Millbank. . . . He thought it was 'all over'—that's what he used to say. He told me so several times."

Fortunately Chamberlain decided to go before any of these plans could mature. Public opinion and the new-found enthusiasm of Labour for Churchill swept him out of office. But the same obstinate sentimentalism which made Churchill recall Fisher to the Admiralty in World War I caused him to turn to Lloyd George as a new candidate for the Cabinet in World War II. It could have been a fatal error.

[1] Lothian believed that Halifax in the Lords and Lloyd George in the Commons would have been an ideal combination.

There was something about Ll. G. which always mesmerised Churchill on occasions. Despite intermittent sharp attacks on his old ally, Winston never forgot that Lloyd George fought tooth and nail against Tory opposition to bring him back into the wartime Coalition Cabinet as Minister of Munitions. Lord Boothby in his memoirs recalls a meeting between Churchill and Ll. G. when the former was Chancellor of the Exchequer and the latter out of office. Churchill told Boothby: "It is a remarkable thing, but Lloyd George hadn't been in this room for three minutes before the old relationship was completely established—the relationship of master and servant."

There are conflicting views of what happened at this time. Mr. A. J. Sylvester says that when Churchill asked Ll. G. in the middle of May whether he would join his Government, the latter was agreeable. But the morning after Churchill took command, Ll. G. was reported to have said: "It would be impossible to be in a Cabinet like that. They would be fighting me."

Correspondence between Churchill and Lloyd George makes it clear that the latter was asked to join the Government and equally obvious that the major obstacle to this from Ll. G.'s point of view was Chamberlain's retention in the Cabinet. Garvin, editor of the *Observer*, had had a talk with Ll. G. and expressed the opinion that he was "still good for six hours a day and it would be six hours of radium". Dr. Thomas Jones told of a lunch party given by Lady Astor at which Lloyd George was present and during which he clearly expected to be invited to high office shortly. But it is more likely that at this time—Chamberlain had not then fallen—Ll. G. still half expected a call to Buckingham Palace. He was anxious to keep everyone guessing as to his real intentions, whether he meant to wait until a call came from the King, or whether he would serve under a new Prime Minister.

Doubtless Ll. G. felt that he would be in a minority in the new Cabinet and that the suggested office of Minister of Agriculture was not particularly attractive. But, as later evidence will show, he still believed there was a chance that the Churchill Government would fall and he would return to No. 10 Downing Street. The outlook was bleak: Belgium had been crushed, France seemed likely to collapse any day and there were still many of the same old incompetents in the Churchill Government.

Meanwhile in Berlin, though Hitler had over-run most of Europe, the military experts still shied away from the project of an amphibious operation against Britain. The men who could be so brave when fighting on land disliked the prospect of attacking even an undefended mole hill if it was surrounded by water. Hitler himself, though more favourable to "Operation Sea Lion", did not think it would be necessary. He was convinced that Britain would either sue for peace, or that the Churchill Government would be overthrown.

This viewpoint was strengthened when Hitler learned through the *Abwehr* that Lloyd George had declined to join the Churchill Government and had addressed a private meeting of certain members of Parliament at which he expressed his fear that "the war cannot be won by Britain" and had talked about the need for a new "Treaty of Amiens".

Not least among the factors which prevented a triumphant Germany from crushing swiftly a disorganised and largely defenceless Britain was the German belief that, by holding her hand, the Third Reich could make it easier to come to terms with the Fifth Column which Hitler was certain was as all-powerful in Britain as it had been in France. The Nazis were specially interested in the extreme nationalist movement in Wales which, shortly before the war, had shown itself violently hostile to the British Government. Allegations that Germany had active sympathisers among a "group of Welsh nationalists" are made in *The German Fifth Column*, by Dr. L. Dejong, a Dutch historian. The author says: "In the spring of 1940 a group of Welsh nationalists lent themselves for this purpose. Six months later it was noted in Berlin that they had developed along the lines of the task set by the *Abwehr*."

It should be made clear that Dr. Dejong's allegations refer to Welsh nationalists and not to the Welsh Nationalist Party. Dr. Dejong's book was compiled with the aid of captured German documents, including diaries of the *Abwehr*. But it is clear from a variety of sources that the German Secret Service had contacts with fanatical sympathisers in Wales who became known as "the Welsh group". Dr. Fritz Hesse, who was Ribbentrop's adviser on British affairs, has since stated that Herr Otto Behne, the putative Gauleiter of Britain, some time before the war had talks with "a young Welsh nationalist to discuss harnessing national forces in Wales in the German interest", while Hauptmann Nikolaus Ritter, former head of the *Abwehr* branch, *Ast-Hamburg*, has recorded that two German agents were dropped near Salisbury in the summer of 1940 to "contact Welsh nationalist circles who had already expressed themselves as willing to help in the event of a Nazi invasion of Wales". Referring to a fire started in an aircraft factory at Denham in April, 1940, the *Abwehr's* official war diary states that this was the "first major sabotage task set for the Welsh agents' group", while a note dated the following August 15th, signed by Major-General Lahausen, says: "The dispatch of agents to take up direct contact with the Welsh group has been approved by me."

Despite all this organisation, carefully supported by the *Abwehr* and the military, the results of these operations were negligible, due largely to the absence of proper briefing for agents working in Wales and lack of suitable training. But there was a definite plan to take Wales by a combination of paratroops and seaborne divisions which were to be based on Ireland. This was "Operation Green", linking up the invasion of Wales with that of Ireland, and it was to have been launched

Lloyd George with Hitler in 1936.

The bridge over the River Dwyfor at Llanystumdwy. *UPI*

Lloyd George's last resting place overlooking the Dwyfor.

Topix Picture Service

at the end of August, 1941. A subordinate project, code-named "Whale", concerned the Welsh part of this operation, and the *Abwehr* diaries reveal that: "An attempt is to be made to set down the agent Lehrer with a wireless operator on the coast of South Wales in order to establish better communications with the Welsh nationalists."

Unfortunately all agents mentioned in the *Abwehr* diaries and other documents are given code-names and it is almost impossible to establish their identity except in certain cases where the very choice of code-name suggests it. General Lahousen, who was responsible for these diaries, is dead and a great many of the documents are either missing or "unavailable" for independent research. Code-names for prominent Britons were frequently being changed during the war, but available details from the *Verbindungsstab* show that in 1939–40 Ll. G. was designated "Mr. Hindhead".

Whereas there is no evidence of Lloyd George being directly connected with any of the attempts to organise Welsh quislings by the *Abwehr*, there was an attempt before the war, organised by Admiral Canaris's intelligence service, to arrange for secret messages to be passed between Ll. G. and certain people in Germany through the pro-Nazi organisation in Britain known as The Link. There were thirty branches of this organisation, whose chairman and founder was Admiral Sir Barry Domville, former Director of Naval Intelligence at the Admiralty. One of these branches was at Hindhead, the village situated close to Lloyd George's estate at Churt in Surrey.

A German woman teacher, who had been assigned to "look after" the Hindhead branch of The Link in 1938, a Fraulein Bumke, told American intelligence officers after the war; "It was not our aim to stir up trouble or to destroy England. The emphasis was on making friends and building up contacts to improve Anglo-German understanding. We knew that if war came, we should be cut off from our contacts in England and we needed to make sure there was a line of communication. I was assigned the mission of making sure that Mr. Lloyd George could get news of our plans and intentions. He was referred to in correspondence as 'Mr. Hindhead'."

There is no doubt that the Germans were still anxious to exploit both Lloyd George and the Duke of Windsor. Volume VIII of *Documents of German Foreign Policy* confirms this. Reports from the German Minister at The Hague on January 27 and February 19, 1940, claim to reveal certain opinions of the Duke of Windsor. He said the Duke was not entirely satisfied with his position as "a member of the British Military Mission with the French Army Command" and that he was disgruntled. "He has expressed himself in especially uncomplimentary terms about Chamberlain, whom he dislikes. Also there seems to be something like the beginning of a *Fronde* forming around W., which at some time might acquire a certain significance."

The Duke has since refuted these allegations. It was stated on his behalf that he "never met or had any communication with Count Zech-Burkersroda [the Minister at The Hague]" and that "the suggestions affecting the Duke in letters are completely without foundation".

Volume X of the *Documents on German Foreign Policy* shows that Ribbentrop and the German Foreign Office were convinced after the fall of France that they could induce the Duke of Windsor—then in Madrid and Lisbon—to stay on in Europe instead of leaving to become Governor of the Bahamas. They were certain that he would lend himself to their peace campaign and that he and Lloyd George could be brought into a secret accord. Their efforts in this direction range from the sinister to the fatuous and, as the book rightly states, "the German records are necessarily a much tainted source. The only firm evidence they provide is of what the Germans were trying to do in this matter and how completely they failed to do it."

An elaborate plot to kidnap the Duke and Duchess was ordered by Hitler and Ribbentrop, and the man chosen to organise it was Walter Schellenberg. It was to take place while the Duke was hunting near the Spanish frontier. He was to have been "inadvertently" lured over the frontier by a ruse and taken to the German Embassy in Madrid. But at the last moment the British had warning of the plot, the Duke cancelled his shooting trip and guards were posted around the villa where he was staying just outside Lisbon. Schellenberg, who went to Madrid to organise this ambitious coup, wrote in his journal: "I had accomplices in the house where the Duke was staying. Servants at table were in my pay and reported to me all that was said."

The two most remarkable features of this astonishing story are, first, that the British authorities allowed the Duke to stay in such an espionage centre as Lisbon and, secondly, the extraordinary credulity and wishful thinking of the Nazis. Von Stohrer, the German Ambassador in Madrid, reported that "Churchill had threatened W. with arraignment before a court-martial in case he did not accept the post [i.e., Governorship of the Bahamas]. . . . The Duke was considering making a public statement and thereby disavowing present English policy and breaking with his brother. . . . The Duke's agreement [for the Germans' future plans] can be assumed as in the highest degree probable."

* * * * *

Fugacious and futile as many of these espionage activities of the Germans must appear in retrospect, they nevertheless illustrate how deep was Germany's misunderstanding of Britain and the British people. For the first two and a half years of the war there was a firm belief in Berlin that Britain could be brought to her knees by creating a Fifth Column and forcing the break-up of the Churchill Government.

The folly of the Duke of Windsor in agreeing to pay a visit to Germany after his Abdication and the enthusiastic pro-Nazi utterances of Lloyd George had flattered the enemy into believing these two men could be manipulated like puppets for paving the way to a new régime in London.

Lloyd George stepped up his criticism of the Churchill Government. He condemned the holding of secret sessions in Parliament—"a pernicious sham". Even after Chamberlain's death, when it seemed he might at last change his mind about joining the Cabinet, he held back. "The difference between Winston and me," he said, "is that when I was Prime Minister I listened to everyone's opinions and then did the opposite. He listens to no one's opinions and then does what they want."

Mr. Kingsley Martin, editor of the *New Statesman and Nation*, has given a particularly illuminating version of Lloyd George's true standpoint at this time.

"I had long conversations with him at this period and the other day unexpectedly turned up a full note of a talk with him after a visit to Churt. The memorandum is undated, but it clearly refers to the dark period before the German invasion of Russia.

"He began almost at once to tackle me about our two leaders in the *N.S. & N.*, which argued that a compromise peace with Hitler would be fatal. He said that if it were a question of survival, he would fight to the last man, etc. He was no pacifist and, if he could win, he would fight it out. But he judged that we could not win.

". . . At best he saw stalemate. 'In a year's time,' he said, 'if we are both alive, you will be sitting here and I shall remind you of this conversation. We shall be weaker and Germany will be stronger. Peace will be more difficult to get, the war will have spread everywhere in the world, causing suffering and destruction beyond imagination, and you will not be a whit nearer solution.'

"I said: 'This is an odd conversation between you and me. In 1917 you proclaimed the knock-out blow and Lansdowne was defeated. I regarded you as the devil and I think I was right. A compromise with *that* Germany was possible, and the results of victory have been what we have seen.'

"'No,' he said, 'I did not proclaim the knock-out blow until I had Asquith's agreement and had inquired from the Germans whether they were willing to evacuate Belgium. I got no answer. And a knock-out blow was justified by a rational calculation. I could see how we could win. And I was right. We did win. This time there is no rational calculation which shows how victory is possible.'

"The memorandum goes on with a full summary of Ll. G.'s argument that in our desperate situation, and with Winston as Prime Minister, negotiation was impossible. 'Winston,' he said, 'likes his war.' He had had much argument with Winston who had shouted 'Never, never, never' when he talked of conversations with the Nazis. But Ll. G. had no positive proposals except to call for a world conference of powers, proclaim the futility of war and invite a general settlement. He thought we might be invaded but not out-and-out defeated. His view was that in such circumstances, if he were not identified with Churchill, he might be England's 'last chance' as a negotiator. As it turned out, Hitler invaded Russia instead of Britain and Ll. G. lived on until Churchill's military victory was assured."

Then in December, 1940, Lord Lothian died. When the question of replacing him in Washington arose, Lloyd George's name was instantly suggested. Here again the evidence is conflicting, for Ll. G. told some people he would not accept the post, but informed others he was seriously considering it. It may well be that he had difficulty in making up his mind. For, with that astonishing ability in one so old to switch from one idea to its opposite, he was, despite his defeatism, often thinking up schemes to prosecute the war more vigorously. Mr. Sylvester has suggested that in World War II Lloyd George's "inferiority complex" soured his outlook and made him intensely jealous of other political leaders. He may have been jealous, but "inferiority complex" is not a phrase one would normally apply to Lloyd George. As in World War I, Ll. G. was at heart only interested in power, and he believed that one way to power was to take the side of those military and naval leaders with whom Churchill, or the Chiefs of Staff, disagreed. Wavell was one, Keyes was another.

In World War II, though his overall view of the prospects of the Western forces was pessimistic, his ideas on strategy and his summing-up of the military situation were sounder than in World War I. His experience was invaluable and, if he had only recaptured some faith in his own countrymen and their cause, he might well have contributed usefully to the war effort instead of remaining a critic. If Germany had not been so rash as to attack Russia, Churchill might have failed; if Japan had not attacked U.S.A., many of Ll. G.'s gloomy forecasts might have come true. In either or both of these events Lloyd George's long-term view could have been right and Churchill's wrong. Despite his age, his ideas for military diversions were quite as bold as some of Churchill's. At heart he was still an "Easterner", though in World War II for "Easterner" one had to read "Mediterraneaner".

Pantellaria was one example of his ideas for Mediterranean diversions. Lloyd George, who discussed this with Roger Keyes, then Chief of Combined Operations, believed that a few not too costly operations which diverted the enemy might restore our prestige, and, even if a settlement had to be made with the enemy eventually, give us more bargaining power. Keyes wanted diversions in Norway and the Mediterranean. He urged an attack by Commandos aimed at two objectives: first, to capture the island of Pantellaria in September, 1940, thus wiping out an Italian strong-point and taking the submarine pens which were menacing the convoys to Malta; second, to land Commandos along the Tunisian coast close to the Libyan border to link up with the advancing column of Wavell's men.

Keyes and Lloyd George in their different ways argued that this could knock Italy out of the war. Ll. G., who had been bitterly critical of Admiral Sir Dudley Pound, the cautious First Sea Lord, pressed his views on Keyes: "The Italians have no stomach for further fighting. If at the same time British naval forces can strike a blow at the Italian fleet, it may deter Franco and prevent the French fleet from falling into German hands. If Britain hesitates now, the Germans will come to the aid of Italy in North Africa. Pound is too much of an old woman. As for the Chiefs of Staff, they are as hesitant as a covey of neurotic cases in a psychiatrist's parlour."

In this Lloyd George was right. Delay and hesitation in 1940 certainly prolonged the war by at least a year. For once Churchill and Lloyd George seemed to have been in agreement. In her book *Geoffrey Keyes, V.C.*, Elizabeth Keyes stated: "Mr. Churchill had proposed seizing Pantellaria in September and my father had been pressing to be allowed to capture the island from October, 1940, onwards, as he was convinced that it was the key to the Central Mediterranean. The island's aerodrome, with its large underground hangars and bombproof steel doors, could have provided fighter cover to protect our convoys as they approached Malta. . . . He [Keyes] . . . knew the fortifications were not particularly formidable. He hoped to see the entire Italian army in Libya cut off and surrendering to General Wavell."

General Sir Leslie Hollis wrote that Admiral Keyes had "fighting spirit in his bones and fear was unknown to him. Every operation he submitted seemed to envisage that he himself would lead the assault. The Chiefs of Staff had some difficult passages with this intrepid Admiral."

Lloyd George was extremely bitter when Churchill, whom he accused of having a "Dardanelles complex", changed his mind about Pantellaria and sided with the Chiefs of Staff. An expedition had been equipped, but it was repeatedly postponed. The Commandos were already embarked to attack Pantellaria in mid-December, 1940, but the Admiralty refused the destroyers to support them.

Depressed after his brief enthusiasm for military diversions, Lloyd George once again relapsed into defeatist mood. Keyes was replaced by Mountbatten as Chief of Combined Operations, and Wavell was baulked in North Africa. The impracticable guarantee to Greece resulted in the denuding of British forces in North Africa and an end of Wavell's magnificent advance across Libya, still one of the most under-rated operations of the war. The Germans came to the aid of the Italians in North Africa, as Ll. G. had forecast, and the attack on Pantellaria was postponed for more than two years.

* * * * *

President Roosevelt in earlier years had a high opinion of Lloyd George, but he was disturbed to read reports in the American Press of July, 1940, that Ll. G. favoured peace with Germany. When the idea of sending Lloyd George to Washington as Lothian's successor was mooted, Roosevelt's first reaction was that it "might take the old man's mind off gloomy things". But, after warnings from the Secret Service, he vetoed the proposal on the grounds that Lloyd George would be a bad security risk. New light has recently been shed on this apparent attempt by Churchill to make Ll. G. Ambassador to Washington in Lord Casey's book, *Personal Experience: 1939–46*. In 1940 Lord Casey was Australian Minister to Washington and he was formally requested to inquire what President Roosevelt thought of the proposal to send Ll. G. to U.S.A. Lord Casey says that he learned on the best authority that Roosevelt's reaction was "consternation" and that any such appointment would be an embarrassment for him.

Mr. A. A. Berle, junior, who was Assistant Secretary of State at the time, says of the proposal: "Everybody had great respect for Lloyd George. He wasn't turned down in any formal sense. We wanted someone who would be very close to the British Government, and it was felt that Ll. G. was no longer intimate with the situation and with the feeling of the then British Cabinet."

The warning that Lloyd George was politically unreliable and a bad security risk had been passed to Roosevelt personally by one of his closest friends, Robert E. Sherwood, the author and playwright. Markedly pro-British and vehemently anti-Nazi, Sherwood had been in touch with certain intelligence agencies in an unofficial but advisory capacity to the President. He had learned of a report from Helga Stultz that Hitler was keenly interested in the proposal to send Ll. G. to Washington and saw "useful possibilities of establishing contact with him in a neutral country".

Sherwood, like Roosevelt, had been favourably disposed to Ll. G. and, though he passed this information on to the President, was not inclined to attach too much importance to it. But Roosevelt took the report seriously, and he valued Sherwood so much that in 1941 he appointed him to the staff of his co-ordinator of intelligence, Colonel William Donovan.

An immediate check on Helga Stultz's reports was ordered by Washington. They produced some surprising results. Fraulein Bumke, the woman who had used the code-name of "Mr. Hindhead" for Lloyd George, had arrived in Tangier, which had become one of the world's chief spy centres. To a retired British army officer in that city, a member of The Link, she confided that the *Verbindungsstab* established contact with Lloyd George through "a tiny group of Welsh nationalists who were agents of the German Secret Service". She claimed that Lloyd George was prepared to negotiate with Hitler, should the Churchill Government fall. The authority for this statement was a former member of The Link in Tangier, and he added that, according to Fraulein Bumke, "Ll. G. would agree to Germany having Tanganyika and possibly other territories in East Africa and he would support German claims to Tunisia rather than those of Italy. But he was emphatic that Japan must be contained by a joint agreement between Britain and Germany."

Helga Stultz provided further enlightenment in a report to Washington: "Hitler has been in a terrible mood. I am sure he will repudiate the German-Soviet Pact. Ribbentrop is most anxious not to upset the Russians, but I do not think his view will prevail. Hess sides with Hitler; he believes that Germany must settle her account with Russia and that by doing this some agreement can be reached with England. Hess is so confident of this that I feel sure he has had important news from England. Lloyd George's name is often mentioned here in a favourable context.

"Hess is contemptuous of the *Abwehr* and is pursuing his own ideas of espionage. He has organised the *Verbindungsstab*, which is so far the only real attempt to build a co-ordinated espionage system. It is interesting that the Welsh section of the *Verbindungsstab* has been set up in Lisbon. The Café Chiado in the Rua Garetta in Lisbon is a rendezvous for their meetings. The Hotel Riff in Tangier is another. One of these intermediaries, a Welshman, uses the code-name of 'Caradoc' and he has urged that the time is now ripe to make a direct approach to Lloyd George. This, he has indicated, will not be easy, but channels of communication with 'Mr. Hindhead' have been kept open."

Churchill must have suspected that there were still prominent people in Britain, even on the fringes of his own nominal supporters, who believed that the best prospect was of an armistice with Germany in return for giving her a free hand against Russia. For this reason he probably did not show his hand until the last possible moment. The flight of Rudolf Hess to Scotland must have caused as much perturbation as delight in Downing Street. Then on the night after Germany marched against Russia, Churchill spoke on the radio: Germany was told that Britain would fight on, with Soviet Russia as an ally.

This was one of the biggest shocks which the German espionage organisations suffered in the war and one from which they never recovered. It marked the beginning of the end for Admiral Canaris. The new espionage body that Hess left behind him disintegrated. For all their fanciful and imaginative planning, their hopes of winning over the Duke of Windsor and Lloyd George, Germany's Secret Services broke down in 1941.

On May 7, 1941, three days before Hess landed in Britain, Lloyd George revealed his unhappiness about the war and his critical attitude towards the Government and the High Command in the House of Commons.

"I know there is such a thing as assistance to the enemy, but there is such a thing as assistance to our side," he said. "If we had more of the facts, we could get more of that kind of assistance."

He stressed that the war was passing through one of its most "difficult and discouraging phases". "The position now is that we have practically no ally. America is not an ally at the present moment at any rate."

Tribute was paid to Wavell: "One of the most brilliant series of successes won by any British general in a long and continuous war."

But in the main Ll. G. was still defeatist. He denounced the idea of the "invasion of Europe in the teeth of an army of ten million highly trained and well-equipped men" as "fatuous".

This drew from the Prime Minister the barbed response that: "It was the sort of speech with which, I imagine, the illustrious and venerable Marshal Pétain might well have enlivened the closing days of M. Reynaud's Cabinet."

For one who had so deeply sentimental a regard for Lloyd George as Churchill the necessity for such a remark must have been painful.

Even after Russia was invaded and America had entered the war, Lloyd George continued to take the gloomiest possible view of events. He did not believe that Russia would survive the Nazi onslaught; he condemned the Churchill-Roosevelt agreement of "unconditional surrender". On this last issue Ll. G. showed a realistic appraisal of what was an underwriting of the anti-German views of Henry Morgenthau. His criticisms of this declaration might have carried more weight if the general tone of his other utterances had been more responsible and less pessimistic, for by early 1943 there were growing forces within Germany which might have been encouraged by a less rigid approach. In private Lloyd George warned that "unconditional surrender" merely played into the hands of the Russians, that it would result in gain to Russia and loss of influence to the West. He also urged that Britain should make some effort to contact those in Germany who wanted to end the Hitler régime—men like Adam von Trott, whom the Foreign Office refused to regard as other than enemies.

The death of Dame Margaret Lloyd George in January, 1941, had been a harsh blow. A snowdrift in Shropshire delayed Ll. G.'s journey by car to reach her bedside in time and when he reached North Wales she had already died. Thus the serenest and purest influence in his life since the death of "Uncle Richard" passed away. Though in later years they had not been together very often, indeed, perhaps because of this, the blow seemed harder to bear. From that day he aged visibly.

On January 16, 1943, he told the political correspondent of the *Manchester Guardian*: "Here we are in the fourth year of the war and we have hardly tackled our main enemy, Germany, at all. I doubt if we are opposing 100,000 Germans in North Africa. The only country that is tackling Germany is Russia. Japan is still fighting on the borders of Australia."

Had this political enigma been in supreme power during those years, anything might have happened. It might well have been that Britain would have followed France and sought an armistice in the summer of 1940. Yet, defeatist, intriguer and scuttler that he was, the fighting spirit was always lurking beneath the surface; he never completely lost the love of doing battle. One could never say for certain that he harboured traitorous instincts, though more than once he was on the verge of revealing something akin to them. Never would he have admitted, even to himself, that they were traitorous.

As the evidence shows, in some ways, even in his late seventies, he was more daring than Churchill when the light of battle took over from the clouds of pessimism. In another mood, had he been in power, he might well have backed Wavell more strongly, supported Keyes and overruled the Chiefs of Staff. It is certain that he would have felt for the prim and prissy Alanbrooke all the pent-up detestation he vented on Robertson, and that Alanbrooke would have come off worse. Lloyd George would never have let Alanbrooke have his own way to the extent that Churchill grudgingly did. That might have been fatal to the course of the war, but one may be sure that Ll. G. would have been prodding his Chiefs of Staff for a short cut to victory. Indeed he might have insisted on the attack on Pantellaria and made sure the Italians were driven out of Africa before the Germans got there. Certainly he would have had no qualms in repudiating the guarantee to Greece. Again, he might have done all these things and precipitated a situation as bad as any in the spring of 1918.

But none of this was to be. The ill-considered guarantee to Greece was honoured, North Africa was temporarily sacrificed and the war dragged on for a longer period. But Lloyd George lived on to see the liberation of France and to drive to London for his last visit to the House of Commons in the summer of 1944 to congratulate the man who had compared him to Marshal Pétain.

The tired old warrior had had his last fling . . . "so hung his destiny, never to rot, while he might still jog on and keep his trot."

23

THE LAST YEARS

> "Ease was his chief disease: and to judge right,
> He died for heaviness that his cart went light:
> His leisure told him that his time was come,
> And lack of load made his life burdensome . . . ."
>
> *John Milton*

As one concludes this quest for the riddle of the Wizard one finds the maze-like path of his tangled and tempestuous career—that "tempestuous journey" which Frank Owen has called it—bringing one back to the bridge over the Dwyfor at Llanystumdwy.

"All things flow," said Bergson, in explaining his philosophy of life force, but there is a backward flow, too—a flow of dissipated energy that withdraws into the River of Forgetfulness, that oblivion of which we read in Virgil. For Lloyd George the River Dwyfor was his River of Forgetfulness and of memories, too. His mind, as he grew older, flowed back into these surroundings and sought there the Nirvana after which all men thirst when they have drawn too far away from the original fountain of their inspiration.

On October 23, 1943, Lloyd George married Miss Frances Louise Stevenson, who had been his private secretary for thirty years. The ceremony was conducted at Artington House Register Office, near Guildford.

The story of their association began when Miss Stevenson was a teacher at the school attended by his daughter Megan. Invited to tea one day when Ll. G., then at the Exchequer, happened to be exceptionally short-staffed, Miss Stevenson volunteered to help him, and Ll. G. was so impressed by her ability that he asked her to stay on as his permanent assistant.

Miss Stevenson inherited the business acumen and efficiency of her Scots father and the good looks and vivacity of her French mother. She had been educated at London University and was an excellent linguist. Following Ll. G. from the Treasury to the Ministry of Munitions and the War Office, she became in 1916 the first woman in history to be secretary to a Prime Minister of Britain.

But shadows swiftly appeared to obscure the brief happiness of this second marriage. Suddenly Lloyd George aged perceptibly and became frailer. His zest for politics ebbed away and his mind and heart turned increasingly towards Llanystumdwy. Perhaps he sensed that he was dying, despite the fact that when the doctors diagnosed the cancer that was slowly eating away his life, they did not tell him. He asked no questions. Sometimes he blamed the war and his own inactivity for his condition; at other times he would mellow and a ghost of the old smile would creep around the now wrinkled and emaciated features.

In September, 1944, he left Churt and went to Ty Newydd, a small farm near Llanystumdwy which he had bought in 1939. At the age of eighty-two he returned to the mountains he loved so deeply and to the Dwyfor which had so often provided him with balm, solace and inspiration. Here he could savour old memories and re-live the past. On warm, bright mornings three old men could be seen standing on the bridge over the Dwyfor exchanging the gossip of the day and recalling their schoolboy pranks. They were John Roberts, a farmer, Evan Elias, a retired insurance agent, and Lloyd George.

Occasionally the old enthusiasm for farming would return. "So the village gets its fruit and vegetables from Liverpool, does it?" he asked. "That's all wrong. We must grow more here." It was pointed out to him that his land, overlooking Cardigan Bay, was too exposed to winds sweeping across the sea. His answer was to plant rows of poplar trees as a wind break. He went round the village, mustering a staff of eight, and planted fruit trees and vegetables.

By late 1944 it was obvious that soon the war in Europe would be over and a general election must be held. The question of whether Lloyd George should stand again was one he could not shirk answering, for the local Liberal Association was becoming restive. Doctors and friends were agreed that he could not stand up to the strain of another election contest; the only hope was whether the Conservative and Labour organisations would agree not to oppose him as a tribute to the most famous living Welshman.

But his name no longer carried the same weight in North Wales. His attitude over the Abdication and his defeatism during the war had told against him. A new generation had grown up, the Liberal-minded of whom were antagonistic to Lloyd George and saw Labour as a more effective vehicle for their aspirations. Evacuation and the influx of English professional men and women had also increased the potential Tory vote. For the first time for more than half a century a Conservative victory seemed in sight and there was a distinct possibility that the Liberals would come third.

Intuitively, Lloyd George must have known there was a revolt against him and that if he stood again he would be defeated. When Churchill, in a mood of sentimentalism, overlooked the fact that a year or two earlier he had compared the old man to Pétain and wrote offering to submit his name to the King for an Earldom, Ll. G. after some hesitation accepted.

But he was also somewhat ashamed of joining the Peers whom he had so bitterly attacked most of his life. He tried to excuse himself on the grounds that perhaps in the Lords "I can make some useful speeches on the problems of a peace settlement".

On New Year's Day, 1945, the Honours List appeared and henceforth David Lloyd George, commoner, became Earl Lloyd-George of Dwyfor. "I am sure he was very sorry," said his secretary, A. J. Sylvester. "He took the peerage after consulting his brother, Dr. William George, because he felt he could not fight another election and did not want to break with Parliament after fifty-five years."

Lloyd George's first suggestion for his title was Arfon Lleyn or Eifon, but this was finally rejected in favour of retaining his own name. When the Earldom was granted, the names of Lloyd and George were hyphenated for the first time, a purely academic point which caused much fussing and pontificating by the College of Heralds. Garter King of Arms had originally insisted that the title should be George only, but he had ceased to be known as George for more than half a century; Lloyd George he always would be, whether hyphenated or otherwise.

In Wales there was bitter regret that he had accepted an earldom. Even Ramsay MacDonald, the secret lover of things aristocratic, had avoided that final devastating blow to the pride of a radical commoner. The Commoner of Commoners had sold his birthright for the doubtful messpot of an Earldom. The man who had brought honours into disrepute had himself committed the final fatuity in accepting a title.

Baldwin of Bewdley in the sole flash of pure wit—whether unconscious or otherwise—he had ever shown, chose as his peer's motto, "With God's help I leap over the wall." Perhaps mindful of the ditches which lay behind Lord Baldwin's walls, Lloyd George went one better than this. From the Druids he took the motto, "Truth against the World."

As his weakness became more marked, he was fretful if no one came to see him. His mind strayed back into childhood, sometimes expressing itself in Biblical allegories that were confusing and confused.

A Nonconformist minister who called on him returned home shaking his head. "I cannot make him out," he said. "His sense of dogma is all mixed up. At times he talks like a Catholic. It was very strange that he should tell me all about his visit to the Pope years before, and how the Pope gave him sweets to take back to Tim Healy. 'Papal sweets,' he muttered. 'You have to hand it to those Catholics. They even make sweets a subject for religion.'"

This same minister told the author some years later: "Lloyd George had a sense, a feeling for religion, but he was not truly a religious man.

He liked a good sermon, but he had very little patience for the rules of religion. I had the impression that as he felt death approaching his mind wrestled with two spirits—the spirit of fear which our Nonconformist ancestors preached, hellfire and vengeance, and the spirit of mysticism like the Catholic possesses. Not long before he died he told me: 'I wish I could have the blind faith of the Catholic.'"

The mind of a dying man is either an open book or a fluttering of pages turned so fast that the words cannot be read. It was the latter with Lloyd George—at least to those apart from his family with whom he talked in these last weeks.

The spring of 1945 burst with all the magic of an early summer in the final days of February; it was as though Nature was heralding the approaching victory. Down to Llanystumdwy came reporters from all over the country to wait and watch for the old man's death. The end came on March 26, on the evening of a perfect spring day.

On the Good Friday he was laid to rest in a place of his own choosing on a bank of the River Dwyfor, near the old road bridge and his house, Ty Newydd. The grave was lined with evergreens brought by workmen on his estate. Long before the time fixed for the funeral, men, women and children flocked to the burial site. Easter holiday-makers from Liverpool and Manchester, from Birmingham and bomb-stricken Coventry, lined the grassy banks of the lane leading from the house to the spinney, where the open grave was situated. On the meadows on the other side of the river thousands had gathered.

The bitter duel between the Church of Wales and Nonconformity had given way to a more Christian spirit of co-operation, for assisting at the service were the Rector of Llanystumdwy and the Welsh Presbyterian and Baptist Ministers.

"A choir of men and women, each wearing a daffodil, began to sing a Welsh hymn," recorded *The Times* special correspondent. "The opening bars . . . brought a hush over the vast assembly and the powerful, melodious cadences swept over the valley. Another of the hymns sung was to the tune of *Tyddyn Llwyn* (cottage in the spinney), written and composed by one of Lloyd-George's friends of his early days."

* * * * *

A memorial service in Westminster Abbey marked the final tribute to the Restless Warrior who had at last found rest. And on the morrow of his death, as the speeches to his memory were made in London, Ottawa, Cape Town, Canberra, Cardiff, Caernarvon and Caerphilly, the magic seemed to return. Some of the tributes have been quoted in an earlier chapter and they show to what extent the magic had flamed again and stirred the minds of great men to extravagant imagery. There were even indignant complaints that the burial had not been carried out in Westminster Abbey. But, as one cynic said, "It would have been like burying the Unknown Quantity beside the Unknown Warrior."

Yet even in death Lloyd-George became a centre of controversy. His will was the subject of prolonged arguments and debating in the Probate Court. On June 6, 1945, the details of the will were announced. To his widow he bequeathed his Parliamentary and other political papers. There were other bequests to his widow and family, with one notable exception, his eldest son, Richard. The new Earl—formerly Major Richard Lloyd George—commenting on the fact that the Earldom carried no emoluments, told the Press: "I shall have to go back to my job as a civil engineer if I am going to have any money. I am left nothing at all in the will. My father was always very disappointed because I would not follow in his footsteps as a politician. That is why he has not left me a bean in his will."

A harsh judgment on an eldest son who had been his mother's favourite. Yet not even old age and approaching death could rob Lloyd-George of a streak of vindictiveness.

There was a sequel to all this in the High Court of Justice, Probate and Admiralty Division, when an application was made for the appointment of an administrator *pendente lite* of the Lloyd-George estate, Earl Lloyd-George being the defendant. The plaintiffs were Countess Lloyd-George, Mr. Gwilym Lloyd George and Mr. J. E. Morris, the executors under the will dated November 12, 1943, and two codicils dated September 2 and September 19, 1944. Earl Lloyd-George entered a *caveat* and opposed the will and codicils. Later it was announced that a settlement out of court had been reached in the dispute over the will and the two codicils. This followed the intimation that an action was listed in which Earl Lloyd-George contested the will and codicils on the grounds of "want of knowledge, lack of testamentary capacity" and that they were "not duly executed". In the Probate Court, Mr. Justice Byrne consented to delete "paragraph 17" from the will.

Mr. W. Latey, for the Earl, agreed when the judge asked: "You say they are offending words which have no testamentary effect?" When Mr. Latey asked that the judge's order should include a direction that "paragraph 17" should not appear in the registry copy of the will, Mr. Justice Byrne replied, "Certainly".

There was much surprise when the published figures showed that Lloyd-George had left only £141,147. This was a considerable sum for a life-long politician to leave, when one bears in mind that in recent years several old colleagues of Lloyd-George had died in relative poverty. But at one time Lloyd-George was reputed to have been worth more than a million pounds and many expected him to leave as much as half a million. A great deal of his capital had been devoted to the development of his model farm at Churt and to improving the farm at Llanystumdwy.

* * * * *

The Lloyd-George legend persisted. There was a demand for the preservation of his birthplace at Manchester. Books about Ll. G. followed one another in quick succession: Jack Jones even performed the seemingly impossible feat of writing *The Man David* in the form of fiction.

Post-war Britain sometimes sighed for the return of his magic touch to relieve the monotony of the tedious "Me-tooism" of the two major political parties. Whatever Lloyd-George had been, he was never a "Me-Tooist", though the deviousness of his policies and his fondness for facing both ways had, ironically enough, been responsible in no small degree for the growing tendency towards "Me-Tooism".

A Committee of the House of Commons was appointed to decide whether a statue to him should be placed "within the precincts of the Palace of Westminster, or in Parliament Square". The House approved a resolution, moved by the Prime Minister (then Sir Winston Churchill) that a monument "with an inscription expressive of the high sense entertained by this House of the eminent services rendered by Earl Lloyd-George to the country, to the Commonwealth and Empire in Parliament and in the great offices of State" should be provided.

"He might have liked it to be as near this chamber as possible," added the Prime Minister. "When the British history of the first quarter of the twentieth century is written, it will be seen how great a part of our fortunes in peace or in war were shaped by this one man."

24

A GLIMPSE BENEATH THE MASK

"O make me a mask and a wall to shut from your spies
Of the sharp, enamelled eyes and the spectacled claws
Rape and rebellion in the nurseries of my face,
Gag of a dumbstruck tree to block from bare enemies
The bayonet tongue in this undefended prayer-piece,
The present mouth, and the sweetly blown trumpet of lies . . .
. . . To shield the glistening brain and blunt the examiners. . . ."

Dylan Thomas

As more than a decade has passed since Lloyd-George's death and as this year marks the centenary of his birth, one might be tempted to say that the time has surely come to assess what he really did shape and how true was the generous tribute made by Sir Winston Churchill mentioned in the last chapter.

A clearer picture of the man has certainly emerged in these intervening years, much that seemed gold has turned to lead, while less well-remembered phases of his life—notably during the South African War—seem more courageous in retrospect than his wartime Premiership. But the clearer picture is at the same time a bewildering image, not so much because of the magic and quicksilver genius which lights it up, but because of the contradictions of that genius, the extraordinary manner in which the facts of his life contradict one another. The mental inconsistencies of the man, especially in times of crisis, frequently rob him of the right to be the architect of any particular policy.

It is not without significance that more space has been given in this book to his earlier speeches than to those of his heyday. The former will live as examples of some of the most splendidly pungent radical perorations of any age. The latter are too often so full of false sentiment and insincerity, so lacking in reasoned argument, so leavened with barely disguised sophistry that they appal one by their triteness, ambiguity and unadulterated humbug. True, when listening to him speak, they never sounded thus: no statesman could mask his insincerity and make it wring the heartstrings more effectively. He could coo like a dove with the same facility that he could roar like a lion. But in cold print these speeches of his hey-day lose their magic. Occasionally in the latter years there was a notable exception, and the speech which helped to bring down the Chamberlain Government in the House of Commons in 1940 was one such example—forthright, unrelenting, fearless and effective.

One cannot help feeling that those early speeches helped to shape a new consciousness in national life. Lloyd-George's homespun imagery, his unerring gift for selecting a simple anecdote to illuminate a political idea did much to bring the political facts of life within the grasp of the man in the street. Also, in the early days, Lloyd-George did as much as any man to prick the bubble of unreasoning imperialism which besotted the British mind at the beginning of the century. Dilke, Rosebery, Asquith and Haldane were great radical imperialists who saw how radicalism could improve and rebuild an Empire and Commonwealth. But Lloyd-George saw the faults and warts of imperialism: he showed them up and, with a devastating wit and repartee, forced men to do some re-thinking on this subject. The fruits of this change which he helped to bring about can be seen today in the very wide measure of agreement between all Parties on colonial problems and the need for speeding up the process of self-government within the Commonwealth. It is also a sad reflection on how power corrupted Lloyd-George that he took so savage and barbarous a course with Ireland, thus setting back the clock which he had so eagerly put forward twenty years before.

It was the part he played in the Boer War which gave Lloyd-George two of his earliest allies in the Press, Robertson Nicoll, of the *British Weekly*—the man who "made" Ll. G., according to A. J. P. Taylor—and C. P. Scott, of the *Manchester Guardian*. C. P. Scott never forgot Ll. G.'s rôle in the Boer War and later he obstinately supported him in many causes regarding which both his intellect and his conscience must have told him to be wary. There was a streak of vanity in C. P. Scott on which Lloyd-George was not slow to play. Whenever Ll. G. spoke in Manchester, Scott was always given a seat close to him on the platform, and Ll. G. was subtle enough never to miss referring to him in his presence as "the world's greatest living journalist". Massingham, another notable journalist of the era, once declared: "To me there are few spectacles more melancholy than that of dear old C. P. Scott drearily dredging in a foul pond for the soul of Ll. G."

When papers and records belonging to Lloyd-George were acquired by Lord Beaverbrook from Countess Lloyd-George, it was announced shortly afterwards that Robert E. Sherwood, the American author, would have access to the papers to write a new life of Ll. G. But the man who was four times a Pulitzer Prize winner, who helped to prepare many of President Roosevelt's speeches and wrote a biography of Harry Hopkins, finally decided to turn down the project.

His reasons for arriving at this decision—in view of what has been mentioned in the chapter on World War II—seemed worth seeking.

Inquiry of his closest friend, George Becker, produced this reply: "The idea of doing a book on Lloyd-George at first attracted Bob because he thought it would lead up to his own book on Hopkins, Roosevelt and Europe. He saw Lloyd-George at first as the architect of post-Victorian Europe, but this he found out was not true.

"To have used Lloyd-George as leading up to Roosevelt would have been artificial. Ll. G. didn't fit into the scheme of things and in the end had no particular interest for Bob."

Nor did the Lloyd-Georgian proposals between the wars do much more than underline the fact that both Tories and Socialists in that era preferred a cheap dole to costly public works. That his proposals did not receive more attention was a national disaster. It was unfair and unfortunate that they were misrepresented and distorted by opponents and allies alike. At the same time, in pursuing his theme for the need for public works and the creation of new fields of employment, by over-enthusiasm he helped to foster the dangerous, demagogic idea that Britain was a bottomless pit of abundance into which one had only to dig to give plenty to all.

On the subject of waging war, Lloyd-George set out to give the impression of vigour, valour and immense drive. The important fact at the time was that he *seemed* to provide all these qualities, and a majority of the nation believed he possessed them. Yet it was by propaganda, dictatorial methods, ruthlessness, deceit, plotting and lying, allied, of course, to his own irresistible personality, that he succeeded in convincing some contemporary writers. History will almost certainly arrive at the conclusion that he did not shape the final victory, but that it came on the very front he had always decried.

The Coalition Government over which he presided after 1918 was, by any judgment, Tory, Liberal or Socialist, a thoroughly bad administration. It was dishonest, unstable, irresponsible, incoherent. It approached the tasks of peace with the mentality of a gambler, betting now on Greece, now on the Black-and-Tans, on "Hang the Kaiser" as an election gimmick and selling honours to boost its funds.

In every age decent people have been exploited by the unscrupulous and self-seeking—Burleigh, Strafford, Clarendon, Shaftesbury, Bolingbroke, Walpole, Chatham, Wellington and Disraeli. But after Disraeli's time there had been a marked improvement in the standards of political conduct of the leaders of the nation, while the integrity of the Civil Service had become a national tradition. It cannot be denied that the corruption and lowering of standards in political morality during the Coalition days was a *malaise* that spread far and wide. It was through the corruption which power brought during this epoch that Lloyd-George most shaped our destinies. He destroyed the Liberal Party which had provided stability for so long and gave Britain the choice of a Labour Party, which was then unfit to rule, and a Tory Party which eschewed its best brains and wallowed in the incompetence and apathy which large majorities bring in their trail. By doing so he forced the nation into a prolonged and bitter class warfare and threw the middle classes to the wolves of the two political collosi, to be wooed and punished in turn.

It may be strongly arguable that modern degeneracy is due rather to decline in talent than to any difference in moral standards—that politicians have been equally dishonest in every age, but that while in the past clever rogues have risen to power, we are now afflicted by knaves of mean ability. Yet this accession of mean ability may indeed be attributed to Lloyd-George, for he became so feared for his astuteness by friend and foe alike that he inspired a preference for dullards and plodders known to be incapable of his cleverness, and thus his successors—Baldwin, MacDonald, Chamberlain, Attlee, Eden and Macmillan (all, in fact, except Churchill, who would never have come back to power except for a wartime emergency)—have all been mediocrities in contrast, naturally gathering about them still lesser men, on the principle laid down in Landor's imaginary conversation between Pitt and Canning: "Employ men of less knowledge and perspicacity than yourself, if you can find them. Do not let any stand too close or too much above; because in both positions they may look down into your shallows and see the weeds at the bottom."

In effect, Lloyd-George disenfranchised the thinking classes, or rather those who are too intellectually honest to be tied irrevocably to the chariots of the Tories or Socialists, leaving them with Hobson's choice in those constituencies where no Liberal or Independent candidate submitted himself. But, worse than this, by his example, his contempt for ethics in political life, he created a *politique dégringolade* of which the Coalition Government of 1918–22 was the symbol. First, this was done by seeking accommodations with his political enemies in a manner that can only be compared to the machinations of Pierre Laval under the Third Republic. Then it was by creating a huge political fund, by selling honours and undisguised nepotism, and, not least, by infiltrating unorthodox and unworthy citizens into the Civil Service.

All this helped to pave the way to the age of the Whips. Both the Conservative and Labour Parties after 1922 used dictatorial powers undreamed of half a century before. The Tory Whips instilled Prussian discipline into their ranks and silenced the honest warnings of Churchill and the murmurings against Chamberlain's vacillations. As for Labour, they expelled anyone with a mind of his own: Cripps and Bevan were hurled into the wilderness when they urged a common front against Fascism. Perhaps the most brutal, callous and typical comment of Labour's official mind was that of Ernest Bevin saying he was tired of listening to George Lansbury's conscience "being hawked from conference to conference".

Since 1922 opposition within the ranks of a political Party has been condemned as treason and conformity has been increasingly demanded. This state of affairs is still draining political life of all constructiveness. The winding-up of the university seats was an example of this. But the real gold in British politics has come from the unorthodox and selfless individualist. It glittered somewhat wickedly in the tirades of John Wilkes, it shone like burnished metal in the heart of Eleanor Rathbone, it sparkled in the polished wit of Labouchere, it warmed with its rich, human glow in the passionate sincerity of James Maxton and the practical Christian beliefs of Sir Richard Acland.

* * * * *

Yet, having made this indictment, the magic of the man remains. Magic does not shape our destinies, but it colours them. And Lloyd-George's greatness lay in his talent for colouring our destinies with vivid phrases, with lighting up the dark corners of our minds with an oratory that stirred the emotions.

With Lloyd-George the phrases flashed like butterflies in the afternoon sun, but they floated away and dissolved like bubbles. T. P. O'Connor wrote that "no orator of his time has been so often translated and so abundantly read by continental countries".

The truth of this is apparent when one realises how un-English these Lloyd-Georgian speeches often are. His phrases have none of the moral appeal of Burke, or the grandeur of Gladstone, none of the massiveness and sense of history which is the secret of Churchill's oratory, nor the cool, almost detached marshalling of facts and the logical development of argument so characteristic of Asquith. There is in his speeches no understatement, so beloved of the English, but in its place the shot-silk of speech, the embroidery of Welsh melody and the rhythms of the English Bible.

Most Prime Ministers of Britain in modern times have found that the long hours and strain of office have not only undermined their health, but severely curtailed their private lives. But Lloyd-George, like Churchill, had a stamina and remarkable physical fitness which defied long hours and unremitting toil. His resilience not only enabled him to relax at will, but to indulge in an uninhibited and varied life in his hours of leisure. Mr. A. J. Sylvester wrote that "a doctor, meeting Lloyd-George for the first time, once told me that everything about him was at least double of an ordinary man. That included not only his good qualities, but his bad".

This particularly applied to one aspect of his private life. Perhaps no Prime Minister of Britain since the days of Palmerston had been so careless of his reputation in private life, or risked so much to satisfy the slightest sexual whim. How he escaped unscathed in a country so prone to outbursts of moral indignation is one of the social miracles of his time. Luck was always with him in his private life so that even the scandals which were perpetually surrounding his name were repudiated as fast as the rumours developed.

He had an insatiable interest in and appetite for women and was fascinated by them from his youth, just as they were equally fascinated by him. This fascination was peculiarly feminine in some ways, rather like that of a slightly ageing actress who is for ever playing Peter Pan. The atmosphere he created was that of Oberon, but beneath the surface the rough, blunt, roguish maleness of Puck was ever ready to jump out and surprise. He also had an uncanny, almost telepathic gift for sensing some subtle affinity for him in even the shyest and most self-effacing of women. It has been recorded by many who knew him that often at a dinner party he would delight in spotting some shy woman he had never met before and then set about bringing her into the conversation and charming her out of her shyness and silence.

His son, Earl Lloyd-George, has said that he can "never forgive" his father "for what he did to my mother. I shall never understand how my mother stood all she did. With one word she could have ruined his political career for ever. But she kept quiet. She must have loved him far more deeply than seems possible.

"They used to say that Charles II was the father of his people, or at least a great many of them. That was true of my father, too. No woman could resist him and he could not resist them. Casanova was just an amateur. Father just couldn't help himself."

No doubt the dangerous combination of religious and sexual obsessions in the North Wales of his youth played a part in shaping the tastes of the young Lloyd-George. There is perhaps nowhere in the British Isles even today where the atmosphere, the social climate and the language is so impregnated with a Rabelaisian delight in the venereal pastimes as in parts of rural Wales. Anglo-Welsh literature can never escape from this preoccupation. But, even allowing for this, Lloyd-George continued until late in life to display a rashness, a ruthlessness and an almost anarchical attitude in his amours. He pursued sexual pleasures with the single-mindedness which another man might devote to chess, to cricket or to painting. For him it was almost a recreation; he was the hunter with the light rein, questing vigorously and purposefully, but light-heartedly and casually, always regarding it as a game, never as a romantic pastime. He would banter, he would tease, he would coax; he never indulged in sentimentalism, or the luxury of a *grande passion.*

On affairs of the heart he left no incriminating letters, or, if he did, all trace has been obliterated. "Letters are the very devil. They ought to be abolished altogether," he told Lord Riddell. He wrote far fewer letters than either Asquith or Baldwin, though as many memoranda as Churchill.

In every big city he visited he delighted in making excursions into what he called "the underworld". It was in much the same spirit as spurred Samuel Bennett in Dylan Thomas's *Adventures in the Skin Trade* to explore the night life of the Metropolis. When the "Jack the Ripper" murders were terrifying Whitechapel and Limehouse in 1888 he made a noctural tour of the area with the late Sir Alfred Davies, a superintendent of the Metropolitan Police, who was born in Caernarvon. The Tories were in power at the time and there was a strong demand that the Home Secretary of the day should be dismissed. Lloyd-George hoped that this fact-finding tour might enable him to find material for more attacks on the Government. Sir Alfred Davies said afterwards: "Mr. Lloyd George showed then what a formidable cross-examiner he could be, and I should welcome him as a detective."

One isolated incident such as the divorce action in which he was involved in the nineties might have been ignored, but during his life others occurred which created the legend in political and social circles that he was an amorous adventurer. His enemies and some sections of the Press went out of their way to remind him that hostile publicity can be the price of dalliance with married women.

In July, 1908, the *Bystander* published a paragraph which commented: "Mr. George has, of course, been overloaded with flattery of late, especially from the fair sex, which is always difficult for a man of 'temperament' to resist. The matter may, of course, be kept quiet. Also, it may not."

An action for libel was brought, an apology and denial were published, and at Ll. G.'s request a donation of £315 was paid to the Caernarvon Cottage Hospital by the magazine in question.

A year later another newspaper, without mentioning Lloyd-George's name, referred to a prominent public figure who was about to be named as co-respondent in a divorce case. Later it stated that the divorce action had been withdrawn as a result of pressure by "friends" at a cost of £20,000. Again Lloyd-George brought an action; again the proprietors of the paper admitted the libel and this time £1,000 damages were paid to charity.

Yet on this occasion Lloyd-George was saved from committing political suicide only by the loyal support he received from Asquith, his Prime Minister. Not only did Asquith offer advice, but he personally interceded with the husband of the musical comedy actress with whom Ll. G. had become entangled. For good measure his son, Raymond, together with Rufus Isaacs and F. E. Smith, were briefed on Lloyd-George's behalf. But had a divorce action been brought it is almost certain that he would have been unable to deny the charges with quite such vehemence as he did in the witness-box at the Old Bailey.

In later life Lloyd-George became more demanding in his quest for feminine company. He was particularly attracted to actresses, and was always anxious to meet any new star who appeared in the theatrical firmament. He frequently attended the Gaiety Theatre shows in which Julia James was acting and, she recalled, he sent her "not a bouquet of flowers, or a necklace, but a cooked chicken".

His interest in actresses was not always an amorous whim, as, no mean actor himself, he had a genuine technical interest in their art. Maud Allen, Lily Langtry and Tallulah Bankhead all aroused his attention. Tallulah Bankhead tells in her autobiography how she met Ll. G. through Lord Beaverbrook. "We went to Ll. G.'s place in Churt. We met the great Welshman in his garden. I was impressed with his charm and gallantry. He cut a rose and handed it to me. Then he took me into his living-room. Spread out on the floor were the London reviews of *The Green Hat*, in which I had opened at the Adelphi the week before."

No other Prime Minister has had such a passion for travel as Ll. G. This is all the more remarkable when one realises that he grew up in an age when it was neither fashionable nor popular for Cabinet Ministers to travel far afield. The early Victorians and those of the middle of the nineteenth century had shown some zest for travel, but after that period even Foreign Ministers rarely went abroad even in their professional capacity before World War I. It was considered beneath their dignity to do so. But Lloyd-George as a young man went to France, South America and Canada. As Cabinet Minister he went all over Europe in quest of ideas and pleasure, while the latter years of his life were spent in such diverse holiday trips as motoring across Europe, hiring a yacht to cruise through the Mediterranean, sometimes visiting Zaharoff, and enjoying the medieval splendours of the entourage of the Pasha of Marrakesh in Morocco, visiting the West Indies, Brazil and Ceylon.

The "physical stamina and sustaining power" of Ll. G., about which Professor Severn spoke, could not last for ever. Lloyd-George worried about this and disliked the idea of growing old.

It was Sir Basil Zaharoff who, well versed in Ll. G.'s weakness for women, provided the answer to this. He introduced Lloyd-George to Dr. Serge Voronoff, a Russian who had become a naturalised Frenchman, and made a fortune out of an operation which was supposed to make old people young again. In the nineteen-twenties and thirties Voronoff made a considerable revenue from men and women who visited his clinic at Mentône to undergo his rejuvenation operation by the grafting of monkey glands. His standard fee for this was a thousand guineas.

This operation was never performed in Britain; the Home Secretary ruled it to be a breach of the anti-vivisection laws. Today it is regarded as out-of-date, having been overtaken by research on the endocrine glands. Lloyd-George was fascinated by Voronoff's experiments and even more by the philosophy which he had evolved from his study of human nature. "The source of life," wrote Voronoff, "is intimately linked with love. Love is the chief aim of life." Voronoff's own aim was to increase the human span to 120 years.

Voronoff stated: "Lloyd-George came to my continental clinic. The whole object of my treatment was to increase both the mental and sexual vigour of the patient. He was then at the critical age for a man—between sixty and seventy, when the glands are wearing out. He was particularly interested not only in my experiments in the human field, but in agriculture, too.

"In 1927 I carried out experiments with sheep on a farm at Tadmit in Algeria and found that grafted sheep gained 22 lb. in flesh and 24½ ounces in wool compared with ungrafted sheep. Lloyd-George was very excited about this idea of creating 'super-sheep'. He championed my experiments among British agriculturists and in 1928 a body of British experts appointed by the Board of Agriculture came to investigate my efforts in this field."

Whether gland grafting proved successful with Lloyd-George, Voronoff declined to say, but nevertheless Ll. G. seems to have believed in the efficacy of monkey glands in whatever form they were presented. He also turned to the new science of hormone-vitamin therapy. Boxes and bottles of capsules containing glandular extracts were delivered to him regularly.

* * * * *

The impromptu humour of Lloyd-George was irrepressible and it took many forms. It did not seem to matter whether it was with adults or children, with wits or bores, it never failed him. He would romp with children and indulge in their games with Gargantuan laughter.

Lord Alness once said: "If you set Mr. Lloyd-George at the dinner table next to his bitterest enemy, man or woman, and heaven knows he has not a few, he will have made a complete conquest of that individual by the end of the meal."

Aboard ship and at dinner parties he was the best of companions. He would invent amusing games, adapting the games to the company. A favourite was "epitaphs", in which each guest had to compose his or her own epitaph. Then there were trick questions. He would ask a Tory M.P., "Who would you rather have as companion on a cruise—Stanley Baldwin or Tallulah Bankhead?" Or to a female passenger he would pose: "If you could take three people to a desert island, who would you choose?"

One evening aboard ship during a cruise the captain, introducing Ll. G., said in a speech: "Some of my passengers don't take the same view of our distinguished guest as I do. One lady said to me today:

'Captain, I marvel that you can welcome that man on board your ship. If I had my way, I would throw him overboard.'"

When it came to Ll. G.'s turn to speak he made the comment: "I was very much interested in the captain's speech, and, in particular, in what he told us the lady said about me. All I can say is that she must be a real lady!"

While writing his *War Memoirs*, Lloyd-George went to Marrakesh to seek peace in the sunshine, and the Pasha of the Moorish city put at his disposal his private golf course which was presided over by Arnaud Massy, a Frenchman who spoke French with a slight Scots accent. The Pasha knew all about Lloyd-George's fondness for women and wished to make a gesture to the statesman. "It was a delicate and somewhat embarrassing mission to pass on this offer to Mr. Lloyd-George," Arnaud Massy told the author. "I felt like a procurer. A villa, which housed some Moorish beauties, had been set aside for Ll. G.'s personal use, but how to name it without giving offence I could not think.

"It was to all intents and purposes a private bordello. I tried to make a joke about it by calling it Mr. Lloyd-George's pavilion. But I need have had no qualms. Lloyd-George gave me a roguish smile and said: 'I think we'd better call it the Nineteenth Hole.'"

* * * * *

Quixotic trains of thought, bantering gaiety in the sunshine, and white-hot, thunderous invective in the gloom; these are the fleeting, kaleidoscopic impressions of a peep behind Merlin's mask. The ability to quote the Scriptures with intense fervour one moment and to bear witness that he denied the existence of God the next. Mr. Frank Owen has described movingly how, when his favourite daughter Mair died at the early age of eighteen, Lloyd-George was in such a state of despair that he declaimed in anger against the very idea of a Creator who could permit such a thing to happen. Others have testified that at that time he was for weeks like a man living with a nightmare, neither sleeping nor caring, neither eating nor talking, except to himself. C. F. G. Masterman described him as "a man who gave the impression of having taken the lid off hell and been overwhelmed by what he saw, a man without faith or hope. I thought he was really going insane."

In his many casual relationships with women Ll. G. nearly always gave the impression of being a shallow philanderer with no deep or lasting emotions at all. The man who could so easily evoke emotion in his speeches seemed, when it came to his own life, to mistrust emotion altogether. He could make emotional appeals to people, but he was never easily moved by emotional appeals to himself and tended always to harden his heart against them, to regard any concession to such as a major weakness. The death of his daughter Mair seems to have been the one occasion in his life when he allowed emotion to overwhelm him.

Dame Margaret, his first wife, was undoubtedly a stabilising influence in his early days. With another woman he might easily have foundered disastrously on the rocks of his own peccadilloes. Her selflessness, humility, forgiveness and, above all, her intense pride in her husband were qualities which sustained this marriage long after it had ceased to have any real or abiding meaning for Ll. G. During the last twenty years of his life he only saw her on occasional visits to North Wales.

If Lloyd-George liked to roam far and wide, his roots were also firmly established in the British countryside. Yet when he became an experimental farmer it was not towards his native Wales he turned first, but to Surrey. Perhaps when in 1921 he bought some land at Churt and built a house there, Bron-y-de, he tried to recapture something of North Wales in the Surrey highlands with their expansive views of heather and gorse. He was for ever developing and improving this new home, borrowing ideas from Hitler's *berghof*, so that he replaced the wall of one room by an immense sheet of glass. He added to his land until he acquired in all about 780 acres, including several farms, and employed about eighty men. It was his proud boast that "I have grown two or three apples where there was only one thistle before, and ten potatoes where there was only one dock". But the fact that he had ample capital with which to experiment and adopt the most modern methods made him fail to realise that every other farmer could not do likewise between the wars. A Lloyd-George farming policy —as distinct from his Land Policy of the late 'twenties—could only have been set up at the price of costly subsidies, restrictive tariffs and even more feather-bedding than the British farmer has today.

* * * * *

Many have tried to interpret the Merlinesque magic, but it has eluded most non-Welshmen. Most try to see Lloyd-George as an Englishman and so fail to understand him. Thus one gets this hasty and unsubtle picture of him by Maynard Keynes, irritated because he is baffled by the magic of the man. . . .

"This extraordinary figure of our time, this syren, this goat-footed bard, this half-human visitor to our time from the hag-ridden magic and enchanted woods of Celtic antiquity. One catches in his company that flavour of final purposelessness, inner irresponsibility, existence outside or away from our Saxon good and evil, mixed with cunning, remorselessness, love of power, that lend fascinating enchantment and tenor to the fair-seeming magicians of North European folk-lore."

It is not an inaccurate picture, though hyperbolic and allowing the

Keynesian zest for sparkle to obscure its purpose. It is a perceptive portrait, but from a narrow viewpoint. The real answer lies much deeper than this. A clue to it is to be found in the development of Anglo-Welsh literature during this century. In a curious way Lloyd-George was the unconscious father of this bastard offspring of the Muses. For in some form or another, by some quirk or foible, he appears again and again in this branch of literature. He peeps out in Caradoc Evans's stories of peasant vice, in the tales of the border animosities of Margiad Evans, and not least in the rumbustious humour of that self-styled "Rimbaud of Cwmdonkin Drive", Dylan Thomas.

Anglo-Welsh literature has enriched the English language with new jewels of rhythm and idiom in the same refreshing way that Lloyd-George himself embellished public speaking. Both the literature and his speeches were born and flourished in periods of social upheaval; both reacted to the broken society that surrounded them, not in a passion of moral fervour but by a purely amoral desire to be iconoclastic, to break "the system", to be lively, jaunty, sardonic and satirical in turn.

Thus Caradoc Evans and Lloyd-George in their respective spheres delighted in shocking their audiences and making them draw in their breath. There is a parallel between Ll. G.'s picture of the squire and the parson "breaking into the poor-box" and Evans's lecherous Chapel deacon bringing home his daughter's corpse on a dung cart.

Professor Gwyn Jones has said: "The contemporary Welsh story is the product of a passionate, rebellious and humorous generation with a huge delight in life and no small relish for death." That generation is not Lloyd-George's generation, but he was of it in spirit—that was the measure of his modernity of outlook. He was that generation's forerunner who, like Dylan Thomas's Uncle Jim, could "set the darkness on fire".

For the Welsh Nonconformists of Lloyd-George's youth the real sources of inspiration were not Christ, or St. Paul, or John the Baptist, but Gladstone, Robert Owen, Mabon; already fundamentalism had been decried and denied. Having denied it, the political and radical elements of these sources were cherished, while the religious and moral aspects were ignored, and the new thinkers—"new lifers" might be an apter phrase—revelled in a secret inner freedom which permitted them to pray and to lust, to sing hymns and tell bawdy stories, to soar to the heights of mysticism and to enjoy being down-to-earth, randy and passionate materialists. The Welsh poets, short story writers and novelists of this century have realised all this and sought to interpret it. For this reason their contribution to literature is not a shallow piece of current reporting, but a three-dimensional portrait of the period from the 1860s to the 1960s.

Search for the magic of Lloyd-George and, even though they cannot capture it, they will provide many clues to the mystery. Through them one will see this magic mellowed from the extreme and biased portrait of Maynard Keynes into something which is human and not "half-human", dishonest only in a desire to be honest with innermost thoughts. Lloyd-George would have agreed with Strindberg that truth is relative. He always marvelled that Bonar Law should resent being called a liar. "Now *I* don't mind," was his comment.

He was akin to the eighteenth-century view of a Welshman—"Full of pride, petulance and pedigree, hot as a leek and amorous as a goat."

And for the man who did not mind being called a liar this verdict is probably the one which Lloyd-George himself in his sunniest moments would have appreciated most.

BIBLIOGRAPHY

A. *GENERAL*

The following biographies of Lloyd George have provided useful, background information

BURBIDGE, WILLIAM F., *The Wizard of Wales.* A biographical sketch of the Rt. Hon. David Lloyd George. John Crowther: London & Bognor Regis, 1943.

CLARKE, TOM, *My Lloyd George Diary.* Methuen & Co.: London, 1939.

DAVIES, SIR ALFRED THOMAS, K.B.E., *The Lloyd George I Knew . . .* supplemented by the story of the Welsh Department. Henry F. Walter: London, 1948.

DAVIES, WILLIAM WATKIN, *Lloyd George, 1863–1914.* Constable & Co.: London, 1939.

DILNOT, FRANK, *Lloyd George: the Man and his Story.* Harper & Bros.: New York & London, 1917.

DU PARCQ, HERBERT, Baron du Parcq, *Life of David Lloyd George.* 4 vols. Caxton Publishing Co.: London, 1912, 13.

EDWARDS, JOHN HUGH, *The Life of David Lloyd George*, with a short history of the Welsh people. 5 vols. Waverley Book Co.: London, 1913–1924.

EVANS, BERIAH, *The Life of Lloyd George.* "Everyman": London, 1916.

GEORGE, WILLIAM, *My Brother and I.* Eyre & Spottiswoode: London, 1958.

JONES, JOHN J., *The Man David.* An imaginative presentation, based on fact, of the life of David Lloyd George from 1880 to 1914. Hamish Hamilton: London, 1944.

JONES, THOMAS, C.H., *Lloyd George.* Oxford University Press: London, 1951.

MAISKY, V., *Lloyd George.* A political character-sketch. Petrograd: 1916.

MALLET, SIR CHARLES EDWARD, *Mr. Lloyd George.* A study. Ernest Benn: London, 1930.

OWEN, FRANK, *Tempestuous Journey.* Lloyd George, his life and times. Hutchinson: London, 1954.

SYLVESTER, ALBERT JAMES, *The Real Lloyd George.* Cassell & Co.: London, 1947.

THOMSON, MALCOLM, *David Lloyd George.* The official biography by M. Thomson with the collaboration of Frances, Countess Lloyd-George of Dwyfor. Hutchinson: London, 1948.

WEST, GORDON, *Lloyd George's Last Fight.* Alston Rivers: London, 1930.

B. *CHAPTERS 1–24*

A check list of books consulted

Chapter 1

BARNES, JAMES THOMAS STRACHEY, *Half a Life Left.* Eyre & Spottiswoode: London, 1937.

GEORGE, RICHARD LLOYD, Earl Lloyd-George of Dwyfor, *Dame Margaret.* George Allen & Unwin: London, 1947.

HAIG, DOUGLAS, Earl Haig, *The Private Papers of Douglas Haig, 1914–1919.* Edited by R. N. W. Blake. Eyre & Spottiswoode: London, 1952.

Chapter 2

COUPLAND, SIR REGINALD, K.C.M.G., *Welsh and Scottish Nationalism.* A study. Collins: London, 1954.

Chapter 4

GARDINER, ALFRED GEORGE, *The Life of Sir William Harcourt.* 2 vols. Constable & Co.: London, 1923.

HALDANE, RICHARD BURDON, Viscount Haldane. *Richard Burdon Haldane:* An autobiography. Hodder & Stoughton: London, 1929.

HAXEY, SIMON, *Tory M.P.* Victor Gollancz: London, 1939.

Chapter 5

ASQUITH, EMMA ALICE MARGARET, Countess of Oxford and Asquith, *The Autobiography of Margot Asquith.* 2 vols. John Lane: London, 1936.

BROODBANK, SIR JOSEPH GUINNESS, *History of the Port of London.* 2 vols. Daniel O'Connor: London, 1921.

GARDINER, ALFRED GEORGE, *Prophets, Priests and Kings.* Reprinted from the "Daily News". Alston Rivers: London, 1908.

HYNDMAN, HENRY M., *The Murdering of British Seamen by Mr. Lloyd George, the Liberal Cabinet and the Board of Trade.* Verbatim report of a speech on this subject delivered April 14th, 1913. The British Socialist Party: London, 1913.

JENKINS, ROY HARRIS, *Mr. Balfour's Poodle.* An account of the struggle between the House of Lords and the government of Mr. Asquith. Heinemann: London, 1954.

MASTERMAN, LUCY, formerly LYTTELTON, *C. F. G. Masterman.* A biography. Nicolson & Watson: London, 1939.

Chapter 6

LINCOLN, IGNATIUS TIMOTHY TRIBICH, afterwards CHAO KUNG, *The Autobiography of an Adventurer*. Translated by Emile Burns. Leonard Stein: London, 1931.

MORLEY, JOHN, Viscount Morley of Blackburn. *Memorandum on resignation, August, 1914*. Macmillan: London, 1928.

MURRAY, ARTHUR CECIL, Viscount Elibank. *Master and Brother*. Murrays of Elibank. John Murray: London, 1945.

NEUMANN, ROBERT, *Zaharoff, the Armaments King*. Translated by R. T. Clark. Allen & Unwin: London, 1935.

RYAN, ALFRED PATRICK, *Mutiny at the Curragh*. Macmillan: London, 1956.

SIMON, JOHN ALLSEBROOK, Viscount Simon, *Retrospect*. The memoirs of the Rt. Hon. Viscount Simon. Hutchinson: London, 1952.

SPENDER, JOHN ALFRED and ASQUITH, HON. SIR CYRIL, *Life of Herbert Henry Asquith, Lord Oxford and Asquith*. 2 vols. Hutchinson: London, 1932.

Chapter 7

ALLEN, FREDERICK LESLIE, *The Great Pierpont Morgan*. Harper & Bros.: New York, 1949.

ARTHUR, SIR GEORGE COMPTON ARCHIBALD, Bart., *Life of Lord Kitchener*. 3 vols. Macmillan: London, 1920.

HOUSE, EDWARD MANDELL, *The Intimate Papers of Colonel House*. Arranged by Charles Seymour. Ernest Benn: London, 1926.

JAMES, SIR WILLIAM MILBURN, G.C.B., *The Eyes of the Navy*. A biographical study of Admiral Sir Reginald Hall. Methuen: London, 1955.

MILLIS, WALTER, *Road to War: America 1914–1917*. Faber & Faber: London, printed in U.S.A., 1935.

MOOREHEAD, ALAN MCCRAE, *Gallipoli*. Hamish Hamilton: London, 1956.

SPEARS, RT. HON. SIR EDWARD LOUIS, Bart., *Prelude to Victory*. Jonathan Cape: London, 1939.

Chapter 8

BAKER, RT. HON. PHILIP JOHN NOEL, *The Private Manufacture of Armaments*. Victor Gollancz: London, 1936.

BALLARD, COLIN ROBERT, *Kitchener*. Faber & Faber: London, 1930.

BETHMANN-HOLWEGG, THEOBALD THEODOR FRIEDRICH ALFRED VON, *Reflections on the World War*. Translated by George Young. Thornton Butterworth: London, 1920.

DAVENPORT, GUILES, *Zaharoff, High Priest of War*. Lothrop, Lee & Shepard: Boston, 1934.

GEORGE, DAVID LLOYD, Earl Lloyd-George of Dwyfor, *War Memoirs of David Lloyd George.* 2 vols. Odhams Press: London, 1938.

LEWINSOHN, RICHARD, *The Man Behind the Scenes.* The career of Sir Basil Zaharoff. Victor Gollancz: London, 1929.

Chapter 9

AITKEN, WILLIAM MAXWELL, Baron Beaverbrook. *Politicians in the War, 1914–1916.* 2 vols. Thornton Butterworth: London, 1928.

—— *Men and Power, 1917–1918.* Hutchinson: London, 1959.

BLAKE, ROBERT NORMAN WILLIAM, *The Unknown Prime Minister.* The life and times of Andrew Bonar Law, 1858–1923. Eyre & Spottiswoode: London, 1955.

COCKERILL, SIR GEORGE KYNASTON, *What Fools We Were.* Hutchinson: London, 1944.

DAVIES, SIR JOSEPH, K.B.E., *The Prime Minister's Secretariat 1916–1920.* R. H. Johns: Newport, Mon., 1951.

GROOS, OTTO, *Der Krieg in der Nordsee.* Berlin, 1920.

HANKEY, MAURICE PASCAL ALERS, Baron Hankey. *The Supreme Command 1914–1918.* 2 vols. Allen & Unwin: London, 1961.

Chapter 10

A COURT, afterwards A COURT REPINGTON, CHARLES, *The First World War, 1914–1918.* Personal experiences. 2 vols. Constable: London, 1920.

"CENTURION", *The Man Who Didn't Win the War.* An exposure of Lloyd Georgism by Centurion. "National Review": London, 1923.

CHURCHILL, RT. HON. SIR WINSTON LEONARD SPENCER, K.G. *Great Contemporaries.* Thornton Butterworth: London, 1937.

EDMONDS, SIR JAMES EDWARD, *A Short History of World War One.* Oxford University Press: London, 1951.

GREY, EDWARD, Viscount Grey of Fallodon, *Twenty-five Years, 1892–1916.* 2 vols. Hodder & Stoughton: London, 1925.

HART, BASIL HENRY LIDDELL, *The Real War 1914–1918.* Faber & Faber: London, 1930.

MACKENZIE, EDWARD MONTAGUE COMPTON, *Athenian Memories.* Chatto & Windus: London, 1940.

MAURICE, SIR FREDERICK BARTON, K.C.M.G., *Intrigues of the War.* Reprinted from the "Westminster Gazette": Loxley Bros.: London, 1922.

SMITH, FREDERICK EDWIN, Earl of Birkenhead, *Turning Points in History.* Hutchinson: London, 1930.

TAYLOR, ALLAN JOHN PERCIVALE, *Lloyd George : Rise and Fall.* Cambridge University Press, 1961.

Chapter 11

CHURCHILL, RT. HON. SIR WINSTON LEONARD SPENCER, K.G., *The World Crisis, 1911–1918.* 6 vols. Thornton Butterworth: London, 1923–1931.

GEORGE, DAVID LLOYD, Earl Lloyd-George of Dwyfor, *The Truth About the Peace Treaties.* 2 vols. Victor Gollancz: London, 1938.

LAUSANNE, STEPHAN, *Le Diable aux Yeux Bleus.* Paris, 1922.

NICOLSON, HON. SIR HAROLD GEORGE, K.C.V.O., *King George V: His Life and Reign.* Constable: London, 1952.

Chapter 12

ALDINGTON, RICHARD, *Lawrence of Arabia.* A biographical enquiry. Victor Gollancz: London, 1955.

FRY, CHARLES BURGESS, *Life Worth Living.* Some phases of an Englishman. Eyre & Spottiswoode: London, 1939.

GEORGE, DAVID LLOYD, Earl Lloyd-George of Dwyfor. *The Truth About Reparations and War Debts.* Heinemann: London, 1932.

KEYNES, JOHN MAYNARD, Baron Keynes, *The Economic Consequences of the Peace.* Macmillan: London, 1919.

LANSING, ROBERT, *The Peace Negotiations.* A personal narrative. Houghton Mifflin Co.: Boston and New York, 1921.

RAYMOND, JOHN, *The Baldwin Age.* Edited by John Raymond, with an essay entitled "Baldwin and the Right" by R. N. W. Blake. Eyre & Spottiswoode: London, 1960.

RIDDELL, GEORGE ALLARDICE, Baron Riddell, *Lord Riddell's Intimate Diary of the Peace Conference and After, 1918–1923.* Victor Gollancz: London, 1933.

STEED, HENRY WICKHAM, *Through Thirty Years, 1892–1922.* 2 vols. Heinemann: London, 1924.

WRENCH, SIR JOHN EVELYN LESLIE, *Geoffrey Dawson and Our Times.* Hutchinson: London, 1955.

Chapter 13

CARR, EDWARD HALLETT, *A History of Soviet Russia.* The Bolshevik Revolution 1917–1923. 3 vols. Macmillan: London, 1950–53.

COLLIER, JOHN and LANG, IAIN, *Just the Other Day.* An informal history of Great Britain since the war. Hamish Hamilton: London, 1932.

DEGRAS, JANE, *Third (Communist) International. The Communist International, 1919–1943.* Documents selected and edited by Jane Degras. Oxford University Press: London, 1956.

EVANS, TREVOR, *Bevin.* Allen & Unwin: London, 1946.

GOTTLIEB, WOLFRAM WILHELM, *Studies in Secret Diplomacy during the First World War.* Allen & Unwin: London, 1957.

HANKEY, MAURICE PASCAL ALERS, Baron Hankey, *Diplomacy by Conference.* Studies in public affairs, 1920–1946. Ernest Benn: London, 1946.

NIKITIN, BORIS VLADIMIROVICH, *The Fatal Years*. Fresh revelations on a chapter of underground history. Translated by D. Hastie Smith. William Hodge & Co.: London, 1938.

THOMSON, SIR BASIL HOME, K.C.B., *Queer People*. Hodder & Stoughton: London, 1922.

—— *The Scene Changes*. Victor Gollancz: London, 1939.

Chapter 14

CROZIER, FRANK PERCY, *Ireland For Ever*. Jonathan Cape: London & Toronto, 1932.

MANSERGH, PHILIP NICHOLAS SETON, *Documents and Speeches on British Commonwealth Affairs, 1931–1952*. Edited by N. Mansergh. 2 vols. Oxford University Press: London, 1953.

O'CONNOR, FRANK, *pseud.* (i.e. MICHAEL FRANCIS O'DONOVAN), *The Big Fellow: a Life of Michael Collins*. T. Nelson & Sons: London, 1937.

OLIVER, FREDERICK SCOTT, *Ordeal by Battle*. Macmillan: London, 1915.

Chapter 15

GAUNT, SIR GUY REGINALD ARCHER, K.G.M.G., *The Yield of the Years*. A story of adventure afloat and ashore. Hutchinson: London & Melbourne, 1940.

KENNEDY, AUBREY LEO, *Old Diplomacy and New* . . . from Salisbury to Lloyd George. John Murray: London, 1922.

SYMONS, JULIAN, *Horatio Bottomley*. A biography. Cresset Press: London, 1955.

Chapter 16

AITKEN, WILLIAM MAXWELL, Baron Beaverbrook, *The Decline and Fall of Lloyd George*. Collins: London, 1963.

ASQUITH, HERBERT HENRY, Earl of Oxford and Asquith, *Memories and Reflections, 1852–1927*. 2 vols. Cassell & Co.: London, 1928.

BOWLE, JOHN, *Viscount Samuel*. Victor Gollancz: London, 1957.

FISCHER, LOUIS, *Oil Imperialism*. The international struggle for petroleum. Allen & Unwin: London, printed in U.S.A., 1927.

SULTAN MUHAMMED SHAH, Aga Khan, *The Memoirs of Aga Khan*. Cassell & Co.: London, 1954.

Chapter 17

MINNEY, RUBEIGH JAMES, *Viscount Addison: Leader of the Lords*. Odhams Press: London, 1958.

THOMSON, SIR BASIL HOME, K.C.B., *The Allied Secret Service in Greece*. Hutchinson: London, 1931.

Chapter 18

MACMILLAN, GERALD, *Honours for Sale.* The strange story of Maundy Gregory. Richards Press: London, 1954.

MORISON, STANLEY, *The History of The Times.* 4 vols. The Times Publishing Co.: London, 1935–1952.

Chapter 19

BURGESS, JOSEPH, *Will Lloyd George Supplant Ramsay MacDonald?* Joseph Burgess: Ilford, 1926.

KEYNES, JOHN MAYNARD, Baron Keynes, and HENDERSON, SIR HUBERT DOUGLAS, *Can Lloyd George Do It?* An examination of the Liberal pledge (to reduce unemployment). The Nation and Athenaeum: London, 1929.

SPENDER, JOHN ALFRED, *Sir Robert Hudson.* A memoir. Cassell & Co.: London, 1930.

Chapter 20

H.R.H. DUKE OF WINDSOR, *A King's Story.* The memoirs of H.R.H. the Duke of Windsor. Cassell & Co.: London, 1951.

Chapter 21

HITLER, ADOLF, *Hitler's Table Talk, 1941–1944.* With an introductory essay by H. R. Trevor Roper. Weidenfeld & Nicolson: London, 1953.

HOLLIS, SIR LESLIE CHASEMORE, K.C.B., K.C.E., *One Marine's Tale.* Andre Deutsch: London, 1956.

SCHMIDT, PAUL, *Statist auf diplomatischer Buehne, 1923–1945.* Erlebnisse des Chefdolmetschers im Auswartigen Amt mit den Staatsmannern Europas. Bonn: 1949.

TABOUIS, GENEVIEVE RAPATEL, *They Called Me Cassandra.* Charles Scribner's Sons: New York, 1942.

Chapter 22

BENNETT, SIR JOHN WHEELER WHEELER, *King George VI.* His life and reign. Macmillan: London, 1958.

BOOTHBY, ROBERT JOHN GRAHAM, Lord Boothby, *I Fight to Live.* Victor Gollancz: London, 1947.

CASEY, RICHARD GARDINER, Lord Casey, *Personal Experiences, 1931–1946.* Constable: London, 1962.

JONG, LOUIS DE, *De Duitse Vijtde Colonne in de tweede wereldoorlog.* Arnhem, Amsterdam, 1953.

KEYES, ELIZABETH, *Geoffrey Keyes, V.C., M.C., Croix de Guerre . . . Lieut.-Colonel 11th Scottish Commando.* George Newnes: London, 1956.

OGLANDER, CECIL FABER ASPINALL, *Robert Keyes.* Hogarth Press: London, 1951.

RIESS, CURT, *Total Espionage.* G. P. Putnam's Sons: New York, 1941.

SCHELLENBERG, WALTER, *Schellenberg Memoirs.* Edited and translated by Louis Hagen. Andre Deutsch: London, 1956.

Chapter 24

BANKHEAD, TALLULAH BROCKMAN, *Tallulah.* My autobiography. Victor Gollancz: London, 1952.

GEORGE, DAVID LLOYD, Earl Lloyd-George of Dwyfor, *The Wit and Wisdom of Lloyd George.* Compiled and edited by Dan Rider. Grant Richards: London, 1917.

KEYNES, JOHN MAYNARD, Baron Keynes, *Essays in Biography.* Macmillan: London, 1933.

C. *SUPPLEMENTARY NOTES TO CHAPTERS 1–24*

References to books cited in Sections A and B of the Bibliography are given by author and chapter

Chapter 1

Churchill tributes to Lloyd George: speech in the House of Commons, 1945, on the occasion of Lloyd George's death.

Earl Lloyd George on "inaccuracies": see GEORGE, RICHARD LLOYD, Section A.

Mr. A. J. Sylvester's comments: see SYLVESTER, ALBERT JAMES, Section A.

Chapter 2

Thomas Charles Williams: conversation with the author.

Several background references from "Baner Cymru Ac Yr Amserau", "North Wales Chronicle" and "Caernarvon & Denbigh Herald", and from mss. from the Welsh National Library.

Moses Roberts: private memoranda and letters.

Aneirin Talfan Davies: an article in the "Western Mail", 1955.

Chapter 3

"I come from the blackest and wickedest Tory parish in the land." It should be noted that Lloyd George again used this phrase in a speech at the Queen's Hall, London, in 1910, when he added: "I believe that my old uncle was the only Liberal in the village."

Michael D. Jones reference: in a thesis on "Nonconformity's Battle in Wales" by the Rev. Thomas Charles Williams.

Diary reference to "M.O.": see OWEN, FRANK, Section A.

Chapter 4

Edwards v. Edwards divorce action: reports in "The Times" (20th July and 13th Aug. 1897), "Caernarvon & Denbigh Herald", "Montgomery County Times".

The letter from Lloyd George to the Caernarvon Liberal Association: "The Times" (29th Nov., 1897).

D. A. Thomas (controversy over Home Rule): told by Lady Rhondda to the author.

Birmingham Riot: quotations from Lord Randolph Churchill and others; also "Birmingham Post", "Birmingham Gazette".

Chamberlain's reply to Labouchere: from material compiled by Labouchere when writing *Liberalism and the Empire* (1900), but not hitherto published.

It is worth noting that Labouchere stated in *Liberalism and the Empire* that the Chartered Company's chief shareholders were "able a little later to unload them (the shares) upon the public at a very heavy profit" and Labouchere estimated these profits as: "Mr. Rhodes £546,376; Mr. Beit £439,520; Beit and Rhodes in joint names £837,964; Rhodes and Beit in joint names £45,600; Rhodes, Rudd and Beit £68,000."

P. C. Stonier's evidence: told to the author and also substantiated in press interviews in "Birmingham Post" and "Birmingham Gazette" (1954).

Chapter 5

Lloyd George and shipowners: see THOMSON, MALCOLM, Section A.

Quotation from Sir Harold Nicolson: from an interview with Kenneth Harris in "The Observer" (12th Nov., 1961).

Mrs. Sydney Webb on Asquith: see MASTERMAN, LUCY, Section B, Chapter 5.

Chapter 6

Haldane and King Edward VII: see HALDANE, RICHARD BURDON, Section B, Chapter 4.

Lloyd George on King Edward VII: see GEORGE, WILLIAM, Section A.

Lloyd George and Algerian oil: see NEUMANN, ROBERT, Section B, Chapter 6. "As long ago as 1915 . . . Lord Murray, sent out by the oil company, S. Pearson & Co., had tried to get an oil concession which was to include over 750,000 hectares . . . in Algeria." Neumann also gives details of Zaharoff's negotiations after the war. For further reference, see *Documents Politiques de la Guerre* (Barthe, Menevèe and Tarpin).

"A classic confusion of orders": see RYAN, Section B, Chapter 6.

Asquith on "panic in the City", and Asquith on the merits of the Servian and Austrian cases, and his comments on his Cabinet on the eve of war, see SPENDER and ASQUITH, Section B, Chapter 6.

Chapter 7

See also *History Today* (May, 1961) for an article by John Terraine entitled "Lloyd George's Dilemma".

"Wait and See" references: Hansard, 3rd March and 4th April, 1910.

Thomas Lamont's reference to H. P. Davison is quoted in *Road to War*: see MILLIS, Section B, Chapter 7.

John Buchan's comment on Lloyd George: see JONES, THOMAS, Section A.

Also consulted: "La Follette's Magazine" and "New York Times" (1914–1916).

Mrs. Asquith's diary notes: quoted in her *Autobiography*, see ASQUITH, Section B, Chapter 5.

Naval intelligence messages: see JAMES, Section B, Chapter 7. James's account further substantiated by Admiral Sir Guy Gaunt.

Leakages of information: see MOOREHEAD, Section B, Chapter 7; Sir Basil Thomson to author.

Bonar Law's alleged offer of Premiership to Lloyd George: see THOMSON, Section A.

Chapter 8

Kitchener's summing up of French's criticism and requests, and Kitchener's view that he and the Prime Minister would have been "hanged on the gallows of public opinion . . .": see SPENDER and ASQUITH, Section B, Chapter 6.

Haldane's letter to Mrs. Asquith: see ASQUITH, Section B, Chapter 5.

Asquith on Lloyd George's demand for control of the liquor trade: see SPENDER and ASQUITH, Section B, Chapter 6.

Armaments industry: see also Report of Royal Commission on the Private Manufacture of and Trading in Arms (H.M.S.O., 1936).

Lloyd George's bargain with Zaharoff: from *Documents Politiques de la Guerre*; cited above, Section C, Chapter 6.

Lloyd George's urging of "neutral intervention" by President Wilson: see MILLIS, Section B, Chapter 7, and HOUSE, Section B, Chapter 7.

Auckland Geddes's statement on the merits of conscription: see SIMON, Section B, Chapter 6.

Chapter 9

See also Admiralty White Paper (Cmd. 2710 H.M.S.O.), "The Times" (December 1916), "Reynolds News" (December 1916).

Asquith's diary notes on Lloyd George's declaration of loyalty: see SPENDER and ASQUITH, Section B, Chapter 6.

John Terraine: see *History Today*, cited above, Section C, Chapter 7.

Lord Beaverbrook on Bonar Law's opinion of Lloyd George: see AITKEN, Section B, Chapter 9.

Events leading up to Lloyd George overthrowing Asquith: for fullest details see AITKEN, Section B, Chapter 9, *Politicians in the War*.

Asquith's letter to Bonar Law: see SPENDER, Section B, Chapter 6.

"Bonar Law had the resolution in his pocket, but never showed it to Asquith": see Blake, Section B, Chapter 9.

Churchill on Lloyd George's seizure of power: tribute in House of Commons on occasion of Lloyd George's death, cited above, Section C, Chapter 1.

Lyautey on Lloyd George and Haig; and Lloyd George's comments to D'Alençon: see *Documents Politiques de la Guerre*, cited above, Section C, Chapters 6 and 8.

Haig on Lloyd George and the Cabinet, and Haig's correspondence with the King and Lord Stamfordham: see Haig, Section B, Chapter 1.

Haldane on Haig: see Haldane, Section B, Chapter 4.

Chapter 10

Balfour compared to "a powerful, graceful cat": see Churchill, Section B, Chapter 10.

Lloyd George on Rhondda: see George, Section B, Chapter 8.

Admiral Gaunt's diary entries: given to the author by Admiral Gaunt.

Reply to Lloyd George's attacks on Haig by Lord Trenchard, Sir Noel Birch and Sir John Davidson: correspondence in "Daily Telegraph" (1936).

Lloyd George on Haig's "gamble" at Passchendaele: see George, Section B, Chapter 8.

Robertson's warning to Haig: see Haig, Section B, Chapter 1.

See same source for Wilson's warning to Haig that Pétain's "charity" was "very cold".

Duke of Northumberland's letter to Maurice: published in *Intrigues of the War*, as was Grigg's reply on behalf of Lloyd George: see Maurice, Section B, Chapter 10.

Countess Lloyd-George's letter: "Spectator" (November 1956).

Miss Maurice's statement was also quoted in the "Evening Standard" (29th Nov., 1956).

Chapter 11

Clemenceau rehearsing his speech to Churchill: see Churchill, Section B, Chapter 10. The essay on Clemenceau mentions, "He uttered to me in his room at the Ministry of War words he afterwards repeated in the tribune: 'I will fight in Paris'."

Gough's dismissal: see Haig, Section B, Chapter 1, and Smith, Section B, chapter 10. Also "Journal of the Royal United Services Institution" (March 1936), an article by Brig.-Gen. Sir James Edmonds. Other sources: interview with General Gough by J. P. W. Mallalieu, M.P., in the "Evening Standard" (1956), and General Gough to the author.

Dr. Jones on Lloyd George's low courage in 1918: see Jones, Thomas, Section A.

Derby's bet with Lloyd George: statement by Lord Derby and *Private Papers of Douglas Haig*: see HAIG, Section B, Chapter 1.

Churchill's statement that Lloyd George "ran the first world war better than I ran the second": see "The Observer" (12th Nov., 1961), interview by Kenneth Harris with Sir Harold Nicolson.

Haig's insistence on a decision in autumn 1918: see war dispatches and HAIG, Section B, Chapter 1.

Lloyd George's peace manœuvres in May–June 1918: see "CENTURION", Section B, Chapter 10, and *Lloyd George and the War* by Independent Liberal (Hutchinson 1917). See also speech made by Arthur Henderson (27th Nov., 1918) in which he revealed that Lloyd George had favoured sending an envoy to the socialistic Stockholm Peace Conference in the summer of 1917, and only drew back at the last moment.

"Hang the Kaiser": see "Bristol Observer", "North Wales Chronicle" (November to December 1918), and Churchill's essay on the Kaiser in *Great Contemporaries*, CHURCHILL, Section B, Chapter 10.

Briand's query to Lloyd George about hanging the Kaiser: see LAUSANNE, Section B, Chapter 11, and *Documents Politiques* . . .

F. E. Smith's statement to J. H. Morgan was disclosed by Professor J. H. Morgan to R. Barry O'Brien and quoted in the "Daily Telegraph".

Chapter 12

Northcliffe's letter to Dawson: see WRENCH, Section B, Chapter 12.

Mme. Gauthier on Ll. G. and Clemenceau: told to author.

Nicolson on Lloyd George: see "The Observer" (12th Nov., 1961), cited above, Section C, Chapter 11.

Lloyd George's demand of Mosul and Iraq from Clemenceau: see ALDINGTON, Section B, Chapter 12, LEWINSOHN, Section B, Chapter 8, and DAVENPORT, Section B, Chapter 8.

Lloyd George at Spa Conference: see *Documents of British Foreign Policy 1919–1939*.

Lloyd George and Albania: see BARNES, Section B, Chapter 1.

Correspondence on offer of Albanian kingship: see Central News, message of 27th Jan., 1925; "Evening Standard" (29th Nov., 1937 and 8th April, 1939) and FRY, Section B, Chapter 12.

Gregory's letter to the unnamed peer is not available for general inspection, and is, of course, the property of the peer.

Chapter 13

Lloyd George to Thomson on Bolsheviks: as told to author by Thomson.

Churchill on Kolchak: see CHURCHILL, Section B, Chapter 10.

Lloyd George on golf links with Briand and Bonomi: see OWEN, Section A.

The Kuhlmann document was found in the files of the German Ministry of Foreign Affairs and is now in the custody of the British authorities. Other documents show that the Kaiser expressed agreement with the contents.

Russian subsidies to "Daily Herald" and Kamenev: see *Documents of British Foreign Policy* . . ., cited above, Section C, Chapter 12.

Chapter 14

King George V and Ireland: see NICOLSON, Section B, Chapter 11.

Ryan's statements: verbally to the author. Greenwood declined the author's request for a comment on this. Thomson and Crozier both concurred with the general gist of Ryan's remarks when questioned by the author, and Crozier substantiates this in his book: see CROZIER, Section B, Chapter 14.

For Simon quotation see SIMON, Section B, Chapter 6.

Some background information on Irish atrocities obtained from COLLIER and LANG, Section B, Chapter 13, and from current press reports in London and Irish papers.

Irish peace talks: see JONES, THOMAS, Section A.

Chapter 15

See also the *Diplomatika Engraphica* (Greek White Book, 1920).

Hankey as "a powerful and catalytic agent": see JONES, THOMAS, Section A.

David Davies: Frank Owen gives some interesting sidelights on David Davies in *Tempestuous Journey*, giving a more vivid picture of the man than is possible in the scope of this chapter: see OWEN, Section A.

"The Round Table" of the period portrays the views of Curtis and Kerr on imperial development and the Commonwealth idea.

J. T. Davies: see JONES, THOMAS, Section A.

Sylvester on Lloyd George: see SYLVESTER, Section A. Sylvester also mentions a visit by Lloyd George to Zaharoff after Lloyd George had ceased to be P.M.

Zaharoff's statements to Rosita Forbes (Mrs. A. T. McGrath): confirmed in a letter from Mrs. McGrath to the author. Some of these statements were published in the "Sunday Chronicle" (29th Nov., 1936).

Maundy Gregory's statement to Thomson: told by Thomson to the author.

Zaharoff's escape from capture by German submarine: see obituary of Zaharoff in "Daily Telegraph" (28th Nov., 1936).

Clemenceau on importance of Zaharoff's information: see *Documents Politiques* . . . and Clemenceau in a letter to M. Rene Tarpin.

Mutual agreement to prevent bombing of arms plants: see *Documents Politiques* . . . and Baker, Section B, Chapter 8.

Thomson's probes into Bolshevik activities: Thomson to author.

Lloyd George's insatiable curiosity for charlatans: Jones, Thomas, Section A.

Bottomley's prosecution: see "Evening Standard" (21st Aug., 1951), "Bottomley and the Victory Bonds Swindle" by Montgomery Hyde: "Since an M.P. was involved, the normal practice would have been for the Crown to be represented by one of the Law Officers . . . but such was the legend of Bottomley's invincibility that Mr. Lloyd George's Government, which was highly nervous about the proceedings, declined to instruct the Attorney- or Solicitor-General for this purpose."

Chapter 16

Zaharoff's Paris meeting with Lloyd George: see Davenport, Section B, Chapter 8, Lewinsohn, Section B, Chapter 8, Neumann, Section B, Chapter 6.

Lloyd George and Zionism and Sir Charles Henry: see Aitken, Section B, Chapter 9, "Men and Power".

Lloyd George and Lawrence: see Aldington, Section B, Chapter 12.

"Give Lawrence the maximum of publicity": Sutherland's own quotation of his master's instructions, made at a Press Conference in March 1919.

Lloyd George's talks with Zaharoff: Zaharoff's statements to Rosita Forbes, and *Documents Politiques . . .*

Chapter 17

Lloyd George and Poincaré: see Jones, Thomas, Section A, Owen, Section A, Thomson, Section A, and Aldington, Section B, Chapter 12.

On the subject of Poincaré's insistence on a military convention and a "guarantee in writing", the following quotation from André Maurois's *Call No Man Happy* is apt: "France liked precise engagements. The English had a horror of them. Poincaré had irritated the English by his inflexibility."

Viscount St. David's indictment of the Greeks: "Daily Express" (27th Sept., 1932).

Chapter 18

Ll. G. and attempt to buy "The Times": see *The History of The Times*, vol. iv.

Younger's strictures on the Lloyd George Fund: see Nicolson, Section B, Chapter 11, and Blake, Section B, Chapter 9.

The astonishing significance of the large sums mentioned in these "honours deals" is the extraordinary amount of spare cash which rich men had available in these days. The extent of this wealth may probably never be known, but most of it was obtained by profits made out of the war. Support for the claims that such profits reached astronomical figures is contained in this letter of 8th Oct., 1921, from Mr. Churchill to Lloyd George. "... The first and greatest mistake in my opinion was leaving the profiteers in possession of their ill-gotten war wealth. Had prompt action been taken at the beginning of 1919, several thousand millions of paper wealth could have been transferred to the State and the internal debt reduced accordingly." (See Appendix IV in *Men and Power* by Lord Beaverbrook.)

Mr. Archie de Bear's statements: see "Sunday Express" (November, 1936); also substantiated in personal interview with the author.

Honours traffic involving Zaharoff: see *Documents Politiques* . . .: statement by M. Barthe (1919) and archives of Turkish Foreign Office (1916–1926).

Also consulted: "The Banker" (1922); "Whitehall Gazette"; and "Morning Post" (1921–1923).

Sir John Stewart sequestration proceedings: "The Times" (5th and 7th July, 1924).

Chapter 19

The author also had access to the private memoranda and papers of Mr. Vivian Phillipps, and has seen *My Days and Ways*, a memoir by Mr. Phillipps which was privately printed for him and is not available for general inspection.

Lloyd George in America: see OWEN, Section A, and THOMSON, Section A.

Lloyd George Fund: see JONES, THOMAS, Section A, and OWEN, Section A.

Lord St. Davids and alleged destruction of papers relating to Lloyd George Fund: see JONES, THOMAS, Section A. It is perhaps worth noting that the present Lord St. Davids has "no knowledge" of this.

Chapter 20

Lloyd George and Maxton: Maxton to author.

Lloyd George as "King's champion" against "Baldwin and Co.": Wickham Steed in letter to author.

Lord Beaverbrook's comments on suppression of letters by Dawson: broadcast review of *The History of The Times* (May 1952).

Chapter 21

Visit to Hitler: see JONES, THOMAS, Section A, and current press reports.

Heinz Linge's statements: see *The Private Life of Adolf Hitler* by Heinz Linge, "News of the World" (Dec.–Jan., 1955–56).

Letter to Conwell-Evans (27th Dec., 1937): see OWEN, Section A.

Ribbentrop's comments on Lloyd George and King Edward: see

Documents of German Foreign Policy, and for further background on wishful German thinking, see War Diaries of Abwehr II (Sabotage and Subversion), at present in the Munich Institute of Contemporary History. The latter is incomplete and contains only extracts of the Diaries.

Helga Stultz's information: obtained from Helga Stultz to author and from Wythe Williams, American war correspondent and editor of "Greenwich Times" (U.S.A.).

Chapter 22

Nicolson on the possibility of King George VI sending for Lloyd George: see "Observer" (12th Dec., 1961).

A. J. Sylvester's statement: see SYLVESTER, Section A.

Garvin's talk with Lloyd George: see JONES, THOMAS, Section A.

Fraulein Bumke's statement: confirmed by Robert E. Sherwood and Otto Kruger (Tangier, 1946).

Kingsley Martin: see "New Statesman" (27th Nov., 1954).

Lloyd George on difference between himself and Churchill: see "News Review" (26th Feb., 1942).

Lloyd George to Keyes: told by Keyes to author. Keyes' comment was: "Lloyd George was still brimful of ideas and astonishingly up-to-date in his outlook. When he was actually propounding his plans—and some of them were very sound—he seemed forceful enough to deserve a place in the Cabinet. The tragedy was that he saw too closely the more sombre side of the war picture and this damped down his enthusiasm so that within a few minutes it was as though one was talking to a different person."

Hollis on Keyes: see HOLLIS, Section B, Chapter 21.

Roosevelt's reaction to proposal to make Lloyd George U.S. Ambassador: Robert Berle, Jnr.

Helga Stultz and Fraulein Bumke: Wythe Williams, Otto Kruger (Tangier), Lt-Col. W. F. Ellis and Helga Stultz in personal interviews with author. Regarding these sources it should be stated that Col. Ellis held an important post in British Intelligence circles and was press attaché at the British Consulate-General in Tangier during World War II, when the then international zone of Morocco was one of the chief espionage centres of the world. Wythe Williams, after establishing a reputation as a foreign correspondent of the "New York Times", launched a newspaper, "Greenwich Times", from Greenwich, Connecticut. Lowell Thomas has paid this tribute to him: "For several years Wythe Williams had most of us guessing. By 'us' I mean those whose occupation it is to deal with the news . . . Wythe proceeded to pull one news rabbit after another out of the hat. He had us . . . not only guessing, but more than slightly sceptical. How could one man, we asked, dig up information not available to the great American wire services, to say nothing of the great newspapers who had their own news-gathering machinery in addition? But, by jingo, history began to vindicate and corroborate him." The secret of Williams' war scoops and how he always seemed to know in advance what the enemy were planning is revealed in part in his book *Secret Sources* (Ziff-Davis Publishing Co., 1943): he had as informants pro-Allied members of Hitler's and Ribbentrop's staffs, and listening posts inside Germany and other enemy territory as well as obtaining the wave lengths which the German General Staff used for field communications for which he had a special radio receiver built. Prior to the U.S. entry into the war Williams published his scoops in "Greenwich Times" and broadcast many others. In 1942 he wrote: "Because of the transmission expenses connected with our exclusive reports from overseas I had always been faced with a considerable overhead. This in turn could be met only by a commercial sponsor, as the radio stations themselves carry no provision for such expenses. Without a sponsor willing to carry the cost, I had to abandon broadcasting over a nation-wide network. Immediately after Pearl Harbour I offered my services on a non-profit basis and they were accepted by an independent New York station. This activity I maintained for fourteen months, whereupon conditions compelled me to suspend it. After Hitler's declaration of war against the U.S., we did not hear from our German friends for a long time . . . By the very nature of things all such information was turned over to the United States authorities and only the data made available for such a purpose were presented in my broadcasts."

For Nazi War Plan for Wales: see also "Western Mail" series bearing this title (25th March–2nd April, 1957).

Adam von Trott: von Trott, a former Rhodes scholar at Oxford, tried in June, 1939, to awaken Chamberlain and Halifax to the possibilities of opposition to Hitler inside Germany. British Foreign Office opinion was sceptical of and even hostile to von Trott—Eden, when asked by Stafford Cripps to consider any smuggled communications from von Trott as *bona fide*, replied that the dossier against Trott was so formidable that he could not concur. Trott was executed for his part in the plot of 20th July, 1944, to assassinate Hitler. See *Documents of German Foreign Policy* for a somewhat incomplete and undeniably biased picture of Trott's activities in Britain.

Chapter 23

Lloyd George and his peerage: see SYLVESTER, Section A, and GEORGE, Section A.

Lloyd George "talking like a Catholic": this was simply a personal impression given to the author in an interview, but it is interesting in view of Owen's statement in *Tempestuous Journey*: "One afternoon, when his wife thought he was asleep, he suddenly opened his eyes and called out: 'The Sign of the Cross! The Sign of the Cross!' "

Chapter 24

Robertson Nicol ("The man who made Lloyd George"): see TAYLOR, Section B, Chapter 10.

George Becker: in a letter to the author.

T. P. O'Connor: "Lloyds Weekly News" (4th Feb., 1917).

Statement by Earl Lloyd-George: see "Sunday Dispatch" (9th Nov., 1958), in an interview with D. E. H. Dinsley.

Lloyd George and letter writing: see OWEN, Section A, and JONES, THOMAS, Section A.

Voronoff's statements: Voronoff to author. Lloyd George had the wool from his sheep made into coats which he sent to friends abroad.

INDEX

The abbreviation q. *has been used throughout when a quotation from the work or person has been used, and the abbreviation* f. *when an illustration faces the page number.*